UKRAINE DURING WORLD WAR II:
HISTORY AND ITS AFTERMATH

EDITED BY YURY BOSHYK

with the assistance of Roman Waschuk
and Andriy Wynnyckyj

Ukraine during World War II

HISTORY AND ITS AFTERMATH

A Symposium

CANADIAN INSTITUTE OF UKRAINIAN STUDIES
University of Alberta
Edmonton 1986

THE CANADIAN LIBRARY IN UKRAINIAN STUDIES

A series of original works and reprints relating to Ukraine, issued under the editorial supervision of the Canadian Institute of Ukrainian Studies, University of Alberta, Edmonton.

Editorial Board:
Bohdan Bociurkiw, Carleton University (Social Sciences)
Manoly R. Lupul, University of Alberta (Ukrainians in Canada)
Bohdan Rubchak, University of Illinois at Chicago Circle (Humanities)

Canadian Cataloguing in Publication Data

Main entry under title:

Ukraine during World War II

(The Canadian library in Ukrainian studies)
Bibliography: p.
Includes index.
ISBN 0-920862-37-3 (bound). – ISBN 0-920862-36-5 (pbk.)

1. Ukraine – History – German occupation, 1941–1944 – Addresses, essays, lectures. 2. Ukraine – History – 1917– – Addresses, essays, lectures. 3. World War, 1939–1945 – Participation, Ukrainian – Addresses, essays, lectures. 4. World War, 1939–1945 – Collaborationists – Ukraine – Addresses, essays, lectures. 5. War criminals – Ukraine – Addresses, essays, lectures. I. Boshyk, Yury, 1950– II. Canadian Institute of Ukrainian Studies. III. Series.
D802.R82U38   1985940.53'37   C85-098965-5

Editorial services and consultant: The Wordsmith Communications

Design consultant: Laurie Lewis, University of Toronto Press

Cover design: Holly Fisher

Printed in Canada

Distributed by: University of Toronto Press
5201 Dufferin Street
Downsview, Ontario
Canada M3H 5T8

He said that there was only one good, namely, knowledge;
and only one evil, namely, ignorance.
Diogenes

CONTENTS

Part III: Documents, 1929–66

PREFACE

The year 1985 marked the fortieth anniversary of the Nazi surrender to the Allies in Europe, the liberation of the concentration camps, and freedom for millions of slave labourers and prisoners of war. With the commemoration of this anniversary has come a renewed interest in bringing Nazi war criminals to justice.

In an attempt to illuminate the historical period and to make the current discussion on war criminals more informed, a symposium was held in Toronto on 2 March 1985 to examine several important aspects of the war in Eastern Europe: the Soviet and Nazi occupations of Ukrainian territory; relations between Ukrainians and Jews; collaboration with and resistance against the occupying powers; as well as Canadian and American perspectives on bringing war criminals to justice.

This volume is based on papers and discussions from the symposium. Part 1 is a scholarly examination of the period 1939–45, from the Soviet and Nazi occupations of Ukrainian territory to the circumstances relating to collaboration and resistance. Part 2 is devoted to a discussion about one of the most important questions of the war's aftermath, one which has become a matter of public debate: the methods and means of bringing alleged Nazi and other war criminals living in Canada and the United States to justice. This discussion rests on the assumption, shared by the contributors to this volume, that all war criminals must be brought to justice; it focuses, however, on the procedures that should be followed, consistent with the legal traditions and practices of Canada and the United States. Most contributors in part 2 abided by the definitions applied at the Nuremberg trials, which established three basic categories of war criminality: responsibility for instigating war; crimes against civilians and soldiers, including the murder of political prisoners, mistreatment of prisoners of war, and the use of slave labour; and, finally, crimes against humanity, with the intention of exterminating entire peoples and nations.

Together with the chronology of major events, glossary, and bibliographical aids, the documents in part 3 provide historical background. They relate directly to the previous parts of the book. Documents of the Organization of Ukrainian Nationalists (OUN) from the 1920s have been included to illustrate the ideology and political nationalism of one of the main political organizations in Western Ukraine during the war. Similarly, materials from the archives of the United Nations Relief and Rehabilitation Administration (UNRRA) have been included to provide a more balanced evaluation of the postwar displaced persons population in Germany and Austria than that found in recent publications.

The modified Library of Congress system of transliteration used by the Canadian Institute of Ukrainian Studies has been applied to the transliteration of Ukrainian and other Slavic references, unless a commonly accepted English-language version exists. Some authors' names have been given in the original language. Thus, for example, the transliterated spelling Volodymyr Kubiiovych appears with his Ukrainian-language publications, but Kubijovyč is used for his English-language publications; this practice also applies to Potichnyj-Potichny, Yevhen-Ievhen, and the like.

Readers might encounter inconsistencies in statistical information, for example, on the number of Ukrainians killed by the Soviet secret police during the 1939 Soviet occupation of Western Ukraine; the number of Eastern Europeans and Soviet citizens who collaborated with the Germans; the precise number of Ukrainian slave labourers; and the scale of human losses in the artificial Soviet Ukrainian famine of 1932–3. Great care has been taken to ensure historical accuracy, but the available statistical information is of varying reliability and conclusiveness. The reasons for this range from the nature of the historical documents to the lack of free access to vital archival records.

Because of these and other limitations, some questions require further study. Among them are the degree to which the Soviet Union's alliance with Germany during 1939–41 later helped the Nazis on the Eastern front; and the extent and reasons for the local population's assistance in the Nazi program of repression and extermination. This volume, therefore, is still the product of research bound by the constraints of analyzing the recent past, the political control of primary sources and information, and a lack of scholarly consensus on several vital issues and events.

The war brought enormous loss of life and hardship to Ukrainians. Of all the republics of the Soviet Union, it was in Ukraine that the Nazis stayed the longest and caused the greatest suffering. The Nazis viewed all non-Aryans and hence Ukrainians as *Untermenschen* (subhumans) whose only task was to serve the needs of the Third Reich. Moreover, the brutality of the war in Ukraine had been clearly planned by Hitler: his soldiers were instructed to abandon the normal rules and codes of military conduct while on the Eastern front. Estimates of the number killed or taken as slave labourers or prisoners of war range from seven to ten million.

Nor did the Nazis treat Western Ukrainians with favour. They were barely tolerated, and then only to the degree to which they fit Germany's plans for war against the Soviet Union. More nationalistic and better organized than their brethren in the Soviet Union, many Western Ukrainians were committed to the destruction of the Soviet state and the creation of an independent Ukraine. Hence, they had their own political agenda and priorities during the war, and this fact always influenced events in this region. Nevertheless, as several contributors to this volume point out, no amount of historical understanding can ever justify the historical fact that, as was true of other peoples during the war, some individuals directly aided and abetted the Nazis in committing crimes against their own people as well as against others.

It is my hope that the articles in this volume will help clarify the complex situation in which Ukraine and Ukrainians found themselves during the war and the controversial issues associated with its aftermath.

The authors, of course, are responsible for their views. Their arguments may cause discomfort to some readers but, as is often said, in coming to terms with the past, we gain a better appreciation of our own moral values and principles. The aim of this book is not to judge but to promote understanding, and thoughtful readers will come to their own conclusions. If, in some small way, this book has been of assistance in this effort, the work will have been worthwhile.

Yury Boshyk
University of Toronto

ACKNOWLEDGEMENTS

The preparation of this volume would not have been possible without the co-operation of the contributors, which is deeply appreciated. Gratefully acknowledged also is the assistance of Roman Szporluk and Romas Vastokas; Wasyl Veryha, who helped compile the chronology of events and made valuable suggestions; David Springer of the Chicago law firm of Kirkland & Ellis, who prepared the legal bibliography; Taras Pidzamecky, who allowed the use of his translations; the staff of the National Ethnic Archives at the Public Archives of Canada; Taras Hunczak, who discovered some of the rare photographs reproduced in this volume; and Myroslav Yurkevich, Boris Balan, Leonid Heretz, James Mace, and Roman Senkus, who provided much useful advice.

Permission to print previously published or forthcoming material was granted by Macmillan Press, London (for Bohdan Krawchenko's essay), and by Peter Potichnyj and Yevhen Shtendera (for selections from their forthcoming book, "The Political Thought of the Ukrainian Underground"). The map by Luba Prokop is courtesy of Bohdan Vitvitsky. Gratitude is also expressed to Petro Sodol, Stepan Welhash, Nestor Mykytyn, Wasyl Veryha, and others for their help in providing photographs. The contribution of Sylvia Pellman and the staff at the Office Works, who very ably handled the word processing, is gratefully acknowledged, as is the assistance of Laurie Lewis at the University of Toronto Press. Thanks are extended to all those who helped organize the symposium: Danylo Husar Struk; Yvonne Ivanochko, Myroslav Bodnaruk, and the Board of Directors of St. Vladimir Institute; Stepan Ilnytzkyj, who made audiotapes of the symposium proceedings and provided copies; Yury Luhovy, Zorianna Hrycenko-Luhova, and their assistants from Concordia University, who videotaped the proceedings; and the following members of the Ukrainian Students' Club at the University of Toronto: Andrij Chabursky, Roman Dubczak, Marta Dyczok, Danylo Dzikewicz, Natalia Lebedynsky, Christine Mushka, Peter Opar, Daria Skidaniuk, and Jeffrey Stephaniuk.

Advice and assistance at an earlier stage was kindly provided by Victor Goldbloom, president, Canadian Council of Christians and Jews; Olga Fuga; Olenka Demianczuk; Halya Kuchmij; Luba Zaraska; John Armstrong; Ihor Kamenetsky; David Roth, American Jewish Committee; the Ukrainian Famine Research Committee (Toronto); Cosbild Investment Corporation; S & B Realty; Yaroslav and Luba Osmak; the So-Use, Toronto, and Buduchnist credit unions; Community Trust; the Taras Shevchenko Foundation; and the Ukrainian Studies Endowment Fund, York University.

Finally, special thanks are owing to numerous individual donors, to Manoly R. Lupul, director, Canadian Institute of Ukrainian Studies, who gave editorial and financial support, and to Roman Waschuk and Andriy Wynnyckyj for their research assistance.

CONTRIBUTORS

MARK R. ELLIOTT, professor of history, Asbury College, Wilmore, Kentucky, is the author of *Pawns of Yalta: Soviet Refugees and America's Role in Their Repatriation* and numerous articles on World War II.

TARAS HUNCZAK, professor of history, Rutgers University, is the author of *Symon Petliura and the Jews: A Reappraisal* and editor of *Russian Imperialism from Ivan the Great to the Revolution; Ukrainian Socio-Political Thought in the Twentieth Century* (with Roman Solchanyk); and *The Ukrainian Insurgent Army (UPA) in Light of German Documents, 1942–45.*

BOHDAN KRAWCHENKO, assistant director, Canadian Institute of Ukrainian Studies, University of Alberta, is the author of *Social Change and National Consciousness in Twentieth-Century Ukraine* and editor of *Ukraine after Shelest.*

ROMAN KUPCHINSKY, president, Prolog Research Corporation, New York City, is the editor of *Pogrom in Ukraine, 1972–1979* and *The National Question in the USSR: Documents.*

MYRON KUROPAS, former special assistant for ethnic affairs to President Gerald R. Ford, is the author of *The Ukrainians in America; To Preserve a Heritage: The Story of the Ukrainian Immigration in the United States;* and *The Ukrainian Americans: Roots and Aspirations* (forthcoming).

DAVID MATAS, a Winnipeg lawyer, is senior legal counsel for the League for Human Rights, B'nai B'rith Canada, and former head of the Canadian Bar Association's International Law Committee. He has written several studies on the Canadian legal system and its role in prosecuting Nazi war criminals allegedly residing in Canada.

PETER J. POTICHNYJ, professor of political science, McMaster University, Hamilton, Ontario, is the co-author (with Howard Aster) of *Jewish-Ukrainian Relations: Two Solitudes*. Among his edited works are *Poland and Ukraine: Past and Present*; *Chronicle of the Ukrainian Insurgent Army* (with Yevhen Shtendera); and the forthcoming *Jewish-Ukrainian Relations in Historical Perspective* (with Howard Aster).

ROMAN SERBYN, professor of history, Université du Québec à Montréal, is chairman of the Ukrainian Information and Anti-Defamation Commission (IADC), Montreal.

OREST SUBTELNY, professor of history and political science, York University, Toronto, is the author of *The Mazepists: Ukrainian Separatism in the 18th Century* and *Domination of Eastern Europe: Foreign Absolutism and Native Nobilities, 1500–1715*.

MYROSLAV YURKEVICH, research associate, Canadian Institute of Ukrainian Studies, University of Alberta, is a specialist on Ukrainian political movements and political thought. He is currently completing a major study of the Organization of Ukrainian Nationalists.

S. PAUL ZUMBAKIS, an attorney in private practice in Chicago, is a member of the American, Chicago, and Illinois bar associations and of the Association of Trial Lawyers in America. He has acted on behalf of defendants in trials initiated by the U.S. Justice Department's Office of Special Investigations.

LIST OF PHOTOGRAPHS

PART I

Ukraine during World War II

1. OCCUPATION

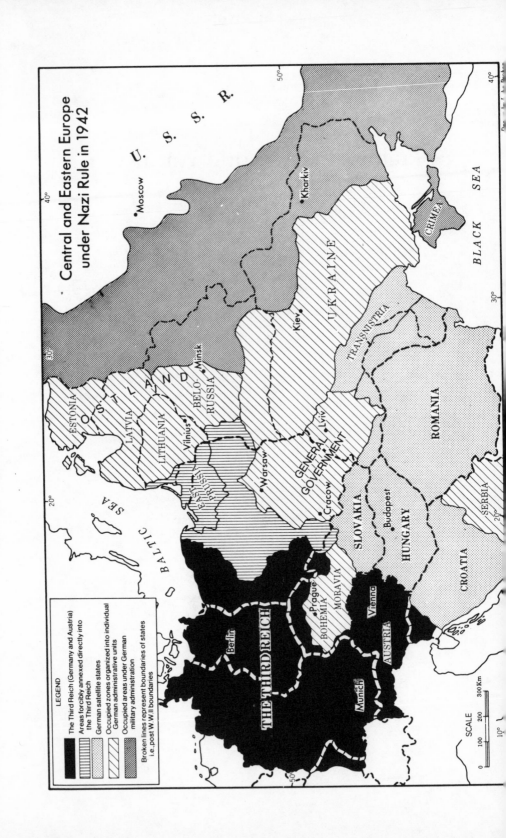

Central and Eastern Europe under Nazi Rule in 1942

LEGEND

- The Third Reich (Germany and Austria)
- Areas forcibly annexed directly into the Third Reich
- German satellite states
- Occupied zones organized into individual German administrative units
- Occupied areas under German military administration
- Broken lines represent boundaries of states i.e., post W.W.II boundaries

U. S. S. R.

•Moscow

•Kharkiv

•Kiev

UKRAINE

CRIMEA

BLACK SEA

OSTLAND

ESTONIA

LATVIA

LITHUANIA

Vilnius•

BELO RUSSIA

•Minsk

EAST PRUSSIA

Warsaw•

GENERAL GOVERNMENT

•Lviv

•Cracow

TRANSNISTRIA

BALTIC SEA

SLOVAKIA

ROMANIA

•Budapest

HUNGARY

SERBIA

CROATIA

THE THIRD REICH

Berlin•

•Prague

BOHEMIA

MORAVIA

Vienna•

AUSTRIA

Munich•

SCALE

0   100   200   300 Km

INTRODUCTION

In 1939, at the outbreak of World War II, the territory inhabited by the Ukrainian people was divided among four states: the USSR, Poland, Hungary, and Romania. Under the Molotov-Ribbentrop Pact, signed in the same year, the USSR seized Western Ukraine from Poland and with the assistance of German diplomacy soon wrested Bukovyna from Romania. In these newly acquired regions the Soviets applied severe measures similar to those which had served to solidify Stalinist rule in the rest of the USSR: national organizations were prohibited; ethnic Poles, politicians, and intellectuals were arrested and deported to Siberia; and preparations were made for the collectivization of agriculture. At the same time, in order to justify their forcible annexation of these territories, Soviet authorities promoted some Ukrainians to managerial and governmental posts that had been denied them under Polish and Romanian rule.

In order to understand fully the war's origins and its unprecedented barbarity, one must look to the 1920s and 1930s. Roman Szporluk, a specialist on Eastern European history and national movements, has argued that World War I and the 1917 Bolshevik Revolution unleashed two major forces that transformed Eastern Europe: political and nationalist exclusivity, and Stalinist class war. These forces led, in turn, to a profound crisis of national identity and legitimacy during the interwar period. Few states, including the Soviet Union, recognized the legitimacy of the Versailles Treaty. At the same time, some of the newly created nation states in Eastern Europe (for example, Poland and Lithuania) focused their political agenda on nation-building, identifying the political interests of the state with a particular national group. Whether the nations of Eastern Europe acted from a fascist, Stalinist, nationalist, or class political perspective, the goal was the same: to change the *status quo*.

But if these nations were recalcitrant, so too were the many minorities in Eastern Europe who did not emerge from World War I with a nation-state of their own and thus felt no allegiance to their new governments. Moreover, the dominant national groups in Eastern Europe and the Soviet Union (especially the Poles and the Russians) did not regard the minorities within their borders as equals but sought their enforced assimilation.

During the 1930s a bitter and at times violent struggle took place among the peoples of Eastern Europe, disguised, in Roman Szporluk's words, as "war by other means."[1] In the Soviet Union, Stalin purged the party of non-Russian cadres, declared war on the non-Russian peasantry, and rescinded rights that had previously been granted to minorities. In Poland, discrimination against the Jewish, Belorussian, and Ukrainian minorities became institutionalized. Poles were encouraged, for example, not to patronize Jewish merchants and shopkeepers, while social mobility, better paying jobs, and education became dependent on ethnic or national background. The culmination of this process were campaigns of violence directed against Ukrainians and the 1937-8 pogroms against Jews. These class and national tensions culminated in the tragic events of 1939-45.

Collaboration with a power seeking to challenge political authority in Eastern Europe and the Soviet Union therefore seemed the only real alternative to some Ukrainians and other minorities. Not owing allegiance to any state, some minorities looked to any political movement, ideology, or state that promised or allowed them national self-determination. Many political groups believed that their own political agenda for national independence could be achieved through the expected struggle between Germany and the Soviet Union.

That this hope proved futile for Ukrainians and others is a matter of historical record. Nevertheless, their motivations must be placed within this historical context. To understand this crisis of legitimacy and identity in interwar Eastern Europe is to better appreciate issues that are still with us today and are the focus of part 1.

Note

1 Roman Szporluk, "War By Other Means," *Slavic Review* 44, no. 1 (Spring 1985): 20-26. For another recent view on this period, see Raymond Pearson, *National Minorities in Eastern Europe, 1848-1945* (London, 1983).

OREST SUBTELNY

The Soviet Occupation of Western Ukraine, 1939–41: An Overview

When the North American media deal with the topic of occupied Europe during World War II, they usually present a predictable, if substantially correct, image of countries overrun by Nazi armies, populations terrorized by the *Gestapo*, summary executions, and concentration camps. The behaviour of the occupied peoples is also depicted in standard fashion: the "good" people invariably resisted the Nazis while the "bad" collaborated. The essence of this version of the war is that the Nazis were the universal and exclusive enemy and that the only acceptable behaviour during World War II was to fight against them.

This position is valid in certain respects but misleading in others. Although the Nazi regime was generally despised, its oppressiveness varied from country to country. Some countries were brutalized more than others. And while a small minority in the occupied lands joined the anti-Nazi resistance or chose to collaborate with the Germans, the vast majority engaged neither in heroics nor in evil deeds. Most people in the occupied lands simply tried to survive. But perhaps the greatest shortcoming of the popular North American view of occupied Europe is the implication that only the Nazis brutalized the lands which they occupied.

Many peoples of Eastern Europe, among them the Estonians, Belorussians, Latvians, Lithuanians, and Western Ukrainians were persecuted not only by the Nazis but also by the Soviets. Tens of thousands were murdered by the NKVD, the Soviet secret police, as well as by the *Gestapo*, and hundreds of thousands more were dispatched to Nazi concentration camps and to the Soviet Gulag. In 1939–41, it was the Soviets who first inflicted the horrors of occupation on much of Eastern Europe. After the Nazi regime was defeated in 1944, the Soviets returned once again to these Eastern European lands with their own brand of inhumanity.

For the Balts, Belorussians, and Ukrainians, foreign occupation during World War II presented a more complex problem than for the other occupied nations of Europe. Some tried to resist both the Nazis and the Soviets. (The Ukrainian Insurgent Army is a case in point.) Others considered this policy unrealistic and argued for the need, no matter how distasteful, of siding with one totalitarian regime in order to withstand the other. Since the Soviets had already occupied their lands once and were about to do so again, they were perceived by many Eastern Europeans as the greater long-term threat; hence the Baltic, Belorussian, and Ukrainian units that fought in the German army on the anti-Soviet front.

Unfortunately, the North American media have shown little appreciation for the unique dilemma of peoples caught between the Nazi and Soviet regimes. They judge the behaviour of Balts, Belorussians, and Ukrainians in World War II according to the political context of Western Europe, where the Nazis were the sole enemy. This approach has led to irresponsible accusations of "collaboration," made by those who had obvious choices in World War II against those whose alternatives were less clear-cut and, consequently, more difficult to make. It is therefore important to focus on the "other side" of the occupation issue during World War II and to examine the conditions prevailing under Soviet rule and during the Soviet occupation of Western Ukraine in 1939–41.

PRELUDE TO OCCUPATION: THE HITLER-STALIN PACT

On 23 August 1939 Nazi Germany and the Soviet Union concluded the Molotov-Ribbentrop Pact, one of the most astonishing treaties of the twentieth century.[1] As a result of the pact, the two heretofore bitterly antagonistic regimes secretly reached an understanding that, in the view of many historians, led directly to the outbreak of World War II. The major components of this treaty were a declaration of non-aggression, friendship, and co-operation; a trade agreement whereby the Soviets were to supply the raw materials necessary for the Nazi war machine in return for German technological help and machinery; and a secret protocol, the most important part of the treaty. This protocol divided Eastern Europe into two spheres of influence: Estonia, Latvia,

Lithuania, Bessarabia, along with Western Belorussia and Western Ukraine (the latter two areas belonged to Poland at the time), were to be handed over to the Soviets, while the remainder of Poland and a part of Lithuania were assigned to the Germans.

Why did Stalin agree to sign a treaty which allowed Hitler to begin the most terrible war in history? Why, in the months that followed, did the Soviets faithfully and regularly supply the Nazi war machine, engaged against the Western Allies, with raw materials? And why did co-operation between the two regimes go so far that officers of the Nazi *Gestapo* and the Soviet NKVD regularly met to deal with matters of mutual interest?[2] In short, why did the Soviets, for a period of almost two years, collaborate with the Nazis?

When these questions are put to the Soviets and their sympathizers, the response is usually that the collaboration was necessary because it served Soviet interests at the time. This view has some validity. In 1939, faced with diplomatic isolation, the Soviet leadership might have felt that it had few options other than to strike a political deal with Hitler. Today, Western scholars and the Western media in general are quite willing to take into account the Soviet dilemma and often obligingly bypass this embarrassing episode in the Soviet past.

This understanding attitude, this willingness to forgive and forget the Hitler-Stalin pact is noteworthy, especially today when the sensitive issue of collaboration has been brought up again, because it reflects a blatant double standard: while Soviet collaboration with the Nazis is explained away by both the Soviets and Westerners, the collaboration of various Eastern European peoples, which was on a much smaller scale, is denounced by the Soviets and the Western media as one of the worst crimes of the century. The same authorities who argue that one must take into account the context of the Hitler-Stalin pact and the problems that the Soviets faced in 1939 find it difficult to appreciate the context in which the Balts, Ukrainians, and others acted and the political dilemmas they had to face. Even more hypocritical is the attitude of the Soviets, who for years have been in the forefront of those who have made accusations of collaborationism.

The impact of the Hitler-Stalin pact on Ukrainians was to assign about 4.5 million Western Ukrainians, most of whom had previously lived under Polish rule, to the Soviet Union, without any choice or consultation. Nothing could have been worse for Western Ukrainians. Of all Ukrainians, they were the most fiercely nationalistic and desirous of independent statehood. And of all the great powers in

Europe, none of whom cared the slightest about Ukrainian national aspirations, the Soviet Union was the most implacable enemy of Ukrainian nationalism and independence. Thus, on basic political issues, Western Ukrainians and the Soviets were uncompromisingly opposed to one other.

Western Ukrainian anti-Sovietism, however, was based not only on political and ideological differences. Only six years earlier, in 1932–3, millions of Ukrainians in the Soviet Union had starved to death as a result of Stalin's determination to carry out collectivization at all costs. And in 1937–8, hundreds of thousands of Ukrainians were either executed or exiled to Siberian concentration camps during the purges.[3] Western Ukrainians therefore had good reason to fear the arrival of the Soviets in Galicia, and their fears proved to be well-founded.

SOVIET OCCUPATION

On 17 September 1939 the Soviet armies entered Western Ukraine. This first Soviet occupation, which lasted twenty-one months, can be divided into two distinct phases.[4] In the early phase the Soviets went out of their way to "win the hearts and minds" of the populace. Actually, they had little choice but to follow such a policy at the outset. Their formal justification for the occupation was that Soviet collaboration with the Nazis in the dismemberment of Poland was motivated by the desire to aid its oppressed minorities, the Ukrainians and Belorussians.

During this initial phase, the Soviets tried to impress Western Ukrainians with their regime's ostensible Ukrainianism. Soviet troops were led into Galicia by a general with an obviously Ukrainian name – Semen Tymoshenko. The segment of the Soviet armed forces that entered Galicia was called the Ukrainian Front. These symbolic gestures were meant to indicate that what was occurring was not a foreign invasion but a case of Ukrainians coming to the aid of fellow Ukrainians. The Soviets also put on a great show of being democratic. On 22 October 1939 they organized an election during which the populace was strongly encouraged to vote for the single slate of candidates supporting the annexation of Western Ukraine to the Soviet Union. (After World War II, similar "democratic" elections would take place in Hungary, Romania, Bulgaria, and Poland.)

Some early Soviet policies, when compared with those of the Poles, were an improvement for the Ukrainians.[5] Ukrainian culture, severely repressed by the Poles, was allowed to flower. Ukrainian became the official language of Western Ukraine. Great efforts were made to improve the school system. And whereas the Poles had discouraged Ukrainians from entering universities, the Soviets allowed Ukrainians to obtain a higher education and Ukrainianized the universities. Health care improved. But perhaps the most popular measure was the Soviet expropriation of the Polish landlords and the promise to redistribute the land among the peasants.

Yet simultaneously with these reforms, steps were taken to deprive Western Ukrainians of the means for political self-expression. When the Soviets first arrived, they undertook a systematic campaign of arrests and deportations eastward of the Western Ukrainian political leadership. Politicians who were not arrested were forced to flee to German-occupied Poland. The largest Ukrainian political parties, which were centrist and relatively liberal, were disbanded. These measures resulted in the elimination in Western Ukraine of individuals and political parties representing middle-of-the-road, liberal tendencies. Western Ukrainians were left with only one viable political organization – the underground network of the Organization of Ukrainian Nationalists (OUN).

Along with the growing numbers of arrests and deportations came other repellent aspects of the Soviet regime. Even before Galicia was formally incorporated into the USSR, the Soviets introduced their own administrative structure and laws. During 1940 they began to dismantle systematically almost all of the educational, cultural, and economic institutions that Western Ukrainians had laboriously developed over generations and in the face of strong Polish opposition. Thus, the occupation forces set out to destroy the entire infrastructure of Western Ukrainian society.[6]

At the same time, the less attractive side of the early Soviet reforms became more evident. Lands that had been expropriated from Polish landlords and "given" to the peasants did not remain in their hands; instead, the Communists forced the peasants to combine their holdings in collective farms. Thus, the same intensely hated collectivization that had cost millions of lives in Soviet Ukraine was imposed on the Western Ukrainian peasantry. At this point, the vast majority of the peasantry, which had long been wary of the invaders, turned against them. The intelligentsia, many of whom were initially pleased by the jobs they found in the educational and cultural institutions, soon realized that they were expected to act as mouthpieces for ever more blatant Soviet propaganda, and that refusal to do so could mean arrest and deportation.

Because of the Western Ukrainians' strong commitment to their church, the Soviets initially treated the Ukrainian Catholic Church with a great deal of circumspection. They did not attempt to ban it but simply imposed what at first appeared to be relatively minor restrictions. However, in time these restrictions became more onerous. Priests were forced to carry special passports identifying them as clergy and were impeded in their attempts to fulfill their duties. The clergy was also saddled with much higher taxes. Anti-religious propaganda, present from the outset, steadily increased. By late 1940 it was evident that the future boded ill for the Ukrainian Catholic Church.

In the spring of 1940 the Soviets dropped their democratic guise, and repressions against both Ukrainians and Poles began on a massive scale. The most widespread and feared measures were the deportations. Without warning, without trial, even without formal accusations, thousands of supposed enemies of the people were arrested, usually at night, packed into cattle cars, and shipped to Siberia and Kazakhstan to work as slave labourers under horrible conditions. Many of the deportees, whose numbers included entire families, perished.

Who were these "enemies of the people"? The first waves of deportees consisted of leading politicians, industrialists, landowners, merchants, bureaucrats, judges, lawyers, retired officers, and priests. Later, in co-operation with Nazi officials, the Soviet authorities also rounded up the families of Ukrainian political activists and the 20–30,000 Ukrainians who had fled to German-occupied Poland. However, anyone vaguely suspected of sympathizing with Ukrainian nationalism was liable to arrest. In the final stages, the deportations, which grew constantly in scale and brutality, seemed to lose all rhyme or reason. People who had relatives abroad or received letters from abroad (and almost every Western Ukrainian had relatives or friends in Canada or the United States), who were visiting friends when they were arrested, who were denounced for purely personal reasons or who, by accident, happened to be in the wrong place at the wrong time, were deported. The fear aroused by the deportations was described by an eyewitness:

During the war all of us had gotten used to the idea of death. When our town was bombed, many people got üsed to the bombing. They said that if someone was fated to die from a bomb, there was no way to avoid it. Therefore, instead of hiding in shelters, they moved about in the streets, oblivious to the shooting. . . . However, these very same people would lose their composure when they heard news that "the Bolsheviks will be shipping more out in the next few days". And no wonder. Those words encompassed one of the most horrible techniques of Bolshevik terror.[7]

The deportations occurred in three waves. In December 1939 they were still selective and encompassed primarily the former leadership and elite. But on 13 and 14 April 1940 a new wave began that included vast numbers of people. "From then on," a survivor wrote, "no one, literally no one, was sure whether his turn would not come the next night." The final and most extensive wave of deportation occurred in June 1941, when the panic-stricken and suspicious Soviets herded thousands of arbitrarily chosen people on trains and shipped them eastward. Estimates of the population losses in Western Ukraine, which must rest on Soviet sources, are obviously difficult to come by. The Ukrainian Catholic Metropolitan Andrei Sheptytsky, in a letter to the Vatican dated 7 November 1941, provided the following statistics: in the Lviv eparchy alone an estimated 200,000 Ukrainians had been jailed, forcibly evacuated, or executed. He put the losses of Ukrainian population for Galicia as a whole at approximately 400,000. The Polish government-in-exile in London placed total population losses for Poles, Ukrainians, and others in the Soviet-occupied areas of the former Polish state at about 1.5 million people.[8]

The deportations, however, were not the worst of what the Soviet occupation inflicted upon Western Ukraine. A journalist who witnessed the final days of this occupation recalled how the NKVD carried out widespread massacres of political prisoners shortly before it fled the invading Germans:

During the twenty-one-month Bolshevik rule in Western Ukraine we had ample opportunities to become well acquainted with all the tricks of the Red regime and all of the repressions it inflicted upon the innocent population. People from Western Europe simply could not imagine the methods which they [the Soviets] applied. However, it was only in the final week of their stay in Lviv that we realized the extremes of horror and sadism that the cruelty of the Bolsheviks was capable of reaching.[9]

Months before the outbreak of the Nazi-Soviet war, the NKVD

began to arrest increasing numbers of people suspected of being potentially politically unreliable. However, the sudden advance of the Germans into Galicia caught the NKVD by surprise, and it did not have time to evacuate prisoners. The solution applied was simple and brutal: during the week of 22–29 June 1941 the NKVD set about slaughtering the inmates of its prisons, regardless of whether they were incarcerated for minor or major offences, or whether they were already convicted or merely awaiting questioning. Major massacres occurred in the following places: in Lviv (about 1,500 victims), in Sambir (about 1,200), in Stanyslaviv (about 2,500), in Zolochiv (about 800), in Chortkiv (about 800), and Dobromyl (about 500). These figures do not include the many small towns and villages where dozens of prisoners died. Thus, an estimated 10,000 prisoners were killed in Galicia. In neighbouring Volhynia, particularly in the towns of Rivne and Lutske, about 5,000 more were executed.[10]

It was not only the numbers of the executed but also the manner in which they died that shocked the populace. When the families of the arrested rushed to the prisons after the Soviet evacuation, they were aghast to find bodies so badly mutilated that many could not be identified. It was evident that many of the prisoners had been tortured before death; others were killed en masse. In Sambir on 26 June 1941 the NKVD dynamited two large cells crammed with female prisoners. In Stanyslaviv three huge cells were stacked to the ceiling with corpses that were so badly decomposed that no attempt was made to bury them. The townspeople simply cemented up the cells. In Zolochiv the people found cells full of mutilated bodies next to torture chambers strewn with tongues, ears, eyes, and tufts of hair.[11] These and similar findings, coming on the heels of months of growing terror, filled Western Ukrainians with a deep revulsion for the Soviets and reinforced their conviction that the Soviets were, and would always be, their worst enemy. These experiences later encouraged Ukrainians to join the German fight against the Soviets, and these bitter memories of 1939–41 impelled tens of thousands of Western Ukrainians to flee their homeland in 1944 when the Soviets were about to occupy it again.

In analyzing the events of 1939–41 in Western Ukraine, three points are most important. First, because Western Ukrainians had to deal with not one but two alien totalitarian invaders during World War II, they were forced to make choices that other peoples did not have to confront. Second, based on very recent and painful experiences – the Soviet crushing of attempts to establish Ukrainian independence in

1917–20, the famine of 1933, the purges of the 1930s, and especially the occupation of 1939–41 – Ukrainians had good reason to view the Soviets as their primary enemy and, after the German defeat at Stalingrad in 1943, as the greatest threat they would face in the future. Third, when many Western Ukrainians chose to side with the Germans to fight against the Soviets, they acted in what they perceived to be their best interests, as have other nations in similar circumstances.

Notes

1 For literature on the pact, see George Kennan, *Soviet Foreign Policy, 1917–1941* (New York, 1960); Adam Ulam, *Expansion and Coexistence: The History of Soviet Foreign Policy, 1917–1967* (New York, 1968); for a Soviet viewpoint, see A.A. Gromyko and B.N. Ponomarev, eds., *Istoriia vneshnei politiki SSSR, 1917–1975*, vol. 1 (Moscow, 1966–).

2 "Dokumentationszentrum des Bundes Jüdischer Verfolgter des Naziregimes," *Bulletin of Information*, no. 25 (1985): 6.

3 On Soviet rule in Ukraine, including the famine and the purges, see Ewald Ammende, *Human Life in Russia* (Cleveland, 1984; reprint); Robert Conquest, *The Great Terror* (Harmondsworth, 1971); Miron Dolot, *Execution by Hunger* (New York, 1985); Hryhory Kostiuk, *Stalinist Rule in the Ukraine: A Study of the Decade of Mass Terror (1929–1939)* (Munich, 1960); Boris Levytsky, *The Uses of Terror: The Soviet Secret Service, 1917–70* (London, 1971); James Mace, *Communism and the Dilemmas of National Liberation: National Communism in Soviet Ukraine, 1918–1933* (Cambridge, Mass., 1983); Semen O. Pidhainy, ed., *The Black Deeds of the Kremlin: A White Book*, 2 vols. (Toronto, 1953–5); and Olexa Woropay, *The Ninth Circle* (Cambridge, Mass., 1983).

4 For further discussion of the Soviet occupation of Western Ukraine, see John Armstrong, *Ukrainian Nationalism*, 2d rev. ed. (Littleton, Colo., 1980); the memoirs of Kost Pankivsky, *Vid derzhavy do komitetu*. (*Lito 1941 u Lvovi*) (New York-Toronto, 1957); Volodymyr Kubiiovych, *Ukraintsi v Heneralnii hubernii, 1939–1941* (Chicago, 1975); the very valuable collection of memoirs of the Soviet occupation edited by Milena Rudnytska, *Zakhidnia Ukraina pid bolshevykamy* (New York, 1958); and Hryhorii Vashchenko, "Vyzvolennia Zakhidnoi Ukrainy bolshevykamy," *Ukrainskyi zbirnyk*, vol. 1 (Munich, 1954), 67–77. See also a useful overview by David Marples, "The Ukraine in World War II," *Radio Liberty Research Bulletin*, Radio Liberty Supplement 1/85, 6 May 1985, 1–26. On the Soviet Union's treatment of Poles and Jews, see the following: Władysław Studnicki, *Das östliche Polen* (Kitzingen-Main, 1953); Z. Sobieski, "Reminiscences from Lwow, 1939–1946," *Journal of Central European Affairs* 6, no. 4 (1947): 350–74; Shimon Redlich, "The Jews in the Soviet Annexed Territories, 1939–41," *Soviet Jewish Affairs* 1, no. 1 (June 1971): 81–90; and Dov Levin, "The Jews and the Inception of Soviet Rule in Bukovina," *Soviet Jewish Affairs* 6, no. 2 (1976): 52–70. Especially enlightening and valuable materials may be found in Irena Grudzinska-Gross and Jan Tomasz Gross, eds., *War Through Children's Eyes: The Soviet Occupation of Poland and the Deportations, 1939–1941* (Stanford, 1981).

5 For a Soviet treatment of their reforms in Western Ukraine, see V. Varetsky, *Sotsialistychni peretvorennia u zakhidnykh oblastiakh URSR* (Kiev, 1960).
6 On the Soviet dismantling of Ukrainian institutions, see Rudnytska, *Zakhidnia Ukraina*, 111–255.
7 Ibid., 453.
8 Cited in ibid., 456, n. 1. Some Polish sources put the estimated number of deportees even higher. For example, Władysław Studnicki, in *Panowanie Rosji Radzieckej w Polsce Wschodniej, 1939–1941* (Warsaw, 1943), argued that as many as 1.8 million were deported from Poland's eastern territories. This estimate, however, seems to be greatly exaggerated.
9 Rudnytska, *Zakhidnia Ukraina*, 465.
10 Ibid., 465–92. Most of the statistics cited by Rudnytska come from reports published in the newspaper *Ukrainski shchodenni visti*, which began to appear in the first week of July 1941. On pages 472–6 Rudnytska provides a list of well-known Western Ukrainians who were either executed or deported by the Soviets. For more statistical information on the numbers of executed, see Volodymyr Kubiiovych, ed., *Entsyklopediia ukrainoznavstva* (Munich-New York, 1949), 583, 587. For an example of the categories of people the Soviet authorities slated for arrest and execution, see the third interim report of the Select Committee on Communist Aggression, House of Representatives, 83rd Congress, 2d session, 1954, entitled *Baltic States: A Study of Their Origin and National Development; Their Seizure and Incorporation into the U.S.S.R.,* International Military Law and History Reprint Series, vol. 4 (Buffalo, 1972), 497–500, which contains translated copies of Soviet instructions to their secret police in Lithuania. Similar lists and instructions were most probably issued to Soviet authorities in Western Ukraine.
11 Rudnytska, *Zakhidnia Ukraina*, 477–91. The Soviet historian Roy A. Medvedev, in *Let History Judge: The Origins and Consequences of Stalinism* (New York, 1971), 248–9, corroborates the information regarding the brutality of Soviet occupation:

A large number of illegal arrests in 1939–41 occurred in Bessarabia, the Western Ukraine, West Belorussia, and the Baltic territories. Besides a few real enemies of the proletariat – agents of the tsarist secret police, reactionary politicians, members of fascist and semifascist organizations – thousands of completely innocent people were repressed. In some of these areas Stalin and the NKVD carried out a criminal deportation: tens of thousands of local people were arbitrarily sent east. This action caused widespread dissatisfaction among the local inhabitants, which led in turn to worse repression. Just before the war, all the prisons of Lvov, Kishinev, Tallin, and Riga were filled to overflowing. In the turmoil of the first days of the war, the NKVD in some cities (Lvov and Tartu, for example), unable to move prisoners, simply ordered them to be shot. The bodies were not even removed, and in Lvov, before the appearance of the Germans, the population came to the prison to identify the dead. This crime caused an outburst of indignation in the western areas, and was very useful to fascist propagandists and the followers of Bandera. The criminal actions of the NKVD were largely to blame for the slow development of the [Soviet] resistance movement against the fascist occupation in the western regions.

BOHDAN KRAWCHENKO

Soviet Ukraine under Nazi Occupation, 1941–4

Ukraine had barely begun to recover from the traumas of the 1930s when it was plunged into World War II. It was the largest Soviet republic to be fully occupied by the Germans and was held longer than the areas of Russia under German control.[1] In the course of the conflict, 6.8 million people were killed, of whom 600,000 were Jews and 1.4 million were military personnel who either perished at the front or died as prisoners of war (POWs). More than two million citizens of the republic were sent to Germany as "slave labour."[2]

By 1944, when the German armies were cleared from Soviet Ukraine, the republic was in ruins. More than 700 cities and towns, representing 42 per cent of all urban centres devastated by the war in the entire USSR, and more than 28,000 villages had been destroyed. Direct material damage amounted to 285 billion rubles (in 1941 prices), or more than 40 per cent of the USSR's losses. But the real cost of the war to the Ukrainian republic, in damage, war effort, and goods requisitioned by Germans, was estimated at an astronomical one trillion two hundred billion rubles (in 1941 prices).[3] During his travels in Ukraine in 1945, Edgar Snow reported that "the Second World War, which some are apt to dismiss as 'the Russian glory,' has, in all truth and in many costly ways, been first of all a Ukrainian war . . . . No single European country suffered deeper wounds to its cities, its industries, its farmlands, and its humanity."[4]

The German advance into Ukraine had been rapid and spectacular. The invasion was launched on 22 June 1941, and Kharkiv, on Ukraine's eastern border with Russia, was captured by 25 October. The Germans encountered an army with little will. One soldier reported, "Only a few small special detachments fought stubbornly. The great majority of Red soldiers was not influenced at all by a spirit of resistance."[5]

The swift defeat of the Soviet troops was a natural consequence of the many weaknesses of Stalin's regime and of the population's experience during the 1930s.[6] The bureaucratic centralization of military decision-making in Stalin's hands also contributed to the collapse.[7] Ignoring the pleas of Ukraine's republican leadership for flexible manoeuvres and for a regroupment of forces in order to draw up new lines of defence, Stalin ordered haphazard, unco-ordinated offensives that led to the encirclement and capture of entire armies.[8]

During the 1936–8 purges, the Red Army suffered terrible blows to its fighting capacity. Almost 60 per cent of army commanders at the corps, division, and brigade levels were either executed or died in prison camps prior to the war. The replacements for the purged officers were unseasoned and less capable.[9] Local authorities, made servile by Stalin's bureaucratic system, did not exhibit the independent initiative demanded by a crisis and retreated instead.[10] As a result, enormous numbers of prisoners were taken by the Germans. As early as November 1941 the Germans held 3.6 million POWs, among whom were an estimated 1.3 million Ukrainians.[11]

In the face of the German advance, Stalin's "strategic plan" was put into effect: "destroying all that cannot be evacuated."[12] Cities, factories, and food supplies were blown up. Tens of thousands of prisoners in the hands of the NKVD were executed.[13] Almost 45 per cent of all cattle owned by collective and state farms were driven across the Ukrainian border to Russia. More than 50,000 factories and plants were dismantled and removed.[14] Of the civilian population, approximately 3.5 million men, women, and children were moved into the interior of Russia and to Central Asia.[15] Since "pull and friends were used to get out ahead of the Germans," it was mostly prominent party and state officials, the labour aristocracy, and the "higher intelligentsia" who were able to leave.[16] Given the Nazis' extermination policies, the evacuation was necessary. However, the administration made little effort to evacuate Jews; only those who were prominent in the Party and in state and other institutions were moved.

The departure of the most well-known members of the Ukrainian intelligentsia produced a leadership vacuum,[17] and the population could therefore not help but think that it was being left to face the Germans alone. This, combined with the widespread destruction accompanying the Soviet retreat, "helped infuriate the population against the Soviet regime."[18]

The initial response of the civilian population toward the Germans has yet to be studied in a systematic way. However, the image of smiling Ukrainians in national costume welcoming the German "liberators" with the traditional bread and salt is grossly overwrought. This stereotype was promoted rather effectively during the Cold War as proof that American psychological warfare directed at the Soviet population would pay huge dividends.[19] Its source was the measured welcome that the residents of the Western regions, annexed by the Soviet Union in 1939, offered the Germans. Popular moods toward the Germans in the Soviet regions during the first days of occupation were "considerably more complex," according to a 9 July 1941 report of the *Einsatzgruppen*, the task forces of specially selected police officials headed by SS officers from Heinrich Himmler's trusted circles.[20]

Judging from eyewitness accounts and interviews with refugees, the vast majority of people were relieved to see the Soviets leave, but they were "completely disoriented" by the rapid turn of events.[21] Most saw "no reason to be overjoyed by the Germans," since common sense dictated that "they have not come to Ukraine to do good."[22] Others, notably some former urban petit bourgeois (small shopkeepers and the like), some intellectuals, as well as peasants whose families had had substantial holdings before the revolution, engaged in "watchful waiting."[23] Their hopes were pinned on the expectation that "Germans are a cultured people," and that the events of World War I – when Germans occupied Ukraine in 1918 and "things were not so bad" – would be repeated.[24] (Tragically, some Jewish artisans also shared this illusion and thought that they would be permitted to open private shops.[25])

The announcement of a positive program in this initial period of uncertainty and confusion would have yielded results for the Germans. Their silence, however, was not an oversight. Giving consideration to the wishes of the conquered peoples would have meant compromising Hitler's goals. Confident of victory, German propagandists were strictly forbidden to say anything about the Nazis' plans for the occupied territories.[26]

The hiatus between the evacuation of Soviet authority and the entrenchment of the German administration lasted approximately two months, from July to September 1941 in most regions. In this short span of time, numerous attempts at the self-organization of Ukrainian society (the establishment of a local administration, schools, and newspapers) were made. In explaining this unexpected activity, which often manifested itself days after the departure of Soviet officials, two factors must be taken into account. The first is the role of Western Ukrainians, several thousands of whom were sent into Soviet Ukraine by their revolutionary nationalist parties. The second was the development of national consciousness among Soviet Ukrainians during the previous two decades.

Western Ukrainian intervention in Soviet Ukraine is intertwined with the story of the Organization of Ukrainian Nationalists (OUN), founded in 1929. The OUN propagated a brand of revolutionary integral nationalism, emphasizing voluntarism, self-sacrifice, discipline, and obedience to the leadership. Apart from a militant attachment to Ukrainian independence, its political and social program was confused, with an unimaginative recast of Italian corporatist ideology within an essentially populist framework.[27] When Hitler took power, a member of the OUN leadership condemned Nazi ideology as imperialist, racist, and anti-Christian.[28] The Soviet-German non-aggression treaty in 1939 and the subsequent Soviet occupation of Western Ukraine, as well as Hitler's backing of Hungary's destruction of the short-lived Carpatho-Ukrainian Republic, whose defence forces the OUN helped organize,[29] reinforced OUN suspicions of German ambitions. Nonetheless, Germany was the only power opposed to the European status quo, and a German-Soviet conflict seemed to be the only way out of the impasse in which Ukraine found itself. For this reason the OUN counted on a new war to give it an opportunity to assert Ukrainian statehood. It prepared for this event by maintaining contact with the *Abwehr*, the German military intelligence service, and by mobilizing OUN cadres.[30]

Soviet rule in Western Ukraine between 1939–41 alienated the Western Ukrainian population without completely destroying the cadres of the nationalist movement. Because of its conspiratorial nature, the OUN survived the Soviet occupation of Western Ukraine better than socialist groups and the large electoralist parties, all of which collapsed. Indeed, the OUN used the opportunity to establish contact with Soviet Ukrainians.[31] The OUN also had members scattered throughout Western Europe. Many lived in German-occupied Poland, having crossed the border when the Red Army entered Western Ukraine.

In 1940 the OUN split. The younger, more radical elements followed Stepan Bandera (the OUN-B), while the others remained adherents of Andrii Melnyk (the OUN-M). Both factions formed expeditionary groups (*pokhidni hrupy*), whose task was to follow the Germans into Ukraine and seize power. The groups were also instructed to organize anti-German resistance if necessary.[32] In 1941 the OUN had close to 20,000 members, half of whom were under twenty-one.[33] It sent about 8,000 members into Soviet Ukraine as soon as the Germans launched their offensive.[34] Of this number, roughly 300 acted as translators with the German forces and were to facilitate the work of expeditionary groups.[35] The rest were formed into small detachments of ten to fifteen members and spread into all areas of Ukraine, where they helped fill the leadership vacuum.

When the expeditionary groups entered Soviet Ukraine, they encountered a population on whom, according to a Western Ukrainian observer, "the era of Ukrainization and the formal existence of a Soviet Ukrainian state had left a great mark."[36] Former members of the Ukrainian Galician Army who were in Ukraine in 1918–9 and who visited the country again in 1941 noted that "national consciousness is now incomparably greater than during the revolution."[37] The rise in national consciousness was also observed in Ukraine's industrial regions, whose human fabric had been transformed by the influx of Ukrainian peasants during the 1930s.[38] In the Donbas (Donets basin), according to a local resident, "the need for Ukrainian statehood was taken for granted."[39] This national awareness served as a basis for common action between Soviet and Western Ukrainians.

The political culture of Western Ukrainians differed markedly, however, from that of their Soviet compatriots and emerged as a point of tension. Western Ukrainian nationalists ignored socio-economic and civil rights issues and viewed the attainment of national independence as a panacea, while Eastern Ukrainians regarded these questions with great concern and rejected the integral nationalist doctrine as elitist, intolerant, and obscurantist.[40]

But at a time when Soviet Ukrainians had no political organizations, and the democratic and socialist parties in both Western Ukraine and in exile in Western Europe were "absent from the scene," "what remained were only the nationalists."[41] People were prepared to work with Western Ukrainian nationalists in establishing a local administration and schools not only because these were essential institutions but also in order to give these institutions a national content. Self-organization at the local level was felt to be the first step toward achieving a national government.[42] The OUN's singleness of purpose and dynamism impressed the still-fragmented Soviet Ukrainian population and was taken by them as a sign that the activity being undertaken would be tolerated by the Germans. That the *Wehrmacht* had left a relatively free hand to the inhabitants in the first month or so reinforced this false belief.[43]

Within a matter of weeks a local administration with various departments responsible for such areas as health and education was established at the municipal, village, and, in some areas, at the *oblast* level. These administrations, many of which were elected, served with the militias as organs of self-government and attempted to rebuild the shattered communities. Since these organs were targeted for control by the OUN, in many regions they became dominated by "separatist elements."[44] Where this occurred, the OUN together with its Eastern Ukrainian sympathizers Ukrainianized the administrations and transformed them into vehicles promoting Ukrainian national goals. The work of some administrations was marred by the factional conflict between the OUN-B and OUN-M, and by Eastern Ukrainians' resentment of OUN members' high-handedness, neglect of social welfare issues, and virulent anti-Russian attitudes.[45] However, as one eyewitness reported, the local administrations were initially headed largely by "honest people, intellectuals, and the [formerly] 'repressed.' There was no talk about them being puppets or German agents. People hoped that they would be the nucleus of a government."[46] Indeed, "the wildest rumours" circulated about the imminent arrival of the former head of the Ukrainian Directory during the Revolution, Volodymyr Vynnychenko (with his Jewish wife), and other well-known socialists who were to head a new government.[47]

Throughout Ukraine many elementary, secondary, and vocational schools were repaired and reopened by community efforts. Wherever possible, universities and institutes renewed their activities. An All-Ukrainian Teachers' Union was founded, which had as one of its principal aims the production of new textbooks.[48] As a result of local initiatives, the school curriculum was revised in order to communicate a Ukrainian national message stressing language, history, and culture.[49] In Poltava, for example, children were taught national songs hitherto forbidden by Soviet authorities.[50] In Voroshylovhrad in the Donbas, a teachers' conference decided to make Ukrainian the language of instruction in all schools.[51] At the start of the German occupation, 115 Ukrainian-language newspapers were founded.[52] Some, such as the Kievan *Ukrainske slovo* (Ukrainian Word) established by the OUN-M, developed a substantial readership, with a circulation of 50,000.[53] Many newspapers "maintained an autonomous position."[54] They carried articles outlining the case for Ukrainian independence, exposés of events of the 1930s, discussions of the works of Mykola Khvylovy and of other cultural figures purged under Stalin, and popular accounts of Ukrainian history.[55] At the same time, scores of theatres and choirs were founded.[56] Peasants began to divide collective farms on the basis of the old principle of family size.[57] Co-operatives and an agricultural bank were established. Roughly two months after the Soviet evacuation, Zhytomyr *oblast*, for example, had an agricultural bank with 11 branches and a co-operative with 140 branches.[58] *Prosvity*, the adult education societies, were created. In the industrial centre of Kryvyi Rih, for instance, the *Prosvita* "was well organized, holding many courses and concerts . . . with branches in dozens of villages."[59] After one concert, attended by thousands of people, the entire audience rose in the spontaneous singing of the Ukrainian national anthem, which had been banned under Soviet rule.[60] In Mykolaiv, in southern Ukraine, the revived *Prosvita* was run by local trade unionists who established it as "the centre of Ukrainian cultural life for the region." *Prosvita* members debated "plans for Ukrainization and the methods to be used."[61] Trade unions were revived. In Kryvyi Rih these unions, together with the newly established Club of Ukrainian Engineers, began to reconstruct the factories and plants as well as to establish forms of self-management.[62] A Ukrainian Red Cross undertook the operation of hospitals and clinics, and it provided assistance for Ukrainian POWs.[63] Religious life began to flourish. The Ukrainian Autocephalous Orthodox Church and the Ukrainian Autonomous Orthodox Church quickly gained support and established thousands of new parishes.[64] Streets were renamed in honour of Ukrainian national heroes, and in urban centres it was noted that "more Ukrainian is being spoken, since people no longer have the same fear of reprisals."[65]

All this activity led to a strengthening of national consciousness. "People began to voice public opinion more freely," according to a former resident of Dnipropetrovske.[66] Nationally conscious individuals came out of hiding.[67] Books and periodicals published during the 1920s and forbidden under Stalin circulated freely and were in great demand. The classics of Ukrainian history could now be read.[68] Teachers spoke openly in schools about national oppression.[69] During countless meetings and rallies hundreds of thousands of people became involved in the debate over Ukraine's future. Judging by contemporary reports, these discussions invariably focused on five "burning questions": the need for Ukrainians to have their own national state; the dismantling of collective farms and the introduction of an agrarian order that would allow peasants to "keep the fruits of their labour"; the "emancipation" of the working class; the reopening and Ukrainization of institutions of higher education in order to give youth opportunities for study; and the release of prisoners of war.[70] Nevertheless, caution and hesitation characterized these organizational initiatives and discussions, as a natural consequence of the atomization of society under Stalin and the often brutal behaviour of German troops.[71] But in this early period the German occupation forces could not possibly penetrate Ukrainian society with anything approaching the same effectiveness as had the Soviet regime or the German civil administration that was to follow. This permitted a movement for national and social emancipation, coming from the grass roots of society, to manifest itself. Indeed, the strong Ukrainian patriotism that arose in response to subsequent Nazi terror can only be understood against the background of the mobilization of the population in this brief period.

On the basis of available information it is difficult to establish the exact composition of the Soviet Ukrainians who emerged as the leadership in this initial period. The composition appears to have varied from region to region. Surviving members of the "old intelligentsia" – those who participated in the 1917–20 revolution, individuals who had suffered repression during the Soviet period, activists of the Ukrainization era (1924–30), former state and trade union functionaries, teachers, members of the younger intelligentsia – all appear to have played an important role. Noticeably absent were the higher Soviet intelligentsia and party functionaries, many of whom had either evacuated or remained passive, fearing German reprisals.[72] Certainly, the expansion of higher education during the preceding decades ensured that, unlike the period of the 1917 revolution, there was no shortage of skilled, trained Ukrainian personnel to assume the management of society. For example, the small town of Zhytomyr, with a population of 40,000 in 1941, boasted more than 500 "very nationally conscious members of the intelligentsia."[73] In this process of cultural-national revival, as already noted, Western Ukrainians frequently found themselves in the roles of initiators and intermediaries. Thus, in Mariiupil (now Zhdanov) in the Donbas, when Ukrainian efforts to found a newspaper were blocked by Russians who remained in charge of the local administration, Western Ukrainians intervened and secured permission for the establishment of the newspaper.[74] Often it was they who called the first meetings and began the political discussion. But their role in the cultural, educational, and economic initiatives was considerably less pronounced than the part they played in the establishment of local administrations and the militias.[75]

The period of national revival "passed like lightning."[76] The first concerted German campaign against Ukrainian national assertion began on 31 August 1941 in Zhytomyr and by the end of September 1941 had engulfed all of Ukraine.[77] The instruments used for the task were the *Einsatzgruppen*.[78] They struck at the cadres of the nascent Ukrainian national movement at the same time as they initiated the slaughter of Jews. First to fall victim in the attack against the Ukrainian movement were members of the expeditionary groups sent by the OUN-B and their Eastern Ukrainian sympathizers. In November, following a mass patriotic rally in Bazar (near Kiev) organized by the OUN-M, which demonstrated the strength of Ukrainian national sentiment and alarmed the Germans, an attack on the OUN-M and its Eastern Ukrainian supporters was launched.[79] By January 1942 most advocates of Ukrainian independence, Western and Eastern Ukrainians alike, who had openly participated in the founding of local administrations, militias, *Prosvity*, co-operatives, newspapers, and schools had been caught in the Nazi net.[80] A "colossal number" were executed in this campaign, which marked the entrenchment of German administration in Ukraine.[81]

Among the Nazis there were important differences of opinion over the formal state structures that should replace the union republics. Alfred Rosenberg, a Russophobic Baltic German who was the Nazis' "theorist" on matters of race and Minister for the Occupied Eastern Territories, favoured the establishment of a series of buffer states dependent on the Reich but exercising a measure of self-government, as a *cordon sanitaire* against Russia. He also advocated cultural policies that would "awaken the historical consciousness of Ukrainians" and serve to mobilize them against Russia.[82] His concepts, however, clashed with the views of the Nazi establishment, which wanted only to colonize and exploit the east. Hitler had spoken against the creation of any kind of Ukrainian state and advocated direct Nazi control over this and other eastern territories.[83] Thus the *Reichskommissariat Ukraine* (the German civil administration) was formed as a branch of the *Ostministerium*, the Reich Ministry for the Occupied Eastern Territories. Since Hitler thought that Ukraine was "undoubtedly the most important Eastern district," he appointed a loyal servitor, Erich Koch, to head the *Reichskommissariat*.[84] Although nominally subordinate to Rosenberg, Koch could ignore the policies of his superior because he was favoured by such powerful figures as Bormann and Goering and had direct access to Hitler. In his inaugural speech, Koch described himself as "a brutal dog," declaring that "for this reason I was appointed *Reichskommissar* of Ukraine." His mission, said Koch, was "to suck from Ukraine all the goods we can get hold of, without consideration for the feeling or the property of Ukrainians."[85] Whatever else can be said of Koch, he was a man of his word.[86]

German policy paid not the slightest attention to Ukrainian national sensitivities. The country was divided: Galicia became a district of the General Government of Poland (the *Generalgouvernement*), while most of Odessa and parts of Vinnytsia and Mykolaiv *oblasts*, as well as northern Bukovyna, were assigned to Romania (which called the region Transnistria) as compensation for Romania's loss of Transylvania to Hungary.[87] Except for the eastern districts near the front, which remained under the jurisdiction of the *Wehrmacht*, Ukraine fell under the direct control of Koch. To emphasize the point that "Ukraine does not exist . . . it is merely a geographical concept," Koch made the small provincial town of Rivne the capital of the *Reichskommissariat*.[88]

A vast German administrative network encompassing all spheres of activity was established in both the *Reichskommissariat* and the regions held by the *Wehrmacht*. As noted by a Soviet source, "in none of the countries hitherto occupied by the fascists was there such a large occupational force and such a numerous occupational apparatus" as in Ukraine.[89] Indigenous administrations operated only on the lowest levels – the village or groups of villages and in towns. Even here they were under the strict control of German supervisory personnel, who could dismiss indigenous staff at will.[90] By far the largest local administration was in Kiev. In 1942 its entire apparatus numbered 2,000 – a trifling figure for a city of 352,000 people.[91] Whereas other groups had national committees that acted as representative bodies, "it was the Ukrainians, alone of the non-Russian nationalities, who most of the time had no German-recognized National Committee."[92] A Ukrainian National Committee was formed only in March 1945 in Germany. If participation in civil administration under German occupation is taken as a measure of the level of collaboration, then in Soviet Ukraine collaboration was the lowest in occupied Europe, if only for the simple reason that the Germans did not allow it.

It should also be pointed out that when Germans used the adjective

"Ukrainian" to describe the local administration and its officials they were referring merely to the territory of Ukraine. In fact, many officials were Russians or local ethnic Germans (*Volksdeutsch*). This was especially the case after individuals with a pro-Ukrainian orientation were repressed.[93] While many who served in the local administration did so only to survive the famine that ravaged urban centres, others did so because they were "opportunists" or because they were "Soviet agents."[94] The national composition of the auxiliary police or militia was also varied.[95] As Ievhen Stakhiv observed sardonically, after the Nazi purges, all that remained of nationalists' efforts to Ukrainize the police was the name and the blue and yellow stripes on their uniforms.[96] The police, some of whom participated in the Nazis' round-up and extermination of Jews, was comprised of the "worst elements of society" and was "detested" by the population.[97]

The police also "contained the strongest Communist infiltration,"[98] a development greatly assisted by the German "practice of retaining the Soviet *militsiia* [police] as a matter of convenience."[99] If one takes into account the systematic penetration of the local administration and police by the Soviets, then the number of people who participated voluntarily in these institutions is thus considerably reduced. By the winter and spring of 1942, according to the official Soviet history of Ukraine, "members of the Communist underground had infiltrated the auxiliary local organs established by the occupiers. Very often these organs were in the hands of Bolshevik agents or Communists."[100] Finally, "only a very few" Ukrainian units were established in the German army. Their numbers have been greatly exaggerated because after the war the Western allies described all of the *Wehrmacht's* eastern units (*Osttruppen*), whatever their national origin, as "Ukrainian."[101]

Another aspect of German policy that provoked mass indignation was the treatment of prisoners of war. Initially, Soviet POWs were segregated according to nationality; some non-Russian prisoners (including Ukrainians) whom the Nazis considered essential for harvesting the crops were released.[102] But after the OUN-B proclaimed an independent Ukraine in Lviv on 30 June 1941, against the wishes of German occupational forces, Berlin reversed its policies in the autumn. Hitler ordered the suspect Ukrainians to be held captive, while allowing the freeing of nationals of the Baltic states to continue.[103]

Soviet POWs, unlike prisoners from the other Allied countries, were held under conditions designed to bring about their death. Paltry food rations, exposure to severe weather, diseases, beatings, and mass executions decimated their ranks. In Khyriv in far western Ukraine only seventeen out of a camp of 8,000 troops survived until 1943; the rest perished from starvation.[104] Of the 5.8 million Soviet POWs who fell into German hands, two million are known to have died. Another million are unaccounted for, and it can be presumed that most of them met a similar fate.[105] The Soviet government, for its part, turned a blind eye to the fate of the POWs. It considered any soldier who fell into enemy hands to be a traitor and not deserving of protection, as International Red Cross officials discovered when they made overtures to Soviet authorities during the war to gain an understanding with the Axis powers regarding captives.[106] Since many of the camps were located in Ukraine, the population soon became aware of conditions in them. Indeed, the Ukrainian civilian population attempted unsuccessfully to bring food to POWs.[107] The "grapevine," a very developed form of communication in the USSR, soon spread information about the conditions of POWs to all corners of the country. The resistance of the Red Army and of the civilian population stiffened as the belief that the Germans were out to destroy the Slavic peoples became widespread. The treatment of POWs was considered by many to have been one of the biggest mistakes the Germans committed.[108] It was certainly not the last.

In agriculture, the striking characteristic of the agrarian order established by the Germans was that they preserved the entire Soviet collective and state farm system, including even work norms, price scales, and administrative machinery. Attempts to dissolve collective farms were "fought with the severest measures."[109] There were, of course, a few "innovations." Notable among these was the renaming of collective farms as "community farms" (hromadski hospodarstva). Some in the German hierarchy, such as Rosenberg and members of the Wehrmacht, argued that Ukrainians would never co-operate with the Germans until land had been distributed among the peasants.[110] In Rosenberg's program for a "new agrarian order," the parcelling out of land to individual peasants was to take place through a transitional arrangement called an "agricultural association" (khliborobska spilka). During this phase peasants would receive a land allotment and be allowed to keep a portion of the harvest from it. Major agricultural operations would still be performed in common, under German supervision.[111] But Koch, backed by Goering's Eastern Economic staff, successfully resisted the implementation of this reform because it would hinder the seizure of surpluses.[112] By the summer of 1943, only

10 per cent of peasant households in the *Reichskommissariat* had received allotments under the agricultural co-operative scheme.[113] Outright distribution of land to the peasantry was not even seriously discussed.[114]

Koch also made certain that Ukraine contributed "to the salvation of European civilization."[115] Of the six million tonnes of grain requisitioned by the Reich from the USSR between 1941–4, five million came from Ukraine.[116] In many regions, grain quotas imposed by the Nazis on collective farms were double the 1941 Soviet norm.[117] If Ukraine's peasantry avoided mass starvation it was because the Germans, following Soviet practice, permitted private plots.[118]

A complex administrative network of German officials supervised Ukrainian agriculture. At the bottom of this pyramid were close to 15,000 *Landwirtschaftsführer* or agricultural leaders, dispatched to Ukraine to supervise the peasants' work. These *La-Führer*, as they were known, ruled collective and state farms as their private bailiwick. In Rivne, for example, they regularly beat peasants who failed to doff their hats.[119] Flogging was introduced for the non-fulfillment of work norms; curfews were imposed; the carrying of pocket knives was prohibited and punishable by death. These were but a few of the many new measures that harassed the peasants.[120] Mass executions as punishment for the peasants' voluntary or involuntary assistance to partisans were commonplace. As part of the Nazi campaign against the resistance, 250 Ukrainian villages and their inhabitants were obliterated.[121]

One consequence of the Nazis' exploitation of Ukrainian agriculture was a disastrous food supply situation in the urban centres. In December 1941 German economic administrators decided to increase the delivery of foodstuffs to the Reich by eliminating "superfluous eaters," namely, "Jews and the population of Ukrainian cities such as Kiev."[122] The reduction of the urban population was achieved by a drastic cut in food rations, the establishment of roadblocks to prevent food from entering towns and cities, and the closing of urban (collective) farm markets.[123] Some of these measures were subsequently repealed. However, by the end of 1943 food rations in Kiev amounted to less than 30 per cent of minimum requirements.[124] The urban population declined drastically. In Kharkiv, it dropped from 850,000 in 1939 to 450,000 by December 1941.[125] During the German occupation 70-80,000 Kharkiv residents died of famine.[126]

One of the most hated aspects of German rule in Ukraine was the

Ostarbeiter or forced labour program. Initially, some Ukrainians volunteered to work in German industry in order to escape famine or to learn a new trade.[127] But the volunteers "were packed into freight cars without food or sanitary facilities and shipped off to Germany. Those who survived were put behind barbed wire and fed only enough to keep them alive."[128] Unlike Western Europeans and even Galician Ukrainian foreign workers, they were treated as social pariahs and were forced to wear a humiliating badge designating them as workers from the East (*Ost*) and were subjected to draconian labour discipline. A month or two after the departure of the volunteers, news of their treatment reached Ukraine, and by the summer of 1941, force had to be used to meet labour quotas. People were arbitrarily rounded up in cinemas, churches, and other public places and shipped to Germany.[129] In the summer of 1942 a mandatory two-year labour service in Germany for all men and women in Ukraine between the ages of eighteen and twenty was decreed.[130] Entire communities suffered severe reprisals for failure to comply with the labour quotas. Of the 2.8 million *Ostarbeiter* carried off to Germany, 2.3 million were from Ukraine.[131]

The occupation had severe consequences for education, culture, and health. The Nazis' approach toward education was quite straightforward. As Hitler explained during his 1942 visit to Ukraine, Ukrainians "should be given only the crudest kind of education necessary for communication between them and their German masters."[132] In January 1942, it was announced that all schools above the fourth grade were to be closed. Only the occasional vocational school survived the implementation of this policy.[133] The printing of school textbooks was strictly forbidden.[134] So far as culture was concerned, most theatres, choirs, and operas were disbanded. The best of that which did survive was reserved for Germans.[135] Of the 115 newspapers founded in the early summer of 1941, only forty remained by April 1942.[136] Judging by the issues that are available in the West, these publications were heavily censored propaganda broadsheets. The publishing of books, journals, and magazines was not allowed.[137] The myriad of Ukrainian national organizations reborn following the Soviet evacuation were banned, from the Ukrainian Red Cross to sports clubs.[138] As for health, it was decided as much as possible to curtail medical services in order to check "the biological power of the Ukrainians," as Koch put it.[139] Policies such as these were utterly incomprehensible to a population on whom the ideology of progress had left such a deep imprint and who accepted as axiomatic the development of educational, medical, and social services.

Ukraine was also affected by Nazi racial policies. The genocide of the Jews has been well researched, but that of the Ukrainians has not been emphasized enough.[140] Unlike in most countries occupied by the Nazis, in Ukraine and Poland assisting Jews was punishable by death. Hundreds in Ukraine were executed for such actions.[141] Nazi racial doctrines toward Jews were qualitatively different from those applied to such *Untermenschen* as Ukrainians. However, by any other measure, Nazi views concerning Ukrainians were extreme. Goering thought "the best thing would be to kill all men in Ukraine over fifteen years of age." Himmler advocated that "the entire Ukrainian intelligentsia must be decimated. . . . Do away with it, and the leaderless mass would become obedient." Koch declared, "If I find a Ukrainian who is worthy of sitting at the same table with me, I must have him shot."[142] Such views resulted in a campaign of terror that has yet to be chronicled: the mass destruction of the Ukrainian intelligentsia, the execution of hundreds of thousands of hostages, the incarceration of countless others in Buchenwald, Auschwitz, Ravensbrück, and other camps where Ukrainians were even denied the right to wear the letter "U" to indicate their nationality.[143] In daily life, in countless ways, including such seemingly petty things as stores and latrines marked "For Germans Only," the message of German racial superiority was driven home.[144]

The "strong hatred" that Nazi actions provoked expressed itself in an affirmation of a Ukrainian national identity.[145] "The German occupation increased national consciousness in Ukraine," commented an eyewitness. "By their behaviour the Germans evoked a reaction in the form of a counter-chauvinism."[146] Another noted that "the idea of Ukrainian independence grew."[147] The national revival of the early months served as a reminder of unrealized ambitions and contributed to this "upsurge of Ukrainian patriotism."[148] In Transnistria as well, where the civil administration was less oppressive than in the neighbouring German-held areas, "the national consciousness of the Ukrainian population was. . . stirred by Romanian behaviour."[149] Nazi policies also gave rise to large-scale resistance movements, both national and Soviet, that were influenced by this new patriotism.

From the military point of view the national resistance movement counted for something only in Western Ukraine. In Volhynia the Ukrainian Insurgent Army (*Ukrainska povstanska armiia* or UPA) was established in 1941. By 1942 it had 15,000 men under arms and controlled a liberated zone of some 50,000 square kilometres and two million people. By 1943, after the UPA had come under the control of the OUN-B, the UPA began to extend its operations to Galicia. By 1944 the UPA had approximately 40,000 members.[150] In Eastern Ukraine, on the other hand, apart from a few forays by the UPA and the emergence of small "independent" guerilla detachments that were either quickly absorbed or, more often than not, destroyed by Soviet partisan formations,[151] the resistance movement did not take the form of armed struggle.[152]

The Ukrainian national resistance was carried out predominantly by clandestine groups engaged in anti-Nazi and anti-Soviet propaganda and agitation.[153] These groups were most successful in Ukraine's industrial heartland, among workers in Dnipropetrovske, Kryvyi Rih, and especially the Donbas.[154] In the Donbas, for instance, members of Bandera's expeditionary groups built an OUN network encompassing a dozen cities. Its organizational core consisted of more than 500 people, with some 10,000 others who could be considered "active sympathizers," that is, supporters who distributed leaflets and the like.[155] This organization was unquestionably more significant than the Communist underground in the Donbas.[156] The ingredients contributing to its success were varied. To begin with, having arrived in the Donbas after the Germans started purging and executing pro-Ukrainian elements in Right-Bank Ukraine (the region west of the Dnieper River), the OUN never attempted to work in the open there. It did not assume control of local administrations. Instead, it remained underground, thus preserving its cadres as well as its resolutely anti-Nazi reputation. Another factor was the readiness of Western Ukrainian OUN members to abandon, under pressure from Eastern Ukrainian workers, the integral nationalist doctrine in favour of a program calling for a radical democratization of socio-economic and political life. The workers in the Donbas, on the other hand, embittered by their exploitation under Stalin, and whose Ukrainian identity Nazi policies had reinforced, were more than willing to support what they called "the struggle to complete the social revolution of 1917 by giving it a concrete national form." Thus, in the Donbas the OUN advanced the slogan "For a Soviet Ukraine without the dictatorship of the Communist Party."[157]

The rise of Ukrainian patriotism during the war was such that even Stalin was forced to concede to it in order to harness its force. Undoubtedly, for him this was merely an expedient to improve the battle-worthiness of the 4.5 million citizens of Ukraine who served in the armed forces in 1941–5.[158] Moreover, the 250,000-strong Soviet partisan force in Ukraine, of whom 60 per cent were Ukrainian,[159] represented a major force; and they, too, had to be permitted to communicate to the population a message somewhat more palatable than the dreary slogans that had previously characterized Soviet propaganda. In concrete terms, Stalin's concessions did not amount to much: Ukraine obtained its own ministry of foreign affairs and was eventually admitted to the United Nations; measures were taken to revive the study of Ukrainian ethnography, archaeology and history; the adjective "Ukrainian" was attached to the names of armies and fronts; and the Order of Bohdan Khmelnytsky was created.[160]

Nonetheless, these concessions had an enormous symbolic significance, for they legitimized the expression of Ukrainian national self-awareness. The opportunity was seized by the Ukrainian intelligentsia and party leaders and transformed into a major propaganda effort. In countless leaflets, posters, meetings, and publications, the historical continuity of the Ukrainian nation was affirmed and its uniqueness stressed. The struggle against Hitler was legitimized not by reference to the Party, to Stalin, nor to any of the other familiar themes. Rather, the traditions of the Ukrainian liberation struggle were invoked.[161] Ukrainians were called upon to fight Hitler in order to defend "our Ukrainian statehood," "our native culture, our native tongue,"[162] or "our national honour and pride."[163] Important concessions to Ukrainians, it was felt, were in the offing.[164] This mood was reinforced by a rumour campaign, initiated by the Soviet underground, to the effect that collective farms would soon be disbanded.[165]

The Soviet Ukrainian intelligentsia and party leadership, which had been caught up in the surge of patriotism during the war, attempted to continue the momentum when the last German troops were chased out of Ukraine in the autumn of 1944. They were immediately stopped by Andrei Zhdanov's crackdown on liberalization, which began in Ukraine in 1946. The focus of this campaign was the struggle against the relaxation of ideological controls during the war, which had led "Ukrainian historians to publish books with a less Russified version of history," "prompted Ukrainian writers to press for freedom from censorship," and allowed others to commit a host of serious "krainian nationalistic errors."[166] The Donbas was singled out as requiring particularly "decisive measures" to correct shortcomings in the ideological sphere.[167] The Soviet Ukrainian citizen could be forgiven for thinking that, *plus ça change, plus c'est la même chose.*

Notes

1 Alexander Dallin, *German Rule in Russia 1941–1945: A Study of Occupation Policies*, 2d rev. ed. (Boulder, Colo., 1981), 107.
2 Stephan G. Prociuk, "Human Losses in the Ukraine in World War I and II," *Annals of the Ukrainian Academy of Arts and Sciences in the United States* 13, no. 35–6 (1973–7): 40; Lucy S. Dawidowicz, *The War Against the Jews, 1933–1945* (New York, 1975), 544; *Ukrainskaia SSR v Velikoi Otechestvennoi voine Sovetskogo Soiuza 1941–1945 gg.*, 3 vols. (Kiev, 1975), 3:153.
3 *Ukrainskaia SSR v Velikoi Otechestvennoi voine*, 3:152, 157–8.
4 Edgar Snow, "The Ukraine Pays the Bill," *Saturday Evening Post*, 27 January 1945, 18.
5 Peter Kleist, *Zwischen Hitler und Stalin, 1939–1945* (Bonn, 1950), 130.
6 Documents from the Smolensk Party archives, which were captured by the Germans during the war and thereafter fell into Western hands, provide much evidence of this. For example, a secret police informant reported the following conversation: "Now, comrades, it appears that war is approaching. Soviet rule will not last long, it will tumble in an instant. . . . People have been robbed and taxed heavily. . . . I, like many others, will not go to defend Soviet rule." Svodka No. 7, I.IV.1933 (OGPU 3/0), Smolensk Archives, reel 20.
7 See S.M. Shtemenko, *Heneralnyi shtab u roky viiny*, 2 vols. (Kiev, 1980), 2:467, passim.
8 See Nikita Khrushchev, *Khrushchev Remembers* (Boston, 1970), chap. 6, and his *Secret Speech* (Nottingham, 1976).
9 Roy A. Medvedev, *Let History Judge: The Origins and Consequences of Stalinism* (London, 1971), 213.
10 Harvard University Refugee Interview Project (hereafter cited as HURIP), no. 441, B6, 1.
11 *Krakivski visti* (Cracow), 11 November 1941; *Oborona Ukrainy: chasopys Ukrainskoi narodnoi revoliutsiinoi armii*, 1 August 1942.
12 M. Suprunenko, "Ukraina naperedodni i v vitchyznianii viini proty nimetsko-fashystskykh zaharbnykiv," in *Borotba ukrainskoho narodu proty nimetskykh zaharbnykiv* (Ufa, 1942), 33.
13 See HURIP, no. 33, B6, 2; *Krakivski visti*, 9 November 1941, 28 December 1941, and 24 February 1942.
14 Akademiia nauk Ukrainskoi RSR, Instytut istorii, *Istoriia Ukrainskoi RSR: Ukrainska RSR u Velykii Vitchyznianii viini Radianskoho Soiuzu, 1941–1945* (Kiev, 1977), 7:69; *Ukrainskaia SSR v Velikoi Otechestvennoi voine*, 1: 359–60.
15 *Istoriia Ukrainskoi RSR*, 7: 69.
16 HURIP, no. 441, B6, 2; no. 32, B6, 1.
17 *Nastup* (Prague), 18 October 1941.
18 HURIP, no. 33, B6, 1.
19 A good example of this genre is Wallace Carroll's "It Takes a Russian to Beat a Russian," *Life*, 19 December 1949, 80–8.
20 Cited by Dallin, *German Rule*, 65n.
21 HURIP, 359, B6, 1.
22 Orest Zovenko, *Bezimenni: Spohady uchasnyka novitnykh vyzvolnykh zmahan* (n.p., 1945), 60.
23 HURIP, no. 441, B6, 2.
24 Ibid., no. 32, B6, 1.

25 Ibid. and no. 441, B6, 2; no. 359, B6, 1.
26 Dallin, *German Rule*, 65; V. Samarin, "The Years of Turmoil: In the German-Occupied Regions of Russia from 1941–1944" (typescript, Research Program on the USSR, Columbia University).
27 See Alexander J. Motyl, *The Turn to the Right: The Ideological Origins and Development of Ukrainian Nationalism, 1919–1929* (Boulder, Colo., 1980); John A. Armstrong, *Ukrainian Nationalism*, 2d rev. ed. (Littleton, Colo., 1980), chaps. 1–2.
28 Ievhen Onatsky, "Ideologichni i taktychni rozkhodzhennia mizh fashyzmom i natsional-sotsiializmom," *Rozbudova natsii* (Prague), no. 5–6 (1934): 142–9. I wish to thank Myroslav Yurkevich for supplying this reference.
29 In early March 1939, at the same time as the Nazis occupied Bohemia and Moravia, Hitler gave Transcarpathia, which had been part of Czechoslovakia in the interwar period, to Hungary as a reward for its alliance with the Berlin-Rome Axis. That same month the Carpatho-Ukrainian people proclaimed the independence of their territory and, with the help of the OUN, took up arms against the Nazi-backed Hungarian invasion. They were defeated, and from 1939 to 1944 this region was part of Hungary. See Peter C. Stercho, *Diplomacy of Double Morality: Europe's Crossroads in Carpatho-Ukraine 1919–1939* (New York, 1971).
30 See Mykola Lebed, "Do zviazkiv OUN z nimetskym viiskom," *Suchasna Ukraina* (Munich), 12 June 1960 and 26 June 1960.
31 See Stephan Hlid, *Fragmenty zhyttia i muk: spohady z chasiv nimetskoi okupatsii Ukrainy* (London, 1955), 17; Armstrong, *Ukrainian Nationalism*, 68.
32 Lev Rebet, *Svitla i tini OUN* (Munich, 1964), 98.
33 Alexander Motyl, "The Ukrainian Nationalist Movement and the Galician Reality," *Meta* (Toronto), no. 1 (1975): 64.
34 This figure includes the expeditionary groups of both OUN factions. Zinovii Matla, *Pivdenna pokhidna hrupa* (Munich, 1952), 22; Lev Shankovsky, *Pokhidni hrupy OUN: prychynky do istorii pokhidnykh hrup OUN na tsentralnykh i skhidnikh zemliakh Ukrainy v 1941–1943 rr.* (Munich, 1958), 12, 63n.
35 This figure includes both OUN factions. Interview with Mykola Lebed.
36 *Krakivski visti*, 16 October 1941.
37 *Ukrainskyi visnyk* (Berlin), 31 August 1941.
38 See Shankovsky, *Pokhidni hrupy*, 17–20.
39 HURIP, no. 356, B6, 3.
40 Differences between Eastern and Western Ukrainians are discussed in ibid. and in no. 446, JO, 67, and no. 102, B6, 5–6. See also Armstrong, *Ukrainian Nationalism*, 108–10.
41 HURIP, no. 356, B6, 1.
42 Ibid. and no. 148, WT, 33; and Oleksander Semenenko, *Kharkiv, Kharkiv* (Munich, 1977), 213.
43 HURIP, no. 356, B6, 2–3.
44 Ibid., no. 56, B6, 3.
45 See Armstrong, *Ukrainian Nationalism*, 108–10.
46 HURIP, no. 33, B6, 3.
47 See HURIP, no. 356, B6, 2 for rumours to this effect which circulated in the Donbas. See also *Ukrainskyi visnyk*, 7 September 1941; Semenenko, *Kharkiv*, 212.
48 *Krakivski visti*, 27 November 1941; *Nastup*, 13 December 1941; *Volyn* (Rivne), 1 October 1942.

49 *Ukrainskyi holos* (Kirovohrad), 1 October 1941.

50 *Holos Poltavshchyny* (Poltava), 7 December 1941.

51 Ievhen Stakhiv, "Natsionalno-politychne zhyttia Donbasu v 1941–1943 rr: na osnovi osobystykh sposterezhen," *Suchasna Ukraina* (Munich), 9 September 1956.

52 *Ukrainskyi visnyk*, 31 October 1943.

53 *Nastup*, 1 March 1942.

54 HURIP, no. 440, B6, 1.

55 *Holos Poltavshchnyny*, 7 December 1941; *Ukrainskyi zasiv: literaturnyi chasopys* (Kharkiv), no. 1 (1942); HURIP, no. 495, B5, 19.

56 *Ukrainska diisnist* (Berlin), 1 November 1941; 1 December 1941.

57 HURIP, no. 314, B6, 1; no. 102, B6, 1, 3.

58 *Nastup*, 13 December 1941.

59 *Krakivski visti*, 18 November 1941.

60 Ibid., 15 November 1941.

61 HURIP, no. 495, B6, 4.

62 Ievhen Stakhiv, "Kryvyi Rih v 1941–1943 rr.," *Suchasna Ukraina*, 22 January 1956.

63 *Volyn*, 24 October 1941.

64 *Nastup*, 13 December 1941; *Ukrainska diisnist*, 20 January 1942.

65 *Krakivski visti*, 18 October 1941.

66 HURIP, no. 102, B6, 2.

67 Interview with Ievhen Stakhiv.

68 Ibid. See also *Ukrainska diisnist*, 1 March 1943.

69 Stakhiv, "Kryvyi Rih."

70 *Krakivski visti*, 3 August 1941; 31 August 1941; and 3 December 1941.

71 Zovenko, *Bezimenni*, 65–6; HURIP, no. 314, B6, 6; Hlid, *Fragmenty zhyttia*, 12–13.

72 HURIP, no. 441, B6, 2, and no. 482, JR, 23–4; *Nastup*, 18 October 1941; *Ukrainska diisnist*, 1 December 1941; *Volyn*, 24 October 1941; *Krakivski visti*, 17 January 1942.

73 *Ukrainskyi visnyk*, 12 October 1942. Population data from *Ukrainska diisnist*, 20 January 1942.

74 *Krakivski visti*, 28 November 1941.

75 Interview with Ievhen Stakhiv; Shankovsky, *Pokhidni hrupy*, 6–14; Armstrong, *Ukrainian Nationalism*, chap. 4.

76 HURIP, no. 356, B6, 3.

77 E. Pavliuk, "Borotba ukrainskoho narodu na skhidno-ukrainskykh zemliakh," Document C 52-1, archive of the Foreign Representation of the Ukrainian Supreme Liberation Council, New York, 2.

78 Armstrong, *Ukrainian Nationalism*, 106.

79 Ibid., 97, 106.

80 Pavliuk, "Borotba ukrainskoho narodu," 1–2.

81 Ibid., 2.

82 For example, Rosenberg supported the establishment of a major university in Kiev. See "Unsigned Memorandum, 16 July 1941," in *Documents on German Foreign Policy, 1918–1945*, 13 vols. (London, 1949–64), 13: 151.

83 "Memorandum by the Chief of the Reich Chancellery, 1 October 1941," in ibid., 319. See also Dallin, *German Rule*, 8, 49, 57.

84 "Unsigned Memorandum, 16 July 1941," in *Documents on German Foreign Policy*, 13: 153.

85 Cited by Jürgen Thorwald, *Wen sie verderben wollen* (Stuttgart, 1952), 74.

86 Koch was captured by the Western powers and turned over to Poland in 1950 for

prosecution as a war criminal. It took Polish authorities nine years to bring him to trial and then only for crimes committed while *Gauleiter* of East Prussia. In 1959 he was sentenced to death, but the sentence was never carried out. He lives under very favourable conditions in the Polish prison of Barczewo. The USSR has never asked for his extradition. The reasons for this unprecedented "humanitarianism" on the part of the Polish and Soviet authorities remain a mystery.

87 For a good discussion of Romanian policies in Transnistria, see Alexander Dallin, *Odessa, 1941–1944: A Case Study of Soviet Territory under Foreign Rule* (Santa Monica, 1957).

88 Cited by Ie. V. Safonova, *Ideino-vykhovna robota Komunistychnoi partii sered trudiash-chykh vyzvolenykh raioniv Ukrainy v roky Velykoi Vitchyznianoi viiny, 1943–1945 rr.* (Kiev, 1971), 91.

89 *Istoriia Ukrainskoi RSR*, 7:141.

90 *Ukrainska diisnist*, 10 November 1942.

91 Ibid., 10 May 1942; *Ukrainskyi visnyk*, 20 September 1942.

92 George Fischer, *Soviet Opposition to Stalin: A Case Study in World War II* (Cambridge, Mass., 1952), 21.

93 Armstrong, *Ukrainian Nationalism*, 113–14n; HURIP, no. 356, B6, 4; no. 59, B6, 3.

94 Ibid., no. 542, B6, 3; no. 356, B6, 4.

95 See Stakhiv, "Natsionalno-politychne zhyttia Donbasu"; HURIP, no. 314, B6, 4; and V. Volodymyrovytch, *L'Ukraine sous l'occupation Allemande* (Paris, 1948), 36.

96 Stakhiv, "Natsionalno-politychne zhyttia Donbasu."

97 HURIP, no. 485, B6, 6.

98 Ibid.

99 Armstrong, *Ukrainian Nationalism*, 218.

100 *Istoriia Ukrainskoi RSR*, 7:157.

101 Fischer, *Soviet Opposition*, 48. According to Hans von Herwarth there were 100,000 Ukrainians serving in the German army. This figure includes Western Ukrainians. See his "Deutschland und die ukrainische Frage 1941–1945" (typescript, Deutsches Institut fr Geschichte der nationalsozialistischen Zeit, Munich), 19. According to Fischer, *Soviet Opposition*, 45, there were some 500,000 former Soviet citizens bearing arms.

102 "Memorandum by an Official of the Department for German Internal Affairs, 6 August 1941" and "Memorandum by the Chief of the Reich Chancellery, 1 October 1941," in *Documents on German Foreign Policy*, 13: 290, 319.

103 Ihor Kamenetsky, *Secret Nazi Plans for Eastern Europe: A Study of Lebensraum Policies* (New York, 1961), 150–1.

104 Zovenko, *Bezimenni*, 672.

105 Dallin, *German Rule*, 426–7.

106 Ibid., 420.

107 *Krakivski visti*, 4 February 1942; Kamenetsky, *Secret Nazi Plans*, 153.

108 HURIP, no. 27, B6, 1.

109 Cited by Clifton J. Child, "The Ukraine under German Occupation, 1941–4," in *Hitler's Europe*, ed. Arnold Toynbee and Veronica M. Toynbee (London, 1954), 638.

110 Ibid.

111 *Novyi chas: orhan Voznesenskoho gebitskomisara* (Voznesenske), 12 July 1943.

112 Child, "The Ukraine," 638.

113 *Volyn*, 10 June 1943.

114 See ibid. as well as the issue for 23 August 1942. *Novyi chas,* 12 July 1943, has a detailed discussion of Koch's agricultural policies that fails to mention the distribution of land. For an excellent analysis of rural life in Soviet Ukraine under German occupation, see *Ukrainskyi visnyk,* 4 April 1943.

115 *Volyn,* 23 August 1942.

116 Tabulated from Dallin, *German Rule,* table 2, p. 374.

117 Z. Shulha, "Borotba ukrainskoho selianstva proty nimetskofashystskykh okupantiv," in *Borotba ukrainskoho narodu,* 39.

118 *Ukrainskyi visnyk,* 4 April 1943.

119 Dallin, *German Rule,* 317.

120 Shulha, "Borotba ukrainskoho selianstva," 38; HURIP, no. 314, B6, 2.

121 *Ukrainskaia SSR v Velikoi Otechestvennoi voine,* 3:152.

122 Cited by Kamenetsky, *Secret Nazi Plans,* 146.

123 Ibid. See also "Kharkov under the Germans" (typescript, Research Program on the USSR, Columbia University).

124 Leontii Forostivsky, *Kyiv pid vorozhymy okupatsiiamy* (Buenos Aires, 1952), 48.

125 *Krakivski visti,* 7 March 1942.

126 Feliks Korduba, "Der Generalplan Ost," *Ukrainskyi istoryk* (Munich), nos. 1–4 (1981): 157.

127 HURIP, no. 314, B6, 2.

128 Carroll, "It Takes a Russian," 82.

129 HURIP, no. 482, B5, 9.

130 *Holos Dnipra: khersonskyi chasopys* (Kherson), 23 May 1943.

131 Tabulated from Dallin, *German Rule,* table 2, p. 452.

132 Kamenetsky, *Secret Nazi Plans,* 106–7.

133 *Volyn,* 1 October 1942; *Ukrainska diisnist,* 10 November 1942.

134 Nikon Nemyron, "Probudzhena v ohni stolytsia Ukrainy," *Suchasna Ukraina,* 2 December 1956.

135 HURIP, no. 102, B6, 8; no. 121, B6, 13.

136 *Ukrainska diisnist,* 5 April 1942.

137 Shankovsky, *Pokhidni hrupy,* 8.

138 See Shankovsky, "Ukraina pid nimetskym chobotom," *Kyiv* (Philadelphia), no. 6 (1954): 275.

139 Cited by Dallin, *German Rule,* 455.

140 See HURIP, no. 33, B6, 3; no. 121, B6, 3; no. 441, B6, 7; no. 542, B6, 1; no. 548, B6, 2.

141 *Nasha strana* (Jerusalem), 2 November 1983. See also HURIP, no. 500, B6-7 for a report of a large number of Ukrainians in Berdychiv executed by the "Ukrainian" police for assisting Jews.

142 Cited by Dallin, *German Rule,* 123, 127, 67, respectively.

143 Mykhailo H. Marunchak, *Systema nimetskykh kontstaboriv i polityka vynyshchuvannia v Ukraini,* 2d ed. (Winnipeg, 1963), 51-2; V.K. and A.T., *Chomu svit movchyt? Ukraintsi v kontsentratsiinykh taborakh Nimechchyny 1940–1945 rr.,* 2d ed. (Paris, 1945–6), 36, 69.

144 HURIP, no. 102, B6, 3; no. 548, B6, 4.

145 Ibid., no. 314, B6, 7.

146 Ibid.

147 Ibid., no. 121, B6, 3.

148 Ibid., no. 441, B6, 8.
149 Alexander Dallin, *Odessa, 1941–1944: A Case Study of Soviet Territory Under Foreign Rule* (Santa Monica, 1957), 290.
150 *Oborona Ukrainy*, 1 August 1942; *Svoboda* (Jersey City), 24 September 1982.
151 *Samostiinyk*, 23 December 1943 (UPA underground publication); Shankovsky, *Pokhidni hrupy*, 192–9; HURIP, no. 542, B6, 7; no. 32, B6, 5; no. 314, B6, 7.
152 In part this was dictated by Eastern Ukraine's terrain which, unlike Volhynia, contained few forests. The wooded areas that could offer cover were in the north, on the border with Belorussia, and were under the control of Soviet partisans.
153 HURIP, no. 548, B6, 6.
154 See Shankovsky, *Pokhidni hrupy*, 132–92.
155 Stakhiv, "Natsionalno-politychne zhyttia Donbasu," *Suchasna Ukraina*, 9 August 1956.
156 Ibid., 23 August 1956. Stakhiv, an OUN organizer in the Donbas, claims that the Donbas Soviet underground did not produce a single leaflet during the German occupation. In fact, two were produced – one by a village Pioneer organization, another by a Komsomol group in Donetske. This is hardly an impressive output given the Donbas's importance in Ukraine. See *Lystivky partiinoho pidpillia i partyzanskykh zahoniv Ukrainy u roky Velykoi Vitchyznianoi viiny* (Kiev, 1969). For a discussion of evidence from Soviet sources regarding the existence of a Ukrainian national underground in the Donbas, see Ievhen Stakhiv, "Do dyskusii pro Oleha Koshevoho," *Suchasna Ukraina*, 3 February 1957.
157 Stakhiv, "Natsionalno-politychne zhyttia Donbasu," *Suchasna Ukraina*, 9 August 1956. See also Pavliuk, "Borotba ukrainskoho narodu."
158 *Istoriia Ukrainskoi RSR*, 7: 509.
159 V.I. Klokov, *Vsenarodnaia borba v tylu nemetsko-fashistskikh okupantov na Ukraine 1941–1944 gg.* (Kiev, 1978), 57; Safonova, *Ideino-vykhovna robota*, 208.
160 *Pravda* (Moscow), 27 May 1944; *Kulturne budivnytstvo v Ukrainskii RSR*, 2 vols. (Kiev, 1959), 2: 56–7; Safonova, *Ideino-vykhovna robota*, 84.
161 See, for example, *Ukraina v ohni: almanakh* (n.p., 1942) and *Lystivky partiinoho pidpillia*.
162 *Ukraina byla i budet sovetskoi: vtoroi antifashistskii miting predstavitelei ukrainskogo naroda 30 avgusta 1942 g.* (Saratov, 1942), 63, 12.
163 Shulha, "Borotba ukrainskoho selianstva," 41.
164 HURIP, no. 121, B6, 3.
165 Ihor Kamenetsky, *Hitler's Occupation of Ukraine, 1941–1944: A Study of Totalitarian Imperialism* (Milwaukee, 1956), 58.
166 Werner G. Hahn, *Postwar Soviet Politics: The Fall of Zhdanov and the Defeat of Moderation, 1946–1953* (Ithaca, N.Y., 1982), 48–9.
167 Safonova, *Ideino-vykhovna robota*, 17.

TARAS HUNCZAK

Ukrainian-Jewish Relations during the Soviet and Nazi Occupations

"The evil that men do lives after them;
The good is oft interred with their bones . . ."
William Shakespeare, *Julius Caesar*

In their attempts to understand Ukrainian-Jewish relations, scholars face several obstacles, the most troubling of which is the reliability and paucity of historical evidence. Because the available sources dealing with the subject are incomplete and often contradictory, it is impossible to reconstruct an objective record of the past. Furthermore, one frequently finds unconfirmed reports and stereotypical judgments which suggest that the matter of Jewish-Ukrainian relations is as much psychological as it is historical. As a result, various writers, using fragmentary and frequently questionable evidence, have created negative stereotypes whose emotional overtones have kept the Jewish and Ukrainian communities in a state of permanent confrontation.

One should also bear in mind that relations between Jews and Ukrainians were almost never free of outside interference – there was always a *third* factor, a dominant power which often exercised a decisive influence. In previous centuries it was Poland and tsarist Russia, while in the twentieth century, particularly in the 1930s and during World War II, Ukrainian-Jewish relations stood in the shadow of Nazi Germany and the Soviet Union. These states exacerbated local social and economic tensions by fostering ideological intolerance and political confrontation.

Apart from these easily definable problems, an invisible wall separating the two communities, based on mutual suspicion, religious prejudice, ethnocentric beliefs and values, and popular myths, prevented Ukrainians and Jews from reaching a genuine understanding. The result has been virtually no communication, with neither group able to rise to a higher moral level so as to understand and empathize with the other's problems and aspirations. Seemingly victims of their own history, both groups are unable – or perhaps unwilling – to free themselves from the past.

This Ukrainian-Jewish dilemma was characterized very perceptively by Howard Aster and Peter Potichnyi, as "two solitudes" in close proximity, yet never neighbours in the real sense of the word.[1]

Milena Rudnytska, political activist and member of the Polish parliament, commented on the estranged relations between Jews and Ukrainians:

[In Galicia] during the interwar Polish period, both the Ukrainian and Jewish communities lived their secluded lives separated by a wall of mutual resentments. It is strange that even political leaders who co-operated with each other in Warsaw maintained neither political nor personal contacts in Lviv. They did not even sit behind a common table in order to explain and decide upon mutual grievances and mutual claims.[2]

World War II brought not only an unprecedented tragedy for the Jewish people but also severe trials for the Ukrainian people. From the moment the war began, Ukrainians in the western regions found themselves without political leadership, as the political parties, which had enjoyed considerable support in the 1930s, dissolved themselves. The resulting power vacuum was gradually filled by a new, dynamic, and rapidly growing force – the Organization of Ukrainian Nationalists (OUN), whose central objective was to create an independent and sovereign Ukrainian state. It was this organization which eventually championed Ukrainian political aspirations during and after the war.[3]

In April 1941 the OUN held its second congress in Cracow. One of the congress resolutions concerned Jews:

17. In the USSR the Jews are the most faithful supporters of the ruling Bolshevik regime and the vanguard of Muscovite imperialism in Ukraine. The Muscovite-Bolshevik government exploits the anti-Jewish sentiments of the Ukrainian masses in order to divert their attention from the real perpetrator of their misfortune in order to incite them, in time of upheaval, to carry out pogroms against the Jews. The Organization of Ukrainian Nationalists combats the Jews as the prop of the Muscovite-Bolshevik regime and simultaneously educates the masses to the fact that the principal enemy is Moscow.[4]

The late Philip Friedman, a respected scholar, concluded that this passage reflected "the classical Nazi anti-Jewish equation of 'Jews-

Bolsheviks'."[5] Friedman, however, oversimplified the problem when he reduced the popular perception of "Jews-Bolsheviks" to a facile Nazi anti-Jewish equation.[6] It is possible that the OUN's resolution could have reflected the views of some Ukrainians, irrespective of Nazi ideology. But what counts most is whether the popular perception (which is deeply buried in many other peoples, particularly in Eastern Europe) was founded in fact.

The popular perception of Jews as agents of Bolshevism resulted in violent mass outbursts against the Jewish people during the initial stages of the German war against the Soviet Union. The violence was more likely a response to a situation – the aftermath of Soviet rule – than to the OUN's political resolution. As Philip Friedman pointed out, the OUN resolution warned "against pogroms on Jews, since such actions only played into the hands of Moscow."[7]

In the course of its two-year struggle against the Nazis, the OUN modified its ideology in several important respects. The changes were formally accepted at the Third Congress of the OUN, held in August 1943, which not only adopted the principle of democracy as the basic tenet of the future Ukrainian state but also modified its stand on the national minorities in Ukraine. The anti-Jewish resolution of the earlier congress was annulled and replaced by a provision calling for equal rights for all national minorities in Ukraine.[8]

The ideas of democracy and equality for all national minorities were restated with even greater clarity in the constitution of the Ukrainian Supreme Liberation Council, established in July 1944.[9] The new organization was to be the revolutionary government directing both the OUN and the Ukrainian Insurgent Army (UPA) in their struggle for Ukrainian independence. The OUN's position vis-à-vis the Jews was disseminated through such official underground party organs as the journal *Ideia i Chyn* (Thought and Action), which published an article instructing OUN members "to liquidate the manifestations of harmful foreign influence, particularly the German racist concepts and practices" against Jews.[10]

This shift in orientation seems to have had practical consequences for Ukrainian-Jewish relations. According to a German report of March 1942:

In Zhytomyr, Kremenchug and Stalino several followers of Bandera were arrested for trying to win over the population to the idea of political independence of Ukraine. At the same time it was established that the Bandera group supplied its members and the Jews working for its movement with *false passports*.[11]

There is also information suggesting that hundreds, perhaps thousands, of Jews entered the ranks of the UPA as physicians, dentists, hospital attendants, pharmacists, and craftsmen. Unfortunately, this evidence is not reliable, and one must rely on testimonies that cannot be verified.[12] What is certain is that some Jews served the UPA in various technical capacities, particularly as physicians.[13]

It seems that the number of Jews in the UPA was large enough to establish special camps where they could work at their trades. According to Friedman, one such camp, near Poryts, Volhynia, contained 100 Jews. A larger camp with some 400 Jews was located in Kudrynky, some twenty miles from Tuchyn, also in Volhynia. At the end of the war seventeen Jews from the Kudrynky camp survived; the rest apparently perished.[14]

Neither the Ukrainian underground movement nor any other organizations thus cultivated anti-Semitic programs or policies. They readily accepted Jews into their ranks and sheltered them from Nazi persecution, despite the popular perception of Jews as promoters of communism.

This perception naturally encouraged anti-Semitic attitudes and played into the hands of the Nazis, who hoped to enlist the various peoples of Eastern Europe – not just Ukrainians – in anti-Jewish campaigns. It was German policy to make violence against Jews appear to be initiated by the local population. An *Einsatzgruppe A* report described the policy:

. . . Native anti-Semitic forces were induced to start pogroms against Jews during the first hours after capture, though this inducement proved to be very difficult. Carrying out orders, the security police was determined to solve the Jewish question with all possible means and determination most decisively. But it was desirable that the German security police should not put in an immediate appearance, at least in the beginning, since the extraordinarily harsh measures were apt to stir even German circles. It had to be shown to the world that the native population itself took the first action, reacted naturally against the oppression by Jews during several decades and against the terror exercised by the Communists during the preceding period.[15]

Thus, the people of Eastern Europe were to act as pawns in the hands of their German masters,[16] and in some instances the people obliged. At the outset of the Soviet-German war this was relatively easy as the retreating NKVD, the Soviet secret police, left behind prisons full of mutilated corpses of Ukrainian youth. From reports of *Sicherheitspolizei und SD*, the German security police, a picture of horror emerges: in Stryi, 150 dead; Lviv, 5,000; Dobromyl, 82; Sambir, 520; Lutske, 2,800; Zolochiv, 700; Lublin, 100; Kremianets, 100–150; Dubno, a "severe blood bath" (*ein schweres Blutbad*); Ternopil, 600; Vinnytsia, 9,432.[17] It is obvious even from this incomplete list that the Soviet authorities perpetrated on Ukrainian soil a crime against humanity deserving of a Nuremberg trial.[18]

The Germans, for their part, were quick to accuse Jews of acting as co-conspirators and perpetrators, while some Ukrainians accused Jews of participating actively. In some cities where the Soviet NKVD had committed mass murders, acts of violence occurred against Jews.

The perception of some Ukrainians was not without substance, since the rather significant level of Jewish participation in the Communist movement and in the subsequent Soviet government is a matter of record. Leonard Schapiro, a distinguished British specialist on Soviet affairs, wrote:

By the time the Bolsheviks seized power, Jewish participation at the highest level of the Party was far from insignificant. Five of the twenty-one full members of the Central Committee were Jews – among them Trotsky and Sverdlov, the real master of the small, but vital secretarial apparatus of the Party. . . . But Jews abounded at the lower levels of the Party machinery – especially in the *Cheka* and its successors, the GPU, the OGPU and the NKVD. . . . It is difficult to suggest a satisfactory reason for the prevalence of Jews in the Cheka. It may be that having suffered at the hands of the former Russian authorities they wanted to seize the reins of real power in the new state for themselves.[19]

The perceptions of Jews by Ukrainians and other non-Jews of Eastern Europe were not new, and the events immediately preceding World War II only exacerbated them. To date, however, there is no thorough study of this important and highly complex question, and it is therefore impossible to render a final judgment about the nature of Jewish and Ukrainian behaviour during World War II. It would be just as outrageous to suggest that the Jewish people as a whole are responsible for the criminal acts perpetrated against Ukrainians by Jews who actively supported the Soviets, as it would be to maintain that Ukrainians as a whole are accountable for the anti-Semitic actions of a few.

Related to this problem is the oft-repeated charge of Ukrainian collaboration with the Nazis during World War II. The issue of ethical behaviour under the domination of foreign power is an old problem.[20] For the majority of people subjected to such occupation, collaboration has always been a question of survival.

During World War II collaboration acquired a pejorative connotation reflected even in its lexical meaning – "co-operation with the enemy." For the definition to apply, however, the enemy must be clear. Western states such as France, Holland, and Belgium lost their national sovereignty as a result of German conquest and occupation; in their case the enemy was readily identifiable. In Eastern Europe and in the territories under Soviet control (apart from the Russian Republic), large segments of the population viewed Soviet authority as an extension of the Russian imperial state and the Soviet Union was therefore a supranational union that masked an occupying power.

Given the high level of national consciousness reinforced by Stalin's tyrannical rule, the population of the non-Russian republics viewed the Soviet government as the enemy and looked to foreign powers, including Germany, for national deliverance.[21] Within this context, a collaborator would be anyone who co-operated with the Soviet authorities. To be sure, the Soviet Union was on the side of the victors, who defined collaborators as those who co-operated with the other side – with either Germany or Japan. These being enemy states, the very concept of collaboration acquired a pejorative connotation. In such circumstances, power becomes the ultimate source of justification.

As a result, collaboration or co-operation with the occupying power became a worldwide phenomenon during World War II. Most leaders in the Philippines, for example, collaborated with the Japanese in establishing the Republic of the Philippines on 14 October 1943.[22]

Collaboration, however, was much more complex in Europe than in Asia. Apart from those who collaborated with the Germans in order to gain power, financial advantage, special privileges, or to lighten the burden of occupation, some in Western Europe found the Nazi ideology attractive. Western European fascist movements had wide support and affected Western societies profoundly, particularly during the German occupation. France, for instance, not only espoused collaboration as its national policy under the Vichy government but also produced several political parties whose goal was co-operation with Germany, and made German victory a cornerstone of their political programs.[23]

In differentiating between ideological and non-ideological collaborators, Bertram Gordon used the terms collaborator and collaborationist. In France collaborationists were committed to the victory of the Third Reich and actively worked toward that end.[24] In Ukraine there were no collaborationists seduced by Nazi ideology or by the seemingly irresistible *Griff nach der Weltmacht* (grasp for world power). Unlike the French, Belgians, Dutch, and Russians, Ukrainians did not establish fascist organizations and youth movements that promoted collaboration with Germany.

Although Ukrainians were not collaborationists, there were certainly many collaborators among them who *volens-nolens* co-operated with the Germans. They paid taxes, delivered grain quotas, went to Germany as labourers, and filled administrative posts. Even more significantly, Ukrainians joined various indigenous auxiliary police formations,[25] and the Galician Division was formed with the intention of being the nucleus of a Ukrainian national army.

What is important, however, is that Ukrainian co-operation was not intended to serve German interests. Documents of the period leave no doubt that the objective of all Ukrainian political groups was to promote Ukrainian national self-interest.[26] Moreover, it was precisely for that reason that the OUN challenged the right of the German occupation authorities to make political decisions on Ukrainian territory.[27] John Armstrong has argued that Ukrainian "collaboration" was pragmatic: the Germans were against the status quo, while the OUN was determined to establish an independent Ukrainian state, regardless of German political plans for Ukraine.[28]

Thus, while the OUN was a factor in promoting collaboration among Ukrainians before the war and during the first phase of the Soviet-German war, it was also the first to oppose German policy actively,[29] thereby negating the very idea of collaboration. The high point of the Ukrainian resistance to German domination was the organization of the UPA, which took up arms against the Nazi occupiers.[30]

Non-political collaboration, whether voluntary or involuntary, active or passive, was, of course, an entirely different matter. Stanley Hoffmann suggests that there were almost as many forms of collaboration as there were practitioners.[31] Moreover, in any occupied country, collaboration was an inescapable fact of life. Although Jews were condemned to extermination, they, too, were forced to collaborate by forming *Judenrats* (councils responsible for helping enforce Nazi orders affecting Jews) and the ghetto police.[32] The ghetto police in particular were forced to perform functions which must have posed some serious dilemmas. Isaiah Trunk described their activities:

. . . They were burdened with the most inhuman tasks . . . to help the German enemy tighten the noose around the necks of Jewish victims. . . . The police collected cash contributions and taxes; they assisted in raiding, guarding and escorting hungry, mentally exhausted people on their way to places of forced labor. . . . The ghetto police sentries formed the inside guard at the ghetto fences. . . . The Jewish police carried out raids against and arrests of inmates destined for shipment to labor camps. . . . In the final stages of the ghettos the Jewish police were called upon to assist in the "resettlement actions". In short, the ghetto police came to be identified with the inhuman cruelty of the Nazi ghetto regime.[33]

The so-called Ukrainian police were also an arm of the German government, since they functioned on the orders of the German authorities and in the interests of the German state. Unlike the Jewish ghetto police, however, whose authority was restricted to Jews, the Ukrainian auxiliary police, at the behest of the Germans, could participate in the persecution of Jews; some even participated in their execution. Like other nations, Ukrainians had their share of scoundrels whose behaviour besmirched the good name of the Ukrainian people, although they in no way represented Ukrainians as a whole. The government merely availed itself of the services of criminal elements, which can be found in every society.

Nonetheless, in both the civil administration and in the indigenous Ukrainian auxiliary police there were decent, and even heroic, people who risked their lives to help Jews. One such individual was Senytsia, mayor of Kremenchuk. With the help of Romansky, a Ukrainian Orthodox priest, Senytsia was able to save Jews by having them baptized and providing them with false documents.[34] An equally interesting case is that of Mr. Wawryniuk who, as a Ukrainian police officer in Lviv, hid a Jewish woman, Clara Zimmels-Troper, in his house. His courageous and selfless act saved her life.[35] These are but two examples for which this author has documentary evidence of Ukrainians in official positions helping Jews survive the Holocaust.

While the Germans pursued their policy of extermination of Jews and Gypsies, the Ukrainian nation was also locked in a struggle against the further depletion of her economic and human resources. According to Soviet data, the Germans destroyed and burned 714 towns and 28,000 villages, leaving some ten million inhabitants of Ukraine without any shelter. Five to seven million civilians and prisoners of war also lost their lives at the hands of the German authorities.[36] Other Ukrainians lost their lives fighting in the German Army, the Red Army, in Soviet partisan groups, and in the UPA. Ukrainians were obviously not disinterested bystanders; whether they wanted to or not, they participated in the tragic drama of World War II.[37]

Many Ukrainians, particularly members of the OUN, perished in concentration camps.[38] In addition, an estimated 2.3 million Ukrainians were taken to Germany, where they worked as forced labourers under the most adverse conditions on the farms and in the factories, which were frequently bombed by the Allies.[39] Among the workers were children, whom the Germans exploited as much as adults. In fact, the plight of children was one of the most tragic chapters of the war. The object of the German policy of *Heu-Aktion* in the territories of Eastern Ukraine was to apprehend 40–50,000 youths between the ages of ten to fourteen, who were earmarked for "the German trades as apprentices to be used as skilled workers after two years' training."[40] Similar action was taken in Galicia, where the objective of the German authorities was to obtain 135,000 labourers. Youths under seventeen were to serve as *SS* auxiliaries while those over seventeen were to be detailed to the Galician *Waffen-SS* Division.[41] Ukrainians therefore experienced a full measure of tragedy at the hands of the Nazis.[42]

Yet in the midst of this inferno there were men and women who risked their lives and the lives of their families to save Jews. The precise number shall probably never be known because most records note those who were discovered and executed by the Germans. Of those not discovered by the Germans very little is known, because many Jews did not consider it proper to come forth to identify their saviours. This author knows of at least two survivors who did not make depositions or public statements, despite repeated urgings to do so.

Philip Friedman suggests that some idea of the Ukrainians who risked their lives to save Jews may be gained from the official German posters which named those executed and gave reasons. The posters show that from October 1943 to June 1944, at least 1,541 Ukrainians were sentenced to death. Many of them were executed for belonging to the OUN and UPA, but approximately 100 had concealed or helped Jews. According to Friedman, the number was substantial, for it reflected a much greater participation.[43]

After the war some efforts were made to gather testimonies about those who saved Jews. Eleven Ukrainians were listed by Joseph Schwarz, who gathered testimonies from Jewish survivors. Among the more spectacular stories was that of Oleksander Kryvoiaza of Sambir, Western Ukraine, who helped save fifty-eight Jews.[44] Roman Biletsky and his father Levko rescued and hid twenty-three Jews in Zavaliv.[45] A Ukrainian forester tells how a group of twenty-five Ukrainians and five Poles helped 1,700 Jews who hid in the forests. Some others hid in the monastery of the Ukrainian Studite order.[46] There were many individual Ukrainians who, *on penalty of death*, tried to help Jews. Relying on memoirs, Philip Friedman enumerates several such cases.[47]

The following letter illustrates individual heroism in defense of Jews:

With regard to the question of attitudes of the Ukrainian population toward the Jews during World War II, I would like to put on record the following facts concerning our family:

1. A Ukrainian priest Kouch . . . in Przemyslany (Peremyshliany), near Lviv, baptized in 1942 my brother and myself in order to provide us with Christian (aryan) papers. He did such things so *en masse* that he himself was arrested by the Germans, deported to Auschwitz, where he was killed.

2. A Ukrainian family Sokoluk (from the village Borshchiv, near Przemyslany) was hiding us (my mother, my brother and myself) for about three months – from June to September 1943 – after the liquidation of the ghetto in Przemyslany and thus saved our lives. They did this completely gratuitously.[48]

In the archives of Israel's Yad Vashem this author was able to identify several other Ukrainians who helped Jews by concealing them or providing them with food. Jona Oliver from Mizeche told of several Ukrainians who were helpful. In addition to Danylo Rybak, Oliver mentioned M. Pachybula, who hid J. Bronsztejn, and another Ukrainian (unfortunately no name is given) who concealed Izie Bronsztejn and five other Jews.[49]

Hermann Zenner, in a lengthy memoir, told of what he observed in Kolomyia, Rohatyn, Horodenka, and Tluste (Tovste). He also recounted his experiences with Franko Solovy, a Ukrainian farmer from Dobki who not only hid Zenner but also helped him to maintain contact with his family.[50] Such self-sacrificing individuals reaffirm one's faith in humanity. What impelled a Ukrainian brother and sister, Orest Zahajkiewicz and Helena Melnyczuk, to hide Egek and Eda Schafler? Wherein lies the "soul of goodness?"[51]

The role of the Ukrainian Church and Metropolitan Andrei Sheptytsky constitutes a special chapter in the history of Ukrainian-Jewish relations. Sheptytsky's courageous stand against the persecution of Jews was probably unequalled in Europe. When the Nazis began to implement their policy of genocide against the Jews, Sheptytsky sent a letter to Heinrich Himmler in February 1942, protesting vigorously against it and the use of Ukrainian auxiliary police.[52] Himmler disliked Sheptytsky's letter and his office returned it to Lviv for appropriate action. The Germans were in a quandary, for Sheptytsky's arrest would have created an explosive situation in Galicia. To retaliate they terminated the activities of the Ukrainian National Council in Lviv, of which Sheptytsky was honorary chairman.[53]

The problem did not rest with the Germans alone. Some Ukrainians, particularly members of the indigenous police, also participated in the persecution and murder of Jewish people. It was basically to them that Sheptytsky addressed his November 1942 pastoral letter, entitled "Thou Shalt Not Kill" (Ne ubyi). Read in all churches instead of the Sunday sermon, the epistle threatened with divine punishment all individuals who "shed innocent blood and make of themselves outcasts of human society by disregarding the sanctity of man."[54]

In his efforts to help Jews, Sheptytsky became directly involved in rescue operations. Using his high office and church organization, he enlisted some 550 monks and nuns in saving the lives of 150–200 Jewish children.[55] The metropolitan's immediate partners in this undertaking were his brother Klymentii, who was the archimandrite of the Studite monasteries, and his sister Josepha, who was mother superior of the nunneries.

One of the boys saved by Sheptytsky, Kurt I. Lewin, son of the Rabbi of Lviv, described the rescue operation:

This labor of saving Jews was possible only because of the cooperation of a small army of monks and nuns together with some lay priests. They gathered the Jews into their monasteries and convents, orphanages and hospitals, shared their bread with the fugitives, and acted as escorts with total disregard of the danger of Jewish company. . . . Some of them, taught and guided by the Metropolitan Andreas, reached a new height in spiritual life, spread the teachings of their great Prince of the Church among the people, and followed his path in all things. They were the ones most active in giving aid and comfort to the hunted fugitives. Others, never completely free of their anti-Jewish prejudice, nevertheless helped Jews because of their abhorrence of German cruelty. There were those who were indifferent, but being summoned to help, obeyed that summons with eagerness and selflessness. All of them, regardless of motive or attitude, equally shared the grave peril, and helped to provide Jews with shelter and food. But most important of all, they gave moral support to those whom they hid, and hunted Jews deprived of every human right and stripped of any sort of protection, were made to feel wanted and thus allowed to regain their faith in humanity. And those monks, nuns and priests kept their faith by their silence. For two long years no outsider knew about the Jews who were hidden in each and every cloister, and even in the Metropolitan's private residence.[56]

Among the fifteen Jews hiding in Sheptytsky's residence were Kurt Lewin's brother, Isaac Lewin, and David Kahane, who spent three years teaching the monks Hebrew and working in the metropolitan's library.[57] Isaac Lewin, whose memoirs recount his meetings with Sheptytsky, recalled a conversation in which the metropolitan told him:

I want you to be a good Jew, and I am not saving you for your own sake. I am saving you for your people. I do not expect any reward, nor do I expect you to accept my faith.[58]

The respect Sheptytsky earned for his work is indicated by Rabbi David Kahane:

[Sheptytsky] was one of the greatest humanitarians in the history of mankind [and] certainly the best friend the Jews ever had. . . . If the Metropolitan was willing to risk his priests, nuns and churches, he was moved by true undiluted Christianity, by love of our Jewish people, and by a sense of national responsibility. He realized that the enemies of the Ukrainian people would lose no time in blaming the actions of pogrom mobs and militia scum on the entire Ukrainian nation. It was therefore the holy and sacred duty of every nationally-conscious Ukrainian intellectual and priest to save as many Jews as possible.[59]

Kurt Lewin admired Sheptytsky's moral fiber, leadership, and commitment to Christian principles: "World War II was an opening to the madness of the world which you see today and it's a privilege for me and for you to be able to see a man [like Sheptytsky]; it's like touching the stars and being inspired by it. . . . It's a ray of humanity at its best, a ray of religion and faith at its strongest."[60]

Besides Sheptytsky's efforts to help Jews, there were many initiatives by individual Ukrainian priests. Father Marko personally saved forty Jewish children.[61] Philip Friedman lists several others who helped Jews in a variety of ways. Indeed, even in the far-off city of Marseilles, a Ukrainian priest, Valentyn Bakst, hid Jews in his church and provided them with forged "Aryan papers," while serving the spiritual needs of Ukrainian dock workers.[62]

The story of Jewish-Ukrainian relations during World War II is therefore a multi-faceted one. Problems between the two groups have their roots in past social, economic, and political relationships, which shaped the perceptions and attitudes of Ukrainians and Jews, placing them in adversarial positions.

Both groups developed collective stereotypes of each other, often of a semi-mythical nature, which not only influenced but perhaps even determined their attitudes and behaviour. It is unfortunate that such stereotypes have been reinforced by writers and scholars who lend them authority and respectability.[63] What seems to be missing in most writings on the subject is restraint, attention to details, historical context, and an understanding of the political aspirations of the other side. Probably no one will ever write a complete history of the tumultuous events of World War II, but we can contribute to it by eliminating misconceptions and distortions which render impossible a balanced view of the past.

Notes

1 Howard Aster and Peter J. Potichnyj, *Jewish-Ukrainian Relations: Two Solitudes* (Oakville, Ont., 1983).
2 Milena Rudnytska, "Pomer dr. Emil Zomershtein, kolyshnii lider halytskykh zhydiv," *Svoboda* (Jersey City), 5 July 1957.

3 For a history of the OUN and its role during World War II, see John A. Armstrong, *Ukrainian Nationalism*, 2d rev. ed. (Littleton, Colo., 1980).

4 *OUN v svitli postanov Velykykh Zboriv, Konferentsii ta inshykh dokumentiv z borotby 1929-1954 r.* (n.p., 1955), 36.

5 Philip Friedman, "Ukrainian-Jewish Relations during the Nazi Occupation," *YIVO Annual of Jewish Social Science* 12 (1958-9): 265.

6 The identification of Jews with Communism stems originally from the period of the Bolshevik Revolution and the Civil War (1917-21). See the study by Arthur E. Adams, *Bolsheviks in the Ukraine: The Second Campaign, 1918-1919* (New Haven, 1963), 142.

7 Friedman, "Ukrainian-Jewish Relations," 265.

8 *OUN v svitli postanov Velykykh Zboriv*, 107-20. See part 3 of this volume, document 9, for a translation of the Third Congress resolutions.

9 Ievhen Shtendera and Petro Potichny, eds., *Ukrainska holovna vyzvolna rada: dokumenty, ofitsiini publikatsii, materiialy*, vol. 8 of *Litopys Ukrainskoi povstanskoi armii* (Toronto, 1980), 36-7.

10 Friedman, "Ukrainian-Jewish Relations," 284.

11 Tätigkeits-und Lagebericht Nr. 11 der Einsatzgruppen der Sicherheitspolizei und des SD in der UdSSR (Berichtszeit vom 1.3. - 31.3.1942), 20, Bundesarchiv, Koblenz, R70/31.

12 The problem of reliable evidence and testimonies is discussed in Friedman, "Ukrainian-Jewish Relations," 284-7.

13 Mykola Lebed, head of the OUN-B in 1941-3, stated: "The majority of doctors in the UPA were Jews whom the UPA rescued from the destructive Hitlerite actions. The Jewish doctors were treated as equal citizens of Ukraine and as officers of the Ukrainian Army." See Mykola Lebed, *UPA: Ukrainska povstanska armia* (n.p., 1946), 35-6.

14 According to Friedman, "Ukrainian-Jewish Relations," 286, B. Eisenstein-Keshev claimed that the OUN-B liquidated the Jews in the camps at the approach of the Soviet army. Freidman expressed some reservations about Eisenstein-Keshev's account: "The report of B. Eisenstein-Keshev is not sufficiently documented and both its figures and events are subject to question. In the middle of June 1943, the UPA was compelled to disband this camp not because of the advance of the Soviet Army, as Eisenstein-Keshev erroneously states, but because of an attack by a German motorized batallion under the command of General Huentzler. Conceivably, the Jewish inmates left behind fell into the hands of the Germans and were exterminated."

15 Einsatzgruppe A, "Comprehensive Report up to October 15, 1941," in *Trials of War Criminals before the Nuernberg Military Tribunals under Control Council Law No. 10* (Washington, D.C., 1949-54), 4: 155-6, 159.

16 Referring to the policy of setting neighbour against neighbour, the Nuremberg military tribunal declared: "Certain *Einsatzkommandos* committed a crime which, from a moral point of view, was perhaps even worse than their own directly committed murders, that is, their initiating the population to abuse, maltreat, and slay their fellow citizens. To invade a foreign country, seize innocent inhabitants, and shoot them is a crime the mere statement of which is its own condemnation. But to stir up passion, hate, violence and destruction among the people themselves aims at breaking the moral backbone even of those the invader chooses to spare. It sows seeds of crime which the invader intends to bear continuous fruit even after he is driven out." See ibid., 435.

17 Der Chef der Sicherheitspolizei und des SD Berlin, der 12 Juli 1941. Ereignismeldung UdSSR, No. 20, Bundesarchiv, R58/214, 4, for the situation in Stryi. SS Brigadier General Erwin Schul, commander of *Einsatzkommando* 5 (of *Einsatzgruppe* C), testified at Nuremberg that 5,000 inhabitants were murdered in Lviv. For his testimony, see *Trials of War Criminals before the Nuernberg Military Tribunals*, 4:518–21. A report of 16 July 1941 states that about 20,000 Ukrainians disappeared from Lviv during Soviet rule. At least 80 per cent of them were members of the intelligentsia. The number of those murdered is estimated at between 3–4,000. See Der Chef der Sicherheitspolizei und des SD, Ereignismeldung UdSSR, Nr. 24, Bundesarchiv, R58/214, 10. For pictures of those murdered, see The National Archives, Washington, D.C., T312/ 617/8308287-8308296. In Dobromyl among those murdered were four Jews. Also in the Dobromyl area several hundred people were murdered in the salt mines, which were filled with bodies. See Der Chef der Sicherheitspolizei und des SD, Ereignismeldung UdSSR. Nr. 24, Bundesarchiv R58/214, 10–11, 13, 15. The figures for Lublin, Kremianets, and Dubno can be found in Der Chef der Sicherheitspolizei und des SD Berlin, den 20. Juli 1941, Ereignismeldung UdSSR Nr. 28, Bundesarchiv, R58/214, 7–9. The German report most likely referred to Lublin, which was under the Nazis in 1939–41, but either to the villages of Liuby or Liublynets, both in Volhynia. The report also indicated that, following the Soviet occupation in September 1939, some 2,000 Ukrainians lost their lives, and about 10,000 Ukrainians disappeared from Ternopil. In Vinnytsia, an international team of physicians examined a mass grave unearthed in 1943 and confirmed that the victims had been murdered by the NKVD in 1937–8. Their findings are contained in *Amtliches Material zum Massenmord von Winniza* (Berlin, 1944).

18 For eyewitness accounts as well as reports from various parts of Western Ukraine, particularly from Sambir (Ivano-Frankivsk), where the NKVD tortured and murdered 1,200 Ukrainians, see Milena Rudnytska, ed., *Zakhidnia Ukraina pid bolshevykamy, IX. 1939–VI. 1941* (New York, 1958), 441–92.

19 Leonard Schapiro, "The Role of the Jews in the Russian Revolutionary Movement," *Slavonic and East European Review* 40 (December 1961): 164–5. A recent Soviet publication provides some information on Jewish participation in the Soviet government; its reliability is unknown. See Avtandil Rukhadze, *Jews in the USSR: Figures, Facts, Comments* (Moscow, 1984), 23.

20 For a very perceptive and concise treatment of this problem, see David Daube, *Collaboration with Tyranny in Rabbinical Law* (London, 1965).

21 This explains why, in 1941, the Ukrainian population welcomed the German army, particularly in the territories of Western Ukraine.

22 José Veloso, a former member of the Philippine Congress, wrote a first-rate analysis of the problem of collaboration, putting it within the context of an occupied country's political, social, and economic realities. See "Collaboration as a National Issue: A Grave Government Problem," *Lawyer's Journal* (November and December 1945). He concluded that (1) anyone who did not actively fight the Japanese collaborated with them of necessity, obeying the law of self-preservation; (2) collaboration helped the people survive oppressive foreign rule; and (3) collaboration was not treason because "service to country in any form and under any circumstances is patriotic, so long as it is for the good of the people. The final judge as to whether the service is loyal or treasonable is the people concerned and they alone, because to them it was rendered" (p. 177). Nevertheless, collaboration was a much more complex matter in Europe than in Asia.

23 For a thoughtful article on this subject, see Eberhard Straub, "Der verdrängte Sündenfall: Die französische Kollaboration und ihre historische Voraussetzungen," *Frankfurter Allgemeine Zeitung*, 19 November 1983.

24 Bertram N. Gordon, *Collaborationism in France during the Second World War* (Ithaca, N.Y., 1980).

25 See Stärkenachweisung der Schutzmannschaft, Stand vom 1. Juli 1942, Abschnitt C, Geschlossene Einheiten, Bundesarchiv, Koblenz, R.19 vol. 266; also Hans-Joachim Neufeldt, Jürgen Huck, and Georg Tessin, *Zur Geschichte der Ordnungspolizei, 1936–1945* (Koblenz, 1957), 3:17, 51, 55, 64–5.

26 For thought-provoking arguments on this controversial issue, see John A. Armstrong, "Collaborationism in World War II: The Integral Nationalist Variant in Eastern Europe," *Journal of Modern History* 40, no. 3 (September 1968): 396–410. Armstrong provides a history and analysis of the OUN and its programs in *Ukrainian Nationalism*, 2d rev. ed. (Littleton, Colo., 1980). See also Taras Hunchak and Roman Solchanyk, eds., *Ukrainska suspilno-politychna dumka v 20 stolitti: dokumenty i materiialy* (New York, 1983), 3:23–43.

27 The most direct challenge to the Germans was the unilateral proclamation of an independent Ukrainian state by Iaroslav Stetsko on 30 June 1941. The Germans considered this act a Ukrainian attempt at a *coup d'état*. Stepan Bandera, head of the OUN, when pressed by a German representative on 3 July 1941 to withdraw the proclamation of a Ukrainian state because the right to do so belonged to the German Army and the Führer, replied that this right belonged to the OUN. Personal archive, NSDAP Nr. 51, "Niederschrift über die Rücksprache mit Mitgliedern des ukrainischen Nationalkomitees und Stepan Bandera vom 3.7. 1941," 11.

28 Armstrong, "Collaborationism"; see also Armstrong, *Ukrainian Nationalism*.

29 The reference here is to the OUN under the leadership of Stepan Bandera.

30 For the most comprehensive source on the UPA, see *Litopys Ukrainskoi povstanskoi armii*, ed. Ievhen Shtendera and Petro Potichny, 10 vols. (Toronto, 1976–).

31 Stanley Hoffmann, "Collaborationism in France during World War II," *Journal of Modern History* 40, no. 3 (September 1968): 375.

32 To be sure, members of the *Judenrats* collaborated with the Nazis, convinced that they were serving the best interests of the majority of the Jewish population. In their desperate situation, they had to face some very difficult ethical questions. These questions were similar to some asked by David Daube, namely, whether a group of women should allow one of their number to be defiled by an oppressor in return for a promise to save the rest. See Daube, *Collaboration with Tyranny*, 2, 69.

33 Isaiah Trunk, *Judenrat* (New York, 1972), 499; see also 500–33.

34 For his subversion of the German policy, Senytsia was executed. See Der Chef der Sicherheitspolizei und des SD, Berlin, den 6. März 1942, Ereignismeldung UdSSR Nr. 177, 3. Bundesarchiv, Koblenz R58/221.

35 Clara Zimmels-Troper lives in Paris. On 8 March 1984 she made a notarized deposition about her survival. A copy of her deposition is in my archives.

36 Akademiia nauk Ukrainskoi RSR, Instytut istorii, *Istoriia Ukrainskoi RSR: Ukrainska RSR u Velykii Vitchyznianii viini Radianskoho Soiuzu, 1941–1945* (Kiev, 1977), 7:512. Bohdan Krawchenko gives a somewhat different figure. In the Canadian Institute of Ukrainian Studies *Newsletter*, February 1985, 16, he states that Ukraine lost 6.8 million of its population. For a study of the Ukrainian losses, in both wars, see Stephan G. Prociuk, "Human Losses in the Ukraine in World War I and II," *Annals of the Ukrainian*

Academy of Arts and Sciences in the United States 13, no. 35–6 (1973–7): 40. For a more recent study of Ukraine's losses, see Wolodymyr Kosyk, "Ukraine's Losses During the Second World War" in *The Ukrainian Review* 33, no. 2 (Summer 1985): 9–19.

37 Ukrainians also fought in the armed forces of Canada and the United States, as well as in units organized by the London-based Polish government-in-exile, particularly the Polish forces under the command of Gen. Władysław Anders.

38 For personal accounts of life in the concentration camps, see Petro Mirchuk, *U nimetskykh mlynakh smerty: spomyny z pobutu v nimetskykh tiurmakh i kontslaherakh, 1941–45* (New York-London, 1957). See also Mykhailo H. Marunchak, *Systema nimetskykh kontstaboriv i polityka vynyshchuvannia v Ukraini* (Rotterdam, 1947).

39 Alexander Dallin, *German Rule in Russia, 1941–1945* (London, 1957), 428–53. For the treatment of Ukrainian labourers, see *Trial of the Major War Criminals before the International Military Tribunal* (henceforth TMWC) (Nuremberg 1947–9), 25: 101–10; TMWC, 3: 416–511; TMWC, 15: 3–310; TMWC, 16: 548.

40 United States, Chief of Counsel for the Prosecution of Axis Criminality, *Nazi Conspiracy and Aggression* (Washington, D.C., 1946), 3: 71–2.

41 Ibid. For further reports on Ukrainian juveniles who were forced into German service, see TMWC, 27: 12–18; TMWC, 14: 501–04; TMWC, 15: 203–05; TMWC, 25: 89–92. See also Zenon Zeleny, *Ukrainske iunatstvo v vyri Druhoi svitovoi viiny* (Toronto, 1965).

42 It is unfortunate that Jewish authors writing about World War II portray the Holocaust only in terms of the Jewish experience. They rarely mention the human losses suffered by Ukrainians, Poles, or Gypsies, thus reducing the profound tragedy almost exclusively to one people. This kind of writing is not only insensitive, but it also makes for poor history. On 20 April 1985, for example, American Gypsy representative James Marks protested that Gypsies were "excluded from the Days of Remembrance observances, even though 500,000 Gypsies were killed by the Nazis." See "Gypsies Protest Exclusion From Holocaust Rites in U.S.," *New York Times*, 21 April 1985. One gets the impression that Jews were the only ones that suffered and that now one should remember only Jews.

43 Friedman, "Ukrainian-Jewish Relations," 288. The originals of the German posters, or official announcements, are in the archives of the Foreign Representation of the Ukrainian Supreme Liberation Council in New York. See also the Harvard University Refugee Interview Project, no. 500, B6, 7 and *Nasha Strana* (Jerusalem), 2 November 1983.

44 See Friedman, "Ukrainian-Jewish Relations," 289.

45 For the story of the reunion of Roman Biletsky with the survivors in New York, see "Pidhaietski zhydy v Niu Yorku viddiachylys ukraintsevi za riatunok," *Svoboda*, 24 February 1978.

46 See Petro Pik-Piasetsky, "Iak ukrainski lisnyky riatuvaly zhydiv," *Svoboda*, 9 April 1955.

47 Friedman, "Ukrainian-Jewish Relations," 290.

48 Letter from Ida Pizem-Karezag to this author, 26 February 1982.

49 See "Uwagi do zeznania Jony Olivera z dn.8.3.1962," Yad Vashem, Jerusalem 03/2233, 9–10,12.

50 See "Erinnerungen des Herrn Hermann Zenner (Steinkohl), Chicago," Yad Vashem, Jerusalem, 03/3389, 20, 25, 71, 124. In fairness to the reports read by this author at Yad Vashem, it should be stated that they tell mainly the story of Ukrainian persecution of

Jews. The reports about righteous Ukrainians are almost an exception to the rule. That, of course, does not mean that all the reports are true. When they deal with specific individuals, be they saviours or persecutors, they are probably true. The historical value of the reports' generalizations is suspect, however, for the writers discuss situations they did not witness or things that it would be almost impossible for them to know. On the whole, the depositions or reports of the survivors are tinted with anti-Ukrainian bias. A classic example is the testimony of Jan Artwinski (Jakob Grinberg): "We travelled on the road to Brody. . . . Before Brody we saw in one forest forty-three Jews who were hanged by their feet. Among them were women, men and juveniles. . . . *It was the work of the Ukrainians* [emphasis added]. The same thing would have happened to us had we met up with them." See "Protokoł zeznania świadka," Yad Vashem, Jerusalem, 03/1556, 3.

51 For some perceptive observations on the subject, see Daniel Goleman, "Great Altruists: Science Ponders Soul of Goodness," *New York Times*, 5 March 1985, C1–2.

52 See Stepan Baran, *Mytropolyt Andrei Sheptytsky* (Munich, 1947), 114–5.

53 Kost Pankivsky, *Roky nimetskoi okupatsii* (New York, 1965), 29–30. Kurt Lewin, who worked in Sheptytsky's library and archives in 1943–4, confirms that he saw the metropolitan's letter and Himmler's rude rebuke telling the metropolitan "not to interfere in affairs which did not concern him." See Kurt I. Lewin, "Archbishop Andreas Sheptytsky and the Jewish Community in Galicia during the Second World War," *Unitas* (Summer 1960): 137–8.

54 Sheptytsky's pastoral letter was published in *Lvivski arkhieparkhiialni vidomosti* 55, no. 11 (November 1942): 177–83. An original translation of the letter into the German (probably by the German Security Service) is in this author's personal archives.

55 Philip Friedman says that some 150 children were saved ("Ukrainian-Jewish Relations," 293), while Rabbi Kahane's figure is 200 children. See Leo Heiman, "They Saved Jews," *Ukrainian Quarterly* 17, no. 4 (Winter 1961): 328.

56 Kurt I. Lewin, "Archbishop Andreas Sheptytsky," 139–40. For other testimonies, see "Mytropolyt Andrei," *Ukrainskyi samostiinyk* (June 1966): 24–36; also Osyp Kravcheniuk, *Veleten zi sviatoiurskoi hory* (Yorkton, Sask., 1963), 97–104.

57 After the war David Kahane went to Israel, where he became chief chaplain of the Israeli Air Force.

58 Philip Friedman, *Their Brothers' Keepers* (New York, 1978), 135–6.

59 Heiman, "They Saved Jews," 325. When David Kahane speaks about the humanitarianism of Metropolitan Sheptytsky and his friendship toward Jews, there certainly is sufficient evidence for such a judgment. When, however, he speaks about political motivations in helping Jews, one must wonder what his source is. It is doubtful whether the basis of Sheptytsky's altruism was political.

60 The interview with Kurt Lewin was conducted by David Mills on 31 May 1968. The original tapes of the interview are in this author's archives.

61 See Heiman, "They Saved Jews," 331.

62 See Friedman, "Ukrainian-Jewish Relations," 294.

63 In this connection, one can note two highly respected Jewish authors, Raul Hilberg and Lucy Dawidowicz. In *The Destruction of the European Jews* (Chicago, 1961), 585, Hilberg wrote: "Little is known about the guard forces of Belzec and Sobibor, except that they numbered in the hundreds and that, again, they were mostly Ukrainian." What is the evidence for such a statement? Lucy Dawidowicz presents an entirely different problem, because she distorts a document. In "Babi Yar's Legacy," an article

that abounds with anti-Ukrainian bias, she states: "According to an official report, *Sonderkommando* 4A – assisted by the staff of *Einzatzgruppe* C, two units of Police Regiment South and the Ukrainian militia – 'executed' a total of 33,771 Jews in two days." What Dawidowicz does is add "and the Ukrainian militia" to the list of those who slaughtered Jews in Babi Yar. By doing this, she distorts the historical record of that tragic event. See Lucy S. Dawidowicz, "Babi Yar's Legacy," *New York Times Magazine*, 27 September 1981, 54. From a German report on the subject, one learns: "Consequently, the Jews of Kiev were requested. . . to appear on Monday, 29 September by 8 o'clock at a designated place. These announcements were posted by members of the Ukrainian militia in the entire city. . . . In collaboration with the group [Gruppen] staff and 2 Kommandos of the police regiment South, the Sonderkommando 4A executed on 29 and 30 September 33,771 Jews." See *Trials of War Criminals before the Nuernberg Military Tribunals* (Washington, D.C.), 4: 148.

PART I

Ukraine during World War II

2. COLLABORATION AND RESISTANCE

PETER J. POTICHNYJ

Ukrainians in World War II Military Formations: An Overview

There is a great deal of confusion about the behaviour of Ukrainians during 1939–45, and it is not limited to non-Ukrainians. Forty years after World War II, some Ukrainians are themselves unclear on issues that affected them four decades ago and have influenced their thinking to this day.

The common view of the war is that of an enormous struggle between the forces of good and evil, in which the former triumphed. It follows from this view that the nations and individuals who were not on the side of the Allies (except, of course, for the neutral countries) must have been on the side of the Axis powers or, worse still, on the side of the Nazis. Whatever does not fit this neat pattern is either overlooked or misunderstood, and so it has been with the present debate over collaboration and war criminality among Ukrainians.

During World War II Ukrainians collaborated with all sides, for two main reasons. First, as one of the world's largest national groups without a sovereign state, Ukrainians did not control their destiny at a crucial time in world history. Second, not unlike Jews, Ukrainians were – and still are – scattered throughout the world; thus in 1939–45 they could be found in all kinds of places and situations.

Since the war's fiercest battles were on Ukrainian territory, it is not surprising that Ukrainians fought in various armies and military formations, in large numbers and on all fronts. In the Soviet army alone were 4.5 million citizens of Ukraine. According to Soviet statistics, 409,668 Ukrainians were awarded medals for bravery in the war; 961 became heroes of the Soviet Union; and 60 per cent of the 250,000-strong Soviet partisan force in Ukraine was Ukrainian.

Thousands of Ukrainians served in the Polish army of General

Władysław Anders and fought with him on the British side in Egypt, Libya, and Italy. Ukrainians also joined the Polish units that advanced with the Soviet army into Poland. Czech units attached to the Allied forces and formed in the USSR had Ukrainian troops. In 1943, of the 15,000 soldiers in the brigade led by General Ludvik Svoboda, 11,000 were Ukrainians. Most of them became members of the brigade after a three-year sojourn in Soviet concentration camps, where they had been kept since 1940. (Thirty thousand Ukrainians had originally fled to the Soviet Union from Subcarpathian Ukraine to escape the Nazi-supported Hungarian occupation of their territory. The Soviet authorities, suspicious of their national consciousness and eager to assure the Germans that the Molotov-Ribbentrop Pact would be honoured, promptly arrested them and sent them to concentration camps.)

Ukrainians served in the Romanian and Hungarian armies, and they played an important role in bringing about peace between the latter and the Ukrainian Insurgent Army (UPA). Ukrainians fought on the side of the Serbian monarchist Draža Mihailović and with Tito's Yugoslav partisans. A large number of Ukrainians served in the American and Canadian armed forces (an estimated 40,000 in the latter). They could also be found in the French Resistance.

World War II Ukrainian military formations fall into three categories: those established on the basis of a political agreement with the German authorities; those organized by the Germans without any regard to political considerations (precise figures on the number of Ukrainians in such units are not available); and those connected with the underground.

To the first category belong the Nationalist Military Detachments (VVN), the Brotherhoods of Ukrainian Nationalists (DUN), the Galician Division of the *Waffen-SS*, Ukrainian units in the Russian Liberation Army (ROA), the Ukrainian Liberation Army (UVV), and the Ukrainian National Army (UNA).

The Nationalist Military Detachments, organized in 1939 by the leadership of the Organization of Ukrainian Nationalists (OUN) (still unified at the time), was put under the leadership of Colonel Roman Sushko. It had the blessing and support of the Germans immediately before the war with Poland, but existed for a very short time, being disbanded when the Molotov-Ribbentrop Pact came into effect. Many of its members later entered the Ukrainian auxiliary police, *Werkschutz* units, and the *Baudienst*. Its real importance lies in its efforts to renew the traditions of the World War I period, when a national legion, *Sichovi striltsi*, became the nucleus of the Ukrainian Army.

The Brotherhoods of Ukrainian Nationalists was also organized with the understanding and support of the Germans. It fought under the auspices of the Bandera faction of the OUN (OUN-B) and was divided into two groups: *Nachtigall* and *Roland*. *Nachtigall* had about 1,000 men in Lviv when a Ukrainian state was proclaimed in June 1941. After the arrest of the OUN-B leadership, both battalions were returned to Frankfurt an der Oder and there organized into Guard Battalion 201, which was sent to Belorussia to combat Soviet partisans. Because of various complaints about the Ukrainians' insubordination, almost all the Ukrainian officers were arrested and the unit disbanded. One officer, Captain Roman Shukhevych, escaped and later became Commander-in-Chief of the Ukrainian Insurgent Army (UPA). He headed the Ukrainian underground until his death in a battle with Soviet MVD troops in March 1950, near Lviv.

The most important and largest regular unit in this first category was the Galician Division, organized in mid-1943 amid much controversy. Initially, the Ukrainian underground strongly opposed its formation, but once the Galician Division became a *fait accompli*, the underground used the division to train its own people. However, the trainees later deserted and rejoined the underground. Many division members also joined the underground after the division's defeat during the Battle of Brody in July 1944. The remaining troups regrouped in 1945 into a division that became the 1st Division of the UNA.

Other units were formed from Red Army prisoners of war. This was the case of the Sumy (Ukrainian) Division, created in late 1941 and early 1942, although without a political agreement with the Germans. The division was nearly destroyed during the Battle of Stalingrad in 1942–3, and its remnants were attached in 1944 to General Vlasov's Russian Liberation Army (ROA). As a result of Ukrainian protests, all Ukrainian units (but not all individual Ukrainians) separated from the ROA and reorganized as the Ukrainian Liberation Army in the spring of 1944.

In early 1945 former Red Army officers and soldiers formed an anti-tank brigade, Free Ukraine, near Berlin. The recruits came mostly from the Berlin fire brigades, 85 per cent of whom were allegedly composed of Ukrainians. The brigade was organized according to geographical region and included, among others, companies from Myrhorod, Lubni, and Chernihiv.

All of the above-mentioned units or their remnants were brought together under one command in early 1945, when the Ukrainian National Committee, headed by General Pavlo Shandruk, was established in Berlin. In a very difficult situation, pressured from all sides, the Germans finally agreed to the creation of the Ukrainian National Army. The core of the army was to be the reorganized Galician Division, which was to become part of the UNA's 1st Division. Although this plan was never fully realized because of Germany's defeat, the Germans' consent to Ukrainian control of these units gave Ukrainians a free hand to negotiate with the Allies at the war's end.

Once removed from the Eastern front, the Ukrainian units were often less than reliable. For example, two guard battalions of the 30th SS Infantry Division, composed of Ukrainian forced labourers in Germany who were pressed into service, were sent to fight the French underground. In late fall 1944 these units deserted to the French side and became part of the *Forces Françaises de l'Intérieur* (the Resistance). The units were first named the Bohoun and Chevtchenko (Shevchenko) Battalions, and later became the First and Second Ukrainian Battalions. Both battalions were dissolved at the request of the Soviet authorities at the end of 1944. Another unit within the French resistance, led by Lieutenant Osyp Krukovsky and composed of the remnants of three battalions of the Galician Division sent to the West for training, immediately tried to desert to the French side. The attempt was thwarted by the Germans but a small group managed to escape in 1944. The rest were shipped back to Germany.

In the second category (formations organized by the Germans without any prior political agreement) were the guard and construction units: *Werkschutz, Bahnschutz, Baudienst, Hilfswillige (Hiwis)*, and the *Schutzmannschaften*, the Ukrainian auxiliary police. They were made up mainly of former Red Army soldiers who joined these units to save their lives, since Soviet POWs were not covered by the Geneva Convention and the Germans treated them most inhumanely.

In the third category were the formations of the Ukrainian underground, composed of those who joined neither the Soviet nor German forces. This third alternative became a possibility only when the brutality of the Nazi regime and its position on the question of Ukrainian statehood was no longer a mystery.

The first underground unit formed was led by Taras Bulba-Borovets. It was variously named the Ukrainian Insurgent Army (UPA), Polissian *Sich*, and the Ukrainian National Revolutionary Army (UNRA). The

UPA originated in 1942. Initially, it was politically connected to the Ukrainian People's Republic (UNR) government-in-exile and was later associated with the OUN-M. It became a popular force so large that in 1944 the Ukrainian Supreme Liberation Council (UHVR) was created to lead the struggle and co-ordinate political activity. By then the UPA had come under the control of the OUN-B and was active well into the 1950s, when it was liquidated by the Soviets.

There are many misconceptions about the underground. One concerns its origins, and the approach to this question in the West has often been oversimplified. Because the underground was created by nationalists, many of whom had earlier served in units associated with the Germans, they were by definition considered fascists. Another misconception relates to its membership, since once the UPA began to operate, it drew on all organized nationalist groups. Many members of the auxiliary police forces, particularly in Volhynia, deserted and joined the UPA, as did members of the Galician Division. As a result, uninformed writers in the West and an absolute avalanche of Soviet publications give the impression that the Ukrainian underground was created by the Germans in order to fight against the USSR and, as such, harboured all kinds of war criminals.

What is overlooked is that the UPA drew its members from all areas of Ukraine and that Red Army soldiers also belonged to it. Many of the UPA's leading officers and political leaders were from areas controlled by the Soviet Union before 1939. Osyp Pozychaniuk, a former *Komsomol* member, was a prominent leader within the UHVR and in charge of its Information Bureau. He was not the only one. In his memoirs, Danylo Shumuk mentions members of the Communist Party of Western Ukraine who eventually joined the underground units.

It is important to re-emphasize that Ukrainians were to be found on all sides during World War II. The main reasons were that Ukraine was one of the largest nations in Europe without an independent nation-state; the territory of the Ukrainian people was divided among four states on the eve of the war; and there existed a large and dynamic Ukrainian diaspora. Ukrainians who were in German military units were there for various reasons, few of which included sympathy for Nazi ideology or racial policies. Most nationalist Ukrainians had a political agenda – an independent Ukraine, which placed them squarely in opposition to the two main adversaries of the region, Germany and the Soviet Union.

References

Armstrong, John A. *Ukrainian Nationalism, 1939–1945*. 2d ed. New York, 1963.

Holovenko, V. "Bataliony 121 i 116." *Visti Bratstva kolyshnikh voiakiv I-oi Ukrainskoi dyvizii UNA*, no. 9–10 (1953): 10–11.

Horbach, Oleksa. "Ukraintsi u viiskovykh formatsiiakh Druhoi svitovoi viiny." In *Entsyklopediia ukrainoznavstva*, 1186–8. Vol. 1, pt. 3. Munich, 1949.

– "Dyviziia Halychyna." In *Entsyklopediia ukrainoznavsta*, 589. Vol. 1, pt. 2. Munich, 1949.

Karov, D. *Partizanskoe dvizhenie v SSSR v 1941–45 gg*. Munich, 1954.

Kleist, Peter. *Zwischen Hitler und Stalin, 1939–1945*. Bonn, 1950.

Kovach, A. *Vlasovshchyna*. Germany, 1948.

Kovpak, Sidor A. *Ot Putivlia do Karpat*. Moscow, 1945.

Kubiiovych, Volodymyr. "Pochatky Ukrainskoi dyvizii 'Halychyna'." *Visti Bratstva kolyshnikh voiakiv I-oi Ukrainskoi dyvizii UNA*, nos. 3–4 (41–2) (1954): 2–5.

Levytsky, Myron, ed. *Istoriia ukrainskoho viiska*. 2d rev. ed. Winnipeg, 1953.

Lysiak, Oleh. "Volynskyi batalion." *Visti Bratstva kolyshnikh voiakiv I-oi Ukrainskoi dyvizii UNA*, no. 3 (1951).

– ed. *Bii pid Brodamy: zbirnyk stattei u trydtsiatlittia*. New York, 1974.

Matla, Zynovii. *Pivdenna pokhidna hrupa*. Munich, 1952.

Medvedev, Dmitrii N. *Silnye dukhom*. Moscow, 1951.

Nebeliuk, Myroslav. *Pid chuzhymy praporamy*. Paris-Lyon, 1951.

Orhanizatsiia ukrainskykh natsionalistiv, 1929–1954. Paris, 1955.

Ortynsky, Liubomyr. "Druzhyny ukrainskykh natsionalistiv (DUN)." *Visti Bratstva kolyshnikh voiakiv I-oi Ukrainskoi dyvizii UNA*, nos. 6–7 (20–21) (1952): 4–5.

OUN v svitli postanov velykykh zboriv, konferentsii ta inshykh dokumentiv borotby, 1929–1954. n.p., 1955.

OUN u viini 1939–1945. n.p., 1946.

Shandruk, Pavlo. "Tse bulo tak." *Visti Bratstva kolyshnikh voiakiv I-oi Ukrainskoi dyvizii UNA*, no. 3–4 (53–54) (1955): 2–6.

Shtendera, Ievhen, and Petro Potichny, eds. *Litopys Ukrainskoi povstanskoi armii*. 10 vols. Toronto, 1976–.

Shuliak, O. *V imia pravdy: do istorii povstanchoho rukhu v Ukraini*. Rotterdam, 1947.

Thorwald, Jürgen. *Wen sie verderben wollen*. Stuttgart, 1952.

Tytarenko, Petro. "Protypantsyrna bryhada 'Vilna Ukraina'." *Visti Bratstva kolyshnikh voiakiv I-oi Ukrainskoi dyvizii UNA*, no. 6–7 (20–21) (1952): 3.

Vershigora, P. *Liudi s chistoi sovestiu*. Moscow, 1951.

MYROSLAV YURKEVICH

Galician Ukrainians in German Military Formations and in the German Administration

During World War II, three Ukrainian formations functioned primarily in Western Ukraine: the Organization of Ukrainian Nationalists (OUN); the Ukrainian Central Committee, which participated in the German administration of the *Generalgouvernement*; and the Galician Division of the *Waffen-SS*, which was formed in April 1943 and surrendered in May 1945.

In Galicia, the most Westernized area of Ukraine, the process of nation-building had found greater expression than anywhere else in the country.[1] As a result of the first partition of Poland (1772), Galician Ukrainians came under Austrian control and benefited from the Habsburgs' divide-and-rule nationality policies. In order to limit the political power of their Polish subjects, the Austrian monarchs encouraged the revival of the Ukrainian Catholic Church, which led to the formation of a Ukrainian clerical, and later secular, intelligentsia. During the period of constitutional rule after 1867, Galician Ukrainians established a strong network of independent cultural and economic institutions, as well as political parties. In 1914, Galician Ukrainians won the Austrian government's permission to establish the Ukrainian *Sich* Riflemen as a distinct unit of the Austrian army. (The *Sich* had been the Cossack stronghold on the lower Dnieper.) With the fall of the Habsburg monarchy in November 1918 and the proclamation of an independent Western Ukrainian People's Republic, the *Sich* Riflemen became the backbone of the Ukrainian Galician Army, which fought the Poles for possession of the territory until the summer of 1919.

Western Ukrainians' commitment to national sovereignty and readiness to fight in its defence distinguished them from their Eastern Ukrainian countrymen, who had been under direct Russian rule since the mid-eighteenth century. Russian absolutism made it impossible for Eastern Ukrainians to approximate the degree of national consciousness attained in Galicia. Publications in the Ukrainian language, for example, were forbidden by tsarist decree in 1863 and 1876. Consequently, until 1917 Eastern Ukrainian political aspirations were for the most part limited to autonomy within a democratized Russian federation.

A turbulent period of independence followed the Russian Revolution of 1917. The Ukrainian People's Republic was unable to withstand the superior forces of Soviet Russia. The latter's indigenous allies, the Ukrainian communists, were prepared, like their nineteenth-century populist predecessors, to compromise with the more powerful Russians.

Galicians reacted to political defeat in a very different manner. In 1921, former soldiers of the *Sich* Riflemen and the Ukrainian Galician Army combined under the leadership of Colonel Ievhen Konovalets to form the underground Ukrainian Military Organization. Throughout the 1920s, it waged a campaign of violence against the Polish administration and Polish colonial settlement in Galicia and Volhynia. (A former province of the Russian Empire, Volhynia came under Polish rule in 1921.) The decision of the Allied Council of Ambassadors, announced on 15 March 1923, to recognize Polish sovereignty over Galicia confirmed Ukrainian nationalists in the view that they would obtain no support for their aspirations from the liberal democracies.

In 1929, at a clandestine meeting in Vienna, representatives of the Ukrainian Military Organization and student nationalist groups in Western Ukraine and Czechoslovakia established the Organization of Ukrainian Nationalists (OUN) (*Orhanizatsiia ukrainskykh natsionalistiv*). Like virtually every European nationalist movement of the interwar period, the OUN explicitly rejected liberal-democratic ideas,[2] and modelled its political program on the Italian corporatist ideal. It called for a national revolution to establish a sovereign Ukrainian state, which was to be ruled by a dictator with the assistance of a national council formed on the basis of corporate representation of citizens. The state was to have the deciding voice in every area of national life, from economics to religion.[3]

Since Ukrainian nationalism had often been denounced by Russians and Poles as an artificial creation inspired by foreign powers, the OUN leadership took care to stress its independence of external models. It further claimed that Ukrainian nationalism differed in principle from

Italian fascism. An editorial note in the OUN's official organ, *Rozbudova natsii* (Development of the Nation), made this point clear:

Fascism is the movement of a *sovereign* people; it is a current that developed out of a *social* environment and fought *for power within its own state*. Ukrainian nationalism is a *national-liberation movement* whose task is the *struggle for statehood*, to which it must lead the *broadest masses* of the Ukrainian people. Accordingly, Ukrainian nationalism not only cannot be identified with Italian fascism, but cannot even be compared too closely with it.[4]

The OUN leadership's orientation toward the Italian model did not imply support for Nazi ideology. The OUN representative in Rome, Ievhen Onatsky, who energetically lobbied Mussolini's government for support of the Ukrainian cause, maintained that German National Socialism was a different ideology from the Italian corporatist ideal.[5] Writing in the OUN's official journal in 1934, he condemned Nazism as imperialist, racist, and anti-Christian.[6] Similarly, the leading OUN ideologue Mykola Stsiborsky devoted a chapter of his major work, *Natsiokratiia* (Natiocracy), to a critique of Hitler's dictatorship.[7]

Yet Germany was a much more powerful state than Italy and far more likely to go to war against the Soviet Union, thereby presenting Ukrainians with an opportunity to win their independence. The OUN leadership therefore called upon its contacts in German military and intelligence circles, attempting to interest them in the Ukrainian cause and providing information about Polish government activities in return for funds to finance OUN operations.[8] Because the German military were considerably more pragmatic than their Nazi masters (Admiral Wilhelm Canaris, head of military intelligence, would eventually foster opposition to Hitler's regime), the OUN leaders tended to discount the racism that motivated the Nazis. They believed it possible to arrange a *quid pro quo* with the Germans: the OUN would mobilize Ukrainian support for the German army in the impending war against Russia in return for German recognition of an independent Ukraine. This belief sustained them in 1939–41, when Hitler's deliberate avoidance of conflict with Stalin led to several major setbacks in Ukrainian nationalist aspirations.

In March 1939, when the Carpatho-Ukrainians took advantage of the destruction of Czechoslovakia to declare their independence, Hitler allowed Hungarian forces to overrun the area. The Carpatho-Ukrainian defence force, organized with the assistance of the OUN, was routed by the Hungarians.[9] Despite this blow, the OUN continued its co-operation with German military intelligence, which sanctioned the creation of a 600-man formation known as the Nationalist Military Detachments (*Viiskovi viddily natsionalistiv*) shortly before the German attack on Poland.[10] The formation, commanded by the prominent nationalist Roman Sushko, was made up of former soldiers of the Carpatho-Ukrainian defence force and members of the OUN living in Germany. After the completion of basic training in the Austrian village of Saubersdorf near Wiener Neustadt, small groups were taken to Germany for further training. Great pains were taken to keep the formation's existence secret. Its soldiers were given German pseud-onyms and forbidden contact with the population. The Ukrainian letters "BBH" on their shoulder patches were interpreted for official purposes as standing for *Bergbauern Hilfe* (assistance to peasants in mountain regions).

Following the German invasion of Poland, the formation was attached to the southern German army group that advanced through Slovakia into Galicia. In accordance with the Molotov-Ribbentrop Pact, however, German forces were ordered to withdraw from Galicia, which was to be occupied by the Red Army. Sushko's detachments, which had already begun to assist Ukrainian refugees from the Soviet advance, were taken aback by the order to withdraw, and in December 1939 the nationalist leadership decided to dissolve the formation.

At the same time, tension between the OUN leaders, who were scattered in Central and Western European cities to escape Polish police repression, and their Western Ukrainian followers had reached the breaking point. The crisis had begun in May 1938 with the assassination in Rotterdam of Ievhen Konovalets, most probably by a Soviet agent.[11] The choice of his successor polarized the older leadership and the younger Western Ukrainian membership, which bore the day-to-day risks of OUN activity and tended to see its superiors as idlers out of touch with the domestic situation. At a conference held in Rome in August 1939 with minimal Western Ukrainian representation, the leaders appointed one of Konovalets's associates, Andrii Melnyk, as his successor. Most of the Western Ukrainian membership refused to acknowledge the appointment and gave its loyalty to the so-called Revolutionary Leadership of the OUN, formed in February 1940 and headed by Stepan Bandera.

As the stronger OUN faction, Bandera's group (OUN-B) attracted the attention of the German army. The OUN-B held a conference in

Cracow in April 1941, adopting a political program that stressed the vital importance of a Ukrainian army to the winning of independence.[12] In the same month, negotiations between the OUN-B leadership and the German military led to the formation of two Ukrainian units codenamed *Nachtigall* and *Roland*. *Nachtigall* trained in Neuhammer in Silesia; its officers were all Germans, but there was an unofficial Ukrainian staff headed by the prominent OUN-B member Roman Shukhevych. Initially, *Nachtigall* consisted of approximately 150 troops, but with the German invasion of the USSR it was expanded to battalion strength.[13] *Roland*, a larger unit than *Nachtigall*, trained at Saubersdorf and was commanded *de facto* by Riko Jary, a member of the OUN leadership who had been particularly close to German intelligence in the 1930s.[14] His chief Ukrainian subordinate was Ievhen Pobihushchy.

The two units were given the collective name Brotherhoods of Ukrainian Nationalists (*Druzhyny ukrainskykh natsionalistiv*) by the OUN-B leadership, which was by no means content to regard them as integral parts of the *Wehrmacht*. In the negotiations that led to the formation of *Nachtigall* and *Roland*, the Ukrainian nationalists insisted on concessions that would guarantee the units' independence and ensure that they would defend Ukrainian interests. The OUN-B leadership was to remain the units' political master, overseeing recruitment, training, and their eventual use in combat. The units were to be deployed exclusively against Soviet forces.[15] When the Germans attempted to have *Nachtigall* swear loyalty to Germany and the *Führer*, Shukhevych lodged a formal protest. Only after this step had been taken and a telephone call made to Bandera were *Nachtigall*'s soldiers able to swear allegiance to Ukraine and the OUN-B leadership.[16] Both factions of the OUN also formed expeditionary groups whose task was to follow the Germans into Ukraine, organize the population independently, and seize power.[17]

When the invasion occurred on 22 June 1941, *Nachtigall* advanced with the *Wehrmacht* to the Galician capital, Lviv, reaching it on 30 June.[18] *Roland* was sent with the German forces to southern Bessarabia. In Lviv, the OUN-B acted immediately to realize its political plans, hastily summoning a "National Assembly" and proclaiming an independent Ukrainian state in the name of Stepan Bandera and his lieutenant, Iaroslav Stetsko, who was given the title "Head of the National Congress."[19] *Nachtigall* was represented at the congress by Shukhevych.[20] The OUN-B also succeeded in obtaining a statement of support from the Ukrainian Catholic primate, Metropolitan Andrei Sheptytsky.[21]

Although the Germans had not been consulted about the proclamation, OUN-B leaders believed that the *Wehrmacht* would accept the *fait accompli* in order to gain Ukrainian support on the Eastern front.[22] They failed to understand, however, that German policy in the East was determined by the Nazi party, which considered Ukraine a territory for German exploitation and colonization; the Nazis regarded Ukrainians, like other Slavs, as subhumans who were to serve them as slaves.[23] Accordingly, the German secret police proceeded to arrest the OUN-B leaders and demand that they withdraw the proclamation of independence. Bandera and Stetsko refused and spent most of the war in German prisons and concentration camps. The Melnyk faction (OUN-M), which had intended to proclaim Ukrainian independence in Kiev, was hunted down before it could proceed with its plan; Melnyk was kept under house arrest and sent to Sachsenhausen concentration camp in 1944. After having arrested the nationalist leaders, the Germans began a campaign of wholesale repression against the OUN, imprisoning or killing as many of its members as they could track down.[24]

Upon the arrest of the OUN-B leaders, Shukhevych addressed a protest to the *Wehrmacht* general staff, but this brought no positive result.[25] The Germans, concerned that *Nachtigall* and *Roland* might rebel against them, withdrew the two units from the front lines to Frankfurt an der Oder, where they were united into a single formation, *Schutzmannschaftbataillon* (Guard Battalion) No. 201. In April 1942 the battalion was sent to Belorussia to fight Soviet partisans.[26] Its formal agreement to fight in the German ranks was to expire at the end of 1942, and the Germans insisted on renewal of the agreement in November of that year. The officers and soldiers refused, claiming that promises to give them equal rights with German soldiers and to provide assistance to their families had not been kept.[27] The battalion was then dissolved, its officers arrested and imprisoned in Lviv. Shukhevych and several companions managed to escape and join the Ukrainian underground. In 1943 Shukhevych became commander-in-chief of the Ukrainian Insurgent Army (UPA) (*Ukrainska povstanska armiia*), remaining at this post until March 1950, when he and his men were surrounded and killed by the Soviet secret police.[28]

The UPA was initiated by an independent activist in Volhynia, Taras Borovets, who established a Polissian *Sich*, which attacked retreating Soviet forces in 1941.[29] Conceiving of this *Sich* as the nucleus of a national army, Borovets allied himself with the OUN-M and, in the spring of 1942, undertook anti-German resistance. By that autumn, however, the OUN-B had begun its own resistance to the Germans and in 1943 managed to seize control of the UPA, which had grown to a peak strength of about 40,000.[30]

Since the UPA was now fighting the Germans, who made a determined but unsuccessful attempt to destroy it,[31] the nationalist underground was obliged to shed any ideological affinities with totalitarianism. In 1943, both the UPA and the OUN-B adopted official programmatic statements condemning Nazi and Soviet imperialism and affirming the nationalist movement's commitment to political pluralism and to the traditional democratic freedoms associated with Western liberalism.[32] The revision of ideology did not come easily, and arguments about it within the émigré OUN-B caused the organization to split in 1954.[33] Nevertheless, the commitment of the OUN-UPA in Ukraine to the new political program was confirmed not only by documents but also by articles from the movement's publicists.[34] It was also attested to by the formation in 1944 of the Ukrainian Supreme Liberation Council (*Ukrainska holovna vyzvolna rada*), initiated by the OUN-UPA, and based on an explicitly democratic, pluralist platform.[35] The UPA continued fighting for an independent Ukraine after the end of World War II and was largely destroyed by 1948 as a result of joint Soviet, Polish, and Czechoslovak efforts.[36] Isolated units continued to fight until 1954, without assistance from any foreign power.[37]

What of Ukrainian participation in the German administration of occupied territory? The only area in which the Germans allowed this to any significant degree during the occupation was in the *Generalgouvernement*, the territory of central Poland to which Galicia had been annexed in 1941. Mindful of Galicia's former status as an Austrian crown land (and therefore German territory) and of the presence there of many *Volksdeutsche* (ethnic Germans), the occupying authorities pursued policies less brutal than those of Erich Koch, who administered the rest of Ukrainian territory as the *Reichskommissariat Ukraine*.[38]

In the ethnically Ukrainian areas of southeastern Poland occupied by the Germans, local Ukrainian committees were established as early as October 1939 to represent the Ukrainian population before the occupation authorities, to assist refugees from the Soviet-occupied areas (who numbered approximately 30,000 by the end of 1939),[39] and to undertake economic and cultural activity previously forbidden by the Polish government. Schools, reading societies, choirs, and theatre groups were established, and some twenty churches were revived.[40] In November 1939 representatives of the local committees met with the head of the *Generalgouvernement*, Hans Frank, who permitted the establishment of an umbrella organization, the Ukrainian National Union (*Ukrainske natsionalne obiednannia*), headed by the prominent geographer Volodymyr Kubiiovych. Frank's favourable attitude may be explained by the hope that Ukrainians and Poles could be played off one against the other and that Ukrainians might be induced to co-operate with the Germans.[41] On 13–14 April 1940 a meeting of local committee representatives approved the leadership of the Ukrainian National Union, which in June became the Ukrainian Central Committee (*Ukrainskyi tsentralnyi komitet*), formally established under Kubiiovych's leadership.[42]

Unlike such wartime collaborators as Quisling, Pétain, and Laval, Kubiiovych was never recognized by the Germans as the head of a civil administration, and the Ukrainian Central Committee had no political standing. The two functions specified in its statute were: (1) the organization and provision of social services; and (2) co-operation with foreign charitable organizations through the mediation of the German Red Cross.[43]

The regulations also required the committee to provide emergency assistance to the population in the event of natural disasters; to assist refugees, homeless children, and young people, the poor and unemployed; to "participate in combating immorality"; to help the families of prisoners of war; and to establish, support, and aid institutions that carried out work of this kind.[44] From 1940 to 1945 the committee, operating with 80-200 staff members, did much to help Western Ukrainians survive the conflict. Through the committee's efforts, approximately 85,000 Ukrainian prisoners of war from the German-Polish conflict were released. It was able to do much less for Soviet Ukrainian prisoners of war, whom the Germans treated with great brutality. In 1943, when the Germans began to kill Ukrainian peasants in the Zamość region for alleged resistance, Kubiiovych wrote a memorandum of protest to Hans Frank and the killing stopped.[45]

Following a disastrous flood and subsequent famine in Transcarpathia in the spring of 1942, the committee was able to save and resettle 30,000 children. By the end of 1943, it had opened 1,366 kitchens that fed about 100,000 people. The committee provided medical care to the population, establishing clinics, disinfection stations, and rest camps, as well as organizing courses for paramedical personnel. A limited amount of assistance was given to Ukrainian labourers and political prisoners in Germany.

Since the German policy on Ukrainian education was not as ruthless in the *Generalgouvernement* as in the rest of Ukraine, the committee was able to establish student residences (in 1943–4, there were 131 residences housing 7,000 students) and provide scholarships (a total of 730, amounting to 1.35 million zlotys, were awarded in 1943). Although the committee had no control over the state-run school system, it did manage to organize teacher-training courses. The committee paid special attention to the needs of young people: it organized more than 100 youth groups, sports clubs, and camps. A network of educational groups was formed. There were sixty by 1944, with a total membership of more than 2,500. In 1943–4, when the Germans forcibly recruited Ukrainian adolescents for construction work and anti-aircraft defence, the committee managed to have them kept together in Ukrainian units.

The Ukrainian Publishing House (*Ukrainske vydavnytstvo*), established in Cracow under the committee's auspices, published school textbooks, classics of Ukrainian literature, works of Soviet Ukrainian writers suppressed in the USSR, and a daily newspaper, *Krakivski visti* (Cracow News). The publishers had to struggle constantly with the German censors, and their work was impeded by shortages of paper.[46] An important feature of the committee's work was the establishment of 808 Ukrainian educational societies with approximately 46,000 members by March 1941. Besides conducting adult-education activities, these societies strengthened the national identity of Ukrainians previously subjected to Polonization. In the economic sector, the committee was able to do very little, because Ukrainian economic institutions were forced to meet production quotas for the German war effort.

In the spring of 1943 the committee became involved in the formation of a Ukrainian division of the *Waffen* (Armed) *SS*. Unlike the *Allgemeine* (General) *SS*, which began in the 1920s as Hitler's bodyguard and grew into an all-powerful secret police in charge of the extermination of Jews, the *Waffen-SS* developed in the course of the war into a combat organization (the term dates from approximately 1940).[47] By the end of the war, the *Waffen-SS* consisted of thirty-eight divisions, of which some were only regiments. Nineteen were composed largely of non-Germans, including Frenchmen, Belgians, Dutchmen, Danes, Norwegians, Latvians, Estonians, Lithuanians, and Albanians.[48]

Originally, the *Waffen-SS* was as exclusive as the *Allgemeine SS* and insisted that recruits be "racially pure" Aryans. After the disaster at Stalingrad on 31 January 1943, the need for cannon fodder overrode ideological considerations.

The initiative for the formation of a Ukrainian division came from the governor of Galicia, Otto Wächter, who agitated constantly for this idea in 1942–3.[49] On 1 March 1943 he personally suggested it to Heinrich Himmler, head of the *SS*, who expressed agreement in principle on 28 March.[50] Hoping that the formation of such a division would improve German policy toward Ukrainians, Kubiiovych supported Wächter's initiative.[51] Wächter held further discussions with German officials, and on 28 April he publicly proclaimed the division's formation and issued a call for volunteers. Shortly afterward, Himmler expressly forbade the use of the designation "Ukrainian" in connection with the division, and the order was strictly enforced within the division's ranks.[52] The formation was initially known as the *SS-Freiwilligen-Division "Galizien"*; on 27 June 1944 its designation was changed to *14. Freiwilligen-Grenadier-Division der SS (galizische Nr. 1)* (14th Volunteer Grenadier Division of the *SS*, 1st Galician).[53]

As head of the Ukrainian Central Committee, Kubiiovych published an appeal to Galician Ukrainians to join the division. He stressed the necessity of facing Ukraine's "most terrible enemy – Bolshevism" with an army "strong enough to destroy the Red monster."[54] Kubiiovych also attempted to gain the support of influential Ukrainians for recruitment to the division. According to his memoirs, those opposed to recruitment argued that Germany's defeat was certain and that the Germans could not be trusted to keep any political promises they made. The formation of a Ukrainian division would only complicate relations with the victorious Western Allies.[55]

Those who argued for recruitment prevailed. They pointed out that if Ukrainians did not participate in the division's formation, the Germans would recruit by force, thereby depriving Ukrainians of any opportunity to influence its character and defend the interests of its soldiers. The Germans offered training and weapons for a large military formation which, in the event of Germany's collapse, could well become the nucleus of an independent national army vital to the winning of Ukrainian sovereignty. The formation of a division could also be expected to strengthen the Ukrainian fact in Galicia and perhaps in other Ukrainian lands, as well as put Ukraine on the political map.[56] Metropolitan Sheptytsky, an outspoken foe of Nazism,[57] declared himself in favour of the division, reportedly telling Kubiiovych that "there is virtually no price which should not be paid for the creation of a Ukrainian army."[58] Sheptytsky designated one of his senior clergymen, Dr. Vasyl Laba, as the division's chaplain.[59] The Ukrainian Autocephalous Orthodox Church also supported the division.[60] The OUN-B did not approve of recruitment but did little to prevent it,[61] while the OUN-M was favourably disposed.[62] The UPA was hostile, dissuading youths from joining and attempting to draw recruits into its own ranks.[63] Once recruitment was under way, however, Shukhevych, the UPA commander, acknowledged the value of a properly trained and armed formation, and he agreed to send recruits back to the division.[64]

In the negotiations which led to the division's formation, the Ukrainians demanded a guarantee that the division would be used exclusively against Soviet forces on the Eastern front. It is not clear whether there was a formal agreement to this effect, but the condition was not seriously infringed.[65] The Germans also agreed to the assignment of Ukrainian chaplains to the division and to the creation of a Military Executive Committee (*Viiskova uprava*) to oversee recruitment and represent the soldiers' interests before the German authorities. The Ukrainians expected Kubiiovych to be appointed head of the Military Committee, but Alfred Bisanz, one of Wächter's senior administrators, was named to the position instead.[66] The imprisoned officers of *Nachtigall* and *Roland* were released to join the division.[67]

A number of the Ukrainians' conditions were not met. The division was not incorporated into the *Wehrmacht*, and senior officers' posts were reserved for Germans alone. The division's commander, General Fritz Freitag, and all the German officers except the chief of staff came from the sole police division in the German armed forces.[68] The division's name contained no reference to Ukraine, and its insignia was not the Ukrainian trident but the Galician lion.[69]

Throughout May and the first half of June 1943, mass meetings were held in Galician towns to announce the division's formation. The response was enthusiastic: some 82,000 men volunteered, of whom 42,000 were called up and 27,000 accepted.[70] Ninety per cent of the recruits were aged between eighteen and thirty; very few had undergone any military training.[71] Ultimately, 13,000 actually became soldiers.[72]

The recruits were dispatched for training on 18 July, and their departure from Lviv was marked by a public gathering at which more than 50,000 Ukrainians were present.[73] Training took place at the Heidelager camp near Dębica in southeastern Poland and, from

February 1944, at Neuhammer in Silesia. Officers were trained at twelve locations throughout Europe.[74] On 30 October 1943 the Ukrainian officers were sent to rejoin the division. There were eleven captains, fifty-three lieutenants, and twenty-nine second lieutenants.[75]

Some recruits to the division were assigned to five police regiments, all of whose officers were Germans, and which underwent training near Gdynia and Białystok and at various locations in France. In the course of their training, some of the soldiers were used against the French Resistance (*Forces Françaises de l'Intérieur*).[76] Having no wish to fight the French, the Ukrainian soldiers made plans to desert to the Resistance but were arrested before they could do so. The train taking them out of France came under fire from Allied bombers, and a number of soldiers managed to escape. Led by Lieutenant Osyp Krukovsky, they joined the Resistance.[77] Following protests from Wächter, the Ukrainian Central Committee, and the Military Committee against the formation of the police regiments, they were dissolved and their personnel returned to the division.[78] The Military Committee also lodged protests against the forced recruitment of Ukrainians to German paramilitary formations and to General Andrei Vlasov's Russian Liberation Army, formed under German sponsorship in 1944. Members of the committee made strenuous efforts to ensure that the Ukrainian recruits were reassigned to the division.[79]

At the end of June 1944 the division was sent to reinforce the 13th German Army Corps near the Western Ukrainian town of Brody. As soon as the Military Committee heard of the assignment, it arranged secret negotiations with Shukhevych, since UPA units were operating in the area. Both parties agreed to keep out of each other's way, to refrain from encouraging desertion to either side, and to assist each other in case of need.[80] On 18 July advancing Soviet forces encircled the corps and destroyed it.[81] Of the division's 11,000 soldiers who fought at Brody, only 3,000 managed to break out of encirclement; the rest were either killed or taken prisoner.[82] Some of the survivors joined the UPA;[83] the remainder were sent to Neuhammer to regroup. The division was replenished with recruits and brought up to a strength of approximately 11,400.[84] In the autumn of 1944 it saw action against Slovak and Soviet partisans in Slovakia.[85]

At this point, a significant political development occurred. The Germans, hoping to mobilize Ukrainian political support for their dying war effort, released Bandera, Melnyk, and other Ukrainian

Bekanntmachung

Wegen Verbrechens nach §§ 1 und 2 der Verordnung zur Bekämpfung von Angriffen gegen das deutsche Aufbauwerk im Generalgouvernement vom 2. 10. 1943 (VOBl. f. d. GG. Nr. 82/43) wurden vom Standgericht beim Kommandeur der Sicherheitspolizei und des SD für den Distrikt Galizien am 20. 1. 1944

zum Tode verurteilt:

1) **Kundreck Paul,** geb. am 14. 6. 1912 in Urycz, Ukrainer, Arbeiter, ledig, wohnhaft in Urycz Nr. 68, wegen Bandenzugehörigkeit,
2) **Dmytryszyn Anna,** geb. Kaczor, geb. im Jahre 1890 in Kruszelnica, Ukrainerin, verh., wohnhaft in Kruszelnica, wegen Bandenbegünstigung,
3) **Kindratyszyn Wladymir,** geb. am 9. 8. 1912 in Podhorodce, Ukrainer, verh., Landwirt, wohnhaft in Podhorodce Nr. 285, wegen Bandenbegünsti_ung,
4) **Zazulinec Nikolaus,** geb. am 25. 2. 1912 in Podhorodce, Ukrainer, Landwirt, wohnhaft in Podhorodce, wegen Bandenbegünstigung,
5) **Maletyn Olena,** geb. Sawczin, geb. im Jahre 1896 in Rakow, Ukrainerin, verh., wohnhaft in Rakow Nr. 62, wegen Bandenbegünstigung,
6) **Lawriw Theodor,** geb. am 16. 2. 1911, in Rakow, Ukrainer, verh., Ostbahnarbeiter, wohnhaft in Rakow Nr. 62, wegen Bandenbegünstigung,
7) **Peczenyj Theodor,** geb. am 1. 2. 1915 in Suchrow, Ukrainer, verh., Bauer, wohnhaft in Suchrow, wegen Bandenzugehörigkeit,
8) **Choma Kornelia,** geb. Stehnicka, geb. im Jahre 1906 in Ottyniowice, Ukrainerin, verh., wohnhaft in Suchrow, wegen Bandenbegünstigung,
9) **Katola Petro,** geb. am 10. 7. 1900 in Suchrow, Ukrainer, Landwirt, verh., wohnhaft in Suchrow Nr. 173, wegen Bandenzugehörigkeit,
10) **Maslaga Anna,** geb. im Jahre 1901 in Dowszka, Krs. Turka, Ukrainerin, ledig, Arbeiterin, wohnhaft in Stryj, Schloßstrasse Nr. 8, wegen Judenbegünstigung,
11) **Peczenyj Olexa,** geb. am 26. 3. 1907 in Suchrow, Ukrainer, verh., wohnhaft in Suchrow Nr. 120, Landwirt, wegen Bandenzugehörigkeit,
12) **Peczenyj Dimitro,** geb. am 26. 10. 1911 in Suchrow, Ukrainer, verh., wohnhaft in Suchrow Nr. 37, Landwirt, wegen Bandenzugehörigkeit,
13) **Sloboda Oleksa,** geb. am 27. 3. 1912 in Suchrow, Ukrainer, Landwirt, verh., wohnhaft in Suchrow Nr. 128, wegen Bandenzugehörigkeit,
14) **Kaszczynec Wladimir,** geb. am 22. 12. 1904 in Skole, Ukrainer, verh., Magazineur, wohnhaft in Skole, Sered-Sala Nr. 25, wegen OUN-Organisationszugehörigkeit,
15) **Dyrkawec Michael,** geb. am 20. 11. 1923 in Korostow, Ukrainer, ledig, Waldarbeiter, wohnhaft in Korostow, Krs. Stryj, wegen OUN-Organisationszugehörigkeit,
16) **Swistun Michael,** geb. am 1. 10. 1923 in Korostow, Ukrainer, ledig, Waldarbeiter, wohnhaft in Korostow, Krs. Stryj, wegen OUN-Organisationszugehörigkeit,
17) **Jaksz Theodor,** geb. am 16. 4. 1889 in Rozanka-Wyzne, Ukrainer, verh., Förster, wohnhaft in Korostow, Krs. Stryj, wegen OUN-Organisationszugehörigkeit, Mord an dem volksdeutschen Förster B a b i j und Überfall auf das Baudienstlager in Swietoslaw,
18) **Uszniewicz Ewa,** geb. Pankiw, geb. am 20. 7. 1905 in Korostow Ukrainerin, verwitwet, wohnhaft in Korostow, Krs. Stryj, wegen OUN-Organisationszugehörigkeit,
19) **Sawczyn Wasyl,** geb. am 27. 8. 1910 in Korostow, Ukrainer, verh., Heger, wohnhaft in Korostow, Krs. Stryj, wegen OUN-Organisationszugehörigkeit,
20) **Iwaszkiewicz Nikolaus,** geb. am 1. 12. 1892 in Suchrow, Ukrainer, verh., Dorfschulze, wohnhaft in Suchrow, wegen Bandenbegünstigung.

Das Urteil an den zu Ziffer 1) bis 10) Genannten ist am 21. 1. 1944 in S t r y j vollstreckt worden, als Sühnemaßnahme für den am 14. 1. 1944 von ukrainischen Banditen erschossenen ukrainischen Polizeimeister

H l a d k i Wladimir, in Daszawa, Krs. Stryj.

Die Verurteilten zu Ziffer 11) bis 20) sind für einen Gnadenerweis in Aussicht genommen.

Freigesprochen wurde:

Maletyn Oleksa, geb. im Jahre 1881 in Rakow, Ukrainer, verh., Landwirt, wohnhaft in Rakow Nr. 62.

Sollten in den nächsten 3 Monaten im Bereiche der Kreishauptmannschaft Drohobycz und Stryj Gewalttaten, insbesondere auf Deutsche, Angehörige der mit dem Großdeutschen Reich verbündeten Staaten oder im Interesse des Aufbauwerkes im Generalgouvernement arbeitenden Nichtdeutschen begangen werden, so wird, sofern die Täter nicht sofort ergriffen werden, das Urteil auch an den für den Gnadenerweis in Aussicht genommen Verurteilten vollstreckt werden, und zwar in der Form, daß für jede Gewalttat an einem der Schutzbefohlenen des Großdeutschen Reiches, der beabsichtigte Gnadenerweis für mindestens 10 der Verurteilten hinfällig wird.

Ist die Tat von kommunistischen Elementen begangen, so werden aus dem Kreise der oben angeführten Personen Kommunisten, ist die Tat von sonstigen irregeleiteten Elementen begangen, so werden von den obenangeführten diejenigen, die diesen politisch nahestanden, von dem Gnadenerweis ausgeschlossen.

Es liegt deshalb in der Hand der nichtdeutschen Bevölkerung durch sofortige Festnahme

oder Veranlassung der Festnahme des oder der Täter
oder durch Einwirkung auf ihnen bekannte, irregeleitete Elemente,
oder durch Anzeigen verdächtiger Personen

dafür zu sorgen, daß das Urteil an den für den Gnadenerweis in Aussicht genommenen Verurteilten nicht vollstreckt wird.

Stryj, den 21. 1. 1944.

Der SS- und Polizeiführer
im Distrikt Galizien.

Proclamation issued on 21 January 1944 by the SS and Police Leader in Galicia informing the local population of death sentences passed against prisoners convicted of OUN and UPA membership and of sheltering Jews. Half of the prisoners had already been executed; the others were being held as hostages, with the promise of a pardon if attacks on Germans ceased.
(*Archives of the ZP UHVR – Ukrainian Supreme Liberation Council, New York*)

political prisoners. In November 1944 a Committee for the Liberation of the Peoples of Russia was formed under the leadership of General Vlasov, and Ukrainians were expected to subordinate themselves to him. Instead, a separate Ukrainian National Committee (*Ukrainskyi natsionalnyi komitet*) was formed on the initiative of Bandera, Melnyk, Kubiiovych and members of the Ukrainian Central Committee, Andrii Livytsky, president-in-exile of the Ukrainian People's Republic, and a committee representing Eastern Ukrainians. The Ukrainian National Committee was headed by Major-General Pavlo Shandruk, a contract officer with the Polish army who had been imprisoned by the Germans in 1940. On 30 January 1945 Vlasov met with Shandruk to offer him a position as his senior military and political deputy, but Shandruk refused.[86] Faced with the Ukrainians' obduracy and unable to bring effective pressure against them, the Germans gave in. On 12 March 1945 Alfred Rosenberg officially recognized the Ukrainian National Committee as the sole representative of Ukrainians in Germany. Five days later, the committee appealed to the Ukrainian people for support and appointed Shandruk commander-in-chief of the Ukrainian National Army, which was to include all Ukrainians fighting in the German armed forces, primarily the Galician Division and the Ukrainian Liberation Army (*Ukrainske vyzvolne viisko*).[87]

The division, which had fought Tito's partisans in Slovenia in early 1945, was sent at the end of March to fill gaps on the Austrian front near Bad Gleichenberg and Feldbach. On approximately 23–4 March Hitler ordered the division to disarm, claiming that he had not previously been informed of its existence and that Ukrainians were untrustworthy allies.[88] The order was not carried out. Shandruk joined the division on 19 April, and on 25 April its soldiers swore a new oath of loyalty to Ukraine and the Ukrainian people.[89] In the first days after the capitulation, General Freitag committed suicide, while Shandruk (by his own account) left the division for Bavaria to make contact with the American forces. Most of the division voluntarily surrendered to the British on 8 May near the town of Radstadt, Austria. Its senior staff officer, Mykhailo Krat, became commander during the division's internment.[90]

With the defeat of Germany and the division of Europe into Soviet and Western Allied spheres of influence, hopes for the restoration of Ukrainian sovereignty had to be abandoned. Ukrainians who had collaborated with the Germans faced prosecution as war criminals and the threat of forced repatriation to the USSR. The soldiers of the

Galician Division were investigated by the British and found to have a clear record. Although Soviet propaganda has attempted to portray the division as a racist, Nazi-inspired formation,[91] no credible evidence has been produced to implicate it in war crimes of any kind. Polish and Soviet charges that the division was involved in the suppression of the Warsaw Uprising of 1944 have been refuted in a recent work by Vasyl Veryha.[92] It is particularly noteworthy that the leading Polish authority on German-Ukrainian relations during the war, Ryszard Torzecki, has accepted Veryha's refutation.[93]

The Ukrainian Central Committee, which was forced to transfer its operations to Germany in order to escape the advancing Red Army, was formally dissolved by Kubiiovych on 17 April 1945.[94] Although the Soviet authorities attempted to have him charged as a leading collaborator,[95] his memorandum to Hans Frank protesting the killing of Ukrainians was introduced as evidence at the Nuremberg trials.[96] The document was eloquent proof that Kubiiovych had sought only to defend the interests of the Ukrainian people.

For many in the West who have come to see Nazism as the historical embodiment of ultimate evil, the very fact of association with the Germans during World War II appears as *prima facie* evidence of ideological agreement with Nazism. Thus, the Canadian war-crimes investigator Sol Littman is reported to have said of the Galician Division, "It is patently ridiculous to call an organization volunteering to do Hitler's bidding 'freedom fighters'."[97] Yet ideological support for Nazism was the least important factor in Ukrainian collaboration with the Germans. Even the OUN, whose ideology was inspired by integral nationalist models in the 1930s, made its collaboration conditional on German recognition of Ukrainian independence. When such recognition was not forthcoming, the OUN turned against the Germans. The Ukrainian Central Committee, for its part, sought to assist the Ukrainian population of the *Generalgouvernement* and protect it from German depredations. As for the Galician Division, those responsible for its creation may have failed to obtain the maximum possible concessions from the Germans,[98] but their motivation was anti-Soviet, not pro-Nazi. When Kubiiovych called on Galician Ukrainians to destroy "the Bolshevik monster, which is insatiably drinking our people's blood,"[99] his rhetoric was doubtless inflated, but his perception of the threat posed to the Ukrainian people by Russian imperialism was, given the historical record, perfectly accurate.

Those inclined to view Ukrainian collaboration with the Germans as a betrayal of Western liberal-democratic ideals would do well to consider the West's own record in this respect. It has recently been established that Western governments were in possession of the facts about the famine deliberately created by Stalin in 1932-3 (which claimed millions of Ukrainian lives) but chose not to protest for fear of harming their relations with the USSR.[100] After Germany's invasion of the Soviet Union, the Western democracies showed no compunction about collaborating with one dictator – Stalin – in order to defeat another who presented an immediate danger. Indeed, many influential Western liberals and socialists were prepared to overlook, excuse, or even cover up Stalin's crimes in the name of "progress."[101] Under these circumstances, Ukrainians committed to self-determination had no chance of obtaining support from the West. Most of them chose to throw in their lot with the perceived lesser of two evils, while a minority carried on the lonely struggle of the UPA, hoping for Western assistance that never came. It was their misfortune, in the final analysis, to have opposed a brand of totalitarianism whose destruction was not on the West's agenda.

Notes

1 For comprehensive discussions of Ukrainian nationalism in Galicia, see Paul Robert Magocsi, *Galicia: A Historical Survey and Bibliographic Guide* (Toronto, 1983), and Andrei S. Markovits and Frank E. Sysyn, eds., *Nationbuilding and the Politics of Nationalism: Essays on Austrian Galicia* (Cambridge, Mass., 1982).

2 On the beginnings of the OUN, see Alexander J. Motyl, *The Turn to the Right: The Ideological Origins and Development of Ukrainian Nationalism, 1919–1929* (Boulder, Colo., 1980). For an overview of interwar Eastern European fascism, see Peter F. Sugar, ed., *Native Fascism in the Successor States, 1918–1945* (Santa Barbara, 1971).

3 The 1929 OUN program is reprinted in *OUN v svitli postanov Velykykh Zboriv, Konferentsii ta inshykh dokumentiv z borotby 1929–1955 r.* (n.p., 1955), 3–16. For a translation, see part 3 of this volume, document 1.

4 *Rozbudova natsii*, no. 8–9 (1929): 262.

5 For details of Onatsky's efforts, see his published diaries: *U vichnomu misti*, 2 vols. (Buenos Aires, 1954; Toronto, 1981).

6 Ievhen Onatsky, "Ideologichni i taktychni rozkhodzhennia mizh fashyzmom i natsional-sotsiializmom," *Rozbudova natsii*, no. 5–6 (1934): 142–9; idem, "Kult uspikhu," *Rozbudova natsii*, no. 7–8 (1934): 162–9.

7 Mykola Stsiborsky, *Natsiokratiia* (Paris, 1935), 49–60.

8 Ryszard Torzecki, *Kwestia ukraińska w polityce III Rzeszy (1933–1945)* (Warsaw, 1972), 128–9; Hans Roos, *Polen und Europa*, 2d ed. (Tübingen, 1965), 147–55. For contacts between the OUN and German military intelligence, see Lev Rebet, *Svitla i tini OUN* (Munich, 1964), 94; and Anatol Kaminsky, *Krai, emigratsiia i mizhnarodni zakulisy* (New York, 1982), 78.

9 For a comprehensive account, see Petro Stercho, *Karpato-ukrainska derzhava: do istorii vyzvolnoi borotby karpatskykh ukraintsiv u 1919–1939 rokakh* (Toronto, 1965).
10 This account of the Nationalist Military Detachments is based on Roman Krokhmaliuk, *Zahrava na skhodi: spohady i dokumenty z pratsi u Viiskovii upravi "Halychyna" v 1943–1945 rokakh* (Toronto-New York, 1978), 7–9.
11 On Konovalets, see Iurii Boiko, ed., *Ievhen Konovalets ta ioho doba* (Munich, 1974); on his assassination, see Ievhen Onatsky, *Shliakhom na Rotterdam* (Buenos Aires, 1983).
12 Text in *OUN v svitli postanov*, 24–47.
13 Krokhmaliuk, *Zahrava na skhodi*, 9; John A. Armstrong, *Ukrainian Nationalism*, 2d rev. ed. (New York, 1963), 74.
14 Armstrong, ibid.
15 *Druzhyny ukrainskykh natsionalistiv u 1941–1942 rokakh* (n. p., 1953), 5–6.
16 *Zlochyny komunistychnoi Moskvy v Ukraini vliti 1941 roku* (New York, 1960), 7; Myroslav Kalba, *"Nakhtigal" (kurin DUN) u svitli faktiv i dokumentiv* (Denver, 1984), 27–9.
17 On the expeditionary groups, see Lev Shankovsky, *Pokhidni hrupy OUN: prychynky do istorii pokhidnykh hrup OUN na tsentralnykh i skhidnikh zemliakh Ukrainy v 1941–1943 rr.* (Munich, 1958).
18 Soviet propaganda has repeatedly charged *Nachtigall* with the murder of civilians upon its entry into Lviv. The civilians in question were Ukrainian political prisoners killed by the Soviet secret police as it prepared to retreat from Western Ukraine. The Soviet charges have been refuted not only by Ukrainian eyewitnesses (*Zlochyny*, 5–15, 46–62), but also by a West German government investigation, carried out in 1960–1, into charges against the chief German organizer of *Nachtigall*, Theodor Oberländer (Hermann Raschhofer, *Political Assassination: The Legal Background of the Oberländer and Stashinsky Cases*, Tübingen, 1964). There have also been charges that *Nachtigall* was involved in the murder of thirty Polish professors in Lviv in July 1941. The leading Polish authority on this crime, Professor Zygmunt Albert, does not rule out the possibility of *Nachtigall*'s participation, but lays the blame squarely on the Germans. See Zygmunt Albert, "Zamordowanie 25 profesorów wyższych uczelni we Lwowie przez hitlerowców w lipcu 1941 r.," *Przegląd Lekarski* 20, series 2, no. 1 (1964).
19 Armstrong, *Ukrainian Nationalism*, 77–80. The text of the proclamation remains a subject of controversy, which turns on the presence in one version of the following sentence: "The newly arisen Ukrainian state will co-operate closely with National Socialist Greater Germany, which, under the leadership of its *Führer*, Adolf Hitler, is creating a new order in Europe and in the world and is helping the Ukrainian people to free itself from Muscovite occupation." For a comparison of the available texts, see S.V. Savchuk, "'Akt proholoshennia Ukrainskoi Derzhavy' 30-ho chervnia 1941 roku," *Novyi litopys* 1, no. 1 (1961): 3–25.
20 *Zlochyny*, 8.
21 Armstrong, *Ukrainian Nationalism*, 80–1.
22 Ibid., 82.
23 For a detailed account, see Ihor Kamenetsky, *Secret Nazi Plans for Eastern Europe: A Study of Lebensraum Policies* (New York, 1961).
24 Armstrong, *Ukrainian Nationalism*, 83, 104–17. See also Petro Mirchuk, *Stepan Bandera: symvol revoliutsiinoi bezkompromisovosty* (New York-Toronto, 1961), 88–9; Dmytro Andriievsky, "Pid znakom Saksenhavzenu," in *Nepohasnyi ohon viry: zbirnyk na poshanu polkovnyka Andriia Melnyka, holovy Provodu ukrainskykh natsionalistiv*, ed. Zynovii Knysh (Paris, 1974), 242–54.

25 *Druzhyny ukrainskykh natsionalistiv*, 55; Kalba, *"Nakhtigal,"* 29.

26 For an account of the battalion's anti-partisan activity, see *Druzhyny ukrainskykh natsionalistiv*, 11–41.

27 Myroslav Kalba, comp., *U lavakh druzhynnykiv: spohady uchasnykiv* (Denver, 1982), 136.

28 The only full-length biography of Shukhevych is Petro Mirchuk, *Roman Shukhevych (Gen. Taras Chuprynka), komandyr armii bezsmertnykh* (New York, 1970).

29 On Borovets, see his memoirs, *Armiia bez derzhavy: slava i trahediia ukrainskoho povstanskoho rukhu* (Winnipeg, 1981), and O. Shuliak (pseud. of Oleh Shtul-Zhdanovych), *V imia pravdy: do istorii povstanchoho rukhu v Ukraini* (Rotterdam, 1947).

30 For the figure of 40,000, see Myroslav Prokop, "UPA z perspektyvy 40-richchia," *Svoboda* (Jersey City), 24 September 1982. The methods by which the OUN-B came to control the UPA, especially the role of the OUN-B security service (*Sluzhba bezpeky*), remain highly controversial. See, for example, the accounts of the disarming of Borovets's formation in *Armiia bez derzhavy*, 267, and "Zaiava ZP UHVR i Obiednannia kolyshnikh voiakiv UPA," *Suchasnist* 22, nos. 7–8 (1982): 165–8.

31 Lev Shankovsky, "Ukrainska povstancha armiia," in *Istoriia ukrainskoho viiska*, 2d ed. (Winnipeg, 1953), 668–73. See also Taras Hunchak, ed., *UPA v svitli nimetskykh dokumentiv*, vols. 6 and 7 of *Litopys Ukrainskoi povstanskoi armii*, ed. Ievhen Shtendera and Petro Potichny (Toronto, 1983).

32 *OUN v svitli postanov*, 9–120; *Litopys Ukrainskoi povstanskoi armii* (Toronto, 1976–), 1:121–31. For the English translations, see part 3 of this volume.

33 The best account is that by Roman Krychevsky (pseud. of Roman Ilnytzkyj), *Orhanizatsiia ukrainskykh natsionalistiv v Ukraini – Orhanizatsiia ukrainskykh natsionalistiv zakordonom i ZCh OUN: prychynok do istorii ukrainskoho natsionalistychnoho rukhu* (New York-Toronto, 1962).

34 The best known UPA publicists were Osyp Diakiv (pseud. Hornovy) and P. Poltava (only his pseudonym is known). For Diakiv's collected articles, see Osyp Diakiv-Hornovy, *Ideia i chyn: povna zbirka tvoriv* (New York, 1968); idem, *The USSR Unmasked*, trans. Walter Dushnyck (New York, 1976). For Poltava's articles, see P. Poltava, *Zbirnyk pidpilnykh pysan* (Munich, 1959). Articles by other publicists reflecting similar points of view may be found in various volumes of *Litopys Ukrainskoi povstanskoi armii* (Toronto, 1976–).

35 "Pliatforma Ukrainskoi holovnoi vyzvolnoi rady," in *Litopys Ukrainskoi povstanskoi armii* (Toronto, 1976–), 8:34–8. The English translation is included as document 11, part 3 of this volume.

36 The best account of the UPA is Shankovsky, "Ukrainska povstancha armiia." See also Yuriy Tys-Krokhmaliuk, *UPA Warfare in Ukraine: Strategical, Tactical and Organizational Problems of Ukrainian Resistance in World War II* (New York, 1972).

37 Lew Shankowsky, "Soviet and Satellite Sources on the Ukrainian Insurgent Army," *Annals of the Ukrainian Academy of Arts and Sciences in the U.S.* 9, no. 1–2 (27–8) (1961): 256. See also Jan Różdzyński, "Wycofując się 'popełniłem samobójstwo'," *Polityka* (Warsaw), 6 October 1984, 14.

38 Koch's policies are discussed in Bohdan Krawchenko's contribution to this volume.

39 Volodymyr Kubiiovych, *Ukraintsi v Heneralnii hubernii, 1939–1941: istoriia Ukrainskoho tsentralnoho komitetu* (Chicago 1975), 47.

40 Ibid., 49–51.

41 Ibid., 61–5.

42 For a list of the committee's executive members, see Volodymyr Kubiiovych, "Ukrainskyi tsentralnyi komitet," in *Entsyklopediia ukrainoznavstva* (Paris-New York, 1955–), 2:3441.

43 Kubiiovych, *Ukraintsi v Heneralni hubernii*, 100.

44 Ibid., 100–1. The remainder of this account of the committee's activity is based on Kubiiovych, "Ukrainskyi tsentralnyi komitet," 3443–5.

45 Text of memorandum in *Trial of the Major War Criminals before the International Military Tribunal*, 42 vols. (Nuremberg, 1947–9), 27:298–324.

46 For a detailed account, including production figures, see Volodymyr Kubiiovych, "Ukrainske vydavnytstvo," in *Entsyklopediia ukrainoznavstva* (Paris-New York, 1955–), 2:3405–7.

47 George H. Stein, *The Waffen SS: Hitler's Elite Guard at War, 1939–1945* (Ithaca, N.Y., 1966), xxx.

48 For a list of *Waffen-SS* divisions, see ibid., 296–8.

49 Robert Arthur Gelwick, "Personnel Policies and Procedures of the *Waffen-SS*" (Ph.D. dissertation, University of Nebraska, 1971), 614.

50 Basil Dmytryshyn, "The Nazis and the *SS* Volunteer Division 'Galicia'," *American Slavic and East European Review* 15, no. 1 (February 1956): 3–4.

51 Volodymyr Kubiiovych, *Meni 70* (Paris-Munich, 1970), 58–9.

52 Dmytryshyn, "The Nazis," 7.

53 Kurt Georg Klietmann, *Die Waffen SS: Eine Dokumentation* (Osnabrück, 1965), 193.

54 Text in Volf-Ditrikh Haike [Wolf-Dietrich Heike], *Ukrainska dyviziia "Halychyna": istoriia formuvannia i boiovykh dii u 1943–1945 rokakh*, trans. Roman Kolisnyk (Toronto, 1970), 225–7. Heike, the division's only *Wehrmacht* officer, served as its chief of staff. The original German version of his account, written in 1947, has been published under the title *Sie wollten die Freiheit: Die Geschichte der Ukrainischen Division 1943–1945* (Dorheim, n.d. [1973]). Reference in this paper is to the Ukrainian edition, which contains additional notes, bibliographic references, and appendices. For the original text of Kubiiovych's appeal, see *Krakivski visti* (Cracow), 16 May 1943. A version of the appeal published in *Lvivski visti* (Lviv) on 6 May 1943 makes reference to "Muscovite-Jewish Bolshevism" and the "Jewish-Bolshevik monster." *Lvivski visti* was under the direct control of the German occupation authorities, while *Krakivski visti* was the newspaper of Kubiiovych's Ukrainian Central Committee; thus it can be assumed that the *Krakivski visti* text – which makes no reference to Jews – is the authentic one. See also part 3 of this volume, document 8.

55 Kubiiovych, *Meni 70*, 59.

56 Ibid., 59–60; Armstrong, *Ukrainian Nationalism*, 171–2.

57 Armstrong, *Ukrainian Nationalism*, 173.

58 Kubiiovych, *Meni 70*, 61.

59 Haike, *Ukrainska dyviziia*, 39.

60 Armstrong, *Ukrainian Nationalism*, 173.

61 Krokhmaliuk, *Zahrava na skhodi*, 24, 40.

62 Ibid., 24; Kubiiovych, *Meni 70*, 61.

63 Haike, *Ukrainska dyviziia*, 38, 48–9.

64 Krokhmaliuk, *Zahrava na skhodi*, 40–1.

65 Armstrong, *Ukrainian Nationalism*, 172.

66 Krokhmaliuk, *Zahrava na skhodi*, 23; for a list of committee members, see p. 22.

67 Kalba, *U lavakh druzhynnykiv*, 143.

68 Haike, *Ukrainska dyviziia*, 29.
69 For a list of demands made by the Ukrainian negotiators, see Krokhmaliuk, *Zahrava na skhodi*, 21–2.
70 Ibid., 34.
71 Haike, *Ukrainska dyviziia*, 25.
72 Ibid., 24.
73 Krokhmaliuk, *Zahrava na skhodi*, 37. Since the division's recruitment was not complete until July 1943, it could not have taken part in the crushing of the Warsaw ghetto uprising (19 April–8 May 1943), as charged by Sol Littman in his article, "Agent of the Holocaust: The Secret Life of Helmut Rauca," *Saturday Night*, July 1983, 23.
74 For a list of locations, see Krokhmaliuk, *Zahrava na skhodi*, 65.
75 In ibid., 73, it is claimed that some 200 Ukrainian non-commissioned officers were sent for officer training, but there is no mention of whether their courses were completed.
76 Haike, *Ukrainska dyviziia*, 47. Recently, Dimitri Simes inflated the police regiments' activity into the charge that "the SS division Galitchina [sic] ...fought for Hitler in France." See "The Destruction of Liberty," *Christian Science Monitor*, 13 February 1985.
77 Myroslav Nebeliuk, *Pid chuzhymy praporamy* (Paris-Lyon, 1951), 195–201.
78 Haike, *Ukrainska dyviziia*, 47.
79 Krokhmaliuk, *Zahrava na skhodi*, 76–7, 87–90.
80 Ibid., 92.
81 On the Battle of Brody, see Haike, *Ukrainska dyviziia*, 62–89 and Oleh Lysiak, ed., *Bii pid Brodamy: zbirnyk stattei u trydtsiatlittia* (New York, 1974).
82 Haike, *Ukrainska dyviziia*, 96.
83 Lysiak, *Bii pid Brodamy*, 79–81.
84 Krokhmaliuk, *Zahrava na skhodi*, 128.
85 Haike, *Ukrainska dyviziia*, 119–44.
86 Pavlo Shandruk, *Arms of Valor*, trans. Roman Olesnicki (New York, 1959), 220–3.
87 For an account of the Ukrainian Liberation Army, see Peter J. Potichnyj's contribution to this volume.
88 Haike, *Ukrainska dyviziia*, 171.
89 Krokhmaliuk, *Zahrava na skhodi*, 176.
90 For the division's postwar history, see Roman Serbyn's contribution to this volume.
91 The most recent Soviet pamphlets on the division are Valery Styrkul, *The SS Werewolves* (Lviv, 1982), and idem, *We Accuse* (Kiev, 1984).
92 Vasyl Veryha, *Dorohamy Druhoi svitovoi viiny: legendy pro uchast ukraintsiv u zdushuvanni Varshavskoho povstannia v 1944 r. ta pro Ukrainsku dyviziiu "Halychyna,"* rev. ed. (Toronto, 1981).
93 Ryszard Torzecki, review of Veryha, "Dorohamy Druhoi svitovoi viiny," *Dzieje Najnowsze*, no. 4 (1981): 206–11.
94 Kubiiovych, "Ukrainskyi tsentralnyi komitet," 3443.
95 Kubiiovych, *Meni 70*, 73.
96 See note 45 above; cf. *Trial of the Major War Criminals*, 12:119.
97 *Alberta Report*, 4 March 1985, 19.
98 This argument is made by Kostiantyn Zelenko in his critique of the division. See "Shche pro dyviziiu 'Halychyna'," *Ukrainskyi samostiinyk* 23, nos. 11–12 (November–December 1972): 26–32; 24, no. 1 (January 1973): 25–32; 24, no. 2 (February 1973): 30–41.

99 Haike, *Ukrainska dyviziia*, 225.

100 Marco Carynnyk, "The Famine the *Times* Couldn't Find," *Commentary*, November 1983, 32–40; idem, "The Dogs That Did Not Bark," *The Idler*, no. 1 (January 1985): 14–20; no. 2 (February 1985): 17–21.

101 On pro-Stalinist opinion in Europe, see David Caute, *The Fellow Travelers* (New York, 1973); in the United States, see William L. O'Neill, *A Better World: The Great Schism. Stalinism and the American Intellectuals* (New York, 1982). There is no comparable work in Canadian historiography.

MARK R. ELLIOTT

Soviet Military Collaborators during World War II

World War II, with its thirty million fatalities, exacted the largest human toll of any military conflict in history. The fighting also scattered nations as never before: estimates of civilians made homeless – forty million – are greater than for any other war. Europe alone had thirty million refugees. The Soviet Union, with more than twenty million dead and another twenty million displaced, witnessed the largest human upheaval of any country. While Siberia and Central Asia received twenty million civilians fleeing European Russia, Germany took well over eight million Soviet POWs and forced labourers.[1]

The *Wehrmacht* overwhelmed the Red Army in the first months of fighting, taking hundreds of thousands of prisoners at a time: 300,000 in the battle of Smolensk in mid-July; an astounding 650,000 in the Kiev encirclement in late September.[2] In 1941, the Germans captured 3–4 million members of the Red Army; for the entire war, approximately 5.75 million.[3] The size of the captive population stemmed in part from the speed with which motorized *Wehrmacht* divisions devoured Soviet territory. The German *Blitzkrieg* advanced from the frontier in late June to the suburbs of Moscow by December 1941. The Germans benefited from Stalin's self-defeating standfast orders, which contributed to the needless capture of millions of Soviet soldiers. In addition, many soldiers disenchanted with the Soviet regime surrendered voluntarily.[4]

Although a Soviet demographer claims that Red Army personnel "perished by the thousands," the deaths actually ran into the millions. Alfred Rosenberg, German commissioner for the Eastern European region, complained to Field Marshal Wilhelm Keitel as early as February 1942 that of 3.6 million Soviet prisoners, "only several hundred thousand are fully capable of working. The overwhelming majority perished."[5]

Belated, grudging improvements in prisoner treatment ultimately saved some souls from extinction, but fatalities in this lost Soviet army of POWs, mostly in the winter of 1941–2, still numbered 2–3 million.[6]

Germany's inhumane treatment of millions of Soviet POWs ranks among the worst atrocities of the war. The disaster resulted from deliberate systematic destruction, neglect, and the lack of international protection for prisoners on the Eastern front. The Nazis methodically singled out special categories for extinction. The most certain to perish were Communist party members, military commissars, Jews, and the ill-defined category of intellectuals.[7]

Given the Nazis' loathing of Slavs, being Russian or Ukrainian offered little protection. Camp commandants often refused to allow civilian donations of food to starving prisoners. This harsh treatment and the primitive conditions in POW compounds came as the first great shock to the population of the occupied regions. If starvation did not overcome the captives, lack of protection from the elements, physical abuse, or epidemics might. In the first year of fighting in the East, almost all prisoner compounds suffered at least 30 per cent fatalities, and in some the rate of attrition approached 95 per cent.[8]

The lack of legal protection under existing international agreements also contributed to the plight of Soviet POWs. The USSR did not sign the 1929 Geneva Prisoner of War Convention, nor did it formally ratify the 1899 and 1907 Hague Conventions on Land Warfare. Soviet spokesmen claimed Moscow's adherence to the turn-of-the-century treaties and invoked all three in arguing German criminal responsibility for POW and civilian atrocities – but without mentioning the awkward lack of official accession in every case.[9]

How much Soviet adherence to the Hague and Geneva conventions would have helped the POWs is open to question. By 1941 Hitler had amply demonstrated his willingness to disregard inconvenient treaties. Moreover, the Eastern races were not reckoned to be much superior to Jews. "As for the ridiculous hundred million Slavs," Hitler declared, "we will mold the best of them to the shape that suits us, and we will isolate the rest of them in their own pigsties, and anyone who talks about cherishing the local inhabitant and civilizing him goes straight off into a concentration camp!"[10]

Heinrich Himmler, powerful chief of Nazi elite troops (SS), shared the Führer's racial convictions. Der Untermensch (The Subhuman), a pamphlet partially written by Himmler, gives a plain statement of the Nazi opinion of Slavs: "Whether under the Tatars, or Peter, or Stalin, this people is born for the yoke." The subhuman, it was explained, resembled a human in certain anatomical respects, but in reality was more closely related to lower orders of the animal kingdom. His natural habitat was the swamp.[11]

The Germans hindered their own war effort by treating Slavs much worse than other POWs. The *Wehrmacht* developed elaborate propaganda to encourage desertion from the Red Army, but the prevailing *Untermensch* philosophy frequently prevented preferential treatment from being accorded to deserters over ordinary POWs.[12] Had it not been for substantial covert opposition to the destruction of Soviet captives, the death rate would have been even higher. Some German officials looked upon the question of decent treatment from a utilitarian perspective. Propaganda chief Joseph Goebbels and some of his coterie, for example, realized that Himmler's crudity in pamphlets like *Der Untermensch* would deeply insult Soviet captives and cripple *Wehrmacht* recruitment in POW camps. The *Untermensch* policy also alarmed intelligence specialist General Reinhard Gehlen, who argued that unless there was an end to the "subhuman" approach to Soviet civilians and POWs, partisan warfare could not be controlled.[13] Also, General Ernst Koestring fought energetically for a more enlightened policy toward occupied Eastern territories. But Koestring became the head of the *Osttruppen* (Eastern troops of Soviet origin) too late to make more than cosmetic reforms in German treatment of Eastern units. Many commanders saved Soviet captives from the harsher regimen of POW camps and Nazi labour drafts by quietly diverting them into auxiliary units. In general, the greater the distance from Hitler, the greater the likelihood that German officials would regard the Soviet population under their control as a potential source of labour. Millions of POWs perished, but the fraction that did survive benefited from individual captors within the *Wehrmacht* who were more utilitarian than racist.[14]

Appalling conditions in the camps no doubt simplified matters for *Wehrmacht* recruiters, since the dangerous step of joining enemy ranks could appeal only to persons in the most hopeless of predicaments. On other occasions, the semblance of voluntary enlistment gave way to conscription. The captors simply handed out German uniforms, even weapons, and only the foolhardy refused.[15]

Nazi *Untermensch* philosophy, which coldly anticipated POW mistreatment and starvation, was not the only official policy accelerating the rate of enlistment among Soviet captives. The Kremlin itself

Osttruppen in German Ranks in World War II: Nationalities and Numbers

I. TROOPS IN GERMAN FRONTLINE UNITS

Unit and/or Nationality	Size and Date	*Pawns*[1]
162nd Turkish Infantry Division[2]	?/June 1943–45;	14/n36
Sumy Division (Ukrainian)	10,000/1942–43	14/n37
SS Halychyna (Galicia) Division (Ukrainians)	17,000/April 1943– July 1944	14/n37
1st Ukrainian Division (reorganization of the above)	10,000/fall 1944– May 1945	14/n37; 173/n36
1st ROA (Vlasov) Division[3]	15–18,000/May 1945	84–85/n23,26
2nd ROA (Vlasov) Division[3]	18,000/May 1945	85/n26
Russians	310,000[4]/December 1942	15/Gehlen, *Service*, 86; Gordon, "Partisan Warfare," 66,67; Thorwald, *Illusion*, 73; OSS, "Reichswehr," 6.
Estonians[5]	10,000/ December 1942	15/Ibid.
Latvians[5]	104,000/ "	"
Lithuanians[5]	36,800/ "	"
Crimean Tatars	10,000/ "	"
Kalmyks	5,000/ "	"
North Caucasians	15,000/ "	"
Georgians	19,000/ "	"
Armenians	7,000/ "	"
Azerbaidzhani Turks[2]	36,500/ "	"
Other Turks[2]	20,550[6]/ "	"
TOTAL FRONTLINE UNITS	Approximately 500,000 (excluding Balts)[7]	14–15/n23,26,36,37

1 Mark Elliott, *Pawns of Yalta: Soviet Refugees and America's Role in Their Repatriation* (University of Illinois Press, 1982). Text page(s) and sources with endnote numbers.
2 There is overlap among various Turkish units.
3 There is overlap between figures for Kaminskii and ROA troops.
4 This figure undoubtedly includes Ukrainians and probably Belorussians as well. Almost certainly this estimate encompasses some of the above division.

contributed to the movement by an ill-conceived decree that branded all captives as traitors simply for having been taken alive. That information only made POWs more susceptible to German suggestions that they take up arms against Stalin.[16]

The employment of substantial numbers of Soviet prisoners in the German war effort began almost immediately after the surprise attack on the USSR, on 22 June 1941. German troop strength did not equal the Soviets' even at the outset of hostilities, and the *Wehrmacht*'s dramatic

II. TROOPS IN GERMAN ANTI-GUERRILLA UNITS

Unit and/or Nationality	Size and Date	Pawns[1]
Graukopf Battalion (Belorussia)	10,000/?	16/n40
Voskoboinikov unit[8] (Lokot, between Orel and Kursk)	20,000/January 1942	16/n41
Kaminskii Brigade[8] (Lokot, Pripet Marshes, Berezina River region, Warsaw)	10,000/1942– August 1944	16/n42,43
Rodionovites	?/1943	16/n45
1st Cossack Division (Russians, Ukrainians)	20,000/June 1944	14/n35
Osttruppen (France) (transferred from anti-guerrilla to combat units)	115,500/fall 1943– summer 1944	17/n46; OSS, "Reichswehr," 7,9,12; OSS Intelligence Report 52267, NA RG 226
TOTAL ANTI-GUERRILLA FORCES including units not enumerated above (most apparently Russian)	Approximately 500,000/ December 1942[7]	16/n39
TOTAL FRONTLINE AND ANTI-GUERRILLA FORCES	Approximately 1,000,000[7]	19/n55

5 Balts fighting in German ranks were not Soviet citizens but were considered part of the *Osttruppen* forces. An unknown number of Western Ukrainian *Osttruppen* likewise had not been Soviet citizens in the interwar period.
6 Volga Tatars [sic], Kazakhs, Turkmen, and Tadzhiks.
7 It is likely that there is some overlap between the frontline and anti-guerrilla unit totals since Germany used some *Osttruppen* in both capacities. Conversely, it is unlikely that all *Hiwis* (auxiliary troops) are included in these estimates.
8 There is overlap in the figures for these units.

advances could not change the fact that its early losses were costly, even if Red Army losses were costlier. The invader's casualties took on dimensions incomparably greater than in earlier campaigns. Up to the Battle of Moscow in December 1941, *Wehrmacht* progress went unchecked and victories were sweeping. Nevertheless, German losses for the summer and fall soared to 800,000. *Hilfswillige* (auxiliary volunteers) quickly became indispensable, constituting up to 40 per cent of some support formations.[17]

At first the Germans used these *Hilfswillige* (or *Hiwis*) in noncombat roles: in paramilitary maintenance, supply, transport, engineer, and labour battalions. But before the summer was out, Red Army volunteers began to appear in regular *Wehrmacht* combat formations, even in small all-Soviet units under German command.[18]

All this movement from POW compounds into *Wehrmacht* ranks had to be done discreetly, for Hitler's proscriptions were explicit. Commanders bent on circumventing early prohibitions against arming Soviet nationals took care to mislead headquarters. Rather than report all captured enemy personnel, shorthanded officers recruited a portion of their catch on the spot, concealed them among their troops, and bypassed prisoner compounds altogether. Some "all-German" units quietly admitted Soviet POWs up to a level of 10 or 15 per cent. In 1942 Hitler reluctantly recognized the presence of ex-Red Army prisoners in German uniforms as a *fait accompli*. Wary of racial contamination and even more so of redefection, he did, however, prohibit the formation of any large-scale collaborator forces from among Red Army prisoners.[19]

This viewpoint prevailed until Nazi advances turned into retreats; and when the Germans began to ignore the original restrictions, they turned first to units of Soviet minority nationalities, thought to be more trustworthy than Russians. A number of such formations, all under German leadership, achieved division size, including a Cossack division within the regular army but supplied by the *SS*, a Turkish division, the Sumy (Ukrainian) Division, and a Galician (Ukrainian) *SS* division. Curiously, the Nazis exempted Cossacks – the Russian empire's frontier warriors of mixed ancestry – from *Untermensch* classification. Pulled from Soviet POW camps, they saw action in German ranks as early as 1941. The *Wehrmacht* deployed some Cossacks in front-line action, but more often assigned them to anti-partisan operations. The majority served in that capacity until well past the war's midpoint.[20]

In the spring of 1943, Hitler authorized the formation of the 1st Cossack Division under General Helmut von Pannwitz. The division's six regiments numbered 20,000 by June 1944. Pannwitz's personal bodyguard of old Cossacks, with their imposing, if antiquated, uniforms, crisscrossed with munition belts, added a novel, even bizarre touch to twentieth-century total war. But the natives of Croatia, where the division first served, saw nothing quaint in the Cossacks' time-honoured ravaging of war zones. Achieving moderate success battling Tito's partisans, they seem to have been even more adept at plundering and pillaging.[21]

Unlike the 1st Cossack Division, the 162nd Turkish Infantry Division maintained a fifty-fifty German-*Osttruppen* personnel ratio, an experiment that worked better than most. In late 1942 troop-training took place at Neuhammer in Silesia, instead of in occupied Soviet territory, since the *Wehrmacht* knew that ready knowledge of German mistreatment of the civilian population damaged *Osttruppen* morale. Primarily engaged in anti-partisan activity, the Turkish Division saw action from June 1943 in Croatia, Istria, and northern Italy.[22]

The *Wehrmacht's* use of ex-Soviet Ukrainians included the 10,000-strong Sumy Division, which fought at Kharkiv and disintegrated at the Battle of Stalingrad in 1942–3. More is known about the SS Galician Division (organized in April 1943 in the district of Galicia), under Soviet control from 1939 to 1941. Soviet forces badly mauled this formation of 11,000 Ukrainians in German uniform at the Battle of Brody in July 1944. A desperate Himmler permitted the unit's reorganization in the fall of 1944. After a stint in Slovakia, it made its way to Austria by the war's end.[23]

The Cossack, Turkish, and Ukrainian divisions accounted for only a fraction of the Soviet Union's national minorities in German uniform and not even all of these groups in enemy ranks. Altogether, at least a score of the USSR's ethnic groups could be found in substantial numbers dispersed in smaller units throughout the *Wehrmacht*, including Finns, Belorussians, Crimean and Volga Tatars, Kalmyks, North Caucasians, Georgians, Armenians, and Azerbaidzhanis.[24]

Russian collaborators did not play nearly as large a role in German combat ranks as did various Soviet minority nationalities. Probably well under half the total of nearly one million Soviet military collaborators were Russian.[25] Because of the Germans' special fear and loathing of them, Russian "volunteers" were recruited in quantity later than other Soviet nationalities, and were relegated to the least responsible positions. From 1941 until well into 1944, they were usually in support roles; when Russian combat units were formed, the *Wehrmacht* carefully scattered them throughout the ranks. When the German-sponsored Russian Liberation Army (ROA) under ex-Red Army General Andrei Vlasov finally did appear, it barely reached division strength by the war's end.

Vlasov's army was inconsequential, but Russians did play an important role in the German military effort – not on the front lines, but in anti-partisan warfare. Here their help was enlisted early and had some effect. Vlasov was fond of saying, "It takes a Russian to beat a Russian." He never got a real chance to prove it, but a substantial number of Germans appreciated the sentiment, as demonstrated by their liberal recruitment of Russian POWs to fight Soviet partisans. The Soviet territory Germany conquered proved too vast for effective occupation, especially since the forests and swamps of northern Ukraine and Belorussia served as perfect guerrilla bases. The *Wehrmacht* quickly turned to native collaborators to help counter Soviet resistance behind the lines. By the end of 1942, the *Wehrmacht* employed about a half million ex-Red Army men in its anti-guerrilla operations, most of whom were Russian.[26]

In Belorussia, the *Graukopf* Battalion (so named for its commander's gray hair) numbered 10,000 at one point.[27] The Germans found an especially efficient collaborator in engineer Voskoboinikov, who ran Lokot, a town of 6,000 and region of 100,000. His territory – between Orel and Kursk – ultimately encompassed 1.7 million inhabitants, which he controlled with 20,000 men and twenty-four tanks. In exchange for local autonomy he killed partisans, collected taxes, and paid regular tribute in provisions. Moscow so feared the experiment that parachutists were sent in to kill him, which they did in January 1942.[28]

After Voskoboinikov's death, the Kaminskii Brigade, the most notorious of all the anti-partisan units, commandeered the Lokot base. In the next nineteen months Bronislav Kaminskii, an engineer like his predecessor, expanded operations into the Pripet Marshes and the forests along the Biarezina River, finally commanding 10,000 troops with as many camp followers.[29] Widely known for his brutal treatment of captured partisans, he vied in cruelty with the *SS* in suppressing the 1944 Warsaw uprising. An émigré wrote, "The Kaminsky [sic] brigade has the most sinister reputation among the Russians and was highly valued by Himmler."[30] Somehow, the brutality of his brigands exceeded what even the Germans would tolerate. Kaminskii was shot by the *SS* in August 1944.[31]

The troops under Gil-Blazhevich, alias Rodionov, were nearly as infamous. Poles and Jews especially had reason to dread the appearance of Rodionov's men. But one act set Rodionov apart from Kaminskii in notoriety: his redefection in 1943, after the tide had turned against the Germans. Moscow rewarded this erstwhile traitor with the Order of the Red Star for the overnight creation of a "partisan region" in northeast Belorussia. It has not, however, advertised the postwar fate of Rodionov's followers, which was imprisonment at best.[32]

Line-crossing was not an isolated phenomenon. Soviet redefectors, either unaware of the harsh reception awaiting them, or dreading it less than remaining in *Wehrmacht* ranks, multiplied in proportion to German defeats. Hitler, viewing the large-scale defection and revolts of 1942–3 as confirmation of his low opinion of Eastern nationalities, ordered *Osttruppen* units disbanded or transferred to another front. Some collaborators, especially *Hiwis*, remained on the Eastern front, scattered throughout the German army (up to twelve per company), but the great majority was moved to other parts of occupied Europe in the early fall of 1943.[33] They were dispersed widely, from the fjords of Norway to the islands of Greece. Earlier, Soviet nationals in German uniform had seen service even farther south, in Libya. The tides of war now scattered *Osttruppen* in every direction: to Norway, Denmark, Holland, Belgium, Luxemburg, and France; into Yugoslavia, Greece, and Crete; and, as the war concluded, into Italy, Austria, and Germany.[34]

In 1943 France became the destination for more *Osttruppen* than any other country. There were 115,500 dug in by D-Day, 6 June 1944.[35] Allied forces were dismayed to find former Soviet soldiers among captured Germans. American intelligence had amassed voluminous data on the *Osttruppen* – not only head counts, but also precise knowledge of unit movements, current locations, even troop morale, but this information rarely filtered down to front-line units, who were bewildered to encounter German POWs who could not speak German.[36]

If American and British officers knew anything at all about the "volunteer" units, they mistakenly labeled them as part of Vlasov's army, which received the most publicity and the least combat experience, boasted of more and amounted to less, than most ex-Soviet contingents in *Wehrmacht* ranks. Throughout most of the war, influential Nazis viewed this movement merely as propaganda. Serious consideration for anti-Stalinist Russians in a viable military capacity came only as a last-minute act of desperation.[37]

The organization and training of Russian forces under Vlasov's authority did not begin until November 1944, and only one division ever became operational. Pieced together from Russian battalions, recent POW recruits, and the remnants of Kaminskii's guerrillas, the 15,000-strong formation fought briefly and ineffectively along the Oder River in mid-April 1945, then moved south against German orders. In a bizarre ending too incredible for fiction, these Vlasovites helped Czech partisans drive the Nazis out of Prague on 6–8 May and then surrendered to the U.S. Third Army, beginning on 10 May.[38]

Soviet collaborator forces under Vlasov were thus inconsequential, but at the same time no nation in Hitler's path provided the *Wehrmacht* with as many recruits as did the Soviet Union. Certainly, its citizens did not find the black logic of Nazism any more appealing than other Europeans. On the contrary, the Slavs, whom Hitler dismissed as subhumans, had more to fear from Germany's racial determinism than any group save the Jews. Rather than any positive attraction to *Wehrmacht* enlistment, large-scale military collaboration on the Eastern front stemmed from the size of the Soviet POW pool to begin with, the absolute wretchedness and brutality of their incarceration, and the grievances of many who had suffered under Stalin's rule.

If all the diverse auxiliary and fighting formations are included, close to one million Soviet soldiers served in German ranks in World War II.[39] This "army of the damned," as an American documentary styled it, amounted to the largest military defection in history.[40]

In terms of ethnic distribution of Soviet nationals abroad in World War II, the displaced were least likely to have been Russians. This was the case for *Ostarbeiter*, POWs, military collaborators, non-returners, and those ultimately repatriated. The largest contingent of displaced persons was Ukrainian. They accounted for 52.6 per cent of all non-returners who had held Soviet citizenship prior to World War II, whereas in 1939 they constituted only 16.5 per cent of the Soviet population. In comparison, Russians amounted to 14 per cent of the postwar emigration yet made up 58.1 per cent of the total Soviet population in 1939.[41]

There are three main reasons for the disproportionately large non-Russian, especially Ukrainian, representation among Soviet nationals abroad. First, Ukrainians were charged with, and persecuted for, "bourgeois nationalism" more often than Russians, particularly during Stalin's purges of the 1930s. This made Ukrainians and other minorities less hostile to Berlin than Moscow, at least initially, before German occupation policies took their toll. Second, the Germans occupied the entire Ukraine, whereas only a portion of the Russian population had to endure German occupation.[42] Third, *Wehrmacht* Army Group North, in direct control of the Germans' one major region of Russian population, vigorously resisted deportations to the *Reich* because forced labour drafts fueled the partisan movement. But in the south, the army had less control over occupation policy; consequently, Nazi manhunts netted hundreds of thousands of Ukrainians.

Dramatic as the story of Vlasov and other military collaborators may be, altogether they accounted for only a fraction of Soviet nationals caught up in the German war effort. Millions more, civilians as well as POWs, had no choice but to work in the *Reich*'s factories and fields. In 1942 alone, the Nazi invaders commandeered two million Soviet nationals to work throughout German-occupied Europe.[43] For the war as a whole, Germany mobilized between 2.8 and 7 million Soviet forced labourers, with nearly 6 million a likely figure.[44] More than 0.75 million died from mistreatment and wretched conditions.[45]

In looking at repatriation statistics, it is important to note that the majority of Soviet citizens returned to the USSR did not collaborate with the Germans. Red Army men captured in *Wehrmacht* ranks accounted for only 17 per cent (about 900,000 of 5,236,130) of Soviet citizens going home after World War II. Even among military repatriates, collaborators constituted less than one-third (29 per cent, or 900,000 of 3,100,000) of the total.[46] That is to say, approximately 71 per cent of surviving Red Army POWs had refused to join German ranks despite vigorous recruitment and horrendous camp conditions. Of five million repatriates, 83 per cent were not collaborators – unless forced labour is defined as collaboration; that, to be sure, is unthinkable.

Without question, the collaborator phenomenon included those who were anti-Semitic and who treated Jews and others condemned to death by the Germans despicably. Some did not share their captors' racial perversions, preferred life to death in POW camps, and fought against Stalin rather than Hitler. Simply put, a Soviet soldier in German ranks did not necessarily constitute a Soviet soldier sympathetic to the German cause. Without an ounce of sympathy for the opportunistic, ruthless Rodionovs and Kaminskiis, it must also be pointed out that other Soviet soldiers chose German uniforms to avoid starvation or a bullet in the head. It is essential, then, to differentiate among the collaborators. The word *pawns* was chosen by this author for the title of his study of Soviet displacement and repatriation in World War II in order to emphasize the plight of so many who, caught between the likes of Hitler and Stalin, had scarcely a prayer or a choice.[47]

Notes

1 Andrei Amalrik, "Victims of Yalta," *Harper's*, May 1979, 91–2; Boris L. Dvinov, *Politics of the Russian Emigration* (Santa Monica, 1955), 5; Mark Elliott, "The Repatriation Issue in Soviet-American Relations, 1944–1947" (Ph.D. dissertation, University of Kentucky, 1974), 10–21; Nancy Eubank, *The Russians in America* (Minneapolis, 1973), 74; Edward A. Raymond, "The Juridical Status of Persons Displaced from Soviet and Soviet-Dominated Territory" (Ph.D. dissertation, American University, 1952), 172.

2 Alexander Dallin, *German Rule in Russia, 1941–1945* (New York, 1957), 69; Albert Seaton, *The Russo-German War, 1941–45* (London, 1971), 125, 130; Boris Shub, *The Choice* (New York, 1950), 50; Sven Steenberg, *Vlasov* (New York, 1970), 4.

3 Amalrik, "Victims," 91; V.P. Artiemev, "Crime and Punishment in the Soviet Armed Forces," *Military Review*, 42 (November 1962): 73; Dallin, *German Rule*, 69, 417, 427; Dvinov, *Politics*, 38; Eugene Kulischer, *The Displacement of Population in Europe* (Montreal, 1943), 152; Norman Luxenburg, "Solzhenitsyn, Soviet Literature and the Returned POWs Issue" (paper presented at the Midwest Slavic Conference, Cleveland, Ohio, 2 May 1975), 4; Vladimir Petrov, *My Retreat from Russia* (New Haven, 1950), 274-5; Shub, *Choice*, 63.

4 Mikhail M. Koriakov, *I'll Never Go Back: A Red Army Officer Talks* (New York, 1948), 128-9. A powerful Soviet novel depicting these disasters is Konstantin Simonov's *The Living and the Dead* (New York, 1962).

5 Boris Urlanis, *Wars and Population* (Moscow, 1971), 172, 176. See also Dallin, *German Rule*, 417; Shub, *Choice*, 63.

6 Jay Warren Baird, "German Home Propaganda, 1941–1945, and the Russian Front" (Ph.D. dissertation, University of Colorado, 1966), 27; Patricia Blake, "Solzhenitsyn: An Artist Becomes an Exile," *Time*, 25 February 1974, 39; Dallin, *German Rule*, 426; Edward L. Homze, *Foreign Labor in Nazi Germany* (Princeton, N.J., 1967), 80; Petrov, *Retreat from Russia*, 274–5; Janusz Sawczuk, *Hitlerowskie obozy jenieckie w Lambinowicach w latach 1939–1945* (Cieszyn, 1974), 226–7; Alexander Werth, *Russia at War, 1941–1945* (New York, 1964), 703.

7 *The Fate of a Man* (Moscow, 1957), 25–6; Dallin, *German Rule*, 418.

8 Oleg Animisov, *The German Occupation in Northern Russia during World War II: Political and Administrative Aspects* (New York, 1954), 28–9; Dallin, *German Rule*, 418.

9 Heinz L. Ansbacher, "The Problem of Interpreting Attitude Survey Data: A Case Study of the Attitude of Russian Workers in Wartime Germany," *Public Opinion Quarterly* 14 (Spring 1950): 126; Dallin, *German Rule*, 445; George Ginsburgs, "Laws of War and War Crimes on the Russian Front during World War II: The Soviet View," *Soviet Studies*, 11 (January 1960): 254; Alexander Pronin, "Guerrilla Warfare in the German-Occupied Soviet Territories, 1941–1944" (Ph.D. diss., Georgetown University, 1965), 36–7; Aron N. Trainin, *Hitlerite Responsibility under Criminal Law* (London, n.d. [1945]), 34–5, 47. The Nazi perspective is at least as self-serving: see Albrecht, "The Legal Situation Existing between Germany and the Soviet Union," appendix I of *German Camps for Russian and Polish War Prisoners*, by Adolph Westhoff, National Archives Record Group (hereafter cited as NA RG) 338, Foreign Military Studies, P-046. Albrecht was chief of the legal branch of the German foreign office.

10 Quoted in Baird, "Home Propaganda," 25–30. See also Homze, *Foreign Labor*, 79; U.S. Chief of Counsel for the Prosecution of Axis Criminality, *Nazi Conspiracy and Aggression* (Washington, D.C., 1946), 8:646; EUCOM, Historical Division, "Displaced Persons" (Carlisle Barracks, Pa., Military Historical Research Collection, 1947), 6; and Jürgen Thorwald, *The Illusion: Soviet Soldiers in Hitler's Army* (New York, 1975), 32–3.

11 Baird, "Home Propaganda," 40–1. See also International Military Tribunal, *Trial of the Major War Criminals* (Nuremberg, 1947–9), 29:122; and Alan Clark, *Barbarossa, The Russian-German Conflict, 1941–45* (New York, 1965), 205.

12 John Buchsbaum, "German Psychological Warfare on the Eastern Front: 1941–1945" (Ph.D. dissertation, Georgetown University, 1960), 97–8; Shub, *Choice*, 63–4. For more on German attitudes toward Russians, see "The German Concept of the Russian

Mind," in Buchsbaum, "Psychological Warfare," 73–85; Francis Sampson, "Paratrooper Padre," *American Ecclesiastical Review* 116 (February 1947): 118.

13 Baird, "Home Propaganda," 29, 39–41.

14 Ibid., 28; Viacheslav Naumenko, *Velikoe predatelstvo* (New York, 1970), 2:381; Thorwald, *Illusion*, 181–2; Office of Strategic Services (OSS), "Use of Soviet Citizens in the Reichswehr," 5, NA RG 59, no. 2297, 13 December 1944; Hans von Herwarth, "Memoirs: 1904–1945" (unpublished manuscript), 229, 231–4; Ernst Koestring, "The People of the Soviet Union," 20–1, NA RG 338, C-035; OSS, "Reichswehr," 1, 9, 11; Hans Seraphim, "Eastern Nationals as Volunteers in the German Army," iv, 95, NA RG 338, C-043; Maj. Gen. Alfred Toppe et al., "Political Indoctrination of War Prisoners," 64, NA RG 338, P-018d; Interrogation Report of General Ernst Koestring, 30–31 August 1945, p. 7, 9, NA RG 165, Shuster Mission. For a description of these interrogations, see Oron J. Hale, "World War II Documents and Interrogations," *Social Science* 47 (Spring 1972): 75–81.

15 George Fischer, "The New Soviet Emigration," *Russian Review* 8 (January 1949): 11; Roy A. Medvedev, *Let History Judge: The Origins and Consequences of Stalinism* (New York, 1971), 467; OSS, "Reichswehr," 17–18.

16 Mark R. Elliott, *Pawns of Yalta: Soviet Refugees and America's Role in Their Repatriation* (Urbana, Ill., 1982), 168–71; Burton, "The Vlasov Movement," 14; Dvinov, *Politics*, 51; Ft. Dix interviews, NA RG 59, 711.62114/8-1045.

17 Animisov, *German Occupation*, 26; OSS, "Reichswehr," 12; Seaton, *Russo-German War*, 175.

18 Baird, "Home Propaganda," 29; Alexander Dallin, "Portrait of a Collaborator: Oktan," *Survey*, no. 35 (January–March 1961): 117; Alexander Dallin and Ralph Mavrogordato, "Rodionov: A Case-Study of Wartime Redefection," *American Slavic and East European Review*, 18 (February 1959): 25; Reinhard Gehlen, *The Service: The Memoirs of Reinhard Gehlen* (New York, 1972), 73–92; Koestring Interrogation, 8; OSS, "Reichswehr," 9; Wladimir W. Posdnjakoff, "German Counterintelligence Activities in Occupied Soviet Union 1941/45," 63, NA RG 338, P-122; Toppe et al., "Indoctrination," 22.

19 Gary Howard Gordon, "Soviet Partisan Warfare, 1941–1944: The German Perspective" (Ph.D. dissertation, University of Iowa, 1972), 63; Koestring Interrogation, 7–8; Koestring, "People"; OSS, "Reichswehr," 1; Posdnjakoff, "German Counterintelligence," 179.

20 Ibid., 92; Gordon, "Partisan Warfare," 62; Herwarth, "Memoirs," 235.

21 Alexander von Bosse, "The Cossack Corps," 6, 8, 17, NA RG 338, P-064; Koestring, "People," 12; OSS, "Reichswehr," 17; Steenberg, *Vlasov*, 116–18, 124; Toppe et al., "Indoctrination," 63.

22 Koestring Interrogation, 8; Seraphim, "Eastern Nationals," iii, 36–37, 41; Thorwald, *Illusion*, 77.

23 Yaroslav J. Chyz, "Ukrainians in America, Political Attitudes and Activities," vol. 10 (American Council for Nationalities Service, Box 5, Minneapolis, 1953); University of Minnesota Immigration History Research Center, Koestring Interrogation, 8; Volodymyr Kubijovyč, ed., *Ukraine: A Concise Encyclopedia* (Toronto, 1971), 2:1087–8; Steenberg, *Vlasov*, 163; Thorwald, *Illusion*, 233–4.

24 Elliott, *Pawns*, 15.

25 Thorwald, *Illusion*, 228.

26 Gordon, "Partisan Warfare," 66, 148.

27 Ibid., 64; Steenberg, *Vlasov*, 52–62.

28 Posdnjakoff, "German Counterintelligence," 81; Steenberg, *Vlasov*, 76–7; Donald B. Vought, "An Inquiry into Certain Aspects of the Soviet Partisan Movement 1941–1944" (M.A. thesis, University of Louisville, 1963), 148.

29 Alexander Dallin, "The Kaminsky Brigade: A Case-Study of Soviet Defection," in *Revolution and Politics in Russia: Essays in Memory of B.I. Nicolaevsky*, ed. Alexander and Janet Rabinowitch (Bloomington, Ind., 1972), 227; " 'Haunted Forests': Enemy Partisans behind the Front," 11, NA RG 338, C-037; Vladimir D. Samarin, *Civilian Life under the German Occupation, 1942–1944* (New York, 1954), 58; John J. Stephan, *The Russian Fascists: Tragedy and Farce in Exile, 1925–1945* (New York, 1978), 27; Vought, "Inquiry," 149.

30 Dvinov, Politics, 57.

31 Clark, *Barbarossa*, 394; Paul Petelchuk, "The National Alliance of Russian Solidarists: A Study of a Russian Freedom Movement Group" (Ph.D. dissertation, Syracuse University, 1970), 76–7; Seaton, *Russo-German War*, 456; Steenberg, *Vlasov*, 79–80, 170–1; Thorwald, *Illusion*, 243.

32 Aleksei I. Briukhanov, *Vot kak eto bylo: o rabote misii po repatriatsii sovetskikh grazhdan. Vospominaniia sovetskogo ofitsera* (Moscow, 1958), 12–13; Dallin and Mavrogordato, "Rodionov"; Col. P.Z. Kalinin, "Uchastie sovetskikh voinov v partizanskom dvizhenii Belorussii," *Voenno-istoricheskii zhurnal*, no. 10 (October 1962): 34–7; Alexander Solzhenitsyn, *The Gulag Archipelago* (New York, 1973), 1:257; Steenberg, *Vlasov*, 106–10.

33 Dallin and Mavrogordato, "Rodionov," 30; Dallin and Mavrogordato, "The Soviet Reaction to Vlasov," *World Politics* 8 (April 1956): 320; Kalinin, "Uchastie," 347; Koestring Interrogation, 8–9; OSS, "Reichswehr," 1, 9, 13, 16; Seraphim, "Eastern Nationals," 93–6; Wilfried Strik-Strikfeldt, *Against Stalin and Hitler: Memoir of the Russian Liberation Movement, 1941–1945* (London, 1970), 174; A.V. Tishkov, "Predatel pered sovetskim sudom," *Sovetskoe gosudarstvo i pravo*, no. 2 (February 1973): 93; Toppe et al., "Indoctrination," 66. Herwarth unconvincingly downplays the defections as a cause for the transfers; see his "Memoirs," 267.

34 OSS, "Reichswehr," 11–12; Seraphim, "Eastern Nationals," 91; Solzhenitsyn, *Gulag*, 1: 246.

35 OSS, "Reichswehr," 7, 9, 12; OSS Intelligence Report 52267, NA RG 226.

36 OSS files, NA RG 226 and 59. See, for example, OSS, "Reichswehr," 4.

37 Dvinov, *Politics*, 82; John Erickson, *The Road to Stalingrad: Stalin's War with Germany* (New York, 1975), 322, 331; George Fischer, "General Vlasov's Official Biography," *Russian Review* 8 (October 1949): 299; Albert Seaton, *The Battle for Moscow, 1941–1942* (New York, 1971), 167, 204; Steenberg, *Vlasov*, 21–8. For Vlasov's biography, also consult Robert B. Burton, "The Vlasov Movement of World War II: An Appraisal" (Ph.D. dissertation, American University, Washington, D.C., 1963); Paul Carrell, *Hitler Moves East 1941–1943* (London, 1964), 430–1, 439–41; Mark Elliott, "Andrei Vlasov: Red Army General in Hitler's Service," *Military Affairs* 46 (April 1982): 84-7; Institute for the Study of the USSR, *Who Was Who in the USSR* (Metuchen, N.J., 1972), 588; B. Osokin, *Andrei Andreevich Vlasov: kratkaia biografiia* (New York, 1966); Petrov, *Retreat*, 274–300; Michael Schatoff [sic], *Bibliografiia osvoboditelnogo dvizheniia narodov Rossii v gody vtoroi mirovoi voiny (1941–1945)* (New York, 1961); Strik-Stikfeldt, *Against Stalin and Hitler*; Thorwald, *Illusion*. For hostile Soviet accounts of Vlasov's career, see Yuri Bondarev, "A Russian View," in *The Last Circle* (Moscow, 1974), 66; Jean

Taratuta, "Tell Me Who Your Friend Is," in ibid., 114; P.A. Zhilin, "How A. Solzhenitsyn Sang of the Vlasovites' Betrayal," in ibid., 104-7; Tishkov, "Predatel," 91–2.

38 Dallin, "Kaminsky," 227; Dvinov, *Politics*, 109; Koestring Interrogation, 11; Petelchuk, "National Alliance," 86; Solzhenitsyn, *Gulag*, 1: 258–9; Tishkov, "Predatel," 95–6.

39 All but a few estimates, and the great majority of the most believable ones, run between 0.75 and 1 million. Furthermore, two Germans intimately involved in *Osttruppen* activities, Vlasov's interpreter, Capt. Wilfried Strik-Strikfeldt, and Koestring, both set the number at one million. Some figures probably include old tsarist émigrés and Baltic nationals, whose homelands were independent prior to World War II. But these minor sources of inflated calculations cannot be compared to Germany's systematic, wholesale underestimates, which the *Wehrmacht* used to hide the extent of Soviet collaboration from a wary Hitler and which makes many approximations conservative. George Fischer, *Soviet Opposition to Stalin: A Case Study in World War II* (Cambridge, Mass., 1952), 108, cites 0.5 to 1 million; Toppe et al., "Indoctrination," 33, cites 0.75 million; Eugene Lyons, *Our Secret Allies, the Peoples of Russia* (New York, 1953), 243, claims 0.8 million, as does David Footman in his introduction to Strik-Strikfeldt, *Against Stalin and Hitler*, 4, and Kubijovyč, *Ukraine*, 2: 1986–87, Gerald Reitlinger, *The House Built on Sand: The Conflicts of German Policy in Russia, 1939–1945* (New York, 1960), 99; Frederick Wyle, "Memorandum on Statistical Data on Soviet Displaced Persons" (Harvard Project on the Soviet Social System, Harvard University, Cambridge, Mass.), cites 0.8 to 1 million; Thorwald, *Illusion*, 228, records 0.9 to 1 million. The figure of one million is cited by *Army of the Damned* (CBS, 1962), by Hans de Weerd, "Operation Keelhaul," *Ukrainian Review* 2 (December 1955): 26, by A.I. Romanov, *Nights Are Longest There: Smersh from the Inside* (Boston, 1972), 127, by Steenberg, *Vlasov*, 104, and by Strik-Strikfeldt, *Against Stalin and Hitler*, 49. Burton, "Vlasov," iv, and Posdnjakoff, "German Counterintelligence," 179–80, both say more than one million; Ernst Koestring, *General Ernst Koestring* (Frankfurt -am- Main, 1966), 324, says at least one million.

40 CBS, 1962. Audio-Brandon Co. rental.

41 The percentages are based on the following calculations: 150,000 Ukrainians and 40,000 Russians among 285,000 non-returners from pre-1939 Soviet territories. This excludes an estimated 220,000 refugees from the annexed Baltic states. Warren W. Eason, "Demography," in *Handbook of Soviet Social Science Data*, ed. Ellen Mickiewicz (New York, 1973), 58; Alex Inkeles and Raymond A. Bauer, *The Soviet Citizen* (Cambridge, Mass., 1959), 39; Eugene Kulischer to Robert Feldmesser, 13 August 1953, "Estimated Ethnic Composition of USSR Migratory Gains and Losses 1939–1951," Harvard Project on the Soviet Social System, Harvard University, Cambridge, Mass.

42 Walter Kolarz, *Russia and Her Colonies* (New York, 1952), 11; and Ivan Bahryany, "Why I Do Not Want to Go 'Home,'" *Ukrainian Quarterly* 2, no. 3 (Spring 1946): 236; John Panchuk to Gallan, 10 June 1945, folder 5, John Panchuk papers, Immigration History Research Center, University of Minnesota, Minneapolis; Animisov, *German Occupation*, 29–30.

43 E.A. Brodskii, *Vo imia pobedy nad fashizmom: antifashistskaia borba sovetskikh liudei v gitlerovskoi Germanii (1941–1945)* (Moscow, 1970), 10; G.A. Kumanev, "Sovetskaia istoriografiia ob uchastii grazhdan SSR v antifashistskom dvizhenii soprotivleniia v Evrope," in *Vtoraia mirovaia voina i sovremennost*, ed. P.A. Zhilin (Moscow, 1972), 262.

44 Baird, "Home Propaganda," 30, claims 2.8 million; Werth, *Russia at War*, 701, says "nearly 3 million"; International Military Tribunal, *Trial*, 41: 186, and Petrov, *Retreat*, 274–5, both say five million; Kumanev, "Sovetskaia istoriografiia," 262, claims almost six million by 1944; Thorwald, *Illusion*, 216, gives six million; Steenberg, *Vlasov*, 174, reports 6–7 million.

45 Amalrik, "Victims," 94; Dallin, *German Rule*, 451–2.

46 Michael K. Roof and Frederick A. Leedy, "Population Redistribution in the Soviet Union, 1939–1956," *Geographical Review* 49 (April 1959): 211, say "five million plus"; George Ginsburgs, "Soviet Union and the Problem of Refugees and Displaced Persons, 1917–1956," *American Journal of International Law* 51 (April 1957): 348, cites 5,115,709; Mikhail I. Semiriaga, *Sovetskie liudi v evropeiskom soprotivlenii* (Moscow, 1970), 327, quoting Gen. Golikov in *Pravda* (Moscow), 4 October 1945, says 5,200,000; Malcolm Proudfoot, *European Refugees, 1939–52* (Evanston, Ill., 1956), 212, cites 5,213,000; Eugene Kulischer, *Europe on the Move: War and Population Changes, 1917–47* (New York, 1948), 308, cites 5,236,000; "Repatriation of Soviet Citizens," *International Labour Review* 52 (November 1945): 533, records 5,236,130; Fischer, *Soviet Opposition*, 111, says 5,326,445. See also Dallin, *German Rule*, 427; A. Nemirov, *Dorogi i vstrechi* (Munich, 1947), 39.

47 Elliott, *Pawns of Yalta*.

PART II

History and Its Aftermath

INVESTIGATING WAR CRIMINALS IN CANADA AND THE UNITED STATES

INTRODUCTION

Part 2 examines issues related to bringing alleged Nazi war criminals living in Canada and the United States to justice.

In the United States, owing to the efforts of several members of Congress, especially Elizabeth Holtzman, a bill (Law 95-549) amending Section 212 (a) 33 of the Immigration and Nationality Act was introduced on 30 October 1978 and signed into law on 19 December 1978. The bill further clarified and extended the class of "aliens ineligible to receive visas and excluded from admission (to the United States)," to include:

Any alien who during the period beginning on March 23, 1933, and ending on May 8, 1945 under the direction of, or in association with:
a) the Nazi government in Germany;
b) any government in any area occupied by the military forces of the Nazi government of Germany;
c) any government established with the assistance or cooperation of the Nazi government of Germany; or,
d) any government which was an ally of the Nazi government of Germany; ordered, incited, assisted, or otherwise participated in the persecution of any person because of race, religion, national origin, or political opinion.

The amendment also provided that adjudicated Nazi persecutors could not evade deportation by availing themselves of a previous immigration law provision authorizing the withholding of deportation if the deportees might be persecuted in the country to which they were ordered deported.

Up to the early 1970s the U.S. government, through the Immigration and Naturalization Service (INS), had filed nine cases against persons suspected of Nazi collaboration or of persecuting the innocent. By the summer of 1977 the INS had established a Special Litigation Unit (SLU) to investigate and prosecute alleged Nazi war criminals living in the United States, but little activity was undertaken. With the passage of the Holtzman amendment, however, the Justice Department transferred the INS to its Criminal Division, where the SLU became the Office of Special Investigations (OSI) on 28 March 1979.

The first director of the OSI was Walter J. Rocker (to March 1980), a former prosecuting attorney at the Nuremberg war crimes trials. He was succeeded by Allan A. Ryan Jr. (April 1980–August 1983), a lawyer in the Solicitor General's office. Today the OSI is headed by Neal Sher. It has a three-million-dollar annual budget and a staff of fifty lawyers, investigators, historians, and linguists.

A recent statement from the OSI notes that 3–400 suspected Nazi war criminals are now under investigation. They are alleged to have come to the United States under assumed identities or to have misrepresented their wartime histories when applying for admission to the United States. The OSI's *Digest of Cases* for 24 May 1985 states that it is now involved in eleven cases relating to denaturalization (the revoking of citizenship on the grounds of false or misleading representations for failure to disclose material circumstances in applying for admission to the United States, which thereby vitiates the accused party's qualifying period for application for U.S. citizenship and renders the citizenship revocable). The OSI also has fifteen cases in the second stage of this process – deportation. Twenty cases are "no longer active" because of deaths or forced departures (deportations), of which there are presumed to have been at least four. In almost all of the above-mentioned cases, the defendants were of Eastern European origin. Up to 1 July 1984, for example, the OSI had forty cases pending against individuals: two were born in Germany; the others were from the Baltic states, Poland, Romania, the Soviet Union, and Yugoslavia.

The activities of the OSI have stirred some criticism from various quarters. Their views need not be summarized here; they are discussed in the papers that follow. But a recent study by the Anti-Defamation League (ADL) of B'nai B'rith provides another perspective.[1]

One of the controversial aspects of the OSI's prosecution activities has been its use of information from the Soviet Union. Some critics of the OSI maintain that this information has been "fabricated," that it has played an inordinate role in OSI prosecutions, and that the Soviet

Signing of the Nazi-Soviet Non-Aggression Pact. Moscow,
August 1939. *From left to right*: Viacheslav Molotov, Joachim
von Ribbentrop, Joseph Stalin.

Bodies of victims of NKVD purges of 1937–8, part of a mass grave
of more than 9,000 bodies unearthed in Vinnytsia 1943.
(*Bundesarchiv, Koblenz*)

Shortly before retreating the Soviet NKVD security police murdered its prisoners. Residents of Lviv try to identify the victims at the main NKVD prison, 30 June 1941. (*Bundesarchiv, Koblenz*)

Metropolitan Andrei Sheptytsky, primate of the Greek Catholic Church in Galicia, 1865–1944.

Andrii Melnyk, leader of the Melnyk faction of the Organization of Ukrainian Nationalists (OUN-M). (*Ukrainian National Federation, Toronto*)

Founding congress of the Organization of Ukrainian Nationalists, Vienna, 1929.

Stepan Bandera, leader of the Bandera faction of the Organization of Ukrainian Nationalists (OUN-B). (*Marika Bandera, Toronto*)

Volodymyr Kubiiovych, leader of the Ukrainian Central Committee in the *Generalgouvernement*.

Alfred Rosenberg, Nazi German Minister for the Occupied Eastern Territories. Hanged in Nuremberg as a war criminal in 1946.

LEFT Roman Shukhevych (Gen. Taras Chuprynka), Commander-in-Chief of the Ukrainian Insurgent Army (UPA), photographed in Western Ukraine in 1947. (*Litopys UPA, Archives*)

Erich Koch, *Reichskommissar* of
Ukraine and *Gauleiter* of East Prussia.
Presently serving a life sentence
in Barczewo, Poland. (*Staatsbibliothek
Berlin*)

ABOVE Otto Wächter, Governor of
the District of Galicia. (*Wasyl Veryha,
Toronto*)

Hans Frank (on left), Governor-
General of occupied Poland and
Western Ukraine, and Alfred Bisanz,
head of the Military Committee of
the Galician Division, address a
meeting in Stanyslaviv, 1943 (*Wasyl
Veryha, Toronto*)

Kommando of *Einsatzgruppe D* upon its arrival in Drohobych, 1–6 July 1941. Mobile killing units such as this one were responsible for the murder of the local population.

Nazi execution of OUN members in
Stanyslaviv, September 1943.

Survivors among the dead after the
liberation of Dora concentration
camp, where Ukrainian and other
political prisoners worked on the
Nazis' "V" rockets. (*Ivan Mykytyn,
former Auschwitz, Buchenwald, and
Dora inmate, Toronto*)

Union's motivation in providing this information has been political and not humanitarian – that it is seeking to discredit its "anti-Communist enemies" who fled in the 1940s, not to bring war criminals to justice. The ADL's view is that these critics have seriously exaggerated the role that Soviet-provided evidence plays in OSI prosecutions because some of the defendants have themselves admitted to their wartime past; moreover, incriminating evidence from Western sources has been vital in these prosecutions.

The ADL has also argued that all Soviet evidence has been subject to "rigorous scientific testing by experts from the U.S. Government and by experts hired by the defendants." It believes that testimonies from Soviet witnesses are reliable because no American, Canadian, or other judges have concluded that witnesses lied or that documents from the Soviet Union were fabricated. This was true in cases tried in West Germany as well as during the 1946–9 Nuremberg trials, when Soviet-provided evidence was used by these courts to prosecute former Nazis. Soviet witnesses are not one-sided in their testimonies, the ADL has claimed, because their testimonies have in some cases helped to clear suspects.

To the ADL, therefore, the use of Soviet-provided evidence is of practical importance and even necessary:

The fact is that the overwhelming majority of civilian deaths at the hands of the Nazis during World War II took place on territory now behind the Iron Curtain (where, for example, *all* of the Nazis' extermination camps were located). Hence, evidence from Soviet-controlled areas, especially documents left behind by the Nazis and captured by Allied Forces, including those of the Soviet Union, is of obvious importance.

For similar reasons, many witnesses still reside in the Soviet Union, Poland, and Soviet-annexed lands.[2]

Critics of the OSI have also argued that to deport any former citizen of Estonia, Latvia, or Lithuania would be tantamount to recognizing the USSR's forcible annexation of the Baltic states, thus contravening the U.S. government's official policy of non-recognition of these Soviet annexations. The ADL, however, maintains that this argument misrepresents and misunderstands both the U.S. Immigration and Nationality Act and official State Department policy. According to the act, adjudicated Nazi war criminals are deported to any country willing to take them, while the State Department is on record as maintaining the non-recognition policy despite deportations from the U.S. to the USSR.

As can be seen, the views of the OSI's critics and its supporters diverge considerably. Both sides have been presented here to allow readers an opportunity to better judge the validity of the arguments presented in part 2.

In Canada accusations have surfaced periodically against residents suspected of having committed war crimes under the Nazi regime. The sources of the accusations have been both within and outside Canada. As in the United States, most of the people in Canada against whom accusations have been made came originally from Eastern Europe, mainly from territories now within the Soviet Union.

To date, no person in Canada has been prosecuted for war crimes. However, in June 1982 Helmut Rauca, a Canadian citizen, was arrested and charged with aiding and abetting the murder of 10,500 Jews in 1941 in Kaunas, Lithuania. Rauca was ordered extradited on 4 November 1982 to stand trial in West Germany. He appealed to the Supreme Court of Canada but later abandoned the appeal. He was extradited and on 28 September 1983 was charged in a Frankfurt court with the murder of the 10,500 Lithuanian Jews. Rauca's case did not, however, come before the court because he died on 29 October in a Frankfurt prison hospital.

In response to renewed calls for a more thorough investigation of accusations against suspected war criminals living in Canada, the Canadian Minister of Justice, John Crosbie, announced in February 1985 the creation of a commission of inquiry whose mandate was to ascertain whether Josef Mengele did or tried to immigrate to Canada; to determine whether there were war criminals living in Canada; and to recommend to the government the steps and measures that could be taken to bring such criminals to justice. The commission, headed by Quebec Supreme Court Justice Jules Deschênes, was to report to the Government of Canada by the end of December 1985. (See Appendix B for the commission's terms of reference.)

Justice Deschênes has encouraged concerned citizens to present their views at the commission's public hearings, and has allowed four organizations to designate representatives to defend their interests: the Canadian Jewish Congress, the League for Human Rights of B'nai B'rith, the Brotherhood of Veterans of the 1st Division of the Ukrainian

National Army, and the Civil Liberties Commission of the Ukrainian Canadian Committee.

In Canada and in the United States extensive media coverage of the OSI and the Deschênes inquiry's investigations into Nazi war criminality has generated considerable public discussion on the substance of the issue as well as its handling by the media.

Notes

1 Anti-Defamation League of B'nai B'rith, "The Campaign Against the U.S. Justice Department's Prosecution of Suspected Nazi War Criminals," ADL Special Report (New York, June 1985).
2 Ibid., 12–13.

DAVID MATAS

Bringing Nazi War Criminals in Canada to Justice

In Canada we have belatedly begun to come to grips with the problem of Nazi war criminals in our midst. For forty years we did virtually nothing. There was only one extradition, that of Albert Helmut Rauca, in 1983.[1] There have been no denaturalizations, no deportations. There were seven Canadian prosecutions in Germany immediately after the war, but there have been none in Canada. Now we are facing a deadline: all the witnesses, all the surviving victims, all the perpetrators of the Nazi Holocaust will soon be dead. If justice is to be done, it must be done quickly.

CONCERNS

The commencement of activity relating to the investigation and trial of Nazi war criminals has caused some concern. Simon Wiesenthal has said that he believes that 218 former Ukrainian officers of Hitler's SS, which ran death camps in Europe, are living in Canada. Sol Littman, a Canadian spokesman for the Simon Wiesenthal Center, said that records prove that twenty-eight Nazi war criminal suspects in Canada belonged to Ukrainian SS units.

Spokesmen for the Ukrainian Canadian community objected to these claims. John Nowosad, president of the Ukrainian Canadian Committee (UCC), stated that the allegations reflect badly on Ukrainians and people of Ukrainian descent born in Canada. Orest Rudzik, past president of the UCC of Toronto, pointed out that many Canadians have the impression that all Ukrainians collaborated with the SS. These community leaders emphasized their desire to see war criminals brought to justice, but they expressed fear of a witch hunt reminiscent of the McCarthy era.

The matter was raised in the House of Commons. Alex Kindy, MP (Member of Parliament) for Calgary East, urged that the efforts to bring war criminals to justice not be allowed to reflect poorly on entire ethnic groups such as the Ukrainian Canadian community. Don Blenkarn, MP for Mississauga South, expressed a similar concern about Canadians of German descent. He claimed that, in an effort to assure the world that Canada does not harbour war criminals, it has seemed to some that the government has set out to castigate the German people. He warned that justice is not advanced by reviving old memories of torture, injustice, and bitterness. He asserted that Canada has an obligation not to suggest that Canadians of German descent are war criminals.

RESPONSE

These fears need not be realized. Indeed, we must try to avoid ethnic slurs in the process of bringing Nazi war criminals to justice. In criminal cases, the accused are usually not identified by their ethnic origin, nor should war criminals be identified in this way. We should not, however, be so fearful of ethnic slurs that we do not attempt to try suspected Nazi war criminals in Canada.

The prosecution of a war criminal is not a prosecution of the people to which he or she belongs; it is prosecution of the individual. When we prosecute other kinds of criminals, we do not normally consider the prosecution a slur or an attack on their community. The notion that war crimes were individual crimes with individual guilt is the very antithesis of the notion of collective guilt. It is the notion of collective guilt – not individual guilt – that is an incitement to hatred.

The Jewish community, which has been pressing for action to bring Nazi war criminals in Canada to justice, has no desire to inflict collective guilt on others, since it has been for millennia the victim of collective guilt for the death of Christ. It was only in 1961, twenty-four years ago, that the World Council of Churches resolved that Christians should repudiate the idea of Jews' collective guilt. In 1965 the Roman Catholic Church's Second Vatican Council declared that what happened to Christ should "not be charged against all the Jews without distinction, then alive, nor against the Jews of today."

When taken to an extreme, this fear of linking ethnic slurs to the Nazis' murder of eleven million innocent civilians (including six million Jews) leads to Holocaust denial. Witnesses in the Ernst Zundel trial testified how they felt better about being German once they believed Zundel's claims that the Holocaust never happened.[2] For example, Armin Auerswald is reported to have testified that "his feelings of guilt for being German were not rooted in reality." Jürgen Neumann is reported to have testified that he did not want his children "to grow up with an unjust stereotype of the Germans, to think badly of their father and grandfather."

An appropriate response to Holocaust denial is not just to inform people about the existence of the Holocaust but also to reject the linkage between the existence of the Holocaust and the perception of an attack on the Germans or any other group. We should approach this matter not as ethnic Jews, or Germans, or Ukrainians, but simply as Canadians who are concerned that the innocent go free and that the guilty are punished, that Canada not be a haven for war criminals. If we have that attitude, we cannot go wrong.

FORGETTING

Mr. Blenkarn maintains that justice is not advanced by reviving old, painful memories. However, it is important to remember the past precisely because justice is denied by repressing of memories of torture and injustice. We owe it to the victims to remember and not to forget their murderers. Bringing the victims' murderers to justice is a small attempt to salvage something from the meaninglessness of their deaths.

Moreover, as the Zundel trial illustrated, we are faced with the problem of Holocaust denial. Forgetting about the Holocaust, not reviving its memory, encourages those who would have the world believe it never happened.

There is, in addition, one regrettable fact: the Nazi Holocaust was not unique. History is replete with tragedy. For example, during the artificial famine in Ukraine in the 1930s the Soviets forcibly exported food and prevented the importation of food; millions starved. Forgetting tragedy means forgetting history.

Today not just one people faces extinction, but the entire human race is threatened with extinction by nuclear holocaust. Jonathan Schell, in *The Fate of the Earth*, wrote that Hitler's attempt to exterminate the Jewish people is the closest event in human history to a precursor of the extinction of the human race. If we are to avoid the ultimate holocaust, we must not forget the Nazi Holocaust. We can learn from it that insane crimes are not prevented from happening just because they are unthinkable; on the contrary, such crimes may be all the more likely to occur for that very reason. We can better understand, to use Schell's words, the "gaping unmendable holes in the fabric of the world" these crimes cause. Though the Jewish people have survived, the *shtetl* culture of Europe has gone and will never be revived. We cannot face squarely the dangers that threaten us by forgetting the disasters we have suffered.

JUSTICE

In my report "Bringing Nazi War Criminals in Canada to Justice," published by the League for Human Rights of B'nai B'rith, I discussed the range of legal options available for bringing Nazi war criminals in Canada to justice. The report is technical in nature, but it has a simple point to make: the crime of murder should not go unpunished; Nazi war criminals in Canada should be brought to justice.

Canada has no statute of limitations for murder. The Canadian government asked the West German government to extend its statute of limitations at a time when the German statute would have had the effect of barring prosecution of Nazi war criminals in Germany. Because they were able to enter Canada after World War II, Canada should not impose a statute of limitations for their crimes. It is an irony of history that their intended victims – Jews fleeing the Holocaust – were denied entry by Canada before and during the war.

Canada has said that the prosecution of war crimes and crimes against humanity constitutes a universal commitment for all states. It has maintained that position year after year at the United Nations, from 1946 to the present. In 1981, at the General Assembly, Canada even proposed that position. It should now do what it has committed itself at the United Nations to do. It must not say one thing abroad and do something else at home. Canada must respect all its basic principles of human rights when bringing Nazi war criminals to justice. No human rights principle requires Nazi war criminals to go free, and Canada would be violating human rights in the grossest way imaginable if it allowed the crime of murder to go unpunished.

There are three important legal issues related to the prosecution of Nazi war criminals: the use to be made of Soviet-supplied evidence; the defence of duress; and the bringing to justice of other, non-Nazi criminals against humanity.

EVIDENCE

First, what is to be made of Soviet allegations? What is to be done with Soviet-supplied evidence? At a meeting I attended of non-governmental organizations with the Canadian delegation to the Human Rights Experts Meeting, held in May 1985 in Ottawa under the Helsinki Accords, Peter Kondra, of the national office of the Ukrainian Canadian Committee, asked: Should we not object to Russian interference in Canadian affairs when Russia gives to Canada a list of Ukrainian criminals, a list of witnesses, but does nothing about its own criminals?

One of the great achievements of the international human rights movement is acceptance of the principle that violations of human rights are not only matters of internal domestic concern but are also matters of international concern. A government is not free to brutalize, to imprison arbitrarily, to terrorize, to torture, to murder its own population, free from international reproach.

The Soviets are quick to charge interference in internal affairs whenever the West raises the question of human rights violations. If Canada were now to mimic Soviet rhetoric, when the Soviets produce lists of Nazi war criminals or lists of witnesses, it would reinforce the Soviets' claim to non-interference when Canada raises other human rights matters with them. Rather than reject Soviet lists or witnesses, Canada should examine seriously all information the Soviets supply, and our seriousness should serve as an example to them when we raise concerns about Soviet human rights violations.

If the Soviets make allegations, Canada should examine the allegations. If the Soviets have witnesses, Canada should examine and cross-examine the witnesses. Canada should make its own assessments, using Canadian standards of justice.

Because Canada has done so little about bringing Nazi war criminals in Canada to justice, the guilty have not been punished nor have the innocent been truly free. We have been left with speculation and a cloud of suspicion.

We cannot do nothing about criminals in our midst simply because the Soviets do nothing about theirs. Rather we should act, and use our own action as an argument for the Soviets' bringing criminals in their midst to justice.

DURESS

Second, there is the question of duress. In a letter to the editor of the

Winnipeg Free Press, Mykhailo Marunchak wrote: "Mr. Wiesenthal's statement about Ukrainian officers who allegedly participated in running death camps is false and unfounded. In some cases, the *Gestapo* used some individuals from local police forces to patrol barracks from the outside and to assist in transportation of prisoners, but all of them served as ordinary robots in such situations. Their services were similar to services of the Jewish police in Jewish ghettos."

Duress is a defence under the Canadian Criminal Code. The actual provision in the code reads, in part: "A person who commits an offence under compulsion by threats of immediate death or grievous bodily harm from a person who is present when the offence is committed is excused for committing the offence, if he believes that the threat will be carried out, and if he is not a party to a conspiracy or association whereby he is subject to compulsion." The defence does not apply to a number of offences, among them murder and attempted murder. The courts have held that the defence does apply to aiding and abetting murder.

The defence of duress is different from the defence of "orders of superiors." By Canadian law, as well as by international law, "orders of superiors" is not a defence.

Whether the defence of duress applies in a particular case depends on the facts of the case. It is not a general defence applicable to all Nazi war criminals. The evidence in some cases has been that if a person did not want to work in or for the death camps, that person would still have to work for the Nazis but would be transferred to another task. The evidence in other cases has been that the accused believed in the genocide that was taking place and participated enthusiastically.

People are not guilty of war crimes simply because of their nationality or ethnic origin. Nor are they necessarily innocent of all war crimes simply because of their nationality or ethnic origin. Only a functioning legal system, where the facts are properly assessed and presented, can distinguish the innocent from the guilty.

OTHER CRIMES AGAINST HUMANITY

Nazi war crimes and crimes against humanity are not the only ones. What should Canada do about other war criminals, other criminals against humanity?

In an address to members of Toronto's Lithuanian community, Romas Vastokas called for a reopening of the Nuremberg trials to bring to light atrocities committed by the Soviet regime. He urged other Eastern Europeans to join in the fight to bring Soviet war criminals to trial.

The Canadian War Crimes Act, which is one legal recourse by which Nazi war criminals in Canada could be brought to justice, is limited to wars in which Canada took part after 9 September 1939. It does not apply to crimes against humanity inflicted outside of the context of war, like the famine inflicted on Ukraine in the 1930s, nor to war crimes in wars in which Canada is not a participant, like the Soviet invasion of Afghanistan.

I proposed to the Canadian Bar Association a resolution that new legislation be passed to allow for prosecution of war crimes and crimes against humanity, whether or not the crimes were committed during wars in which Canada has been or may be engaged. That resolution passed the 1981 bar convention and now represents the policy of the association.

More recently, in my capacity as national chairman of the League for Human Rights of B'nai B'rith Canada, I proposed a similar amendment to Bill C-18, the so-called drunk-driving bill, which came before the House of Commons. The bill proposed adding to the list of extraterritorial offences already in the Criminal Code the offences of hostage-taking and theft of nuclear materials. The league suggested adding to the list war crimes and crimes against humanity. The amendment could have the effect, as well, of allowing civilian trials for war crimes. The War Crimes Act provides for military trials. The amendment would prevent the raising of some technical objections that have been raised to the use of the War Crimes Act and the Geneva Conventions Act.

The Standing Committee on Justice and Legal Affairs has already ruled that it will refuse to hear witnesses on this proposal, on the grounds that the proposal is not germane to the bill. It is an indication that the proposal itself will be ruled out of order. It would be a ruling I would regret.

Aleksandr Solzhenitsyn wrote in the *Gulag Archipelago*: "When we neither punish nor reproach evildoers, we are not simply protecting their trivial old age, we are thereby ripping the foundations of justice from beneath new generations."

In Canada there is a trial going on right now – not a trial of a Nazi war criminal but of the Canadian justice system. If Canada is not to be left with a permanent stain on its justice system, we must act to bring Nazi war criminals to justice.

Notes

1 Albert Helmut Rauca, a former *SS* officer, was extradited to West Germany in 1983 to face war crimes charges. He was accused of aiding and abetting the execution of 10,500 Jews in Kaunas, part of occupied Lithuania, in 1941. Rauca died in a West German prison before being brought to trial. (Ed.)
2 In March 1985 Ernst Zundel was tried and convicted in Toronto on charges of knowingly spreading false information about the Holocaust. In a series of publications Zundel had denied that the German genocide of Jews had taken place. (Ed.)

ROMAN SERBYN

Alleged War Criminals, the Canadian Media, and the Ukrainian Community

In response to the recent widespread allegations and attacks against Ukrainians outside Ukraine, as well as the biased handling of Ukrainian topics by the Canadian media, a media watch group was formed in Montreal, the Information and Anti-Defamation Commission (IADC) of the Ukrainian Canadian Committee.[1] The following analysis of the treatment of Ukrainian issues by the Canadian media is based on material gathered by the IADC and on its experience in public relations.

On 7 February the Hon. John Crosbie, Minister of Justice and Attorney General of Canada, announced the establishment of "an independent commission of inquiry . . . to conduct . . . investigations regarding war criminals in Canada," to be headed by Mr. Justice Jules Deschênes.[2] The document outlining the commission's terms of reference consists of two parts: a preamble of three paragraphs, and instructions concerning the prerogatives and the functioning of the commission, elaborated in eleven points.[3] The first two paragraphs refer specifically to Nazi crimes; there is mention of Josef Mengele and of "the activities of Nazi Germany."[4] The third paragraph speaks of bringing to justice "any such criminal currently residing in Canada." This paragraph can be interpreted to include all war criminals, both Nazis and others. The rest of the document, which defines the commission's mandate, is couched in general terms, without specific reference to Nazi crimes.

This author's reading of the document is that the present inquiry into the presence in Canada of alleged war criminals was brought about by the efforts of the Jewish community to flush out Nazi war criminals. Since almost all the crimes against the Jewish people committed during

World War II were perpetrated under the aegis of the Nazi regime, it is understandable that the Jewish community would tend to identify "war crimes" with "Nazi crimes." However, war crimes were committed not only under the authority of Nazi Germany. Countless atrocities against the civilian population were also committed by Communists and by criminal collaborators in the service of the Soviet Union. Limiting the work of the Deschênes Commission only to Nazi criminals is selective and incomplete justice, and it cannot be the intention of the Canadian government. That is why the rest of the terms of reference of the Deschênes Commission should refer to all war crimes and war criminals.

Various members of both the Ukrainian and Jewish communities have stressed the necessity of bringing all war criminals to justice. In a recent publication, Mr. David Matas, senior counsel for and former chairman of the League for Human Rights of B'nai B'rith, wrote: "Though this report looks at the particular problem of bringing Nazi war criminals to justice, the author, of course, believes that all war criminals, all criminals against humanity, should be brought to justice."[5] Although this author agrees fully with his statement, and wishes to emphasize that each ethnocultural community may rightly be preoccupied with the crimes committed against its members, a Canadian commission must not discriminate in pursuit of justice. It must deal with all alleged war criminals, irrespective of the regime on whose behalf the crimes were committed. Unfortunately, the media has taken a narrower view of the problem.

The day after Mr. Crosbie announced the formation of the Deschênes Commission, news about it began to appear in Canadian newspapers. On 8 February 1985 the *Globe and Mail* carried a story from Ottawa with the headline, "Ottawa Sets Up Commission to Pursue Nazi War Criminals." The opening paragraph made it clear that the commission was to deal only with Nazi war criminals. Other newspapers took the same approach, mentioning only Nazi war crimes and Nazi war criminals. That same day, the *Winnipeg Free Press* printed allegations by Simon Wiesenthal, head of the Documentation Center in Vienna, and Sol Littman, a Canadian journalist, to the effect that there were still 2,000 Nazi wartime collaborators alive in Canada of the 3,000 who originally came to this country. Ukrainians figure prominently in the article, as they do in the lists of alleged criminals prepared by Mr. Wiesenthal and the Soviet Embassy.[6]

However, the news item that most upset the Ukrainian community was an Israeli radio interview with Mr. Wiesenthal carried by all the Canadian media. The first report, published on 10 February by the *Toronto Star*, noted: "The Israeli radio quoted Mr. Wiesenthal as saying he believes 218 former Ukrainian officers of Hitler's SS (elite guard), which ran death camps in Eastern Europe, are living in Canada."[7] This quotation, in one form or another, appeared in newspaper, radio, and television reports across Canada. It encompassed all the elements of sensationalism: "SS," "Hitler," "elite guard," "death camps," and, of course, "Ukrainians." It was also false and defamatory.

Mr. Wiesenthal's interview begs several questions. First, for the historical record, most Ukrainians who served in the SS did so in the Galician Division, which was not an "elite guard" but a *Waffen* or combat unit. It was used once on the Eastern front against the Soviet forces; it was never used to guard concentration camps. Moreover, both Soviet and British screening teams cleared the division of any participation in war crimes. The immigration to Canada of individual division members was sanctioned by the federal cabinet after considerable deliberation and further investigation by the Royal Canadian Mounted Police.[8] Second, it was grossly unfair of the Canadian media to give such prominence to Mr. Wiesenthal's radio interview in Israel, containing questionable information that damaged the Ukrainian image, while failing to cover a press conference organized a few days later by the Ukrainian community in order to refute some of the allegations. There was nothing about the press conference on the Canadian Press (CP) wire service, nor did the Canadian Broadcasting Corporation (CBC) have anything to say on the "National," an evening news feature program, or during its morning radio show the next day.[9]

Moreover, there is a discrepancy between the reported Israeli radio interview and the article on the same topic in Mr. Wiesenthal's *Bulletin of Information*. The following passage from the *Bulletin* throws a very different light on the issue:

Shortly before the parliamentary elections in Canada, the Documentation Center submitted a *list of 218 SS officers who had been volunteers* of the Ukrainian SS-division and of general SS formations, to Canada's Solicitor General, Robert Kaplan.

Out of these *218 SS officers, none had been registered dead* after the end of war nor was anyone, to the Documentation Center's knowledge, in Europe by that time. *Since Canada happens to be the most favoured immigration country of*

Ukrainians, there is a possibility that at least some of these former SS officers may have emigrated there. Up till 1953, former SS men were barred from entering Canada by Canadian law. We presume, however, that many Ukrainians managed to bypass this restriction by withholding information about their wartime past from the Canadian immigration authorities. This is particularly likely to have been the case during the Cold War period.[10] [emphasis added]

Whatever the merits of the list of 218 officers, Mr. Wiesenthal's statement in the *Bulletin* is quite different from that reported in the Israeli radio interview. Why had this discrepancy not been pointed out to the media by the office of the Solicitor General?

The allegations by Mr. Wiesenthal, Mr. Littman, and the Soviet Embassy provoked a lively response from the Ukrainian community. "In Edmonton," wrote the Montreal *Gazette*, "Ukrainian-Canadian academics Bohdan Krawchenko and Myroslav Yurkevich demanded that Nazi-hunter Sol Littman prove his allegation that Alberta is a haven for Ukrainian war criminals. The allegation is historically doubtful and a slur on all Ukrainian-Canadians, they said."[11] It is of some interest to note that the CP wire service was the source for this short item. The Montreal *Gazette* used it, but the Toronto *Globe and Mail*, Canada's national newspaper, ignored it. Protests came from other centres as well, and some were reported by the media.[12]

When all the pieces of the unfolding saga of alleged war criminals in Canada are put together, a pattern emerges. There is a shift in emphasis and focus. "War criminals" are reduced to "Nazi war criminals," and "Nazi criminals" become strongly identified with "Ukrainians." The Galician Division's identity as a combat unit (*Waffen SS*) is ignored, and a false identity as Hitler's elite guard is forged. The distinction between "war criminals" and "*alleged* war criminals" is completely blurred, and the two terms are used interchangeably. Ukrainians are never mentioned as having suffered either from Communist or Nazi oppression. They are rarely credited with saving Jews from extermination, and never is it mentioned that many Ukrainians lost their lives for giving shelter to Jews. In this way the Canadian media contributes to the emergence of a new image of Ukrainian Canadians. Gone are the men in sheepskin coats, and a new breed of sinister, criminal collaborators with the Nazis begins to appear. Is it any wonder that the Ukrainian community feels insulted, trapped, and on the way to becoming a scapegoat for a new witch hunt?

The treatment by the media of the current accusations against

Ukrainians is not surprising if one examines how the media has been manipulated in recent years. Simon Wiesenthal's Documentation Center has contributed its share to the denigration of Ukrainians outside Ukraine. In an interview given to the *Jerusalem Post* in 1979, and later reported in Canada, Mr. Wiesenthal blamed the Ukrainian community for the Canadian government's inaction on war criminals residing in this country. According to the *Suburban*, "He [Mr. Wiesenthal] attributes the attitude of the Canadian government to the fact that Ukrainians, who make up most of the war criminals" – in other interviews Mr. Wiesenthal puts the number of war criminals at 800 to 1,000 – "are the second largest ethnic minority in Canada" (elsewhere he speaks of one million Ukrainians in Canada). "They have political clout and no party wants to alienate them."[13] What kind of documentation and information centre makes such blunders in basic, easily verifiable data, and then uses this faulty information to construct outrageous accusations? There are some 530,000 Ukrainians in Canada, not one million; they are not the second-largest ethnic group but come far behind German Canadians and Italian Canadians. If any ethnic community has political "clout" in Ottawa, it certainly is not the Ukrainians. Anyone who is the least knowledgeable about federal politics knows the relative weight of the lobbying powers of the Jewish and Ukrainian communities. The Canadian government meets with representatives of the Canadian Jewish Congress (CJC) and communicates with the Ukrainian Canadian Committee (UCC). The existence of the Canadian Parliamentarians' Group for Soviet Jewry and the establishment of the Deschênes Commission speak for themselves. Mr. Littman should brief the head office in Vienna more thoroughly.

Another example illustrates the unreliable character of Mr. Wiesenthal's testimony and accusations. Last year Professor Taras Hunczak gave a lecture in Montreal on the topic of wartime collaboration, and then had an interview with the *Gazette* on the same subject. The article provoked a full-scale debate on the pages of the *Gazette*, and Mr. Wiesenthal was one of the participants. He wrote, "The one million [sic] Ukrainians living in Canada can easily keep their distance from the few *dozens* [sic] or *hundreds* of persons who committed crimes against innocent people."[14] Such disregard for precision when dealing with the grave accusation of war crimes is striking. The letter does have a redeeming quality – Mr. Wiesenthal's distinction between political and criminal collaboration: "The political collaboration of the Ukrainians with the Nazis is on another level and cannot be mixed with collaboration in crimes which lead to murder and mass murder of innocent people." If only Mr. Wiesenthal would remember this distinction and apply it when making statements about Ukrainians.

One last point about Mr. Wiesenthal. In 1979 the Soviets attacked him for Zionist propaganda. The article appeared in the Kiev newspaper *Radianska Ukraina*, but it is well known that decisions to publish attacks of that nature are not made locally, but in the centre of Soviet power.[15] Mr. Wiesenthal is accused of nothing less than collaboration with the Nazis. As proof, it is alleged that in 1941, forty Jewish intellectuals were arrested in Lviv, and among them was Mr. Wiesenthal; thirty-nine perished and only Mr. Wiesenthal was allowed to live. The conclusion was obvious: Mr. Wiesenthal bought his life with service to the Nazis. This author does not know if anyone has ever seriously invoked this "testimony" against Mr. Wiesenthal; it may be a partial or a complete fabrication by the Soviet authorities. But the point is that if Mr. Wiesenthal, his followers, and other Nazi hunters are so eager to use Soviet information and sources then perhaps they could look into this allegation.

We have seen how the Canadian media have misled the public with biased reporting on the question of the alleged war criminals residing in Canada. One would expect that readers of Ukrainian Canadian newspapers would be better served. Unfortunately, this is not the case. Ukrainian newspapers do not provide their readers with the necessary information to form a meaningful opinion. News analysis is also inadequate if not completely lacking. In this respect, the *Canadian Jewish News* (CJN) is much superior to the Ukrainian newspapers. Ukrainian editors, journalists, and the Ukrainian community as a whole should take the CJN as a model of ethnic journalism and learn from it. All of the news in the CJN is pertinent to the Jewish community, and all of the news that is pertinent to that community is reported by the CJN. The material is up to date and the events are analyzed from a Jewish perspective.

In a recent lecture in Montreal, Lucy S. Dawidowicz elaborated the idea that Jews, especially educated Jews, often see themselves from a non-Jewish or even an anti-Jewish perspective. She attributed this phenomenon to the fact that much of the literature dealing with Jews, even when it is written by Jews themselves, is composed in that vein. Whether that observation is applicable to North American Jewry today, it is difficult to say; but if, *mutatis mutandis*, it was applied to Ukrainians outside Ukraine, it would prove quite useful.

Because the Ukrainian press is so inadequate and the Ukrainian Canadian community so passive, they have both contributed – by sins of omission rather than commission – to the emerging image of the "Ukrainian Nazi collaborator" in Canada. The attitude of the Ukrainian Canadian community – from its leaders in the UCC down to individual members – is roughly this: the outrageous allegations against Ukrainians are so ridiculous that they discredit themselves and the best thing to do is to ignore them and they will soon be forgotten. This attitude has proven damaging to our reputation. We can no longer afford to ignore such racist slurs as that of Larry Zolf, who accuses Canadians of Eastern European background of harbouring "quasi-fascist nationalism," even when he tries to pass this off as satire.[16] The Ukrainian Canadian community did not effectively handle the Communist disinformation distributed in Winnipeg in the form of a pamphlet entitled "Winnipeg's Nazi Suspects." That piece of despicable hate literature, claimed to be the work of a group of Jewish, Ukrainian, and native-born Canadians, was obviously meant to foment strife between the Ukrainian and Jewish communities. On the back cover of the pamphlet there was even a passage in Hebrew so that Ukrainians would not fail to blame Jews for the propaganda. The obvious thing for Ukrainians to do was to have the UCC contact the Canadian Jewish Congress, issue a joint condemnation of this hate literature, and then turn the matter over to the police for investigation and prosecution; but they did not. Why not?

A word should also be said about the overzealous Nazi-hunters in Canada who do no honour to their ethnic community and whose tactics are unworthy of the cause they claim to serve. The strong-arm tactics advocated by Edward Greenspan are not only surprising coming from a lawyer but seem to contravene the very basis of our judicial system. In February 1984, Mr. Greenspan advocated that "pictures of the war criminals should be published in a book listing all the allegations against them and widely distributed to bookstores, libraries and homes of their neighbours."[17] Still more recently, Greenspan maintained that the "ex-Nazis among us should not have a moment's peace."[18] Milton Harris, president of the CJC, was rightfully indignant at such tactics; what is surprising, however, is that Mr. Harris seems to be concerned primarily with the threat of libel suits and not with the moral aspect of such a witch-hunt.

Many Ukrainians outside Ukraine feel that they are becoming scapegoats in the renewed hunt for Nazi war criminals. The danger is very real. Ukrainians are easy targets: they are economically weak, they have little political clout (Mr. Wiesenthal's opinion to the contrary notwithstanding), and their access to the media is limited. While most other ethnic groups can get some help and backing from the country of their origin, Ukrainians cannot count on Ukraine or the government in Kiev to speak in their defence or in the defence of Ukraine itself, for that matter. In fact, the expressed intention of the Soviet leaders in Moscow and their collaborators in Kiev is to undermine, defame, and ultimately destroy Ukrainians outside Ukraine. It is these Soviet authorities, who have themselves shown so little zeal in bringing the real war criminals to justice (the notorious Erich Koch lives comfortably in prison in Poland), who are now most eager to provide Western Jewish Nazi-hunters with lists of names. This collaboration is most disturbing and cannot but be suspected and questioned by Ukrainians.

It is time for Ukrainian Canadians to stand up in defence of their rights, of their reputation, and of their image. They must react to the distortions in the media and establish a better documentation base. Most important, they must establish a meaningful dialogue with the Jewish community. Had the lines of communication between the two communities been kept open, many of the present difficulties could have been avoided. An excellent forum for Ukrainian-Jewish dialogue is the Canadian Council of Christians and Jews, since its *raison d'être* is to promote harmonious relations between Jews and Christians (in this case Ukrainians) and to eliminate animosity among Canadian ethnocultural communities.

Much has been said about the visible minorities in Canada. Ukrainian Canadians are an invisible minority, but there is no reason for them to remain an inaudible minority as well. They must speak up, shed whatever vestiges they still have of the fears and inferiority complexes imposed on them by history. They must adjust to the North American way of life and take advantage of all the opportunities available to them.

The image of the Ukrainian community is closely linked to the public perception formed by the media. Ukrainian Canadians must develop contacts with the media, on the level of the individual citizen and on the level of an organized community. They must undertake affirmative action. They need individual activists and organized groups to lobby by all possible means with the media and with the government.

However, every dark cloud has a silver lining, and the recent attack on Ukrainians is no exception. The allegations, accusations, and slurs may prove to be a blessing in disguise. Ukrainians outside Ukraine have not had a rallying issue since the freeing of Valentyn Moroz from Soviet prison. The fiftieth anniversary of the great artificial famine in Ukraine aroused the community, but its impact was by no means as great as that of commemorations of the Holocaust by the Jewish community. Now the Ukrainian community has a new issue which, it is hoped, will leave some permanent marks on its maturation as an ethnocultural group within Canada.

Notes

1 Besides monitoring and interacting with the media, the IADC provides background information on current issues of interest to the Ukrainian community. To this end the IADC has put out a quarterly bulletin (two issues have appeared to date), and has established a dialogue with representatives of the Jewish community through the Canadian Council of Christians and Jews.

2 *Commons Debates* (Ottawa), 7 February 1985, 2113.

3 See Appendix B for the commisssion of inquiry's terms of reference. (Ed.)

4 Ministry of Justice and Attorney General of Canada, news release, 7 February 1985.

5 David Matas, *Bringing Nazi War Criminals in Canada to Justice* (Toronto, 1985), 98.

6 "Alleged War Criminals Believed in Winnipeg," *Winnipeg Free Press*, 8 February 1985.

7 "Nazi Hunter Wiesenthal Says Ottawa Ignored His Twenty-Eight Suspects," *Toronto Star*, 10 February 1985.

8 After having surrendered on 8 May 1945 to the British near Radstadt, Austria, as "Surrendered Enemy Personnel" (SEP), the 1st Ukrainian Division was interned in a SEP camp near Rimini, Italy. There the soldiers were subjected to screening by the British and Soviet authorities; both cleared the division of any war crimes. In spring 1947 the process of transferring the division to the United Kingdom began. The Ukrainian Canadian Committee and its affiliated organizations made efforts to encourage the Canadian government to allow individual members of the division to immigrate to Canada. On 31 May 1950 the federal cabinet sanctioned their immigration after carefully ascertaining that no war criminals were among those wishing to come to Canada. However, the Canadian Jewish Congress claimed to have evidence of the division's involvement in war crimes. The cabinet then asked the British Foreign Office and the RCMP for further clarification of the division's history and membership. By 25 September 1950, convinced of the correctness of its previous decision, the cabinet reaffirmed that former division members would be allowed to immigrate to Canada. Thus, after many screenings and much vetting of the division's history and membership, former division members came to Canada legally. For a detailed history of the division's immigration to Canada, see Myron Momryk, "Ukrainian Displaced Persons and the Canadian Government, 1946–1952" (unpublished paper). See also Gordon B. Panchuk, *Heroes of Their Day* (Toronto, 1983). Documents relating to the division, its screening, and immigration to Canada can be found in part 3 of this volume.

9 A telegram was sent by the IADC to the CBC requesting an explanation of this attitude, but no answer was received. A follow-up letter also went unanswered.

10 *Bulletin of Information* (Vienna), no. 25 (31 January 1985): 1.

11 Don MacPherson, "Anti-Semitic MPs Might Have Hurt Nazi-Hunt: Activist," *The Gazette* (Montreal), 12 February 1985.

12 "Ukrainian Community Incensed over War-Criminal Allegations," *The Globe and Mail* (Toronto), 14 February 1985; "Veterans Deny War Crime Allegations," *Edmonton Journal*, 14 February 1985; "Ukrainian Community Leaders Fear Effects of Nazi Reports," *The Globe and Mail*, 15 February 1985; "Ukrainian-Canadians 'Disturbed' by Nazi Accusations, Chief Says," *The Gazette*, 16 February 1985.

13 "Canada Shelters Ex-Nazis, Wiesenthal Says," *The Suburban* (Montreal), 31 October 1979.

14 *The Gazette*, 9 May 1984; emphasis added.

15 *Radianska Ukraina* (Kiev), 20 November 1979.

16 See the critique of Larry Zolf's book, *Survival of the Fattest*, in the IADC *Bulletin* (Montreal), 2, no. 1 (1985): 11–12.

17 "Greenspan Attacks Inaction on War Crimes," *The Jewish Times* (Toronto), 10–23 February 1984.

18 *Canadian Jewish News* (Toronto), 21 February 1985.

S. PAUL ZUMBAKIS

Co-operation between the U.S. Office of Special Investigations and the Soviet Secret Police

In *The Name of the Rose*, Umberto Eco, scholar and author, discusses the burden borne by an inquisitor or prosecutor. Eco cautions the reader against zealous prosecutors, who, he maintains, may be more dangerous to society than alleged criminals: "If a shepherd errs, he must be isolated from other shepherds, but woe unto us if the sheep begin to distrust shepherds." His warning is most appropriate today, since in the United States the "sheep" are beginning to mistrust the "shepherds." In the Department of Justice, and particularly in the Office of Special Investigations (OSI), the sheep and the very system may become victims of the zealous shepherds.

The dangers posed by overzealous prosecutors were apparent to the Founding Fathers when they drafted the U.S. Constitution, especially the Bill of Rights. They realized that nothing is more dangerous than the abuse of governmental power by the misuse of the rule of law. To ensure that future generations of Americans would not become the victims of their government, the Founding Fathers included safeguards for individual rights.

After observing both the operation of the OSI and the lack of congressional and administrative supervision for several years, I am convinced that individual rights and the right to a fair trial are not being respected by the OSI. One of the most striking illustrations of this problem is the OSI's use of Soviet, that is, KGB "evidence" in the cases of alleged Nazi war criminals and collaborators. Of the seventeen deportation cases pending today in the United States, thirteen rely almost solely on Soviet evidence. There are twelve denaturalization cases, and all twelve rely on Soviet evidence.

The relationship between the OSI and the KGB must be assessed within the framework of several historical, political, and moral issues. Only then is it possible to appreciate the danger of co-operation with the KGB and the damage that can result from such co-operation.

Because the goals and behaviour of the *Gestapo* were immoral, one reason for the creation of the OSI was to investigate and bring to justice American citizens who collaborated with the *Gestapo*. It should, however, be remembered that the Soviet security police, which were responsible for the deaths of millions of innocent Soviet citizens, also worked closely with the *Gestapo* in 1939–41, when the Molotov-Ribbentrop Pact was in effect. Therefore, co-operation with the Soviet security forces (known today as the KGB) is an immoral act, especially in light of the war crimes committed during World War II.

It is also important to realize that political cases in the Soviet Union are under the exclusive control of the KGB, not the courts or the judicial system. Trials against dissidents are considered political or state security cases; for example, the KGB initiated the proceedings against Victor Krasin, a Jewish dissident, and negotiated the judgment, the sentence, and the parole.[1] The Soviet Union views OSI cases as political or security cases,[2] and these are also under KGB supervision. Thus OSI collaboration with the Soviet judicial system is, in effect, co-operation with the KGB. This relationship should not be condoned by civilized countries.

FACT AND FICTION

How does the OSI explain its use of Soviet documentation? Whenever lawyers complain – to the American Bar Association, to the president of the United States, to Congress, or to the press – that the OSI is dealing with the KGB, the OSI responds it is dealing with "the Soviet system of justice." It insists that it is dealing with Soviet procurators and with the courts, and the KGB is never mentioned. It claims that it is dealing with the judiciary. However, in the Liudas Kairys case, tried in Chicago two years ago, it was established from the first day that the KGB led the investigations in the Soviet Union;[3] this is part of the court record. Moreover, OSI experts have established that all the archives and all the material in the archives belong to and are controlled by the KGB. The witnesses that the Soviets produce for depositions are in the complete and sole protection and custody of the KGB, which decides who is to be a witness. They brief the witnesses and control their testimonies, from beginning to end. After nearly six years of OSI investigations, however, the KGB has not produced a single witness or document for the defence. Everything produced for the OSI supports the prosecution. For the OSI to maintain that it is dealing with the Soviet court system is a travesty: the Soviets themselves, in a major article in *Izvestiia*, wrote about the KGB's leading and initiatory role in OSI cases.[4]

Whenever the OSI is criticized by Congress, attorneys, or the press, it claims it operates under U.S. federal rules of civil procedure. But what are civil procedures in the United States are criminal procedures in the Soviet Union. This difference is an important one, for under Soviet criminal procedures, all witnesses and those who might bear witness are under the complete "protection" of the KGB. Some witnesses have testified many times, their testimony changing according to which "notorious Nazi" is being tried. In contrast to North America, in the Soviet Union it is impossible to obtain the records of previous testimony, for the KGB decides which records will be accessible to lawyers.

Perhaps the most important flaw in the way in which depositions are taken in the Soviet Union is that American lawyers do not have the right to engage in proper cross-examination. Although the OSI has repeatedly declared that American lawyers have this right, they have been unable to ask the simplest questions in so-called discovery depositions. A wide range of questions may be asked under U.S. rules, but none that may embarrass witnesses who are lying or that aim at refreshing the memory of witnesses with respect to previous testimony. Lawyers are also not allowed to question how long the KGB has coached witnesses. The person judging whether a particular question is allowed is not a U.S. judge but a KGB procurator. Yet the OSI has had the audacity to tell the press and Congress that it has followed federal procedures during cross-examination!

CO-OPERATION BETWEEN THE OSI AND THE KGB

What are the dangers of collaboration with the KGB? First, by allowing the KGB to co-operate openly with the American government, the KGB is allowed to compare itself with the CIA. Even though there is a world of difference between them, by publicizing that it is doing the work of the OSI, the KGB becomes legitimate in the eyes of the Western world.

The second major danger of co-operation with the KGB is that it gives the Soviet Union an opportunity to rewrite history. From the cases before the U.S. courts, it is clear that the KGB determines which defendants will be tried in the United States. It appears that the KGB sends documents from the Soviet Embassy to the OSI, and the OSI then follows up on the basis of this evidence. With the selection of documents and witnesses solely in the hands of the KGB, history can be adjusted to the Soviet Union's point of view.

EVIDENCE OF DAMAGE

Damage has been done in several areas. First, dissidents and "refuseniks" in the Soviet Union are demoralized. When the OSI sends people to the USSR, uses the Soviet court system, and openly co-operates with the KGB, the message it sends to dissidents is that the United States respects the system that convicted them. This is a victory for the KGB. Moreover, dissidents in the Gulag are not divided by religion or nationality. Not only are they united, but they are also dismayed to see the Soviet Union split North American communities by pitting Jews against Ukrainians and Christians against Jews; this only weakens concern for dissident opposition to the Soviet system.

Second, by fanning outrage against Nazi atrocities and appearing to provide damning evidence against the perpetrators, the Soviet Union can deflect attention from its own miserable historical record. It no longer need be held to account for the years of terror during Stalin's rule. Similarly, with the Ukrainian, Lithuanian, and Estonian communities in the West under attack, the story of what the Soviets did to these peoples in the past is less likely to be believed or even heard.

The future is not without hope, however. Three courts in the United States have found that KGB-produced evidence is unacceptable in U.S. courts. For example, in a recent appellate court decision, the following points were made:

The prosecution of the case resulted from an unusual cooperative effort of the Office of Special Investigations and Soviet authorities. The court next spoke to the difficulties of Soviet involvement: "The Soviet authorities are outside of the jurisdiction of the United States judicial system. Consequently, it is impossible to provide the usual safeguards of trustworthiness of evidence having its source in the Soviet Union. This becomes a matter of concern for two reasons. First, the Soviet authorities have a strong motive to ensure that the government succeeds in this case. Second, the Soviet criminal and judicial system is structured to tailor evidence and produce results which will further the important political ends of the Soviet state at the expense, if need be, of justice in a particular case."

The motive the court alluded to in the above passage is the desire of the current Soviet government to discredit emigres who fled Eastern Europe in the face of the impending Soviet advance toward the end of the Second World War.[5]

If co-operation with the KGB is immoral, then it damages everyone – Christians, Jews, Americans, and Canadians. It becomes a cancer in the judicial system. In the words of my colleague, Mr. David Matas, "If we bend the law for a particular purpose, we establish a dangerous precedent. We weaken our moral position and dilute the impact of the moral point we wish to make that what the Nazi war criminals did was wrong."[6]

It remains to be seen whether Canada will be more careful than the United States has been. Now we have a cancer – you have only a cold.

Notes

1 Victor Krasin, "How I Was Broken by the KGB," *New York Times Magazine,* 18 March 1984.
2 *U.S. v. Kungys,* 571 F. Supp 1104 (D.C. J.J., 1983).
3 See, for instance, the deposition of Irwin Weil, *U.S. v. Kairys,* NO. 80 C 4302 (N.D. I.L. 4 June 1981).
4 *Izvestiia,* 25 February 1983.
5 *Laipenieks v. I.N.S.,* 750 F 2d 1427, 9th Cir. 1985.
6 David Matas, *Bringing Nazi War Criminals in Canada to Justice* (Toronto, 1985).

ROMAN KUPCHINSKY

Nazi War Criminals: The Role of Soviet Disinformation

In 1973 a lengthy diatribe against the Ukrainian emigration by the then head of the Writers' Union of Ukraine, Leonid Novychenko, appeared in the Soviet newspaper *Literaturnaia gazeta*. In it Novychenko mentioned an article about Soviet youth that had been published in an émigré journal. After denouncing the article, Novychenko got to the essence of his attack: the writer for the émigré publication was a Ukrainian Nazi who, during World War II, had edited a pro-German, anti-Semitic, fascist paper. Although he alleged that I was the author of the article, I cannot recall editing such a newspaper in 1943 – one year before I was born.

When I mentioned the problem to a Soviet representative, the Soviets checked their records and deleted the obvious misinformation. However, a new entry was then placed into the file – that I was a war criminal in Vietnam – and this charge began appearing in the Soviet media. If, sometime in the future, the United States ever comes to rely upon Soviet evidence to try American "war criminals" of the Vietnam War, I shall no doubt figure on some list given by the Vietnamese government to the Justice Department, and thirty Vietnamese "witnesses" will come forward to identify me as a murderer of women and children in some hamlet.

There are numerous designations one can use when talking about such incidents. One is misinformation based upon error. Another is disinformation, which is the premeditated use of false data in order to compromise or discredit a person or nation. A third is repetition of a false statement. Some of these distortions are unavoidable (about 75 per cent are due to lack of knowledge); others are due to repetition of a false statement that appears in a journalist's file on a given topic and is then used as background material for an article. A small percentage is pure disinformation, provided by someone with the intention of discrediting an opponent.

There has been a long and concerted campaign on the part of the KGB to sow disinformation in the West about Ukrainian émigrés and their alleged role in war crimes in order to discredit not only the nationalist, anti-Soviet Ukrainian community but also the organizations for which the alleged war criminals work, and in particular the agencies involved in providing information to closed societies: Radio Liberty, Radio Free Europe, Radio Canada International, and Voice of America. By supposedly proving that former war criminals staff these organizations, the Soviets discredit the organizations in the eyes of the West and in the eyes of their listening audiences inside the USSR and Eastern Europe.

The disinformation department of the KGB, Section "D," was formally organized in 1959, when the KGB was reorganized. The major target of the section was not émigré groups but the countries of the NATO alliance; its aim was to create discord among the partners. In 1969 the Fifth Directorate of the KGB was formed, whose mission was to combat internal and external anti-Soviet groups. The purpose of the Directorate's Eighth Section was to undermine émigré groups. In Ukraine the Institute for the Study of Foreign Countries was formed in Kiev, as a KGB institution, to study Ukrainian émigré communities. Members of this institute who come to Canada on scholarly exchanges are directly involved in disinformation against Ukrainian Canadians.

Section "D" became active immediately after its formation. In December 1959, anti-Semitic slogans appeared on the walls of Jewish synagogues in Cologne, West Germany. Soon afterwards, similar slogans appeared in other German cities and then in other countries – England, France, the United States, and Australia. In Germany alone, police counted 833 anti-Semitic incidents within a period of three weeks. Letters denouncing the rebirth of nazism and fascism in West Germany, written by reputable authors, were published in numerous newspapers. Questions were raised about the United States' relationship with a Germany that still had fascist elements. It is important to note that no anti-Semitic slogans appeared in any East German cities. Germans in the People's Democracy were blameless in this respect; the only "bad" Germans were living in West Germany.

After three weeks, the campaign ended. Not one anti-Semitic slogan appeared. The West German police arrested two men, both members of a pro-Nazi group in West Germany. It turned out that both were members of the East German secret police, sent to West Germany with the express purpose of instigating an anti-Semitic campaign in order to discredit the Federal Republic. A few years afterward, a Soviet KGB officer defected to the West and told how he had been involved in the planning of this campaign.

The mechanics of such a campaign are relatively simple; the results, while not earth-shattering, are impressive. The only role the secret police have to play is to instigate. The world does not lack those who are all too willing to carry out anti-Semitic campaigns. All they need is an excuse and a push. This is exactly what happened in Germany in 1959 and early 1960. Almost all the letters to the editor were genuine. People were outraged by the campaign and rightfully protested in the press. A handful of the letters were insertions, to give a political line to the protest – an anti-NATO analysis, if you will.

Several factors are instrumental in the creation of these campaigns and of an image that is used to promote a given political line. For example, when Andrei Sheptytsky, metropolitan of the Ukrainian Catholic Church, died in 1944, his funeral was attended by the first secretary of the Communist Party of Ukraine, Nikita Khrushchev, who laid a wreath on the tomb. In 1944 the Soviet government was trying to win the loyalties of the Western Ukrainian population, and this concession was needed. However, by 1946–7, when the forced liquidation of the Ukrainian Catholic Church was in progress, Sheptytsky was portrayed as a Nazi henchman and all Uniates as "war criminals and collaborators." Although Sheptytsky had, in fact, sent letters to the pope and to Himmler protesting the liquidation of Jews in Ukraine and had personally helped save Jews, the Soviet propaganda machine began an enormous campaign to discredit him. The reason was simple: it was not in the interests of the USSR to portray a Ukrainian patriot (which Sheptytsky most definitely was) as an anti-Nazi. The political line was that *all* Ukrainian nationalists were pro-Nazi, the metropolitan included. The other factor in this disinformation campaign was to show in some way that the Ukrainian Catholic (Uniate) Church was collaborationist – which it was not – and to help justify the liquidation of the church in 1946. However, the ultimate target of the campaign were Ukrainians who did not want to be under Soviet rule.

It should be clear that the Soviet motivation for these operations was not to promote peace and justice. The demand to bring war criminals to trial, while noble in itself, plays a minimal role in the disinformation game. For example, in the mid-1970s, when Simon Wiesenthal made statements in defence of Soviet political prisoners and dissenters, the Soviet press began a vicious campaign of disinformation about him. The campaign was launched primarily in the Soviet Ukrainian press in order to set Ukrainians against Jews – a tactic the Soviet regime has employed numerous times. In the anti-Wiesenthal campaign of the 1970s the following statement appeared in the Soviet press:

According to the people who met with Wiesenthal during the war, he had secret contacts with the Nazis. After the war, this idea was confirmed by members of the European resistance. Wiesenthal worked for Canaris (the head of German military intelligence), gathered espionage information in Western Ukraine, and later was an agent for the Hitlerites in the Jewish ghettos where people were being prepared for the death camps like Auschwitz. After the war, Wiesenthal came into contact directly with American intelligence and his main mission was to prepare German agents for U.S. intelligence.[1]

In this case, the disinformation was for internal Soviet consumption. The presentation of Simon Wiesenthal as an espionage agent was inserted to reinforce the Soviet stereotype of the Jew as an agent, an outsider, someone not to be trusted. Interestingly enough, it was done in a book whose entire purpose was to combat what the Soviets saw as an increasingly dangerous problem – the beginnings of a rapprochement between Jews and Ukrainians in the West.

There is sufficient evidence to show that any dialogue between Ukrainian émigrés and the Jewish diaspora and Israel is considered a dangerous development by the Soviet government. The best method to combat this is to raise the spectre of Ukrainian anti-Semitism within the Jewish community in order to subvert any contacts. When a Ukrainian-Jewish dialogue began in America in the 1960s and early 1970s, the Soviets began to interfere in several ways.

First, KGB agents in New York (embassy officials and residents) were given a list of questions and topics to discuss with their contacts in the Ukrainian community. This list consisted mainly of questions dealing with Ukrainian-Jewish relations and the names of the people trying to promote a dialogue. The next step was the circulation of an anonymous leaflet within the Ukrainian community that accused Ukrainian leaders of "having sold out to the Jews." The leaflet was printed in Kiev, brought over by diplomatic pouch, and mailed from different Western countries to Ukrainians in the West. It consisted of anti-Semitic and pro-nationalist slogans and contained anti-Semitic cartoons. As far as Soviet disinformation goes, it was a weak effort when one considers that, a few years ago, the KGB produced an issue of *Newsweek* and distributed it on a mass scale in Third World countries.

The KGB is playing a role in the matter of war criminals – not the major role by any means, and people should not become paranoid about it. Nonetheless, it is playing a role and its participation is evident from some of the available evidence. In one case, the Soviet Embassy in Ottawa mailed a list of alleged war criminals to a reporter from the McGill University newspaper, the *McGill Daily*. To my knowledge, the list has not been released, but according to a press report, Mr. Alan Shefman, national director of the League for Human Rights of B'nai B'rith, said: "There are people listed who are not war criminals, but whom the Soviets just don't like." It would be surprising if this type of list was sent only to the *McGill Daily*.

In Winnipeg and other cities a photocopied brochure has been circulated that attacks Ukrainians who served in the Galician Division. It was circulated during the showings of a film produced in Canada on the Ukrainian famine of 1932-3. On the last page of the leaflet is a paragraph in Hebrew – the implication being that Jews produced the leaflet.

At the same time, several misleading articles have appeared in the American and Canadian press about the Galician Division. For example, the *Christian Science Monitor* recently published an article by Dimitri Simes which deals with the broadcasting policy of Radio Liberty, the U.S.-government-funded radio station broadcasting to the USSR.[2] Simes stated that the Ukrainian desk of Radio Liberty broadcast a program favourable to the division and added: "The SS Division Galitchina [sic] whose Ukrainian volunteers fought for Hitler in France, among other places. . . ." The program Simes referred to was aired on 12 February 1984 and quoted a German diplomat, Hans von Herwarth, who had very impressive anti-Nazi credentials and was involved in the anti-Hitler conspiracy of 1944.

In quoting from Herwarth, the broadcast stated: "The Organization of Ukrainian Nationalists and the Ukrainian Insurgent Army urged enlisting in the *Halychyna* Division for clearly ulterior motives, that is, in order that as many Ukrainians as possible should possess modern weapons." This statement is quite different from what Mr. Simes included in his article. Moreover, the Galician Division never saw action in France. Yet Mr. Simes, an émigré from the USSR (this is not mentioned in the description of Simes in the *Christian Science Monitor*), can publish such nonsense and the *Monitor* does not bother to check the facts. What one sees here is even more dangerous than simple disinformation. It is a multi-faceted attack legitimized by a respectable newspaper.

One line of attack is against the Galician Division, the other is alleged Ukrainian anti-Semitism. According to Mr. Simes, the Ukrainian desk broadcast a program that said, "Jewish pogroms in Ukraine during the Civil War, however unfortunate, should be understood in the context of Jewish support for the Reds." This remark totally distorts what was actually broadcast. On 13 January 1984, a program mentioned the pogrom in Proskuriv. It noted that often after terrorism by the Bolshevik *Cheka*, in which "important posts were occupied by Communists who were Jews... the population generalized the circumstances and identified Bolshevism with the Jews, which was a huge mistake." A different section of the broadcast dealt with an incident in Mykolaiv in southern Ukraine. The program recounted a scene in which a rabbi spoke for Jews: "Regretfully, among the Jewish population, especially the young, there were 'apostates' who went along with the Bolsheviks. But there were also among young Ukrainians people who were on the side of the Bolsheviks. So we should not hold the Jews responsible for the transgressions and political fanaticism of a certain part of the Red youth." The passage notes that "the whole crowd shouted approval" of the rabbi's statement.

A third line of attack in Mr. Simes's article is directed at Radio Liberty. The numerous instances of misinformation, distortions, and omissions, when put together, leave the impression that Radio Liberty is staffed by former Nazis, Ukrainian anti-Semites, and fanatical right-wingers, cold warriors bent upon declaring war on the USSR.

It must be re-emphasized that Soviet disinformation is not behind every bush and is rarely a deciding factor in a given situation. But it can influence people's thinking, especially on such an emotional issue as war criminals, when Western prosecutors are all too ready to accept Soviet evidence provided by KGB investigators. If KGB evidence has been rejected in the trials of dissenters like Mykola Rudenko, Anatolii Shcharansky, and others, why has such evidence been accepted in the cases of alleged war criminals?

Evidently, many people are ready to hear what they want to hear and the KGB is more than ready to provide them with material. This serves the purposes of the Soviet government very well. It is amazing to read in Soviet books that "the Soviet Union provided the U.S. in the past six years with materials about 140 war criminals," or "competent employees of the Committee for State Security (KGB) of the USSR said in an interview how many examples there are of factual evidence gathered by us and given to jurists of other countries in order to uncover war criminals." These passages were written by official Soviet representatives. They are confirmed by government officials. In the *New York Times* (23 September 1984), the head of the Office of Special Investigations (OSI) of the U.S. Justice Department said that most of the information upon which OSI cases are built comes exclusively from Soviet authorities.

Yet contradictions do exist. In his book *Quiet Neighbors*, Allan A. Ryan Jr., the former head of the OSI, wrote: "The Soviets have never attempted to tell OSI who [sic] to investigate." Soviet sources say the opposite. Ryan's book mentions a Ukrainian named Vasyl Yachenko, living in the United States, who supplied the Immigration and Naturalization Service with a list of seventy-three names of alleged Ukrainian Nazis living in the United States. According to Ryan, Yachenko told the U.S. Immigration and Naturalization Service that he obtained these names from documents in Soviet archives and in interviews with editors of Soviet Ukrainian newspapers. Ryan says that Yachenko is a pseudonym used in order to protect the source's privacy and admits that some Ukrainians felt that Yachenko was a Soviet sympathizer! Yet Ryan never met with Yachenko, and no steps were taken to see how he got this list and how a private citizen could get access to such Soviet sources.[3]

As for the Soviets never attempting to tell the OSI whom to investigate, let us take the case of Karl Linnas, an Estonian who allegedly was a supervisor at a concentration camp in Estonia. The Soviet government began demanding his extradition in 1961. I do not want to judge whether Linnas was innocent or guilty – but there is no need to say that the Soviets never intervened when in fact they initiated the investigation.

Although disinformation plays a role in such cases, not all the evidence provided by the Soviet Union is false. A good part of the initial evidence provided to the OSI would have been accurate in order for the KGB to establish some credibility. The real Soviet aim is to have the émigré communities defend a genuine war criminal and thus discredit themselves in the eyes of American and Canadian society.

This is precisely what is happening today. Confusion exists; evidence is mixed; and emotions are beginning to take over. Ukrainians are set upon Jews; Jews begin to suspect every Ukrainian of being an anti-Semite. Ukrainians begin raising the cry of Jewish Bolsheviks, and so on.

Ukrainians above all should be interested in having Ukrainian war criminals prosecuted. Looking at *Gestapo* records, one sees that the Germans used their Ukrainian collaborators against the Ukrainian underground that was fighting the Germans. They were also used in actions against Jews. Both crimes are not to be forgiven. But because the Ukrainian underground, the Ukrainian Insurgent Army (UPA), fought on two fronts – against the Nazis and against the Soviets – it became a target for Soviet disinformation and covert action. The Soviets have never released the names of the Ukrainians who worked with the *Gestapo* and were used to combat the UPA. They are living very quietly and very happily in the Soviet Union today.

Notes

1 L.V. Hamolsky, *Tryzub i "zirka" Davyda* (Dnipropetrovske, 1975), 152. See also Lev A. Korneev, *Klassovaia suchasnost sionizma* (Kiev, 1982). Korneev states that "were it not for the Zionist-Nazi alliance, the number of victims, including Jews, in the Second World War would of course have been less." In a review of Korneev's book, Howard Spier commented that Korneev's "message is that Jews are at least partly responsible for the slaughter of Russians, Ukrainians, and other Soviet nationalities by the Nazis – a vicious charge indeed in Soviet conditions." See *Soviet Jewish Affairs* (London) 14, no. 2 (1984): 74–8.

2 Dimitri Simes, "The Destruction of Liberty," *Christian Science Monitor*, 13 February 1985.

3 Allan A. Ryan Jr., *Quiet Neighbors: Prosecuting Nazi War Criminals in America* (New York, 1984), 103–4. Mr. Yachenko is thought to be Michael Hanusiak, editor of the pro-Soviet New York newspaper *Ukrainski visti* (Ukrainian News). Mr. Hanusiak is the author of *Lest We Forget* (Toronto, 1976), a book about alleged Nazi war criminals published by the Communist Party of Canada's Progress Books.

MYRON KUROPAS

Ukrainian Americans and the Search for War Criminals

Had the Soviet Union paid a once highly placed and visible U.S. government official to write a book aimed at discrediting anti-Communism among Americans of Ukrainian, Lithuanian, Latvian, and Estonian descent, especially those who fled Communist oppression after World War II, it would have received more than its money's worth from Allan A. Ryan Jr., former director of the Justice Department's Office of Special Investigations (OSI), and the author of *Quiet Neighbors: Prosecuting Nazi War Criminals in America*.[1]

The ostensible purpose of his book is to alert Americans to the "thousands" of Nazi war criminals who came to the United States after World War II, and to justify the OSI's efforts to prosecute and to deport them. It appears, however, that Ryan has an entirely different purpose: to cast a long, dark shadow of doubt over the European past of all displaced persons, to question the integrity of those humanitarian Americans who assisted them in their flight from the Soviet Union, and to resurrect the spurious notion that the USSR was as dedicated to making Europe safe for democracy as was the United States.

Ryan writes that 116,000 Baltic and Ukrainian DPs, and 53,000 *Volksdeutsche* came to the United States after World War II. "If even five percent of those people had taken part in persecution [of Jews]," Ryan argues, then more than 8,000 Nazi war criminals entered the United States. After admitting that such estimates are hardly scientific ("Indeed, they are speculation dressed in very light clothing"), Ryan nevertheless reaches the incredible conclusion that these numbers "give a certain perspective to the question of how many Nazi persecutors came to the [United States]" (p. 27). Although Ryan offers no documentation for the figure of 5 per cent, it is precisely this type of supposedly rigorous documentation that the book jacket lauds and on which Ryan builds his case.

"The Displaced Persons Act of 1948," Ryan writes, "was a brazenly discriminatory piece of legislation, written exclusively to exclude as many concentration camp survivors as possible and to include as many Baltic and Ukrainian and ethnic German Volksdeutsche as it could get away with. . . . Had Congress tried to design a law that would extend the Statue of Liberty's hand to the followers and practitioners of Nazism, it could not have done much better than this without coming right out and saying so" (p. 16). Ryan reaches this outrageous conclusion by arguing that "preferences went to groups with known patterns of collaboration," and that as a result of pressures to process as many as possible quickly, individual investigations were unreliable (p. 27). Both of Ryan's theses are fallacious.

That some Ukrainians collaborated with Germany is undeniable. But their numbers were significantly smaller than those of the Italians, who were allied with Hitler until 1943. The Soviet government itself actively collaborated with Hitler from 1939 to 1941. The Vichy government of France came to an understanding with the Nazis and provided human and material resources for the German war effort. Belgium, the Netherlands, Norway, and Denmark all had small but enthusiastic fascist parties both before and during the Nazi occupation. The major difference was that while Western Europe regained its independence after the war, the people of Eastern Europe remained enslaved. As a result, Western Europe had few refugees while Eastern Europe had millions.

Preference in the United States was given to those groups who had suffered twice, first under the Soviets and then under the Nazis. Ryan never mentions this in his discussion of displaced persons, leaving the distinct impression that the displaced persons fled their homelands with the Germans because they were supportive of the Nazi cause and not because, having once tasted life under Soviet rule, they were willing to leave everything behind in order not to live under Moscow's hand.

Ryan somewhat reluctantly admits that it would be wrong to leave the impression, as he puts it, that "a majority of Ukrainian, Baltic or Volksdeutsch [sic] immigrants had taken part in Nazi crimes. The number who had actually taken part in persecution, as opposed to those who had been merely sympathizers, was almost certainly a small part." He concludes ominously, "no one will ever know how small."

The impression left with the uninformed reader is that there were many Ukrainian and Baltic Nazi sympathizers in Europe, that those who actually persecuted Jews were probably in the minority, but that the size of this minority will never be known. Although Ryan makes clear that he is only interested in the persecutors who live in the United States and not the sympathizers, his message to uninformed Americans is that even if the OSI has not identified the Ukrainian or Balt who lives in their neighbourhood, that Ukrainian or Balt may still be, if not a Nazi criminal, at least a Nazi sympathizer.

Ryan offers little evidence to substantiate his allegation that investigations of displaced persons in Europe were lax. It is a matter of record that every applicant under the Displaced Persons Act was checked by the FBI, the counter-intelligence corps of the U.S. Army (which included twenty-one separate investigating steps), the OSS, the Provost Marshal General of the U.S. Army in Germany, the Berlin Document Centre, the Fingerprint Centre in Heidelberg, various consular officers especially assigned to the DP program, the Immigration and Naturalization Service of the Department of Justice stationed overseas, and special American investigators assigned to screen escapees from Communist countries. Although it is possible that some war criminals could have squeezed through this network, such an elaborate system can hardly be labelled "cursory and unreliable."

Nor is there any truth to Ryan's suggestion that the provision in the DP Act allocating 30 per cent of the slots to farmers was put into the legislation specifically to favour Ukrainians. In reality, the provision was inserted because few Americans were willing to work on farms after World War II. Wages were low and farm jobs went begging. Responding to veterans' fears that the DPs would compete with them for jobs in the cities (this was the major reason why the American Legion was opposed to the DP Act), Congress hit upon the farming proviso as a kind of compromise. Few Ukrainians were agricultural workers and only those who could not find sponsors elsewhere ended up on farms.

Another serious criticism of Ryan's book is that it subtly but unmistakably helps legitimize the Soviet perspective regarding displaced persons, World War II, and the aspirations for freedom of Ukrainians and Balts. Ryan points out that some Americans were opposed to the DP Act because they feared the United States would become a haven for former Nazis, and he provides citations from the *Congressional Record*, the *New York Times*, and the *New York Post* to substantiate his point. What Ryan fails to mention, however, is the fact that the most vociferous opponents of the DP Act were America's Communists, who were among the first to label indiscriminately all refugees from Communist terror as "Nazi collaborators." He also chooses to ignore the results of a special subcommittee report of the House Committee on the Judiciary, entitled "Displaced Persons in Europe and their Resettlement in the United States," submitted to Congress on 20 January 1950. Supported by staff experts, subcommittee members visited various DP camps, making personal contacts and unscheduled visits, holding hearings with free exchange of questions and answers, and attending briefings by military and civilian personnel. Investigating charges of widespread fraud, falsification, and forging of documents by prospective DPs, the subcommittee reported that "the number of screening agents, screening sessions, interrogations and checks that a displaced person must pass before reaching the United States is so extensive that the chance of a fraudulent statement or a forged document to slip through is practically nil." Based on their findings, subcommittee members concluded that "the majority of allegations regarding misrepresentation can be safely classified either as rumours or as deliberate misrepresentation intended to serve a definite purpose."

Ryan's bias is further revealed when he describes America's fear of Communism immediately after the war as "hysterical over-reaction." While there were excesses, especially in the outrageous allegations of Senator Joseph McCarthy, the United States was hardly overreacting to the Soviets when Soviet forces refused to leave Eastern Europe and permit free elections as they had promised to do, when Greece was in danger of falling to Soviet-backed Communist partisans, when the Soviets blockaded U.S. highway and rail access to Berlin, when Soviet-backed North Korea invaded South Korea, and when Soviet spies were stealing American atomic secrets.

Another example of Ryan's leanings is his description of the negotiations which led to Soviet Procurator General Roman Rudenko's agreement to supply documents and witnesses to the OSI. The Soviets, writes Ryan, were somewhat annoyed "that their earlier efforts to supply information on Nazi criminals in the United States were seemingly ignored by American authorities." Since the war, Rudenko reminded Ryan, the Soviets have held many trials, but the United States has held none. Ryan admitted this, and his compatriots reminded Rudenko about the U.S.-USSR alliance during World War II.

Writes Ryan, "the mood became noticeably more relaxed. We were no longer the Soviet Union's 1980 adversary. We were representing Russia's wartime ally, the common ally of the Hitlerites" (pp. 78–9). Ryan either ignores or is totally unaware of the fact that the Soviets co-operated with the Hitlerites and became America's wartime ally only because the Hitlerites did not trust them and invaded the Soviet Union in a surprise attack. A tragic irony, hopelessly lost on Ryan, is that every one of the land seizures the Soviets initiated while allied with Hitler, including Lithuania, Latvia, and Estonia, remained in their possession at the end of the war. The Soviets were not fighting Hitlerism to destroy it, but to take its place.

And what about the witnesses the Soviets produced for Ryan? Were any of them allowed to testify in the United States? Of course not. All depositions had to be videotaped in the Soviet Union and all testimony was translated into Russian "for official purposes." And who were these witnesses? Ryan writes that many were former Nazi collaborators who had been tried by the Soviets, had served jail sentences (somewhere between three to eight years), and had long since been released and resumed their lives in the Soviet Union and in Soviet society. How, during the Stalin era, could known Nazi collaborators be sentenced and released after only three years?

Throughout his book Ryan reserves such pejoratives as "brutal" and "bestial" almost exclusively for Ukrainians. As Taras Hunczak has pointed out in a review of *Quiet Neighbors*, Ryan is not above distorting citations to attribute German bloodthirstiness to Ukrainians even when the actual reference cited – Raul Hilberg's *The Destruction of the European Jews* – mentioned violence on the part of ethnic Germans and not Ukrainians.[2] Reading Ryan's book, one can easily get the impression that Ukrainians were even more consistently ruthless than Germans in their treatment of Jews. But as Hilberg himself points out, when it came to killing Jews, Ukrainians "had no stomach for the long-range, systematic German destruction process."[3]

Finally, Ryan seems to be totally oblivious of the fact that Ukrainians suffered grievously under German rule. Ukrainians are Slavs, and according to Nazi doctrine, Slavs were *Untermenschen* (subhumans) who were to be exploited and then eliminated. Some 2.3 million Ukrainians were shipped to Germany as slave labourers during the war and an additional 3.9 million Ukrainians (including 0.9 million Jews) were civilian victims of the Nazis.

Nor does Ryan seem to be aware of the Ukrainian Insurgent Army

(UPA), which fought so valiantly against Nazi oppression. Conservatively estimated by the Germans themselves to be a force of 40,000, the UPA represented a resistance movement on a par with any partisan group then operating in Nazi-occupied Europe. Even the French underground had no more than 45,000 fighters in the whole of France prior to the June 1944 Allied invasion of Europe.

Because I consider it an abomination that some Ukrainians were involved in slaughtering Jews simply because they were Jews, I was prepared to accept at face value OSI evidence against those Ukrainians Ryan chose to prosecute. I was ready to applaud the OSI's efforts to expose Ukrainian mass murderers, because Ukrainians who have committed heinous crimes should never find sanctuary in our community. Having read Ryan's book, however, I now have more questions than answers. If Ryan can be so wrong, so biased, so tendentious about so many historical events, how right can he be about Ukrainian "Nazis"? If Ryan chose to ignore, suppress, or distort so much evidence regarding all Ukrainians, how can we believe in his integrity regarding some Ukrainians?

In writing his book, Ryan had it within his power finally to put to rest Ukrainian American concerns regarding what they believe is the beginning of a vicious Soviet disinformation campaign aimed at defaming the entire Ukrainian American community. That he failed to do so discredited him, the OSI, and the U.S. Department of Justice. Ryan, however, is no longer with the OSI. He has been travelling around the United States, appearing on various talk shows and being interviewed extensively by national newspapers.

It appears that the current defamation campaign is the tip of the iceberg. It is an iceberg that began in 1933 when the United States first recognized the USSR. This occurred during the height of the Ukrainian famine, in 1932–3. It should also be recalled that both in the United States and in Canada, the Ukrainian community had great hopes that someday Ukraine would gain independence. It is no coincidence that it was not until the 1930s, when the Soviet Union had an ambassador in Washington, D.C., that Ukrainian Americans came under attack for their advocacy of a homeland free from Communist oppression.

The 1930s and 1940s were a period of extraordinary Communist growth and infiltration in the United States and Canada. Accusing Ukrainians of being Nazis, Communists and their fellow travelers launched a disinformation campaign that, at least in the United States, seriously hampered efforts to work on behalf of an independent

Ukrainian state. The campaign severely damaged the credibility of the Ukrainian National Association and the Organization for the Rebirth of Ukraine (ODVU), two powerful organizations, and all but destroyed the United Hetman Organization. It was not until the war ended that their reputations were restored. Only then did most Americans realize what the aims of the Soviet Union were. Only then did the American authorities realize that not all displaced persons who refused to return to Ukraine were war criminals whose forced repatriation was mandated by the Yalta Agreement. All of this, of course, has long been forgotten. The Soviets have not forgotten, however, and it is for this reason that I believe that what we see in Ryan's book is really an intensification of an ongoing Soviet defamation campaign against our community.[4] The campaign was renewed in America some five years ago, and in my opinion, we Ukrainian Americans handled it poorly. In essence, we did three things wrong.

First, we never clearly and unequivocally acknowledged that *some* Ukrainians were undoubtedly involved in the murder of Jews during the Nazi occupation of Ukraine. It was never clear in our minds that our problem was not the guilt of Ukrainian war criminals but the group culpability which their proven guilt could visit upon us if our community did not dissociate itself from their crimes as quickly as possible.

Second, we believed that if we ignored the problem, it would go away. When Ryan began to identify alleged war criminals by their ethnic origins, we suffered in silence. No one expressed outrage. No one screamed.

And finally, we did not reach out to other groups. We did not reach out to Lithuanians, Latvians, Estonians, or Jews to say, "We need to discuss and share our common experiences. We need to know what your concerns are and you need to know ours." At the same time, Ukrainians need to realize that the Simon Wiesenthal Center for Holocaust Studies in Los Angeles, which is now in the forefront of the Ukrainian defamation campaign in both Canada and the United States, does not represent all North American Jews. The Wiesenthal Center has come under some criticism in Jewish circles recently, and there is reason to believe there will be more. The reality is that with its increasingly irresponsible behaviour, it serves neither the cause of finding and prosecuting Nazi war criminals nor the cause of Ukrainian-Jewish understanding. The only beneficiary is their common adversary, the Soviet Union, which has consistently strived to drive a wedge between the two peoples.

Having observed the approach to the same problem taken by Canada, it is heartening to see that the American mistakes have not been repeated. On the contrary, Ukrainian Canadians have condemned Ukrainian war criminals who participated in the wanton slaughter of Jews, have tackled the defamation campaign head on, and have reached out to other groups.

Notes

1 Allan A. Ryan Jr., *Quiet Neighbors: Prosecuting Nazi War Criminals in America* (New York, 1984).
2 Taras Hunczak, *Ukrainian Weekly* (Jersey City), 17 February 1985; see also Ryan, *Quiet Neighbors*, 10; Raul Hilberg, *The Destruction of the European Jews* (Chicago, 1961), 206.
3 Hilberg, *The Destruction of the European Jews*, 330.
4 For a more recent example of distortion, see Charles Higham, *American Swastika: The Shocking Story of Nazi Collaborators in Our Midst from 1933 to the Present Day* (New York, 1985); and my review, "New Book Based on Soviet Disinformation," *Ukrainian Weekly* (21 April 1985).

Discussion

On the day of the symposium a news conference was held to allow the Toronto press an opportunity to question the speakers.

QUESTION (*Globe and Mail*):
The U.S. Justice Department has been under a great deal of criticism from a number of groups for the methods they have used and some of the details of their prosecutions. Many allegations of KGB and Soviet disinformation have been made. Where is the evidence that this is going on?

D. MATAS:
The way to assess conflicting claims and allegations is through a proper court procedure, according to Canadian standards of justice. One of the unfortunate consequences of the fact that the media have not mobilized themselves to do something about war criminals in our midst until now is that we do have these allegations hanging in the air without any appropriate means of assessment. I do not think that we should take Soviet allegations or information at face value. But we should not reject them out of hand either. If the witnesses are supplied by the Soviets, we must subject them to examination and cross-examination. Subject all their information to assessment by Canadian courts, by Canadian standards of justice, and then we will come to a conclusion that will be accepted generally in Canada.

S.P. ZUMBAKIS:
This is a serious and pivotal point as far as we in the United States are concerned. The court system is not the place where we can try the

issue. We have compiled a booklet containing samples of evidence of linkage between the U.S. Office of Special Investigations [the OSI] and the KGB. We feel the linkage is very clear, but it is not something that we can prove in every case in a court trial. We recommended to the U.S. Congress that it investigate and hold hearings. But, for some reason, Congress is very reluctant to investigate the charges of linkage. We feel that the proper way to investigate this is not in the courts, but in hearings.

The evidence pointing to a linkage is absolutely clear. The documentation is clear. Soviet dissidents, whether they are Christians or Jews, will testify to the fact that the KGB is running these shows. The KGB has even said so in *Izvestiia* and *Pravda*. My answer is that Parliament or Congress has to investigate this.

QUESTION (*Toronto Star*):
Would anyone like to comment on whether Canada, as a society, has been aggressive enough in trying to find the real criminals: in trying to weed them out of the immigration process, finding methods of exposing them and prosecuting them.

D. MATAS:
In answer to your question about whether we have been aggressive enough, I do not think we have been. We have deported no one and started no deportation proceedings. We have denaturalized no one and started no denaturalization proceedings. We have prosecuted no one in Canada and started no prosecution proceedings. There has been only one extradition – of Rauca – who was extradited some thirty years after he came here. His extradition came twenty years after it was requested by the Federal Republic of Germany. We have just started some activity in this area with the Deschênes Commission, so what we have done is very little, very late, and very unsystematic.

R. SERBYN:
An issue that has not yet been raised and that seems to have been ignored by the press are the terms of reference of the Deschênes inquiry. Although the preamble specifically mentions Nazi war criminals, the terms of reference are general. Yet somehow the press focused only on Nazi war criminals. During the two years of Soviet occupation in Western Ukraine prior to June 1941 (as the conference speakers pointed out), many crimes were committed by Soviet authorities. We should investigate all alleged war crimes.

R. VASTOKAS:

Two weeks ago I made a speech to the Lithuanian community in which I suggested, after adducing evidence to attest to Soviet war crimes, that we think about convening Nuremberg Two. It was largely a philosophical exercise, but I think it brings attention to a subject that has long been overdue. A week after the speech, I received a list of Soviet war criminals living in Canada, which I will be passing on to the RCMP.

The mandate of the Deschênes Commission must be expanded to incorporate not only Soviet war criminals but also all war criminals. That the commission has focused on Nazi war criminals has frightened the ethnic communities, particularly when they have been accused of harbouring war criminals. This is most unfortunate.

QUESTION (*Toronto Star*):

Would you include then, for example, Vietnamese war criminals?

R. VASTOKAS:

Absolutely. I spoke to Allan Lawrence, the former Canadian attorney general, and he agreed that the mandate should be expanded to include all war criminals residing in Canada, no matter what their race or creed.

S.P. ZUMBAKIS:

One striking problem that we have in the United States on that point is that almost all of these cases are against former residents of Eastern Europe. Yet we know that France, Spain, and Italy had official fascist parties. We have millions of Germans in the United States, yet the only people who are targeted are the people who come from behind the Iron Curtain. That, to the Eastern European ethnic communities, is unfair. Some American communities are being persecuted, when we should be prosecuting all who officially participated with the Nazis in crimes against humanity. I hope you do not make the same mistake in Canada.

QUESTION (*Globe and Mail*):

Are you suggesting that some of the people who have been prosecuted and ordered deported or were stripped of their citizenship are not guilty? Some would argue that the U.S. Justice Department's evidence is very strong; others would insist that it is very weak and that it is all fabricated by the KGB. Are you suggesting that just because they are from countries from behind the Iron Curtain, they are not guilty?

S.P. ZUMBAKIS:

What I am suggesting is that when the OSI investigates 800 individuals in the United States and of that number, 750 happen to come from behind the Iron Curtain, there is a problem. Many Germans doing business in the United States were in the SS. They are allowed to live in the United States, whereas someone who was remotely connected to anything German has been singled out by the OSI. For the most part, however, the fingerpointing has come from the Soviet Union; that is alarming.

I agree with David Matas that all war criminals should be prosecuted. However, right now we have selective prosecution and persecution. Some cases have merit, while several have no merit at all. Some people are not being tried for war crimes but for misrepresenting their wartime history on a report form forty years ago. In one case a man was tried against whom there was no evidence that he committed any war crimes. Everything is guilt by association. But technically he did not spell out exactly what he did during World War II and technically the court is right in deporting him.

QUESTION (*Toronto Star*):

Why do you prefer a congressional or parliamentary inquiry to court cases?

S.P. ZUMBAKIS:

I have been referring to the OSI because it speaks for the American government on the matter of war crimes. Its typical answer is: "You have a forum. You have a trial, and in the trial you can prove that the documents are forged, that the witnesses are improper. You have a chance." In fact, you do not have a chance.

To give an example, one case was taken on by Kirkland and Ellis, one of the largest law firms in the United States. They took it on as a matter of principle, on a *pro bono* basis. Up to the time of the trial, they had spent $755,000 to defend this individual. How many people could defend themselves at such expense? These are civil cases in the United States. We do not have the right to jury, to appointed counsel, or to get paid for our expenses. Nor do we have the right to inquire or get any information from the Soviet Union, which is the source of most OSI evidence. It is not a fair proceeding. Also, in a typical case, the OSI produces from 500 to 2,000 pages of documents. It costs about $500,000 just to examine the documents in order to prove forgery. No defendant has that kind of money. The OSI maintains, however, that defendants have a chance. Yet if a defendant cannot prove that there are forgeries, then there are no forgeries.

M. KUROPAS:

I would like to mention the U.S. experience, and specifically Allan Ryan, the former head of the OSI. In his book, *Quiet Neighbors*, are numerous exaggerations and distortions. Where is Mr. Ryan's integrity when he writes:

The Displaced Persons Act of 1948 was a brazenly discriminatory piece of legislation, written to exclude as many concentration camp survivors as possible and to include as many Baltic and Ukrainian and ethnic German Volksdeutsche [sic] as it could get away with. Had Congress tried to design a law that would extend the hand to the followers and practitioners of Nazism, it could not have done much better than this without coming right out and saying so.

This statement is outrageous, because it suggests that the major purpose of the Displaced Persons Act was to provide a haven for Nazis; and, as Mr. Zumbakis noted, he singled out Ukrainians and Balts.

T. HUNCZAK:

Concerning American procedures, I want to mention the case of Frank Walus in order to illustrate how a miscarriage of justice can occur. This man was accused by Simon Wiesenthal of having killed Jews. There were witnesses produced by the Israeli police who came to Chicago. The man was found guilty. But he always maintained that he was innocent, that he was a victim of Nazi tyranny. His lawyer went to Germany and found that he had been working as a forced labourer for a farmer. Obviously, this is one case in which a document could be produced. And what if there had been no document?

Even so, an innocent man's reputation was tarnished. A newspaper in Chicago wrote that the thing to do with Walus was to tie him up and throw him in the middle of the ocean. He lost his friends, his neighbours.

S.P. ZUMBAKIS:

There was a strong indication that the government had a list of witnesses that would have exonerated Walus. Now the man is $200,000 in debt and his health has been destroyed. The case was tried in the press. Everywhere he was referred to not as a Polish immigrant, but as a Nazi. The man was totally destroyed before he had his first day in court.

QUESTION (*Toronto Star*):
But is that not true of the situation with a parliamentary commission or royal commission? For example, we had the Grange Royal Commission under which people did not have the protection of the Canada Evidence Act. They could not testify and be exempt from incriminating themselves. They did not have the right to have their counsel paid for by the government. It cost them fortunes. They lost their reputation. And in the end, the commission itself was ineffective. The commission could not point a finger at anyone, and so it could not clear anyone, either.

D. MATAS:
Parliamentary commissions have their place, as do the courts. An investigative commission is an appropriate beginning with general situations, where a systematic study is necessary. We do have one here with the Deschênes Commission, of the sort perhaps that my neigh-bour would have liked to see in the United States. The courts are an appropriate forum for determining the guilt or innocence of individuals, and it is inappropriate for the Grange Commission, or any other commission, to do so. In the United States there is no legal aid available the way there is in Canada. Even here, the availability of legal aid may vary from province to province, and that may become a problem in a particular case. But we should not sell our justice system short. The way to get around selective prosecution is to make sure that we have systematic prosecution rather than no prosecution at all. The Deschênes Commission, as well as the Canadian government, will be as thorough and systematic as possible about this matter.

M. YURKEVICH:
One point about terminology: it makes no sense to refer to Eastern Europeans, who were regarded by the Germans as subhuman, as "Nazi" war criminals; they were not allowed to join the Nazi Party. This is an inaccurate usage one often encounters in the press, and it should be avoided.

QUESTION (*Toronto Sun*):
Would you have any evidence of Nazi war criminals of German origin living in the Soviet Union or Eastern Europe?

T. HUNCZAK:
That is a different problem. The Soviet Union began to plan its occupation of Germany with the *Bund der Deutschen Offizieren* [Union of German Officers], which was formed immediately after the Battle of Stalingrad. At that time they created a committee for "Free Germany." And many, particularly those formerly in the security services who were not known for their niceties, found their way all the way to the top echelon of the East German security police.

M. YURKEVICH:
In his paper Bohdan Krawchenko noted that Erich Koch, the former *Reichskommissar* of Ukraine, is still in the Polish prison of Barczewo. According to Polish dissident sources, the conditions of his imprisonment are extremely humane. He has a TV, receives magazines from West Germany, and receives all the medication he requires from the West. This man was tried by a Polish court in 1959, but for offences he committed as *Gauleiter* of East Prussia. Sentence was suspended because he was ill. He has been in prison ever since. The Soviet Union has never demanded his extradition from Poland to face trial for the crimes that he committed as *Reichskommissar* of Ukraine.

S.P. ZUMBAKIS:
In a recent case, a German scientist, Rudolf, decided not to fight denaturalization and deportation. He went to Germany on his own. He was a NASA scientist who had received several awards in the United States. Allegedly he was a Nazi collaborator because he worked in Peenemünde, where slave labour was used. After the war the Americans recruited as many scientists as they could, including Werner von Braun, to build our rockets. The Soviets got the rest. So if Rudolf was guilty, certainly the Soviets have at least half of their scientists who should be deported somewhere.

QUESTION (*Toronto Sun*):
How well prepared, in terms of experience and judgment, are the OSI officers who travel to the Soviet Union and compile the documentation?

T. HUNCZAK:

On the basis of my discussions with a lawyer from the OSI who travelled to Lutske and to Lviv [in Soviet Ukraine], the translators were provided by the Soviet prosecutor's office. Also, a member of the prosecutor's staff was always present. That may not answer your question directly, but indirectly it does: if we had someone from the United States who spoke Ukrainian, that person could have asked direct questions. The translators were from the prosecutor's office. It is not in pursuit of justice; it is an arm of the KGB. So the "witnesses" answered the questions as the questions were posed.

If you read Mr. Ryan's *Quiet Neighbors*, in which he discusses how the OSI got the agreement for investigating war criminals in Moscow, his enthusiasm is evident. He says the agreement was reached because he met Procurator General Roman Rudenko. Here is an example of the perception of an American lawyer who was also head of the OSI: "How could a man like Procurator General Rudenko have survived the Stalinist purges?" Clearly, Ryan is innocent of historical realities. Rudenko was one of the architects of the Gulag. Such naiveté is alarming.

Another point: the OSI has a yearly budget of three million and a staff of fifty lawyers, investigators, historians, and linguists. Yet from the time it was established until Ryan's book was written, only nineteen people were proven guilty, and even their guilt is questionable.

QUESTION (*Globe and Mail*):
Would you prefer that no such process existed? Would you prefer that none of these people were pursued?

T. HUNCZAK:
War criminals must be brought to justice. But this society should be able to design a process whereby you can provide the individual with the due process of law. The Soviets are polluting our judicial system by providing fragmentary, questionable evidence.

M. KUROPAS:
Something should also be said about the witnesses. First, in his book Ryan mentions that all the witnesses who spoke in Ukrainian or Lithuanian had their testimony immediately translated into Russian by a translator supplied by the Soviet Union. So the question arises, did

the translation reflect what was actually said? Second, Ryan points out that many of the witnesses were purportedly [Nazi] collaborators who, after the war, were tried by the Soviets and received three to eight years for collaborating with the Nazis. Now, this was during Stalin's time. Can you imagine a known Nazi collaborator receiving three to eight years and then being allowed to resume his place in Soviet society? All Nazi collaborators whom the Soviets caught were either shot or sent immediately to the Gulag for twenty-five years.

s.p. zumbakis:
There are two ways that witnesses are gathered by all sides. In some cases – and these are rare – the OSI has a list of witnesses that it wants to interview behind the Iron Curtain. When the OSI approaches the Soviet authorities the latter decides whether or not the OSI can take a deposition. The OSI is not allowed to speak with the witnesses. Most of the witnesses come as a result of the OSI saying, "We have a Nazi and we need witnesses against him." The KGB provides the witnesses, the forum, and the interpreters. In the Juozas Kungys case, for instance, there were more than 100 false translations. There is very strong evidence to indicate that the OSI knew that the translations were wrong. But they still submitted them to the court.

In another case in Chicago, the one defended by Kirkland and Ellis, a question was asked of a witness who was brought in 800 miles from Russia to Riga to give a deposition. When the poor old man was dragged in, the cameras were set on him and the proceedings videotaped. Intourist guides (according to U.S. government studies, they are part of the KGB) were the interpreters. The question was: "Who prepared you for this deposition, for this question?" His answer in Lithuanian was "The KGB." The translation was "nobody." But that is only part of the problem. Where the documents are concerned, no one from the United States – whether from the defence team or the OSI – had access to them.

question (*Toronto Sun*):
Do they produce originals [of the documents]?

s.p. zumbakis:
They eventually show the originals; the KGB decides which documents are to be provided. No one sees the archives. There may be 500 numbered documents, and the KGB produces one document from a

series or pack of correspondence. That document the OSI takes as gospel. As any trial attorney or researcher knows, if you have a hundred documents, and you only choose one, you may have the wrong impression, especially in light of the fact that the Germans (from 1943 on) knew that they were in trouble. They knew they would be tried in the West. They knew they would be accused of war crimes and they started a formal reorganization of guilt. Some SS officers testified at their own trials. They claimed to be appalled at Ukrainians or Lithuanians for killing Jews, because SS officers would never act in that manner. In the case of Kazys Palciauskas, a Florida resident, the court listened to that kind of evidence and wrote in the opinion that SS divisions and the *Gestapo* came to Lithuania to "save" the Jews from the Lithuanians.

Sometimes we are allowed to examine the document, sometimes not. We usually see a fifth-generation photocopy. To examine documents is extremely expensive. If it is an important document, we are allowed to examine it only at the Soviet Embassy, on their terms. In one case we hired experts, but they were not allowed to take the document outside to examine it in the sunlight, which is the best way. Ink samples could not be taken. The question of forgery arose because there were twenty-three erasures on the document, including the signature line, the date of birth, and the place of birth. The key document had twenty-three erasures, and the investigators were not allowed to examine either the chemical or fibre composition of the paper! These are the kind of documents we are dealing with.

PART III

Documents, 1929–66

1. Resolutions of the First Congress of the Organization of Ukrainian Nationalists

28 JANUARY – 2 FEBRUARY 1929

I. GENERAL OUTLINE

1. Ukrainian nationalism is a spiritual and political movement arising from the inner nature of the Ukrainian Nation in the period of its fierce struggle for the foundations and goals of creative existence.
2. The Ukrainian Nation is the basis for every activity and the aim of every aspiration of Ukrainian nationalism.
3. The organic tie of nationalism with the nation is a fact of the natural order and upon it is based the entire understanding of the existence of a nation.
4. The nation is the highest type of organic human community which, in addition to its psychological and social diversity, has its own unique internal form, created on the basis of similar natural location, common historical experience, and an unremitting urge to realize itself in the completeness of intense efforts.
5. The internal form of the nation is the basic agent of its dynamic continuity and, at the same time, the principle of its synthetic formation. This principle gives the life of a nation, throughout its historical development, an integral spiritual definition which is marked by its various concrete-individual expressions. In that sense, the internal form is the ideal of the nation which establishes and facilitates its historical rise.
6. Historical rise [sic] – the external expression of the constant relevance of the national idea – reflects the undiluted ideal of the nation. The unseen ideal comprises the nation's urge to sustain itself in the system of global reality, in the role of a directly active subject having the broadest sphere of influence on its surroundings.
7. On the path to its self-realization in the form of the greatest intensity of historical meaning, the nation numerically increases its inventory of biological and physical strength with the simultaneous expansion of its territorial base; in this connection, there takes place within it a process of constant reformulation of various ethnic elements into a synthesis of organic national unity; in view of this, the nation always finds itself in a state of domestic growth.

8. The prominent force-oriented means for the growth of a nation is its spiritual longing, expressed through the production of cultural values which, from one side, consolidates the internal community of a nation and, from the other, exerts a centrifugal influence on the surroundings. Culture is not only the creator of national individuality and external distinctiveness, but it is the first among the directly active agents on the periphery of the spiritual strength of a nation.

9. The condition which protects a nation's lasting active participation in the world structure, and which conforms most closely to the comprehensive interests of national life, is the political organization known as the sovereign state.

10. The state is an external form of the interrelation of all the productive forces of a nation. This external form reflects the fundamental qualities of the state and in that manner permits its normal development in all possible ways; the state which is the ever-present definition of the nation by the form of organizational interaction of forces, locked into an organic entity, or system, outwardly differentiated, as an independent collective unit.

11. Through the state, the nation becomes a full member of world history, for only in the form of a state does the nation possess the internal and external criteria of a historic entity.

12. The state form of life most accurately affirms the concrete expression of the national ideal's creative character. For this reason, the primary natural aspiration of a nation is to delineate the borders of its state activities so as to cover the entire region of its ethnic distribution. By these means, the nation forms its entire physical organism into a state. This is the most important and most elementary foundation of its future.

13. In view of its state of political captivity, the chief aim of the Ukrainian Nation is the creation of a political-legal organization, to be called the Ukrainian Independent United State.

14. The fundamental condition necessary for the creation, consolidation, and development of the Ukrainian state is: that the state be an expression of the national being, combining the greatest creative efforts of all the constituent organs of the nation. Thus, the state would reflect their organized interrelations on the basis of the integralism of social forces with their rights and duties, which are determined in relation to their significance to the entirety of national life.

15. Ukrainian nationalism derives practical tasks for itself from the foremost principles of state organization. These tasks are to prepare for the realization of the national idea through the united efforts of Ukrainians committed to the ideas of a nation-state organized on the principles of active idealism, moral self-discipline, and individual initiative.

16. The first stage and first executor of the tasks of Ukrainian nationalism is the Organization of Ukrainian Nationalists, created by a Congress of Ukrainian Nationalists and constructed on the principles of all-Ukrainian representation, non-partisanship, and monocracy.

II. STATE STRUCTURE

1. The form of the Ukrainian state's government will reflect the progressive

stages of the state construction of Ukraine, these being: national liberation, state consolidation, and development.
2. In the period of the liberation struggle, only national dictatorship, created in the process of the national revolution, will be able to preserve the internal strength of the Ukrainian nation and its greatest resistance to external forces.
3. Only after the renewal of statehood will a period of internal reorganization and transformation into a monolithic state body take place. In this transitional stage, it will be the duty of the head of state to prepare the creation of the highest legislative organs. The legislative organs will be created on the principle of representation from all organized social classes, taking into consideration the diversity of individual lands which will constitute the Ukrainian State.
4. At the head of the reorganization of the state will be the head of state (chosen by a representative assembly), who will appoint the executive, which will be responsible to him and to the highest legislative body.
5. The basis of the administrative system of the Ukrainian State will be local self-government; each region will have its own separate representative legislative body, summoned by the organized local social classes and by its own executive.

III. SOCIO-ECONOMIC RESOLUTIONS

1. *Introductory Theses*

1. The Ukrainian State will strive to attain national economic self-sufficiency, increase natural wealth, and protect the material livelihood of the population, through expansion of all branches of the national economy.
2. The economic life of the country will be built upon the basis of the co-operation of the state, co-operatives, and private capital. Individual sectors of the national economy will be distributed among them, and will become the object of their simultaneous and equal labour, to the extent that this will benefit the whole of the national economy and be in the interests of the state.

2. *Agricultural Policy*

1. The interests of the national economy of Ukraine are served by the existence and development of the village farm.
2. The expropriation of feudal lands without compensation, conducted in the period of the revolution in Eastern Ukraine, will be confirmed by the state authorities through legislation, the force of which will extend to all areas of the Ukrainian State.
3. The state authority will institute correctives in the distribution of land in Eastern Ukraine, necessary in view of the spontaneous, unordered character of the division of the lands expropriated in the revolutionary period.
4. The state will ensure the development of agricultural productivity and the protection of the prosperity of the peasantry through support for the middle peasantry.

5. Village farming will be built upon the right of private ownership of land, limited by the state regulation of free sale and purchase of land, with the aim of precluding the excessive reduction or increase in the size of land holdings.
6. The state authority will by all means promote the efficiency of village farms and their adaptation to markets; support the expansion of agricultural co-operatives; offer the rural economy more inexpensive production credit; care for agricultural and agri-educational matters, as well as for the protection of farmers' production by state insurance.
7. Forest lands will be expropriated without compensation and will be transferred to the state or to municipal governments. Only small lots, unsuitable for nationalization or municipalization, will remain in the hands of private owners.
8. Agricultural migration will be regulated through the accommodation of the surplus rural population into national production and through the proper implementation of colonization.
9. City lands and real estate will remain in the hands of private owners. The state and the municipal government will regulate urban construction and will avoid housing crises and land speculation by way of concentrating, in their own hands, the necessary regulatory land funds.

3. Industrial Policy

1. The state will encourage industrialization of the country in order that the aims of economic independence and development at all levels, dictated by the needs of national defence and employment of the surplus rural population, be achieved.
2. Enterprises in branches of industry essential to the existence and defence of the country will be nationalized. Other enterprises will be left to the private capital of individuals and associations in keeping with the principles of free competition and private initiative. In certain cases, defined by law, the state will have the right of pre-empting private investors in the acquisition of co-ownership of private enterprises.
3. The state will encourage the rationalization of all types of industry, particularly their mechanization, and the preparation of professional cadres and technical workers in order to satisfy the demands of contemporary technology.
4. In order to increase the rural population's prosperity and to prepare skilled workers for industry, the state will assist the development of cottage industries in the form of production co-operatives.
5. The state will ensure the organization of production and retail artisans' co-operatives, supporting artisans within the limits which suit the contemporary character of production and the markets.

4. Trade Policy

1. Trade operations within both internal and external markets will be distributed among the private sector, co-operatives, and the state. The

state will control trade in the products of nationalized industry and major types of transportation.
2. In order to secure a normal internal process of trade distribution, the state will also ensure the most favourable conditions in world markets for Ukrainian products and manufactured goods and for the external defence of the national economy, and it will use means of a protectionist and favourable character which will be applied in the form of tariffs and trade agreements.

5. Finance Policy

1. The tax system will be operated on the principle of a single, equitable, progressive, and direct tax, with the exception of a limited number of indirect taxes.
2. The state will undertake the development of banking in all branches of the economy. The National Bank will be an institution independent to the greatest possible extent from purely political activities, and will be accountable to the executive and citizenry.
3. The matter of the payment of state debts which the Ukrainian state acquires as part of the debt of the occupying states will be settled in accordance with the principles of justice within the framework of economic capacity.

6. Social Policy

1. Regulation of interrelations between social groups, particularly the right of binding arbitration in matters of social conflict, will belong to the state, which will ensure co-operation between the productive classes of the Ukrainian Nation.
2. Members of all social groups will have the right of coalition, on the basis of which they will unite into professional organizations, with the right to syndicate in accordance with territorial principles and branches of the economy. These will have their representation in government.
3. Employers and employees will have the right to free personal and collective agreements in all matters which concern their mutual interests, within the framework of legislation, and under the supervision of the state.
4. In private and state industrial enterprises elective councils will be created with representation from entrepreneurs, managers, and workers, with the right to oversee and monitor the technology of production.
5. Workers' councils will be established in agricultural, industrial, and trade enterprises, as representative organs for the settlement of workers, relations with trade unions, employers, and the state. Particularly, they will themselves, or in understanding with the professional organizations, conclude collective agreements. In industrial enterprises they will take part in production councils.
6. Employers and employees will have the right to resolve disagreements between them by way of third-party hearings. In the event that an agreement cannot be reached, there remain the rights to strike and to lockout. Binding settlement of conflicts will belong to the state's arbitration bodies.

7. The standard work day will be eight hours, which the state will attempt to shorten, conditions permitting.
8. Recognizing the basic right to choose one's work, the state will encourage productivity, first by passing legislation establishing conditions for skilled labour and small business and by regulating the internal workings of enterprises, particularly in the disposition of jobs and technical processes; and second, by accomplishing the same with the aid of supervisory bodies and other state institutions.
9. In accordance with state regulation of public and private employment offices, the state will ensure provision of material assistance to the unemployed, which will be distributed indirectly by professional organizations from funds collected from workers and employers. In exceptional cases defined by law, this aid will come from the assistance funds of communities and the state.
10. The state will institute a single organization of general insurance, compulsory for all classes of society, which will simultaneously take upon itself the responsibility of supporting all citizens over sixty years of age who do not have their own means of support.

IV. FOREIGN POLICY

1. The realization of the postulate of Ukrainian statehood requires the activization of the internal political life of the Ukrainian people, to be manifested externally to gain recognition of the Ukrainian cause as a decisive force in Eastern European political affairs.
2. Complete expulsion of occupying forces from our lands in a national revolution, enabling the development of the Ukrainian Nation within its boundaries, can only be assured by an independent military establishment and a purposeful policy of alliances of political action.
3. Ukrainian foreign policy will realize its task by making alliances with those nations that are hostile to Ukraine's occupiers and discard in principle the traditional method of Ukrainian politics of making the liberation struggle dependent on one or another of the historical enemies of the Ukrainian Nation. Ukrainian foreign policy will also realize its tasks by properly utilizing the international forum in order to achieve an active role for Ukraine in international politics.
4. In pursuing its external policy, the Ukrainian state will strive to achieve the greatest defensive borders that will include all Ukrainian ethnic territories and guarantee its economic self-sufficiency.

V. MILITARY POLICY

1. The organization of Ukrainian military power will be gradually developed, and its form will change in response to the three stages of the political condition of the Ukrainian nation: enemy occupation, national revolution, state consolidation.
2. Under enemy occupation, the preparation of the Ukrainian popular masses for armed combat, particularly the preparation of organizers and the education of leaders, will be taken over by a separate military body.

3. Only military power, which relies on an armed nation prepared to fight stubbornly and valiantly for its rights, will be able to free Ukraine from occupation and facilitate the organization of the Ukrainian State.
4. The defence of the organized state will be taken over by a single, regular, classless, national army and navy which, alongside territorial Cossack formations, will be formed on the basis of conscription.

VI. CULTURE AND ART

1. The Ukrainian State will strive to raise the level of culture and civilization in Ukraine by sanctioning a cultural process built on the foundation of free cultural activity, and on the spiritual nature of the Ukrainian nation, its historical traditions and contemporary achievements. The Ukrainian State will also strive to root out the detrimental influences of alien domination in the cultural and psychological life of the nation.
2. Only the development of cultural works and artistic currents that are associated with healthy phenomena in the Ukrainian Nation's art and with the cult of chivalry, as well as those which have a voluntaristically creative approach to life, will be able to awaken the healthy urge of the nation to power and might.

VII. EDUCATION POLICY

1. The administration and maintenance of education as an instrument of raising the national masses in a national-state spirit, and the implementation of a school system which would raise the development of the education of the Ukrainian nation to the necessary level, will reside with the state.
2. At the foundations of national education lies a system of Ukrainian state, compulsory, and free comprehensive schools, which will thoroughly guarantee the harmonious development of the person and include practical, vocational training.
3. Private educational institutions and foreign education will be allowed with state permission in each individual case, and will be under the supervision of state officials.

VIII. RELIGIOUS POLICY

1. Believing the religious question to be a personal matter of the individual, the Ukrainian state will adopt a position of full freedom of religious conscience.
2. Recognizing the fundamental separation of church and state, the government – while preserving the necessary supervision of church organizations – will co-operate with Ukrainian clergymen of various faiths in matters concerning the moral upbringing of the nation.
3. In schools, the teaching of religion of those faiths which do not display denationalizing tendencies will be allowed.
4. The Ukrainian state will assist the development of a Ukrainian national

church independent of foreign patriarchs, and the Ukrainianization of religious faiths active in Ukraine.

IX. THE ORGANIZATION OF UKRAINIAN NATIONALISTS

1. Taking the ideal of a Ukrainian Independent and United State as the basis of its political activity, and not recognizing all those acts, agreements, and institutions which consolidated the dismemberment of the Ukrainian nation, the Organization of Ukrainian Nationalists places itself in categorical opposition to all those powers, domestic and alien, which oppose actively or passively this stand of the Ukrainian nationalists, and will act against all political endeavours of individuals and collectives which deviate from the above-mentioned principles.

2. Not limiting its activities to any one territory, but striving for the domination of the Ukrainian national reality on all Ukrainian lands and in foreign territories populated by Ukrainians, the Organization of Ukrainian Nationalists will pursue a policy of all-Ukrainian statehood without giving it a partisan, class or any kind of socially limited character, and directly opposes this policy to all party and class groupings and their political methods.

3. Supported by the creative elements of the Ukrainian citizenry and uniting them around the Ukrainian nation-state ideal, the Organization of Ukrainian Nationalists sets out as its task to make healthy the inner relations of the nation, to extract state-creating efforts from the Ukrainian nation, to expand Ukrainian national power to its full proportions and, in this way, act to guarantee the great Ukrainian Nation a fitting place among the world's other nation-states.

Source: OUN v svitli postanov Velykykh Zboriv, Konferentsii ta inshykh dokumentiv z borotby 1929–1955 r. (The OUN as Reflected in Resolutions of the Grand Assemblies, Conferences, and Other Documents from the Struggle, 1929–1955) (n.p., 1955), 3–16. Translated by Taras F. Pidzamecky, Roman Waschuk, and Andriy Wynnyckyj.

2. The Ten Commandments of the Ukrainian Nationalist (Decalogue)

JUNE 1929

1. You will attain a Ukrainian State, or die in battle for it.
2. You will not permit anyone to defame the glory or the honour of Your Nation.
3. Remember the Great Days of our struggles.
4. Be proud of the fact that You are the inheritor of the struggle for the glory of Volodymyr's Trident.
5. Avenge the deaths of the Great Knights.
6. Do not speak about matters with whom you can, but only with whom you must.
7. Do not hesitate to carry out the most dangerous deeds, should this be demanded by the good of the Cause.
8. Treat the enemies of Your Nation with hatred and ruthlessness.
9. Neither pleading, nor threats, nor torture, nor death shall compel You to betray a secret.
10. Aspire to expand the power, wealth, and glory of the Ukrainian State.

Source: OUN v svitli postanov Velykykh Zboriv, Konferentsii ta inshykh dokumentiv z borotby 1929–1955 r. (The OUN as Reflected in Resolutions of the Grand Assemblies, Conferences, and Other Documents from the Struggle, 1929–1955) (n.p., 1955), 16. Translated by Taras F. Pidzamecky, Roman Waschuk, and Andriy Wynnyckyj.

Note

The Decalogue was the OUN's statement of principles, which every OUN member was expected to memorize. It was written by a leading member, Stepan Lenkavsky (1904–77), and first published as an insert in the underground newspaper *Surma* in the summer of 1929.

In the original 1929 version of the Decalogue, the published text begins with: "I am the spirit of the eternal natural force which protected you from the Tatar hordes and placed you on the frontier of two worlds to create a new life." Several other sections read differently from the version translated here, and it is not known when the newer version became official. The different sections are: "(7) Do not hesitate to commit the greatest crime, if the good of the Cause demands it"; (8) "Regard the enemies of Your Nation with hate and perfidy"; (10) "Aspire to expand the strength, riches, and size of the Ukrainian State even by means of enslaving foreigners." See Petro Mirchuk, *Narys istorii Orhanizatsii ukrainskykh natsionalistiv*, vol. 1, *1920–1939* (Munich-London-New York, 1968), 126–7; and Alexander J. Motyl, *The Turn to the Right: The Ideological Origins and Development of Ukrainian Nationalism, 1919–1929* (Boulder, Colo., 1980), 142–3. (Ed.)

3. *Einsatzkommando* Order against the Bandera Movement

25 NOVEMBER 1941

Einsatzkommando C/5
der Sicherheitspolizei und SD
-Kdo-Tgb. Nr. 12432/41

O.V., 25 November, 1941
G.R.S.

To the Outposts in: Kiev
                           Dnipropetrovske
                           Mykolaiv
                           Rivne
                           Zhytomyr
                           Vinnytsia

Re: OUN (Bandera Movement)

It has been established beyond doubt that the Bandera movement is preparing an uprising in the *Reichskommissariat* with the final goal of creating an independent Ukraine. All functionaries of the Bandera movement are to be arrested immediately and, after a thorough investigation, are to be secretly liquidated as looters.

This letter is to be destroyed immediately after being read by the Kommando leader.

                           [illegible signature]
                           SS-*Obersturmbannführer*

Source: Roman Ilnytzkyj, *Deutschland und die Ukraine, 1934–1945: Ein Vorbericht* (Germany and Ukraine, 1934–1945: A Preliminary Report), 2 vols. (Munich: Osteuropa-Institut, 1956), 2:338–9. Translated by Roman Waschuk.

4. Letter from Alfred Rosenberg to General Keitel on Nazi Treatment of Soviet Prisoners of War

28 FEBRUARY 1942

... The fate of Soviet prisoners of war in Germany is, on the contrary, a tragedy of the greatest dimensions. Of the 3.6 million prisoners of war, today only several hundred thousand are completely fit for work. A large portion of them have starved to death or have died of exposure because of the inclemency of the weather. Thousands have also succumbed to typhus. It is obvious that the feeding of such masses of prisoners of war will encounter difficulties. Nevertheless, had there been a certain amount of understanding for the aims of German policy, death and demoralization on such a scale could have been avoided. For example, according to reports we have received, within [the former boundaries of] the Soviet Union, the civilian population was completely prepared to supply food for the prisoners of war. Several understanding camp commandants followed this route with success. In the majority of cases, however, the camp commandants forbade the civilian population from supplying the prisoners of war with food and preferred to leave them to die of starvation. The civilian population was also not allowed to give food to the prisoners of war during their march to the camps. Indeed, in many cases, when hungry and exhausted prisoners of war could no longer continue with the march, they were shot before the eyes of the horrified civilian population and their bodies were left to lie where they fell. In many camps, no shelter at all was provided for the prisoners of war. They lay there, exposed to the rain and snow. They were not even provided with the equipment to dig themselves foxholes or caves. Systematic delousing of prisoners of war in the camps and of the camps themselves has obviously been neglected. Utterances have been heard, such as: "The more of the prisoners who die, the better it is for us." The result of this approach is that typhus has become widespread through the release or escape of prisoners of war and has claimed victories from among the German *Wehrmacht* and the civilian population, even in the old Reich. Finally, one must also mention the shootings of prisoners of war which, in part, were carried out on the basis of viewpoints which are devoid of any political sense. [. . .]

The treatment of prisoners of war seems to be founded to a great extent on completely incorrect notions about the peoples of the Soviet Union. One encounters the view that the peoples become increasingly inferior, the further east one goes. If the Poles must be treated harshly then, so the argument goes, the same applies on a much larger scale to the Ukrainians, Belorussians, Russians and, finally, the "Asiatics". . . .

Source: International Military Tribunal, *Trial of the Major War Criminals before the International Military Tribunal*, 42 vols. (Nuremberg, 1947–9), 25: 156–61. Translated by Roman Waschuk.

Note

Alfred Rosenberg joined the Nazi Party in 1919. He was the party's official "philosopher" and a leading proponent of Nazi racial theory and of the *Führer* mystique. In 1941 he became Minister of the Occupied Eastern Territories. At the Nuremberg Trials he was condemned to death as a war criminal and executed in 1946. (Ed.)

5. Memorandum from Alfred Rosenberg to Adolf Hitler on Nazi Policy toward Ukrainians

16 MARCH 1942

A variety of partly mutually contradictory requests from the *Wehrmacht* High Command which are based on opinions expressed by the *Führer* have induced me to ask the *Führer* to make a decision in the following question of principle as well as political tactics.

The aims of German policy, notably in Ukraine, have been set by the *Führer*: the exploitation and mustering of natural resources; the settlement of Germans in certain regions; no artificial intellectualization of the population, but rather the maintenance of its capacity for work; otherwise, a general lack of interest in the remaining internal developments. As a consequence of this, there arise for the future fixed and, depending on circumstances and the behaviour of the population, harsh governmental measures for the securing of German interests. Certain persons have seized upon this view and come to the conclusion that it should be stated everywhere possible using drastic phraseology, such as: "a colonial people that, like the Negroes, should be handled with the whip," "a Slavic people which must be kept as ignorant as possible," "the establishment of churches and sects so that they may be played off against one another," etc. This talk has continued to circulate despite a directive approved by the *Führer* to the *Reichskommissar* of Ukraine, and all those who have visited Ukraine have reported about the consequences of this talk, namely that it is precisely this repeatedly displayed contemptuous attitude that often has worse effects on the willingness to work than all other measures. The representatives of the *Wehrmacht* have urgently requested that we see to the pacification of the Ukrainian population so as to hinder sabotage and the formation of partisan bands. It seems to me that talk of this sort harms rather than serves the German interest. Having continuously observed things in the Occupied Eastern Territories, I believe that German policy can have a certain, perhaps even contemptuous opinion of the characteristics of the subject peoples, but that it is not the task of the German political representation to proclaim measures and views which will, in the end, drive the subject population to sheer desperation, instead of encouraging the desired productive labour. The frequently-made reference to India seems entirely wrong to me in *this* respect. England exploited India to a great extent and divided it into power-groups, but it never *broadcast* this division and exploitation. On the contrary, it has instead emphasized for decades what *benefits* it has brought to the land and has, by means of some concessions, created a basis for this sort of propaganda.

While we must, as part of our internal policy, openly and aggressively announce to our entire people our antagonistic aspirations towards others, the political leadership in the East should remain *silent* at times when German policy dictates harshness; it should keep silent about its perhaps disparaging view of the subject peoples. Yes, an intelligent German policy can, under certain circumstances, achieve more for German interests by means of insignificant concessions and a little human kindness than by means of overt, unthinking brutality.

Because the results of the earlier approach have been manifesting themselves everywhere, despite many admonitions, I intend to send the *Reichskommissar* of Ukraine the attached decree. I ask the *Führer* to decide about this memorandum and the draft decree.

Source: International Military Tribunal, *Trial of the Major War Criminals before the International Military Tribunal*, 42 vols. (Nuremberg, 1947–9), 25: 97–8. Translated by Roman Waschuk.

6. Erich Koch on the Economic Exploitation of Ukraine

26-8 AUGUST 1942

... The *Gauleiter* came directly from *Führer* Headquarters and brought with him extraordinarily complimentary words of thanks from the *Führer* for the work of the *La-Führer* [agricultural leaders]. He described the political situation and his tasks as *Reichskommissar* as follows: There is no free Ukraine. The goal of our work must be that the Ukrainians work for Germany and not that we ensure the happiness of the people. Ukraine must deliver that which Germany lacks. This task must be carried out without regard for losses. In every country in Europe, the situation is better than it is here. Food supplies in the Reich are based on ration cards. The black market is limited in its extent. Among other peoples, the black market is the basis, and ration cards are issued as a supplement. The food situation in Germany is serious. Production is already falling under the influence of the bad food situation. An increase in the bread ration is a political necessity in order to carry on the war victoriously. The quantities of grain which are lacking must be procured from Ukraine. The *Führer* has made the *Gauleiter* personally responsible for ensuring that these quantities will be secured. In view of this task the feeding of the Ukrainian civilian population is of absolutely no concern. Through its black marketeering, it lives better than we think. There can be no discussion about the new levies. The *Führer* has demanded 3 million tonnes of grain from Ukraine for the Reich, and this must be provided. He does not wish to hear discussions about the lack of transportation facilities. The transport problem must be solved through one's own inventiveness.

Source: International Military Tribunal, *Trial of the Major War Criminals before the International Military Tribunal*, 42 vols. (Nuremberg, 1947–9), 25: 317–18. Translated by Roman Waschuk. Koch's speech was included in a secret, unsigned note about a conference held in Rivne on 26–28 August.

7. Memorandum from Erich Koch to Alfred Rosenberg on Harsh Measures Adopted in Ukraine by the German Administration

16 MARCH 1943

The Ukrainian émigrés have, meanwhile, also succeeded in gaining influence in the Bandera and Melnyk movements, so that today both of them act in an intentionally anti-German fashion. "Prosvita," to the extent that it exists, is also used as a front organization for Ukrainian chauvinists. For examples of this, please see SD reports. Proof of this has been produced in Rivne, Dunaivtsi [Dunajezy], Kamianets-Podilskyi and Kiev. In Kiev, the Ukrainians, including those who belonged to German social circles, had prepared to assassinate the *Generalkommissar* by poisoning. Ukrainian teachers from "Prosvita" have joined resistance groups, as for example in Kamin-Kashirskyi (see SD report for 27 and 31 June 1942). I gather from the most recent SD reports that, under the mild hand of the German leadership of the operational front zone, a sort of Ukrainian national government could be formed at the "Prosvita" in Kharkiv. I point out in connection with this that, apart from the gentlemen in your Main Political Affairs Section, it was always the representatives of the rear area services in the operational front zone who demanded a different treatment of the Ukrainians than that which occurred in my *Reichskommissariat*. The Ukrainian nationalists from Kharkiv have now been evacuated to Kiev. There they have told [our] reliable Ukrainian informants that very soon a world conference of Ukrainians will take place. They speak of a change in Germany's Ukrainian policy in the coming weeks. They demand independent military units for Ukraine. They insist that the newspapers appearing in my *Reichskommissariat* should be edited in a Ukrainian national spirit, and declare that, if these demands are met, they are ready to demonstrate a conditional loyalty to the Germans.

The Ukrainian émigrés make up a separate chapter of my political work. It must, unfortunately, be stated that here, too, there are differences in political attitude between your ministry and myself. It is not prejudice that has shaped my negative attitude to the Ukrainian émigrés but extensive experience during my activities in Ukraine. . . .

I refer, for example, to the New Year's message of the UNO [19] 42/43, which demonstrates political impudence.[1] It contains no greetings, but crass political demands: the demand for national freedom and state independence. The demands are simultaneously mixed with threats, in the event that the Ukrainian claims would not be complied with.

I was strengthened in my attitude towards the émigrés by a statement made by the *Führer*, passed on to me through official channels, to the effect that these émigrés demoralize the people, and that he would have had them shot at the beginning of the Eastern campaign if he had had a clear idea of their attitude then. I regret that this clarity has not yet made its way into all departments of your ministry. . . .

Source: International Military Tribunal, *Trial of the Major War Criminals before the International Military Tribunal*, 42 vols. (Nuremberg, 1947–9), 25: 270–2. Translated by Roman Waschuk.

Note

1 The UNO New Year's message refers to the *Ukrainske natsionalne obiednannia*, a Ukrainian social and cultural organization in Germany under OUN-M influence. (Ed.)

8. Appeal to Ukrainian Citizens and Youth by the Ukrainian Central Committee President on the Formation of the Galician Division

6 MAY 1943

The long-awaited moment has arrived when the Ukrainian people will again have the opportunity to come out with gun in hand to do battle against its most grievous foe – Bolshevism.[1] The *Führer* of the Greater German Reich has agreed to the formation of a separate Ukrainian volunteer military unit under the name SS Riflemen's Division "Halychyna."

Thus we must take advantage of this historic opportunity; we must take up arms because our national honour, our national interest, demands it.

Veterans of the struggles for independence, officers and men of the Ukrainian Galician Army! Twenty-two years ago you parted with your weapons when all strength to resist had ebbed. The blood of your fellows who fell on the Fields of Glory calls upon you to finish the deed already begun, to fulfill the oath you swore in 1918. You must stand shoulder to shoulder with the invincible German army and destroy, once and for all, the Bolshevik[2] beast, which insatiably gorges itself on the blood of our people and strives with all of its barbarity to arrive at our total ruination.

You must avenge the innocent blood of your brothers tortured to death in the Solovets Islands camps, in Siberia, in Kazakhstan, the millions of brothers starved to extinction on our bountiful fields by the Bolshevik collectivizers.

You, who followed the thorny but heroic path of the Ukrainian Galician Army, understand more than anyone what it is to fight in the face of uneven odds. You realize that one can only face an enemy such as Red Moscow shoulder to shoulder with an army capable of destroying the Red monster.

The failures of the anti-Bolshevik forces of the European Entente in the years 1918 to 1920 testify irrevocably that there is only one nation capable of conquering the USSR – Germany. For twenty-two years you waited with sacred patience for the holy war against the barbarous Red hordes menacing Europe.

It goes without saying that, in this titanic struggle, the fate of the Ukrainian people is also being decided. Thus, we must fully realize the importance of this moment and play a military role in this struggle. Now the battle is not uneven, it is not hopeless. Now, the greatest military power in the world stands opposed to our eternal foe.

Now or never!
Youth of Ukraine!
I turn to you with particular attention and call upon you to join the SS Riflemen's Division "Halychyna." You were born at the dawn of the great age, when the new history of Ukraine began to be written in crimson Blood and golden Glory.

When your fathers and elder brothers, first and alone in all of Europe, took up arms against the most fearful enemy of Ukraine and of all humanity;

When your brothers, inflamed as you are now, first wrote into history the peerless heroic deeds at the Battle of Kruty;[3]

When your brothers covered themselves with the glory of the first Winter Campaigns against the Bolshevik monster;

When they, in the midst of a newly "peaceful" Europe, were the first to go forth against the Bolshevik invader in the second Winter Campaign, writing into history the heroic deeds of the Battle of Bazar;[4]

It was then that You, our Youth, were born, then that You grew, as across the whole of Ukraine revolts rose up against the Bolshevik invader, who by ruin, famine, exile, torture, and murder strove to wipe our nation from the face of the earth. Then You, our Ukrainian Youth, laid your colossal sacred sacrifices on the altar of your Fatherland. You burned with the sacred fire of love for it, hardened your spirit for it, readied yourself for the right moment of reckoning by arms. With longing in your heart, with glowing embers in Your soul, You waited for this moment.

And now this moment has come.

Dear Youth, I believe that your patriotism, your selflessness, your readiness for armed deeds, are not mere hollow words, that these are your deep-set feelings and convictions. I believe that You suffered deeply and understood the painful experiences of the past struggles for independence, and that You culled from them a clear sense of political realism, a thorough understanding of the national interest and a hardy readiness for the greatest of sacrifices for it. I believe in You, dear Youth, I believe that You will not idle while the Great Moment passes by, that you will prove to the whole world who you are, what you are worth, and what you are capable of.

Ukrainian Citizens!

I call upon you for great vigilance. The enemy does not sleep. In the memorable years of 1917–19, enemy propaganda lulled our people with lofty words about eternal peace, about the brotherhood of nations. Now this propaganda aims to tear weapons from our hands once again, and disseminates among us countless absurd slogans, groundless conjectures, febrile dreams. You know where this propaganda originates. You know its purpose. Counter it decisively, even when it comes forth under a Ukrainian guise, guilefully exploiting the uninformed and confused among the Ukrainian people. You know the value of arms, and thus I believe that, with God's assistance, You will worthily pass the test of political maturity to which history has put you.

Ukrainian Citizens!

The time of waiting, the time of debilitation and suffering has come to an end. Now, the great moment of armed deeds has also come for our people. Side by side with the heroic army of Greater Germany and the volunteers of other

European peoples, we too come forth to battle our greatest national foe and threat to all civilization. The cause is sacred and great and therefore it demands of us great efforts and sacrifices.

I believe that these efforts and sacrifices are the hard but certain road to our Glorious Future.

Dr. Volodymyr Kubiiovych
President
Ukrainian Central Committee

Source: *Krakivski visti* (Cracow News), 16 May 1943. Translated by Andriy Wynnyckyj.

Notes

1 In the daily newspaper *Lvivski visti* (Lviv), 6 May 1943, the words "Muscovite-Jewish Bolshevism" were inserted here, whereas in Kubiiovych's original version, from which this translation is taken, no such wording exists. The original version, with minor grammatical changes, can also be found in the weekly newspaper, *Krakivski visti*, 16 May 1943. The reasons for the differences between the Lviv and Cracow texts lies in the fact that the Lviv newspaper was under the careful scrutiny of Georg Lehmann, a Nazi official in charge of the press in Galicia. The Lviv newspaper was an official organ of the Press and Journal Publications Branch of the *Generalgouvernement*, whereas the Cracow newspaper was the organ of Ukrainske Vydavnytstvo, an independent commercial publishing concern with very close ties to the Ukrainian Central Committee headed by Kubiiovych. It should also be noted that press censorship was somewhat more lenient in Cracow than it was in Lviv. For more details, see Kost Pankivsky, *Roky nimetskoi okupatsii 1941–1944* (New York–Toronto, 1965), 91–92, 116–18, 276, 344–5. (Ed.)

2 The words "Jewish-Bolshevik monster" appear in the *Lvivski visti* version. See note 1. (Ed.)

3 This battle took place on 29 January 1918, when a force of 600 Ukrainian cadets attempted to stop a 4,000-strong Red Army force along the Moscow-Bakhmach-Kiev railway line. Almost all the cadets were killed, and their deaths became a symbol of selfless patriotism and sacrifice. (Ed.)

4 An engagement of the Second Winter Campaign or "November Raid" of 1921. The government and army of the ousted Ukrainian People's Republic, exiled in Poland, decided to initiate a military campaign against the Bolsheviks. On 17 November the Ukrainian army was surrounded by the Red Army at Bazar; 443 soldiers were taken prisoner and 359 were shot. (Ed.)

9. Programmatic and Political Resolutions of the Organization of Ukrainian Nationalists' Third Congress

21–5 AUGUST 1943

The Organization of Ukrainian Nationalists is fighting for an independent, united Ukrainian state and for the right of every nation to lead a free life in its own independent state. The only way to effect a just solution to the national and social problem in the world is to bring an end to the subjugation and exploitation of one nation by another and to establish a system of free nations existing in their own independent states.

The OUN is fighting against imperialism and against empires, for within empires, one ruling nation culturally and politically subjugates and economically exploits other nations. For this reason, the OUN is fighting against the USSR and against Germany's "New Europe."

The OUN is resolutely fighting against both internationalist and fascist national-socialist programs and political concepts, because they are the tools of imperialist policies of conquest. Thus, we are opposed both to Russian Communist Bolshevism and German National Socialism.

The OUN is opposed to any nation, intent on fulfilling its imperialist goals, "liberating," "taking under its protection," or "into its care" other nations, for these deceptive phrases conceal a repugnant reality: subjugation, coercion and plunder. For this reason, the OUN will struggle against the Russian-Bolshevik and German plunderers until it rids Ukraine of all "protectors" and "liberators," until it attains an independent, united Ukrainian state in which peasants, workers and intellectuals will be able to live and develop in a free, prosperous and cultured manner.

The OUN is for the full liberation of the Ukrainian people from the Russian-Bolshevik and German yoke; it is for the establishment of an independent, united Ukrainian state free of landowners and capitalists, as well as of Bolshevik commissars, NKVD agents and party parasites.

In the Ukrainian state, the governing power will regard serving the interests of the people as its highest duty. Since it will have no plans for conquest, nor any subject countries or oppressed nations within its state, the national government of Ukraine will not waste time, energy or financial resources on establishing an apparatus of oppression. The Ukrainian national regime will direct all economic resources and all human energies toward establishing a new political order and a just social system, toward building up the economy of the country and raising the cultural level of the people.

Within the ranks of the OUN, Ukrainian peasants, workers, and intellectuals are fighting against their oppressors for an independent, united Ukrainian state, for national and social liberation, for a new political and social order:

1.a) For the destruction of the Bolsheviks' and the Germans' exploitative system of serfdom in the organization of the rural economy. Since the land is the property of the people, the Ukrainian national regime will not impose on farmers any one method of working the land. In the Ukrainian state, both individual and collective work on the land will be permitted; the method will depend upon the will of the farmers.

  b) For a free transfer to peasants in western Ukrainian *oblasts* of all lands held by landowners, monasteries and churches.

2.a) For state ownership of large-scale industry and co-operative ownership of small-scale industry.

  b) For the participation of workers in the direction of factories; for directors to be chosen on the basis of expertise, rather than on the commissar-party principle.[1]

3.a) For a universal eight-hour work day. Overtime will have to be consented to freely – like all work in general – and will have to bring the worker additional wages.

  b) For fair wages for work; for the participation of workers in the profits of commercial enterprises. Every worker will receive a wage sufficient to meet the material and spiritual needs of his entire household. During the period when annual financial reviews of commercial enterprises are carried out, every worker will receive the following: in co-operative enterprises – a dividend (his share of the yearly profits): in state-owned enterprises – a premium.

  c) For freedom in work, a free choice of profession, and free choice of the place of work.

  d) For free trade unions. For the abolition of the Stakhanov work method,[2] socialist competition, increasing norms and other methods of exploiting workers.

4. For freedom in the trades; for the right of tradesmen to unite voluntarily in workmen's associations; for the right of the tradesman to leave the association in order to pursue his work on an individual basis and to dispose freely of his income.

5. For state ownership of large business; for co-operative and private ownership of small business; for free marketplaces.

6. For full equality of women with men in all the rights and obligations of citizenship; for free access for women to all schools and all professions; for the fundamental right of women to engage in physically lighter work, so that women will not be obliged to ruin their health by seeking employment in mines and other heavy industries. For state protection of motherhood. Fathers will receive, in addition to wages for their work, a supplementary payment for the support of their wives and of children

who have not yet reached the age of majority. Only in these conditions will women have the opportunity to carry out their important, honourable and responsible duties as mothers and educators of the younger generation.

7.a) For compulsory secondary education. For raising the educational and cultural level of the population by increasing the numbers of schools, publishers, libraries, museums, cinemas, theatres, and similar institutions.

   b) For increased advanced and professional training: for a continual growth of cadres of highly qualified specialists in every field of human endeavour.

   c) For free access by young people to all institutions of higher learning. For ensuring students' ability to pursue their studies by providing stipends, food, accommodation, and the equipment necessary for education.

   d) For a harmonious, all-round development of the younger generation in the moral, intellectual and physical spheres. For free access to all the scientific and cultural achievements of mankind.

8. For respect for the work of intellectuals. For creating material conditions for intellectual work that will ensure the well-being of the intellectual's family, so that he can be free to devote himself to his cultural and creative work and constantly increase his knowledge and raise his intellectual and cultural level.

9.a) For full protection of all workers in old age and in case of illness or handicap.

   b) For the establishment of universal health care; for the expansion of the network of hospitals, sanatoriums, health resorts and rest homes. For expanding the medical cadres. For the right of workers to have access, without payment, to all health institutions.

   c) For special state protection of children and youths; for an expansion of the network of nurseries, kindergartens, sanatoria and recreation camps; for the inclusion of all children and youths in the programs of state institutions dedicated to care and education.

10.a) For freedom of the press, speech, thought, convictions, worship and world-view. Against the official imposition on society of any doctrines or dogmas with regard to world-view.

   b) For the freedom to profess and practice any religion which does not run counter to the morals of society.

   c) For the separation of church organizations from the state.

   d) For cultural relations with other nations; for the right of citizens to go abroad for education, medical treatment or in order to learn about the life and cultural achievements of other nations.

11. For the full right of national minorities to cultivate their own national cultures.

12. For equality of all citizens of Ukraine, whatever their nationality, with regard to the rights and obligations of citizenship; for an equal right for all to work, remuneration, and rest.

13. For a free, fully Ukrainian culture; for a spirit of heroism and a high moral standard; for civic solidarity, friendship and discipline.

II. POLITICAL RESOLUTIONS

1. *The International Situation*

1. The present war is a typical war between competing imperialist powers for domination of the world, for a new division of material wealth, for the acquisition of new sources of raw materials and markets and for the exploitation of labour.

2. The warring imperialist powers are not bringing the world any progressive political or social ideas. In particular, Germany's so-called "New Europe" and Moscow's "Soviet Union" are a denial of the right of nations to free political and cultural development within their own states; instead, they bring all nations political and social enslavement. For this reason, a victory for the imperialist powers in the current war and an organization of the world according to imperialist principles would bring only a momentary pause in the war and would soon lead to new collisions between the imperialist powers over the division of war spoils and to new conflicts. At the same time, the liberation movements of the nations subjugated by the imperialist powers would become the seeds of new conflicts and revolutions. Thus, a victory for the imperialist powers in the present war would lead to chaos and to further suffering for millions of people within the captive nations.

3. At this time, the present imperialist war has entered a decisive phase, which is characterized by:
   a) the exhaustion of the imperialist powers,
   b) an increase in the contradictions between the imperialist powers,
   c) a growth in the struggle of the captive nations.

   At the same time, the present war is serving as an external auxiliary factor, bringing nearer the time of the outbreak of national and social revolutions inside the captive nations.

4. The reactionary and anti-popular plans of German racist imperialism to enslave other nations, the Germans' terroristic practices on occupied territories and the captive nations' battle against the so-called New Europe have hastened the complete political collapse of German imperialism. Now, as a result of the blows dealt by her imperialist opponents and of the liberation struggle waged by the captive nations, Germany is also nearing an inevitable military defeat.

5. Bolshevik Russia, ideologically and politically compromised and materially weakened, is making use of the Germans' terroristic policy on occupied territories and of the provisions supplied by the Allies for continuing the war.

   Only the fear of German occupation and the internal Stalinist terror are compelling the soldiers of the Red Army to continue fighting. The enormous losses of human life and military equipment are deepening the internal crisis of the Russian imperialist regime. The shortage of food in the country, along with the landing of the Allies in Europe, and the threat posed as a result to Soviet plans, are compelling the Bolsheviks to accelerate their own offensive. The aim of the Bolsheviks is to pursue, under the guise of their so-called defence of the fatherland, revived Slavophilism,[3] and pseudo-revolutionary rhetoric, the goals of Russian imperialism, that is, to gain dominion over Europe and, eventually, the entire world. The point of departure for the fulfillment of Moscow's imperialist plans is Ukraine, with all her natural wealth. Further bases for fulfilling the plans of Russian imperialism are the Balkans, the Baltic region, and Scandinavia.

6. In spite of the differences that exist among the Allies, they are waging the war for the destruction of their rivals, above all, of German imperialism. The Allies' next task is the destruction of Japanese imperialism. In order to bring about the destruction of these opponents, the Allies are making use of Russian imperialism and will attempt to do so as long as possible. At the same time, the domination of Europe by the Bolsheviks is not in the interest of the Allies and they are attempting in the present war to weaken, and eventually destroy, Russian imperialism. The continuation of the war on the eastern front and the mutual destruction of German and Russian imperialism are in accord with the interests of the Allies. The goal of the Allies – especially Britain – on the European continent is the defeat, or at least the substantial weakening, of all the imperialist states of Europe and the establishment of an order which would guarantee them a decisive voice in Europe and give free rein to Anglo-Saxon political and economic influences. In order to attain these goals, the Allies are gaining control or are attempting to gain control of the most important bases around and inside Europe (Sicily, the Apennine and Balkan peninsulas, Scandinavia and the Caucasus).

7. The captive nations and their struggle for liberation constitute one of the most important elements in the further development of the current political situation. The military superiority of the imperialist powers at the present moment still prevents a full manifestation of the powers of the captive nations. But in measure with the deepening of the war crisis, the strength of the captive nations is increasing and the moment of national and social revolutions is approaching; the captive nations are becoming a new, decisive political factor. Only on a platform of a new political concept with regard to the captive nations, a concept which, in opposition to the imperialist powers, guarantees every nation the right to its own national state and grants it social justice, can a just order be built and a lasting peace maintained among nations.

8. The approaching military collapse of Germany in the East and the complete ideological and political bankruptcy of Soviet imperialism have set the captive nations of the East the task of fighting against imperialist oppressors in order to rebuild the East along the new principles of freedom for nations, autonomy in free, independent states and the liberation of nations and individuals from political oppression and economic exploitation. Only by way of national and social revolutions, waged by the captive nations of the East for the sake of new progressive ideas and struggle against imperialism, can Russian Bolshevik imperialism be destroyed.

9. Ukraine stands at the centre of the present imperialist war. Russian and German imperialists are fighting for the domination and exploitation of

Ukraine. At the same time, Ukraine, as the bearer of progressive ideas to all the captive nations, is becoming a decisive factor in the preparation of revolutions in the East. Ukraine is the first country in the East to have raised the flag of resolute struggle by captive nations against the imperialists, and she will begin the period of national and social revolutions. Only through a common struggle of the Ukrainian people with those of other captive nations of the East can Bolshevism be defeated. The rebuilding of an independent, united Ukrainian state will guarantee the rebuilding and permanent existence of the national states of other nations of eastern, southeastern and northern Europe and of the captive nations of Asia. Only with the existence of a Ukrainian state can permanent existence be guaranteed for those nations which, in mutual understanding and co-operation based on the principles of the right of every nation to have its own state, a just social order and economic independence, oppose all the covetous plans of hostile imperialist powers. In this way, lasting peace and the peaceful national, social, and cultural development of these nations will be guaranteed.

Source: Peter J. Potichnyj and Yevhen Shtendera, eds., *The Political Thought of the Ukrainian Underground* (forthcoming); reprinted with permission. See also *Ideia i chyn* 2, no. 5 (1943): 1–10 (partial text). Original copy: archives of the Foreign Representation of the Ukrainian Supreme Liberation Council, New York; photocopy: archives of *Litopys UPA*.

Notes

1 This is a reference to the *nomenklatura* system, one of the main instruments of political control in the USSR. Positions in state, economic, and social institutions and organizations are filled exclusively on the recommendation of party organs by persons from special lists compiled for that purpose. (Ed.)

2 The Stakhanov movement was a form of "socialist competition" that attempted to establish high records of productivity. Formally, it was considered a voluntary expression of workers' initiative, but in reality it was organized by directives from above. (Ed.)

3 Slavophiles were the nineteenth-century conservative Russian intelligentsia. (Ed.)

10. What is the Ukrainian Insurgent Army Fighting For?[1]

AUGUST 1943

The Ukrainian Insurgent Army (UPA) is fighting for an independent, united Ukrainian state and for the right of every nation to lead a free life in its own independent state. The only way to effect a just solution to the national and social problem in the world is to bring an end to the subjugation and exploitation of one nation by another and to establish a system of free nations existing in their own independent states.

The UPA is fighting against imperialism and against empires, for within empires, one ruling nation culturally and politically subjugates and economically exploits other nations. For this reason, the UPA is fighting against the USSR and against Germany's "New Europe."

The UPA is resolutely fighting against both internationalist and fascist national-socialist programs and political concepts, because they are the tools of imperialist policies of conquest. Thus, we are opposed both to Russian Communist Bolshevism and German National Socialism.

The UPA is opposed to any nation, intent on fulfilling its imperialistic goals, "liberating," "taking under its protection," or "into its care" other nations, for these deceptive phrases conceal a repugnant reality: subjugation, coercion, and plunder. For this reason, the UPA will struggle against the Russian-Bolshevik and German plunderers until it rids Ukraine of all "protectors" and "liberators," until it attains an independent, united Ukrainian state in which peasants, workers, and intellectuals will be able to live and develop in a free, prosperous, and cultured manner.

The UPA is for the full liberation of the Ukrainian people from the Russian Bolshevik yoke; it is for the establishment of an independent, united Ukrainian state free of landowners and capitalists, as well as of Bolshevik commissars, NKVD agents, and party parasites.

In the Ukrainian state, the governing power will regard serving the interests of the people as its highest duty. Since it will have no plans for conquest, nor any subject countries or oppressed nations within its state, the national government of Ukraine will not waste time, energy, or financial resources on establishing an apparatus of oppression. The Ukrainian national regime will direct all economic resources and all human energies toward establishing a new political order and a just social system, toward building up the economy of the country and raising the cultural level of the people.

Within the ranks of the UPA, Ukrainian peasants, workers and intellectuals are fighting against their oppressors for an independent, united Ukrainian state, for national and social liberation, for a new political and social order:

1. For the destruction of the Bolsheviks' exploitative system of serfdom in the organization of the rural economy. Since the land is the property of the people, the Ukrainian national regime will not impose on farmers any one method of working the land. In the Ukrainian state, both individual and collective work on the land will be permitted; the method will depend upon the will of the farmers.

2.a) For state ownership of large-scale industry and co-operative ownership of small-scale industry.

   b) For the participation of workers in the direction of factories; for directors to be chosen on the basis of expertise, rather than on the commissar-party principle.[2]

3.a) For a universal eight-hour work day. Overtime will have to be consented to freely – like all work in general – and will have to bring the worker additional wages.

   b) For fair wages for work; for the participation of workers in the profits of commercial enterprises. Every worker will receive a wage sufficient to meet the material and spiritual needs of his entire household. During the period when annual financial reviews of commercial enterprises are carried out, every worker will receive the following: in co-operative enterprises – a dividend, in state-owned enterprises – a premium.

   c) For freedom in work, a free choice of profession, and a free choice of the place of work.

   d) For free trade unions. For the abolition of the Stakhanov work method,[3] socialist competition, increasing norms, and other methods of exploiting workers.

4. For freedom in the trades; for the right of tradesmen to unite voluntarily in workmen's associations; for the right of the tradesman to leave the association in order to pursue his work on an individual basis and to dispose freely of his income.

5. For state ownership of large business; for co-operative and private ownership of small business; for free marketplaces.

6. For full equality of women with men in all the rights and obligations of citizenship; for free access for women to all schools and all professions; for the fundamental right of women to engage in physically lighter work, so that women will not be obliged to ruin their health by seeking employment in mines and other heavy industries. For state protection of motherhood. Fathers will receive, in addition to wages for their work, a supplementary payment for the support of their wives and of children who have not yet reached the age of majority. Only in these conditions will women have the opportunity to carry out their important, honourable, and responsible duties as mothers and educators of the younger generation.

7.a) For compulsory secondary education. For raising the educational and cultural level of the population by increasing the numbers of schools, publishers, libraries, museums, cinemas, theatres, and similar institutions.

b) For increased advanced and professional training: for a continual growth of cadres of highly qualified specialists in every field of human endeavour.

c) For free access by young people to all institutions of higher learning. For ensuring students' ability to pursue their studies by providing stipends, food, accommodation, and the equipment necessary for education.

d) For a harmonious, all-round development of the younger generation in the moral, intellectual, and physical spheres. For free access to all the scientific and cultural achievements of mankind.

8. For respect for the work of intellectuals. For creating material conditions for intellectual work that will ensure the well-being of the intellectual's family, so that he can be free to devote himself to his cultural and creative work and constantly increase his knowledge and raise his intellectual and cultural level.

9.a) For full protection of all workers in old age and in case of illness or handicap.

b) For the establishment of universal health care; for the expansion of the network of hospitals, sanatoria, health resorts, and rest homes. For expanding the medical cadres. For the right of workers to have access, without payment, to all health institutions.

c) For special state protection of children and youths; for an expansion of the network of nurseries, kindergartens, sanatoria, and recreation camps; for the inclusion of all children and youths in the programs of state institutions dedicated to care and education.

10.a) For freedom of the press, speech, thought, convictions, worship, and world-view. Against the official imposition on society of any doctrines or dogmas with regard to world-view.

b) For the freedom to profess and practice any religion which does not run counter to the morals of society.

c) For the separation of church organizations from the state.

d) For cultural relations with other nations; for the right of citizens to go abroad for education, medical treatment, or in order to learn about the life and cultural achievements of other nations.

11. For the full right of national minorities to cultivate their own national cultures.

12. For equality of all citizens of Ukraine, whatever their nationality, with regard to the rights and obligations of citizenship; for an equal right for all to remuneration and rest.

13. For a free, fully Ukrainian culture; for a spirit of heroism and a high moral standard; for civic solidarity, friendship, and discipline.

Ukrainian Insurgent Army
August 1943
Republished 1949

Source: Peter J. Potichnyj and Yevhen Shtendera, eds., *The Political Thought of the Ukrainian Underground* (forthcoming); reprinted with permission. Original copy: Folio of Leaflets, archives of the Foreign Representation of the Ukrainian Supreme Liberation Council, New York; photocopy: archives of *Litopys UPA*; reprinted in Litopys UPA (Toronto, 1978), 1: 126–31.

Notes

1 This is a revised edition of the document "What is the Revolutionary-Liberationist UPA Fighting For?" initially signed by the OUN leadership. (Ed.)
2 The reference is to the *nomenklatura* system, one of the main instruments of political control in the USSR. Positions in state, economic, and social institutions and organizations are filled exclusively on the recommendation of party organs by persons from special lists compiled for that purpose. (Ed.)
3 See document 9, note 2. (Ed.)

11. Platform of the Ukrainian Supreme Liberation Council

11–15 JULY 1944

1. The Ukrainian national-liberation movement, the establishment of an independent Ukrainian state, and the struggle for its consolidation in the years 1917–21 deepened the national consciousness and increased the political activity of the Ukrainian masses.

   The collapse of the Ukrainian state as a result of foreign conquest, which was brought about by insufficient internal unity of the Ukrainian national forces, made it easier for foreigners to gain dominion over Ukraine. This foreign domination has been marked by unprecedented oppression, massive plunder of the Ukrainian people, a return of peasants and workers to a state of true serfdom, merciless exploitation, and the extermination of millions of people by means of famine and terror. These terrible and bloody times, twenty-five years in duration, have taught the Ukrainian masses that no foreign political and social system will bring benefit to them, and that only the establishment of their own national sovereign state will guarantee a normal life and development of the nation and its culture and the material and spiritual well-being of the masses.

2. The present war between two enormous imperialist powers, Soviet Russia and Nazi Germany, is being waged primarily for domination over Ukraine as a point of departure to dominion over Eastern Europe and even all of Europe. Both these powers have as their policy the total colonial exploitation of Ukraine and her population. Having seized all the material and economic resources of the Ukrainian people, they mercilessly exterminate the leading national forces in Ukraine, destroy the national culture and the national consciousness of the masses, and colonize the country with foreigners, while exterminating great masses of the Ukrainian population or transporting them beyond the borders of Ukraine.

3. Nevertheless, this war is also debilitating our enemies and bringing them to a state of social and political disintegration. As a result, conditions are favourable for liberation struggles on the part of the captive nations and their ultimate victory is facilitated.

4. Under these circumstances, it is essential that:

a) in the vortex of the present total war, the Ukrainian people and their leading cadres be protected from extermination;
b) the Ukrainian people be led to battle for their liberation and for their own sovereign state.

For the fulfillment of these tasks, it is necessary that there be a single, pan-Ukrainian national front, organized by uniting all the active, national Ukrainian forces which are endeavouring to establish a sovereign Ukrainian state, and that there be a single governing centre.

For this reason, on the initiative of the Ukrainian Insurgent Army (UPA), which was formed in the process of the Ukrainian people's armed struggle against the plunder and coercion of the peaceable Ukrainian population by the forces of occupation, a pan-Ukrainian governing centre has been established, comprising representatives from all regions of Ukraine and all Ukrainian political circles, under the name *Ukrainian Supreme Liberation Council.*

I. GOALS AND DUTIES OF THE UKRAINIAN SUPREME LIBERATION COUNCIL

1. To unite and co-ordinate the activities of all the pro-independence liberation forces of the Ukrainian people in all the territories of Ukraine and outside these territories in a national-liberation struggle against all the enemies of the Ukrainian people, in particular, against Soviet Russian and Nazi German imperialists, for the establishment of an independent, united Ukrainian state.
2. To determine the ideological program of the Ukrainian people's liberation struggle.
3. To direct the entire Ukrainian national-liberation struggle until sovereignty and the establishment of independent government organs in the Ukrainian state are attained.
4. To represent, in its capacity as the highest pan-Ukrainian governing centre, the current political struggle of the Ukrainian people, both inside the country and abroad.
5. To bring into being the first government of the Ukrainian state and to convene the first nation-wide Ukrainian representative body.

II. FUNDAMENTAL PRINCIPLES OF THE IDEOLOGICAL PROGRAM OF THE UKRAINIAN
SUPREME LIBERATION COUNCIL

The preservation of a nation's life, national unity, and culture constitutes the primary and highest goal of any sound national organism. A sovereign national state is the chief guarantee of the preservation of a nation's life, its normal development, and the well-being of its citizens.

For this reason, the Ukrainian nation should, at this time, dedicate all its powers to the establishment and consolidation of its own state.

All politically active Ukrainian agencies should consolidate their forces in the struggle for an independent Ukrainian state, laying aside all disputes of a social and political nature because, until an independent state is attained, these disputes remain in the realm of theory.

The struggle for a national independent state can be successful only if it is carried out independently of the political influences of foreign powers.

Accordingly, the Ukrainian Supreme Liberation Council bases its activity on the following principles:

1. The Ukrainian Supreme Liberation Council aspires to the re-establishment of an independent, united Ukrainian state on all Ukrainian territories by means of a revolutionary struggle against all the enemies of Ukrainian sovereignty, in particular, against the Soviet and German forces of occupation. The Ukrainian Supreme Liberation Council endeavours to work in co-operation with all those who favour such independence.
2. The Ukrainian Supreme Liberation Council is founded on the principle of complete political independence from the influences of foreign powers and agencies.
3. The Ukrainian Supreme Liberation Council unites all the leading political groupings that favour political sovereignty for the Ukrainian state and political autonomy in the Ukrainian struggle for independence, regardless of their ideological world-views or political and social orientation.
4. To achieve the union of Ukrainian national-liberation forces in the battle for an independent, united Ukrainian state, the Ukrainian Supreme Liberation Council adopts the following political and social platform:
   a) guarantee of a popular, democratic method of determining the political order of the Ukrainian state by means of universal popular representation;
   b) guarantee of freedom of thought, world-view, and belief;
   c) guarantee of the development of Ukrainian national culture;
   d) guarantee of a just social order in the Ukrainian state, free of class exploitation and oppression;
   e) guarantee of the genuine rule of law in the Ukrainian state and of the equality of all citizens before the law;
   f) guarantee of citizenship rights to all national minorities in Ukraine;
   g) guarantee of the right of equal educational opportunity for all citizens;
   h) guarantee in the labour sector of the right of all citizens to the free exercise of initiative, regulated by the demands and needs of the totality of the nation;
   i) guarantee of freedom in methods of working the land; designation of a minimum and maximum size for individual farms;
   j) socialization of the basic natural wealth of the country: the land, forests, water, and underground resources; transfer of arable land to farmers for permanent agricultural use;
   k) nationalization of heavy industry and heavy transport; transfer of light industry and the food industry to co-operatives; guarantee of the right to wide-scale, free co-operation on the part of small producers;
   l) guarantee of free trade within limits set by legislation;
   m) guarantee of the free development of trades and of the right to establish individual workshops and enterprises;
   n) guarantee of the right of freedom in work for workers engaged in physical and intellectual occupations and a guarantee of the protection of the interests of workers by social legislation.

5. The Ukrainian Supreme Liberation Council will wage its struggle for an independent, united Ukrainian state in alliance with all the captive nations of Europe and Asia which are fighting for their own liberation and which recognize Ukraine's right to political independence.
6. The Ukrainian Supreme Liberation Council is striving for accommodation and peaceful co-existence with all of Ukraine's neighbours on the basis of mutual recognition of the right of each nation to its own state on its ethnic territories.

Source: Peter J. Potichnyj and Yevhen Shtendera, eds., *The Political Thought of the Ukrainian Underground* (forthcoming); reprinted with permission. Original copy (carbon copy of a typescript): archives of the Foreign Representation of the Ukrainian Supreme Liberation Council, New York, no. 7-2; photocopy: archives of *Litopys UPA*.

Note

This document was adopted by the First Grand Assembly of the Ukrainian Supreme Liberation Council on 11–15 July 1944. (Ed.)

12. Declaration on the Formation of the Ukrainian National Committee and the Ukrainian National Army

MARCH 1945

The Ukrainian National Committee (UNC) has come into being by the will of Ukrainian citizens who now reside in Germany and in countries allied with it.

The formation of the UNC is a new page in the socio-political life of Ukrainian citizens, who, governed by a pervasive love for the Homeland, desire to see their Fatherland freed of its invader.

The UNC is the spokesman of these hidden sentiments in our citizens and it firmly strides along the path which leads to the formation of a sovereign nation-state.

To this end, the UNC is organizing the Ukrainian National Army (UNA), whose purpose is to renew the armed struggle for Ukrainian statehood.

The UNA, in Ukrainian uniform, under the national flags sanctified by the battles of the past, under the command of its own Ukrainian officers, will stand under the ideological and political leadership of the UNC. Its ranks will be filled primarily by Ukrainians in the German Army and in other military and police formations.

The building of a nation-state requires Ukrainians of sound body and mind who are deeply nationally and socially conscious. To further this goal, the UNC will ensure the protection of all Ukrainians in Germany, equalization of rights of Ukrainian workers with those of their counterparts of other nations, and primarily will ensure their widest possible religious, moral, cultural, and material welfare. The UNC will also ensure the release of all political prisoners.

Foreign and ancient borders separating the individual Ukrainian lands have generated differences in thought and deed. These must disappear in a unified march to a common goal. The UNC wishes to speed up this process of unification of the Ukrainian populace, not only through a wide-ranging educational policy but also by a united Ukrainian approach to all matters.

The UNC will co-operate with National Committees of other nations enslaved by Muscovite Bolshevism who are fighting, as are the Ukrainian people, for Independence and Freedom.

The UNC will staunchly strive to perform the duties placed upon it by Ukrainian citizens, and it will perform them with confidence, providing that every consciously Ukrainian individual concentrates all of his efforts on the Common Struggle for a Common Victory.

Major-General of the General Staff Pavlo Shandruk
Head, Ukrainian National Committee

Professor Volodymyr Kubiiovych and Oleksander Semenenko
Vice-Presidents, Ukrainian National Committee

Petro Tereshchenko
Acting General Secretary, Ukrainian National Committee

Sources: Ukrainskyi shliakh (Ukrainian Pathway) (Vienna), 30 March 1945; reprinted in Volf-Ditrikh Haike (Wolf-Dietrich Heike), *Ukrainska dyviziia "Halychyna": istoriia formuvannia i boiovykh dii u 1943–45 rokakh* (The Ukrainian Division "Galicia": A History of Its Formation and Military Actions in 1943–45) (Toronto, 1970), 236–7. Translated by Andrij Wynnyckyj.

13. U.S. Army Guidelines on the Repatriation of Soviet Citizens

4 JANUARY 1946

RESTRICTED
HEADQUARTERS
U.S. FORCES EUROPEAN THEATER[1]

AG 383.7 GEC-AGEd   (Main) APO 757
                                                          4 January 1946
SUBJECT: Repatriation of Soviet Citizens Subject to Repatriation Under the Yalta Agreement

TO: Commanding Generals:
    Third U.S. Army Area
    Seventh U.S. Army Area
    Berlin District

It is the policy of the Government of the United States, pursuant to the agreement with the Soviet Union at Yalta,[2] to facilitate the early repatriation of Soviet citizens remaining in the U.S. Zone Germany,[3] to the Soviet Union. In the execution of this policy you will be guided by the instructions which follow:

1. Persons who were both citizens of and actually present within the Soviet Union on 1 September 1939 and who fall into the following categories will be repatriated without regard to their personal wishes and by force if necessary:

   a) Those captured in German uniforms.

   b) Those who were members of the Soviet Armed Forces on and after 22 June 1941 and who were not subsequently discharged therefrom.

   c) Those charged by the Soviet Union with having voluntarily rendered aid and comfort to the enemy, provided the Soviet Union satisfied the U.S. Military authorities of the substantiality of the charge by supplying in each case, with reasonable particularity, the time, place, and nature of the offenses and the perpetrator thereof. A person's announced resistance to this repatriation or acceptance of ordinary employment in German industry or agriculture shall not of itself be construed as constituting rendition of aid and comfort to the enemy.

2. Every effort should be made to facilitate repatriation of persons who were both citizens and actually present within the Soviet Union on 1 September 1939, but who do not fall into any of the classes defined in Par 1. In the case of such persons, however, you are not authorized to compel involuntary repatriation. With respect to these persons you will:

   a) Permit Soviet authorities, on their own request and responsibility, free access to these persons for the purpose of persuading them to return voluntarily and assisting them to do so.

   b) Take such practical steps as you may deem appropriate to minimize the development of organized resistance to repatriation, such as the segregation of known leaders of resistance groups, the separation of existing groups into smaller groups, and such other practical measures you may deem appropriate to prevent continuance or recurrence of organized resistance.

   c) Continue vigorous efforts to prevent the dissemination of propaganda of any kind designed to influence these persons against repatriation.

3. You are authorized to permit in your discretion Soviet authorities to have access to persons not specified in Pars. 1 and 2 who are claimed to be Soviet citizens by the Soviet Union, for the purpose of persuading them to return to their homes under practical arrangements which exclude the use of force, threat or coercion.

4. Efforts should be continued to facilitate the transfer to the Soviet Union of all persons who since 1 September 1939 have been given the right to become Soviet Nationals, who affirmatively make this choice, and who indicate that they desire the transfer.

5. The Soviet Authorities will furnish from time to time lists and addresses of Soviet Nationals who are charged with collaboration with the enemy and who are subject to the provisions of Par 1 (c) above and who are not subject to the provisions of Par 1 (a) or 1 (b). Upon receipt of these lists the District Commanders will take measures to collect the individuals listed therein and place them in camps, where they will be held pending screening and examination of charges against them. If addresses given are erroneous Military Authorities will not be required to conduct a search.

6. So much of letter this headquarters, file number AG 383.7 GEC-AGO, subject: "Release of Soviet Citizens subject to Repatriation Under the Yalta Agreement from Employment by Germans in the U.S. Zone", dated 17 November 1945, as provides that "no Soviet citizen subject to repatriation under the Yalta Agreement will be provided for after 1 December 1945 in any displaced persons camp except camps under Soviet administrations" is rescinded.

BY COMMAND OF GENERAL McNARNEY:

s/ L.S. OSTRANDER
t/ L.S. OSTRANDER
Brigadier General, USA
Adjutant General

1 Incl: List of names furnished by Russian Mission

DISTRIBUTION
1- Third U.S. Army Area
1- Seventh U.S. Army Area
1- Berlin District (Less incl)
5- O/Mil Gov (U.S. Zone) (Less incl)
1- AG Opns (Less incl)
1- AG Record (Less incl)

Reproduced by Hq, Third U.S. Army 19 January 1946

Source: United Nations (UNRRA) Archives, New York. PAG-4/3.0.11.0.1.4:3, "Repatriations."

Notes

1 The U.S. Zone in Germany, as well as the Bremen enclave and the U.S. sector of Berlin, was under the command of the United States Forces European Theater (USFET), with headquarters at Frankfurt. The functions of military government, at first exercised by USFET, were later undertaken by the Office of Military Government, United States (OMGUS), a separate organization with headquarters in Berlin. USFET retained jurisdiction only in matters relating to disarmament and demilitarization, security, displaced persons, and matters unrelated to civil control in Germany. OMGUS exercised a general surveillance over all German internal affairs, operating increasingly through approved German administrative agencies and personnel. (Ed.)

2 The meeting of the "Big Three" (Churchill, Roosevelt, and Stalin) in Yalta in the Crimea was held 4–11 February 1945. Zones of occupation for Germany were agreed upon, the Soviet republics of Belorussia and Ukraine received separate membership in the United Nations, but disagreements over the future of Poland remained unresolved. The allies agreed that all non-German, United Nations nationals in wartime Germany, Austria, and elsewhere were to be repatriated immediately to their homelands.

At the war's end the Soviet authorities claimed that some 5.5 million Soviet citizens were residing in the former Reich. Included in this figure were about one million Soviet prisoners of war and about two million forced labourers. According to the Yalta agreement, Soviet citizens were to be gathered together, housed separately, subjected to Soviet law, and handed over to Soviet officials. Being unclear about the exact meaning of "Soviet citizenship," the Western Allies indiscriminately transferred a total of 2,272,000 people to Soviet authorities by September 1945. Many of these were forcibly repatriated and were not, in fact, Soviet citizens when the war broke out in 1939 but of Polish, Czechoslovak, and other citizenship.

By the end of December 1945 and the beginning of 1946, the Western Allies, especially the Americans, changed their approach and declared that forcible repatriation would be limited to specific categories and would be carried out under the conditions outlined in document 13. It is estimated that out of the 5.5 million, about 500,000 former Soviet citizens remained in the West. (Ed.)

3 At the time of the German defeat, the major Allied powers agreed that Germany and Austria should be completely occupied and that German political, economic, and

cultural life should be controlled until the Allied objectives for Germany had been achieved.

The unconditional surrender of the German High Command on 7 and 8 May 1945 was followed on 5 June by the assumption of supreme authority with respect to Germany by the governments of the United States, the USSR, the United Kingdom, and France. Exclusive of the areas east of the Oder-Neisse line, Germany was divided into four zones to be administered separately by the four powers. The Soviet Union controlled the northeastern provinces between the Oder-Neisse and Elbe rivers, Britain the northwest, and the U.S. the southern areas. France received control of two Rhineland states in the American sector. The commanders of the four sectors formed the Allied Control Council which, by unanimous decision, ruled Germany during the first months of occupation. However, by the end of 1945 the Allied Control Council lost power, and American, French, British, and Soviet commanders assumed supreme authority in their zones. "Greater Berlin" was occupied jointly, with each power occupying a sector of the city. (Ed.)

14. U.S. Army Procedures for the Forcible Repatriation of Soviet Nationals

22 JANUARY 1946

RESTRICTED
HEADQUARTERS
THIRD UNITED STATES ARMY

AG 383.6 GNMCY

APO 403
22 January 1946

SUBJECT: Procedure for Repatriation of Russian [Soviet] Nationals
TO: See Distribution

In order to prevent suicides or disturbances among Prisoner of War Russian Nationals who are being forcibly repatriated to Russia the following added precautions will be taken:

1. *Precaution prior to shipment date*
   a) As little publicity as possible will be given to their forced repatriation.
   b) Russian Nationals will not be shipped until they have been cleared by both the Russian Liaison Officer[1] and an American Screening Team, under provision of Letter, Headquarters, United States Forces European Theater, dated 4 January 1946, AG 383.7, Subject: "Repatriation of Soviet Citizens subject to Repatriation Under the Yalta Agreement".
   c) Guards will be thoroughly oriented that these prisoners are desperate characters.
   d) Every effort will be exerted to insure that adequate anti-suicide and escape measures are taken.
   e) Russian Nationals will be segregated in groups of 10 or less for ease of handling.
   f) A showdown inspection will be held in which all possible weapons, knives, razors, glass, etc., are confiscated. If practicable window glass should be removed from windows or screened in to prevent its use as a weapon.

2. *Preparation of train*

If rail movement is to be made, train should be prepared as follows:

a) A partition across each end of the car to separate guards from prisoners and make escape of prisoners impossible (see sketch attached).

b) A field telephone system from car to car should be installed. This should be connected to the engine and to the guard reserve car.

c) The minimum train guard requirements should be as follows: 3 officers, so that one officer is on duty at all times. 4 EM (Enlisted Men) in each box car (2 on duty at all times). Reserve equal to 2% of the number of Prisoners of War shipped.

d) Train guard should be equipped with normal weapons except as follows: (1) Rifles or carbines will be substituted for pistols for all EM. (2) At least 25% of weapons will be automatic type, that is, Browning Automatic Rifles or sub-machine guns.

e) Train guard will be thoroughly oriented.

3. *Loading of prisoners of war*

a) Prisoners will be loaded as quietly as possible. Not more than one hour advance notice should be given prisoners and they will not be told where they are to go. After being alerted for shipment they must be watched constantly.

b) Prisoners must be loaded by American personnel only. Polish Guards may assist in perimeter defense only.

c) Russian Liaison Officer and sufficient interpreters must be present.

d) Fire trucks, Medical Officer and assistants must stand by.

e) Guards should operate as platoons under their normal leaders. It is desirable to have 2/3 of this group armed with night sticks and 1/3 with automatic weapons. A numerical superiority of three to one in the particular sub-group being loaded is necessary. An adequate reserve armed with gas masks, tear gas and smoke must be available. Plans to use tear gas in an emergency should be formulated.

f) The loading operation will be under the command and personal supervision of a competent officer of Field Grade.

4. *Precaution during the rail shipment*

a) Destination will be notified of nature and expected time of arrival of the shipment in sufficient time to allow reception arrangements at destination.

b) Adequate guard will be posted at all times to prevent suicide and escape.

c) Officer in charge will control the movement from the engine cab. Train will not be halted at places favorable for Prisoners of War to escape.

d) Reserve will be alerted and dismounted at all halts and be prepared to act in case of emergency.

e) Latrine facilities inside the car will be provided. Except in trips of more than 72 hours Prisoners of War will not be unloaded.

f) Every precaution against suicide enroute will be taken.

g) Under no circumstances will Prisoners of War be unloaded at night.

h) Train guard is responsible for Prisoners of War until they are turned over and receipted for by Russian authority or the Prisoners of War have been turned over and receipted for at point of detraining by an adequate United States troop unit which assumes responsibility for turnover to Russian authority.

BY COMMAND OF LIEUTENANT GENERAL KEYES:

s/R.A. KNECHT
t/R.A. KNECHT
1st Lt AGD
Asst Adj Gen

1 Incl: Diagram of Railroad Car

DISTRIBUTION
"A" plus
20 copies to 1st Inf. Div.
20 copies to 3rd Inf. Div.
20 copies to 9th Inf. Div.

Source: United Nations (UNRRA) Archives, New York. PAG-4/3.0.11.0.1.4:3, "Repatriations."

Note

1 Russian Liaison Officers were Soviet officials in the Main Administration for the Repatriation of Soviet Citizens, established in October 1944, and better known as the Soviet Repatriation Commission. Although headed by General Golikov, the commission was actually under the authority of the secret police – the NKGB (the People's Commissariat for State Security) within the USSR and Soviet-occupied territory, and SMERSH ("Death to Spies") abroad. The commission, based primarily in the West, received its directions and some of its staff from SMERSH's Main Administration of Counterintelligence (GUKR). (Ed.)

15. Why the Displaced Persons Refuse To Go Home

MAY 1946

REPORT OF THE REPATRIATION POLL OF DISPLACED PERSONS
IN UNRRA ASSEMBLY CENTERS IN GERMANY FOR THE PERIOD
1–14 MAY 1946: ANALYSIS OF NEGATIVE VOTES

GERMANY
MAY 1946   Attachment 8

The following analysis of reasons why approximately 82% of the displaced persons voted not to return home is based solely on their own statements and on summary analyses prepared by the town directors, who, through daily contact with the DPs are best fitted to analyse their present position with regard to repatriation.[1] Observations contained herein should in no way be construed as representing the views of the UNRRA staff in Germany. They are the views of the private individuals in the centers, and are included for the purpose of presenting a comprehensive picture of the group motives, personal motives and repatriation desires of the displaced persons.

Due to the tremendous number of ballots received and the variety of replies in a multitude of languages, it has been impossible to make an accurate numerical calculation of the different reasons. The percentages quoted in this report are therefore based on the most reliable estimates available.

It is interesting to note that nationals of so-called Western countries give both personal and economic reasons for not going home now, while the Eastern Europeans generally fall back on political factors as their primary explanation. The Eastern Europeans seem to show a real fear in their replies, the fear increasing the further east the home of the voter. Nevertheless, there is reason to believe that, among many of these people, the political explanation serves merely as a convenient justification and cover for underlying motives which are essentially personal and economic. Camp directors throughout Germany point to a general impression of demoralization and inertia among the Poles particularly, a reluctance to leave a comparatively secure and comfortable existence for a life of toil and hardship in their war-torn country.

Annex "A" contains some typical replies from the principal nationalities.

Germany
May 1946   Attachment 8

ESTONIANS, LATVIANS, AND LITHUANIANS[2]

The displaced persons from the Baltic countries of Estonia, Latvia, and Lithuania submitted an almost unanimous vote against repatriation. They can be considered as a single group, since their backgrounds are similar and all of their replies express the same unwavering determination not to return to their homelands as long as they are occupied by the Russians.

The principal groups among the Balts come from the so-called "middle" and "upper-middle" classes. Many are well educated and enjoyed the prosperous, independent life of the average intellectual, professional or businessman before the war. Others were independent farmers, small artisans or craftsmen. They started coming into Germany in large numbers in 1941–42, when the Germans first occupied the Baltic lands. It is difficult to determine how many of them came voluntarily, seeking better jobs, and how many were actually deported to Germany. It is significant, however, that very few of this group were persecuted by the Nazis, and that practically none of them have returned home. The bulk of the "displaced" Balts, however, appear definitely to have entered Germany in late 1944, fleeing, not from the enemy, but from the Russians.

Their primary objection to repatriation is based on political reasons. Approximately 90–95% of them express an outspoken antagonism toward "Communism as a way of life" and especially toward "the Russian occupation of their countries." (It is interesting to note that some of the answers were anti-communistic as opposed to anti-Russian, but the majority made no distinction between the two.) Most of their reasons are not a mere parrot-like repetition of political propaganda which characterizes the Polish vote, but arguments apparently based on personal experience during the Russian occupation of 1940/1 when relatives and friends were "transported to Siberia in sealed cars without food or water, never to be heard of again." They express the fear that the same may happen to them if they return. Some refer to the time the Communist party was voted into power in a "free election," held after all the parties but one were dissolved, in which everyone was forced to vote.

The actual replies on the ballots vary from a guarded "our country is occupied" to ferocious denunciations of "Russian dictatorship." Such words as "sadism," "reign of terror," "bestial," "murderous" etc. appear frequently in the descriptions of Communism. A few quoted Molotov's statement made in 1940 to the effect that the Baltic nations must be destroyed. About 30–40% of the Baltic DPs state that they have lost relatives or friends, either killed or deported by the Russians. There is no way of telling whether or not this figure is accurate, but their reasons for not desiring repatriation seem to be motivated by a real fear of personal persecution, deportation or even death at the hands of the Russian secret police.

Closely linked with the political reasons for not desiring repatriation are the economic ones. These were mentioned by approximately 60% of the Balts, usually as a secondary factor, in connection with the communistic regime. Only about 10% based their primary reason for not returning on economic factors. A large number of these DPs were accustomed to a fairly high standard of living before the war. "The confiscation of all private property" has reduced many formerly well-to-do Balts to a position where they could not hope to return to their previous way of life. A number of the Baltic farmers, particularly Lithuanians, claim to have had their land taken away from them during the Russian occupation and were forced to join "Kolchozes" [kolkhozy] or farming communities. They now refuse to return. The uncertainty of being able to buy food at normal prices, the shortage of houses, the prospect of unemployment and the unfavorable currency exchange, all vital problems to the Poles, seem to be relatively insignificant factors contributing to the anti-repatriation desires of the Balts, who for the most part have not considered repatriation seriously enough to think about these problems.

In addition to the fear of economic persecution, the fear of religious persecution is also mentioned as a secondary reason for not wanting to go home. Some mention the days in 1940/1 when they "weren't allowed to go to church"; some fear reprisals for their former membership in religious organizations, while others merely state that "in my country today religion is suppressed and the institution of marriage does not exist."

The majority of the Balts sincerely want to return, provided they can return to a "free, democratic country." Some of them are optimistic enough to state that they "expect" to go home as soon as a democratic government is established. A group of Latvians and Lithuanians in one camp have reluctantly accepted the present situation in their former countries as final and are hoping to immigrate to either the U.S., Canada or Africa. However, the majority of Balts seem to be waiting in Germany for the "occupation" of their countries to end, for there is very little mention of resettlement as a solution to the Baltic "hard-core" problem.[3]

POLES[4]

With very few exceptions, the Poles in the U.S. and British Zones gave political reasons for their negative votes in the repatriation poll. The three basic complaints, repeated again and again, were the "presence of Russians in Poland," "the Communistic Warsaw government," and "the lack of personal freedom in Poland." Although most of the Poles claimed the same reasons for not wanting to go home, it is clear from the comments on their ballots that they did not all have the same motivation for their answers. In general, the Poles who quoted political reasons can be broken down into three groups.

The first and smallest of these groups is made up of those so-called leaders and intellectuals who have an ideological conception of Poland as a "free democracy" and refuse to return under present conditions. They claim to abhor the thought of "Communism" in Poland, the "Russian-dominated Warsaw government," the "occupation by Russian troops," the alleged repression of democratic freedom, and feel that they can do more for their fatherland by not returning now. A few described the conditions under which they would return: "When the Atlantic Charter is applied;[5] "When the Russians leave;" "When General Anders returns;"[6] "When Democracy has been established as in England." Some feel that since they have not returned home before now, they will be suspected and possibly persecuted regardless of their innocence of collaboration. This first group is the only one which mentions terroristic treatment by Russians and fear of reprisals should they return. On the whole the fear of persecution does not play the same important role in the Polish answers as it does in those of the Balts, the Russians and the Polish-Ukrainians.

The second group consists of people who have private political reasons for fearing repatriation. The largest number in this group are those whose homes were located east of the Curzon line in that part of Poland which has been annexed to Russia.[7] The loss of their homes to Russia makes them feel an even stronger nationalistic tie with Poland, so that they invariably refuse to return to their homes and become Soviet citizens. If any of them would agree to go back to Poland they would probably be sent to the newly annexed western provinces which are now being settled by the Poles.[8] This cannot properly be called repatriation, but rather "pioneering" in an unfamiliar land, far from friends and relatives. Most of the DPs now being maintained in camps in Germany seem to lack a pioneering spirit to set forth and build a new home and a new life in an area where conditions are reported to be difficult.

The third and by far the largest group of the so-called political refugees (estimated roughly at about 60% of the total negative vote), are those who cannot definitely make up their minds to return. It must be remembered that the majority of these people have had little or no education to speak of, have not suffered political persecution which would shape their ideology, and are incapable of forming mature political opinions for themselves. They are subject to outside influences and as a result, their minds change almost every day, reflecting current slogans circulating in the camps. It is among this group that you find the stereotyped answers, such as "Poland is not free," "the Russians are occupying Poland," and "Poland is Communistic," indicating that the voters have been propagandized, either in the past, or that there was a planned campaign on the part of their leaders to furnish the DPs with the same answers for the poll. The vote of this group should not be taken as a final indication of their desires. Most of them are agricultural workers, small independent farmers and factory hands who have a strong patriotic feeling for Poland, regardless of her political complexion. The team directors who commented on this group felt that most of them would eventually return to Poland if given a little more encouragement and if removed from the political influences hindering their repatriation.

The influences which are affecting the majority of those potentially repatriable Poles seem to be similar in all of the camps, and are centered around the camp leaders, who were elected by a free vote, the members of the Polish guard units and the Catholic clergy.[9] These political and clerical leaders have been successful in persuading a large number of Poles that it is against their interests to return home until their country is "freed from the Russians." The Polish-Ukrainians who are unanimously opposed to repatriation have also had an effect on the other Poles, as well as the demoralized group who have lost all ambition and are content to stay in the camps, leading a comparatively comfortable life, until forced to make a decision. Three other factors which have recently had an unfavorable effect on the Poles' desire to be repatriated are Hoover's speech describing starvation in Poland, Churchill's "iron curtain" speech and the dissension at the foreign ministers' conference at Paris.[10]

Over half of the Poles quoted economic factors as a secondary reason for not wanting to go home. These factors are probably more basic than the political ones in determining repatriation desires of the Polish DPs. The Poles in Germany are not entirely cut off from their homeland. They maintain contact through newspapers, letters, radio broadcasts and friends who have returned to Germany after having been repatriated. From these sources they receive a description of destruction in the towns and cities, shortages of food, clothes and housing, unemployment and the general economic insecurity of life in present-day Poland.

These Poles who believe they have lost all of their former possessions naturally hesitate to return to their war-torn country where they fear they cannot earn a living. Their feeling of economic insecurity is expressed in the following typical comment by a Polish farmer: "At my house now, no horse, no cow, no pig – only a picture of Stalin on the wall." The desire to remain in their present condition of comparative security is quite natural on the part of these people, who were suddenly taken from a state of slavery and placed into an artificial society where they are cared for without having to work. Many of them who could not maintain the same standards of living at home will continue to live in the assembly centers as long as they exist.

Many of the Poles have not been content to live idly, however, but have found some measure of real economic security in the form of employment. This is particularly true in the French Zone where a large number of DPs live and work in the German communities. The fact that a large percentage of Polish DPs are employed in the local economy in the French Zone is reflected in the ballot, for only 64% gave political reasons, the rest economic or personal reasons for wanting to stay in Germany.

Very few of the Poles gave only personal reasons for not wanting to go home. Among those who did are the people who have lost their homes, their families and their friends as a result of the war and have nothing to which to return. They don't appear to have the courage to face the future alone in a destroyed country, and many of them want to start life anew in a western land, preferably the U.S. or Canada. They are waiting hopefully for a declaration of emigration opportunities by the governments of these countries. Another group of DPs have family ties which are holding them here. They are engaged or married to Germans, to DPs of another nationality or to members of the Polish Guard Units stationed in Germany and are unwilling to break up their families to return home. Others can't be repatriated now for health reasons. Either they are old or sick or are staying with sick relatives, until they can be moved. Some mothers don't want to expose their infants and small children to the uncertain conditions in Poland, but prefer to remain in Germany until after the harvest. Others will return when their personal affairs are settled. Included in this group are those awaiting news from home or abroad before they set out to join relatives, and some who are still trying to locate lost members of their families who were deported to Germany during the war.

A very small number of Poles, chiefly the elderly people from the eastern provinces, gave fear of religious persecution as their main reason for not going home. This factor was mentioned, however, on a number of ballots in connection with political reasons.

Despite repeated instructions from UNRRA directors, this group insists on describing itself as "Polish-Ukrainian" or "Ukrainian Stateless".[11] The constant dissemination of nationalistic propaganda has completely alienated them from the idea of adherence to either Poland or Russia, and thereby has eliminated all chance for a voluntary repatriation of Ukrainian peoples. Like the Poles, they give mainly political reasons for not wanting to return home but they are generally more violent in their attacks on Russia, and express fear of forced labor conditions, even "deportation to Siberia," should they dare to return. Some give supposed first hand accounts of previous persecution, such as "I don't wish to be repatriated to the Ukraine because my father was killed by the communists for his political and religious ideas and I was sent to Siberia, and had to stay for five years in a concentration camp." About 10% of the Ukrainians included in their reasons descriptions of the absence of political, cultural, religious and personal freedom at home, while others compared "Bolshevik totalitarianism" with Nazism.

They claim that their country is occupied and since they do *not* wish to become citizens of the USSR, they have in effect no fatherland to which to return. Some stated that they want a free, autonomous Ukrainian state, even within the boundaries of the new Poland. An important factor in this separatist movement has been the activity of the Greek-Orthodox clergy, who constantly use their strong influence against repatriation. As a logical consequence of this clerical influence, and the fact that Ukrainians are predominantly orthodox [sic], they seem to be much more concerned over the lack of religious freedom than do the Poles.

A few of the Ukrainian DPs lost large land holdings in the collectivization of estates by the Soviet government, so that they have a bitter personal enmity toward the new economic system. Others merely stated their dislike for a system where there is no private property.

The few Russians who are still left in Germany belong in three distinct categories, two of them comprising political refugees who refuse to return to Soviet Russia. The first group represents those Russians and Russian-Ukrainians who came to Germany during the war as volunteers, deserters, forced laborers or POWs. They express a hatred for Communism and the "dictatorship" in Russia and would rather stay in Germany for the time being. Eventually they hope to emigrate to one of the western countries, when opportunities are available.

The second group is composed of White Russians and other Russian emigrants from 1919–20, displaced persons left over from the last war, who never adopted a new citizenship. A few of them hold Nansen passports, while others claim that theirs were lost or taken away by the German authorities.[12] Their return to Russia is out of the question, as the majority of the older men were active counter-revolutionists, and fear reprisal by the Communists, and the younger ones, the children who were born abroad, have never lived in Russia and have no desire to go to the country from which their parents are exiles.

The third group all gave personal reasons for not going home, such as illness or marriage to Germans, Poles or other DPs.

YUGOSLAVS

The Yugoslavs in UNRRA camps are mostly Royalists and therefore opposed to repatriation for political reasons.[13] Like the Balts and Poles, they claim a passionate love for democracy (which they interpret to be a restoration of the monarchy). On the other hand they represent a different problem from the Poles and Balts who are afraid to go home, since the Yugoslavs are for the most part ex-POWs who still consider themselves as part of King Peter's army. They do not accept their present status as a lasting one but are hoping for the chance to go home and fight Tito. In one center in the U.S. Zone, for instance, the Yugoslav leader began the poll with a spirited declaration that he and his men were soldiers, wished to be soldiers and had no plan to go anywhere, or do anything else. He then suggested that UNRRA send them all home to fight the Tito government.

The following explanation from one of the ballots is typical of the general feeling of the Yugoslav DPs. "We were determined to fight against Hitler's Germany for high principles of democracy and freedom. Now the war is over; instead of democracy and freedom we have a dictatorship in Yugoslavia. We expect nobody's charity or any reward. What we expect and claim is the most elementary right to choose our own form of government. This was proclaimed in Article 3 of the Atlantic Charter."

JEWS[14]

The Jews in UNRRA centers in Germany expressed a unanimous desire to immigrate, the majority of them either to Palestine or to the U.S. By far the largest number of Polish and Ukrainian Jews express a desire to go to Palestine. This desire can easily be understood in the light of strong nationalistic feelings among the eastern Jewry already prevailing before the war, coupled with the racial persecution at the hands of the Nazis, not to mention some of their own countrymen during the war. Tragic personal histories on the ballots present vividly the reasons for not returning. It is now impossible for the Jews from Eastern Europe to return to their large Jewish communities for so many of them have been wiped out, and tales of continued anti-semitism drift in daily with new refugees coming out of Poland, seeking refuge in UNRRA centers in Germany. Although many would perhaps prefer to go to some western country, the emigration quotas to these lands will be so low as to allow only a trickle of immigrants to enter. Palestine appears to be the only solution to their problem. Hundreds of ballots showed just one word as an explanation for not returning home: "Palestine."

The German Jews are also anxious to emigrate, most of them to Palestine but a large number have relatives abroad whom they wish to join in such countries as the U.S., Canada, Great Britain, France, Sweden or South America. Like the Polish and other Eastern European Jews these people feel that they can't settle down again in the country which is a constant reminder of their personal tragedies. Some even stated that they feared history would repeat itself in Europe and that they or their children might have to go through the same sort of persecution should they remain in Germany now.

CZECHS

Although there are only about 2,000 Czechs still in Germany, a large percentage of them are staying for the same political reasons as the Poles, namely fear of Communism and the repression of personal freedom. Some fear a war in the near future and state that Czechoslovakia is too close to Russia for any measure of comfort, should a war break out.

In some cases their homes were in that part of Slovakia annexed to Russia, and they are afraid or unwilling to become Soviet citizens.[15]

On the whole the Czechs are not as violent as the Poles in their criticism of their home government, or in their refusal to return home. It is interesting to note that about 25% of them are holding up their decision pending the outcome of the Czech national vote, whereas a much smaller percentage are looking forward to emigration.

The reasons why the remaining Czechs don't want to return are personal. Some are sick, or are staying with sick relatives, some are married to Polish DPs while others are still searching for lost relatives in Germany. In addition, there is a small number who are employed by UNRRA, or the Military and have the permission of their national liaison officers to remain temporarily in the DP centers.

WESTERN EUROPEANS, BRITISH, U.S., AND SMALLER GROUPS

The small number of these nationals are staying in Germany solely for personal or economic reasons. Either they are married to Germans or other DPs whom they are not yet allowed to take home with them, or else they wish to settle in Germany where they have economic interests. The last reason is particularly true in the French Zone where many of the DPs are living privately and can carry on a fairly normal life in the German community. A few individuals are probably collaborators who are trying to hide in Germany, while others have lived in Germany for some time before the war, and do not wish to move. As in the case of the Czechs, many of the Western Europeans are working for UNRRA or the military authorities with the permission of their national liaison officers. These jobs offer more security than they could find at home. Several Frenchmen, Italians and Dutchmen say that they fear to return to the present unstable economic conditions in their countries. They know of the shortages of food, clothing and employment possibilities and prefer to stay in Germany under comparatively favorable conditions until the situation in their homelands improves. In the British Zone there are small numbers of Dutch bargees [bargemen] who will return as soon as the canals and waterways are opened.

Some so-called Armenians (including some "Turks" and "Iranians") fear religious persecution in their homelands.

Germany   Attachment 8
May 1946   Annex A

TYPICAL NEGATIVE REPLIES ON THE BALLOTS
OF THE PRINCIPAL NATIONALITY GROUPS

I. ESTONIANS, LATVIANS, LITHUANIANS

1. "Under the present circumstances I do not want to return, for I know well enough who is ruling behind the 'iron curtain' and what kind of life the people lead in this 'most liberal country'."
2. "I am not a Communist."
3. "I have already been a political deportee to Siberia for four years."
4. "I am a mother and I want to raise my child myself."
5. "My country has ceased to exist."
6. "In Estonia, Latvia and Lithuania there is no democratic government."
7. "I cannot return. My brother, sister, father and mother were deported to Siberia because they did not go to the poll to vote for the Communists."
8. "Russia."
9. "I have never been a Russian citizen and I am not interested to serve in the Russian army. Further I don't recognize the one-party system."
10. "Stalin."
11. "In all countries occupied by the USSR people are physically and morally suppressed."
12. "My country is occupied by the Bolsheviks."
13. "In 1940 my father was arrested and killed because he was a Russian officer under the Czars. My mother was sent to Russia, then I escaped."

II. POLES

1. "Poland is not free."
2. "The Russians are dominating the Polish Government."
3. "Quoting Mr. Churchill's speech: an 'iron curtain' is hanging from Stettin to Trieste. Behind it an ignorant slave state is hidden from the eyes of us all, etc." – "I am a Democrat, not a Communist."
4. "Communist dictatorship. No freedom of personal opinion. Russians annihilate everything that is not Russian and communistic."
5. "Stalin annihilates people as well as Hitler."
6. "I don't trust Stalin and his government in Poland."
7. "Uncertain situation in Poland. The presence of the Soviet Army is dangerous to the freedom of my country."
8. "I don't agree with the policy of the Government and the persecution of the church and the lack of private property and freedom."

9. "I am afraid of Stalin, I am afraid of Siberia. Poland is not free."
10. "After the election of a democratic government, I shall return home."
11. "The Russians occupy that part of Poland where I lived. My home and family are gone."
12. "I can't find my family."
13. "I am ill and tired after the hard work in Germany."
14. "If I go back I am sure they will kill me or send me to Siberia."
15. "They sent part of my family to Siberia and confiscated our farm."
16. "I have been persecuted by the Communists and condemned for exile to Siberia. I don't want to try to live under the Communists again."
17. "My husband is not going back home and so I don't want to go."
18. "When I get a letter from my family saying that they are alive, then I shall return home."
19. "Because there is starvation in my country."
20. "My family is in America. I shall wait until I can also go there."

III. POLISH-UKRAINIANS

1. "I don't want to live under dictatorship and terror."
2. "I am against violations and terror in the USSR. I am against men who persecute religion, who turn peasants into slaves. I am against the one-party system."
3. "Two of my brothers were killed. My parents died in jail after being there a long time. My brother was sentenced to forced labor."
4. "My homeland is at present occupied by Soviet Russia, which follows the policy of general terror against those who are opposed to the communistic system. They persecute religion (Greek-Orthodox); bishops and priests are sent to Siberia. Catholic churches are closed. Because of these reasons I will not return."
5. "I don't agree with the totalitarian system in the USSR. Galicia belongs now to the USSR. I never was, neither am, nor wish to be a citizen of the USSR. Persecution of the Greek-Orthodox Church."

IV. RUSSIANS [SOVIET CITIZENS]

1. "I don't agree with Stalin-terror and oppression of people. The system has nothing to do with democracy."
2. "I have been persecuted by the NKVD since 1929. Most of the time I have been obliged to live under a false name."
3. "Democracy in the Soviet Union exists only on paper. There is only freedom to vote for the candidates of the Communistic Party and for its resolutions."
4. "The Soviet regime is not a Russian government. The main idea of the Soviet government is a world revolution."
5. "Communism is even worse than Nazism."
6. "In the Soviet Union there is no free work nor any private property. There is only forced, slave-like labor in the kolchoz [sic] (Government farms) and in the factories or businesses, all run by the Government."

V. JEWS

1. "Palestine is my Fatherland."
2. "Poland is covered with Jewish blood; even now the Poles are persecuting Jews. We can visit the cemeteries, but we cannot live there. Therefore I want to immigrate to the U.S. to join my relatives in the best democracy in the world."
3. "I have nobody left at home."
4. "My husband was murdered by the Germans. I spent three years in the KZ (concentration camp). My relatives are in foreign countries. They will take care of me."
5. "All my relatives were killed in Auschwitz. I can't live among the murderers of my parents."
6. "Because of anti-Semitism in Poland, and I have no family left there."
7. "Because Poles and Ukrainians are killing Jews."
8. "I am the only survivor of a family of eight. I have no relatives in Europe. I am miserable and want to join relatives in America. I have an affidavit."

VI. WESTERN EUROPEANS AND SMALLER GROUPS

1. "At present there is no job, life is too expensive in France and as I am alone, I have nothing to look forward to at home."
2. "I will not be sent back because I have no job and no home." (Dutch)
3. "I don't want to go back to Greece, because I have no job and there is a food shortage."
4. "I am married to a Pole, but the Dutch Government won't allow her to come home with me. I shall wait in Germany."

Source: United Nations (UNRRA) Archives, New York. PAG-4/3.0.11.0.1.4:2, "Council Resolution 92 etc."

Notes

1 After following a policy of encouraging outright repatriation of "former Soviet nationals" and others whose homelands came under Soviet control after 1945, the United Nations Relief and Rehabilitation Administration (UNRRA) found that about one million displaced persons (DPs) under its care refused to be repatriated. Approximately fifty-two nationalities were among these DPs, and they were dispersed among 920 camps in Germany, Austria, and Italy. Not fully understanding their reluctance, UNRRA officials in the U.S. Zone of Occupied Germany decided to conduct a secret poll among the DPs, during 1–14 May 1946. Each DP was handed a sheet and asked to answer the following questions: (1) what nationality do you claim?; (2) do you wish to be repatriated now? (yes/no); (3) if your answer to 2 is "no," explain your reasons in the space below.

No exact figures on the total number of respondents were given by UNRRA, but the poll gave UNRRA and the U.S. military authorities their first comprehensive understanding of the difficulties involved in repatriation. Although some facts and analyses in the report are inaccurate and misleading, the document does shed light on why DPs did not want to return home after the war. (Ed.)

2 Granted sovereignty in 1919, the Baltic states of Estonia, Latvia, and Lithuania were included in a plan secretly arranged by Nazi Germany and the USSR for dividing these states into spheres of influence. In the secret protocol of the Nazi-Soviet Pact, 23 August 1939, Finland, Estonia, and Latvia were ceded to the Soviets. By the Nazi-Soviet friendship treaty, 28 September 1939, Lithuania was similarily brought under Soviet domination. Profiting from the German advance of May-June 1940 on the Western front, Soviet troops overran all the Baltic states, including the Lithuanian border strip reserved for Germany by the friendship treaty. On 15 June 1940 Soviet forces entered Lithuania, and two days later they were in Latvia and Estonia. In August 1940 the USSR officially incorporated these states into the USSR as the fourteenth, fifteenth, and sixteenth Soviet republics.

After the German invasion of the USSR, the three countries, together with part of Belorussia, constituted the *Reichskommissariat Ostland*, under the direction of *Gauleiter* Heinrich Lohse, and were deprived of their autonomy. With the end of the war, attempts to reconstitute independent governments failed and the Red Army restored the political situation of 1940. By 1946 there were an estimated 190,400 Balts under UNRRA care. (Ed.)

3 These were persons considered to be non-repatriable, either because they were unacceptable to their country of origin or were unwilling to be repatriated. (Ed.)

4 On 1 September 1939 Poland was invaded by Germany and on 17 September by the Soviet Union. Polish army units were soon forced to surrender to the Germans or the Red Army. According to the 28 September 1939 agreement between Ribbentrop and Molotov, Poland was divided along the Narva-Bug-San rivers; that is, approximately along the Curzon Line (see note 7). In the German sphere, some territories were incorporated directly into the Reich, and the central part of the country was organized under the General Government of Occupied Poland.

On 7 May 1945, the day the Germans capitulated, Poland was split between a Polish government recognized by the Western Allies and a Polish Committee of National Liberation recognized by the USSR. A solution of sorts was worked out with the creation of the Provisional Government of National Unity in Moscow in June 1945. On 5 July 1945 the major Western powers withdrew recognition of the London-based Polish government-in-exile. (Ed.)

5 The Atlantic Charter was a statement of fundamental principles for the postwar world order, issued jointly by Roosevelt and Churchill after meetings during 9–12 August 1941 in Argentia Bay, Newfoundland. The main terms were: (1) a renunciation of territorial or other aggrandizement by the United Kingdom and the United States; (2) opposition to territorial changes contrary to the wishes of the people immediately concerned; (3) support for the right of peoples to choose their own form of government. On 15 September 1941 it was announced that fifteen nations fighting the Germans and Italians (including the USSR) had endorsed the Atlantic Charter. Stalin, however, added a proviso: "Considering that the practical application of these principles will necessarily adapt itself to the circumstances, needs, and historic peculiarities of particular countries, the Soviet Government can state that a consistent application of these principles will secure the most energetic support on the part of the government and peoples of the Soviet Union." (Ed.)

6 Władysław Anders (1892–1970), a Polish Army commander, was wounded and

captured by the Soviets in September 1939 and released in July 1941. He then formed an army of 75,000 citizens of Poland (including non-Poles) who fought on the British side in the Near East and participated in the capture of Monte Cassino in May 1944 and of Bologna in April 1945. Anders was politically allied to the Polish government-in-exile based in London and headed by General Sikorski. (Ed.)

7 The Curzon Line refers to a proposal to settle the disputed frontier between Poland and Russia, put to the Poles by Lloyd George, the British Prime Minister, on 10 July 1920, and then dealt with by Lord George N. Curzon, the British Foreign Secretary. The line or demarcation stretched from Grodno, through Brest-Litovsk and Przemyśl, to the Carpathians; it would have excluded from Poland the lands inhabited predominantly by Belorussians, Ukrainians, and Lithuanians. The Poles rejected the proposal and subsequently secured territory twice as large as that suggested by Lloyd George. After the Nazi-Soviet Pact of 1939, the Curzon Line (with minor variations) became the boundary between the German and Soviet spheres of occupation. In 1945 it was accepted by the Polish Government as the frontier with the USSR. (Ed.)

8 At the Potsdam conference of 17 July–2 August 1945, the Allies agreed that Poland would occupy the German areas east of a line following the Oder and Neisse rivers, from the Baltic Sea to the Czechoslovak frontier. Former eastern territories of interwar Poland were taken by the USSR, and about 1.4 million Poles left this territory in 1946–7 to settle in regions taken from the Reich. (Ed.)

9 The term Polish guard units refers to displaced persons recruited to guard American supply depots and other installations. (Ed.)

10 On 9 February 1946 Stalin gave a speech in which he argued that, despite the end of hostilities, there was to be continued vigilance; there was to be no peace at home or abroad. Churchill delivered the Western reply at Fulton, Missouri on 5 March 1946. He argued for close co-operation among the world's English-speaking peoples, because "from Stettin in the Baltic to Trieste in the Adriatic, an iron curtain has descended across the continent," allowing "police governments" to rule Eastern Europe. The month of March 1946 is seen by many historians as the beginning of the Cold War.

At the Paris conference of Allied foreign ministers in May 1946, the USSR accused the United Kingdom of imperialism for its suppression of the Greek rebellion and criticized the Netherlands for its repressive actions in Indonesia. The British foreign minister, Ernest Bevin, responded by accusing the Soviet Union of imperialism. These disputes prevented any agreement from being reached at the conference. (Ed.)

11 At the end of the war, approximately 2.5–3 million Ukrainians were in the Third Reich. Some were prisoners of war who had served in the Polish or Red Army; most had been forced labourers in Germany. A smaller number were political refugees and concentration camp survivors. An estimated two million Ukrainians found themselves in the occupied zones under Supreme Headquarters, Allied European Forces (SHAEF) in Austria, Germany, and Italy. After voluntary and forcible repatriation about 250,000 remained and they refused to be repatriated. About one-third were former citizens of the Soviet Union before 1939; the remaining two-thirds were from other countries, primarily from Poland.

Official UNRRA and other statistical information on the exact number of Ukrainians is, however, not entirely reliable for several reasons. The Allies used citizenship rather than ethnic origin to classify DPs, but because Ukrainian DPs came from the prewar territories of Poland, Czechoslovakia, Romania, and the Soviet

Union their citizenship varied accordingly. Also, the fear of repatriation was so great that many, especially those from Soviet Ukraine, did not reveal their true nationality. In time, a change in designation by officials was precipitated by the Polish government because it insisted that Ukrainians from Poland be separated from "true" Poles, arguing that Poland did not want Ukrainians back since their former lands had been ceded to the USSR. Furthermore, they were to be repatriated to the USSR. On 6 July 1946 Poland and the USSR concluded an agreement to exchange Ukrainians in Poland for Poles in the USSR. Moreover, UNRRA and other authorities were not consistent in their use of the term "Ukrainian." Officially, Ukrainians were not designated by UNRRA as a separate nationality until the summer of 1947; however, even before then, local UNRRA officials sometimes did allow refugees to designate themselves as Ukrainians. For these reasons, official UNRRA statistics underestimate the number of Ukrainians (100,000) and Soviet citizens (10,000) while overestimating the number of Poles (275,000). (Ed.)

12 In 1921 Fridtjof Nansen (1861–1930), Norwegian explorer and later politician, became the first head of the League of Nation's High Commission in Connection with the Problem of Russian Refugees in Europe. After World War I, an estimated 800,000 refugees from tsarist Russia were scattered throughout Europe; most refused to return to Bolshevik-controlled Russia. Mandated to deal with this major problem, Nansen called a conference in Geneva at which sixteen nations were represented. An agreement was reached to issue for Russian refugees a special travel document, to be known as the "Nansen certificate" or "Nansen passport." By 1928 fifty-one governments had agreed to issue and recognize this passport for refugees from Russia and elsewhere. The passport gave the holder League of Nations protection and guarantees that they would not be arbitrarily treated or forcibly repatriated to the Soviet Union. (Ed.)

13 The Royalists were supporters of King Peter II, who ascended the Yugoslav throne in 1934. On 27 March 1941 he assumed full royal powers when a coup d'état in Belgrade overthrew the regency, but he had to flee on 6 April when the Germans attacked Yugoslavia. He established a government-in-exile in London that supported the Serbian officer, Dragoljub (Draža) Mihailović and his Chetniks. King Peter made an accommodation with the Communist partisans led by Josip Broz (Tito) in August 1944 but was deposed in November 1945.

In 1946 there were about 150,000 Yugoslav refugees, most of whom were dispersed in UNRRA and military camps throughout Italy. Among them were monarchists, Serbian Chetniks, Croatian nationalists (Ustashi), and former partisans united in their opposition to Tito's regime. The Yugoslav government was particularly adamant in demanding their forcible repatriation. (Ed.)

14 In December 1945 UNRRA listed only 18,361 Jews as receiving assistance in various zones in Germany. By June 1946 the number had reached 97,333, and in June 1946, 167,531. The combined total of Jews under UNRRA care in Italy, Germany, and Austria was close to 250,000 in June 1947. (Ed.)

15 Some of these Czechoslovak citizens were no doubt Ukrainians (Lemkos) from the eastern provinces of Carpatho-Ukraine (Ruthenia), ceded to the USSR after the war. It was an area of about 8,800 square kilometres with a population of approximately 850,000. Not wishing to take part in the "voluntary" transfer to the USSR, these Ukrainians fled primarily to the U.S. Zone. (Ed.)

16. Report on the Screening of Ukrainian Displaced Persons

22 AUGUST 1946

UNRRA LIAISON OFFICE
9TH INFANTRY DIVISION HEADQUARTERS, AUGSBURG

Military – 7484 Augsburg   22 August 1946

SUBJECT: Report of Screening of Ukrainian Displaced Persons

TO: General Brown, Deputy Director, German Operations
   UNRRA Central Headquarters, Arolsen

   Attention: Mr. Edward Reich, Operations

1. In reply to your telephone conversation of several days ago, I wish to make the following report about the screening progress of Ukrainian Displaced Persons in the American Zone.

2. The latest weekly report of screening in 9th Division area, which includes Districts 1, 2 and 5, shows more than 88,000 persons screened. It is impossible to obtain an accurate breakdown of the number of Ukrainians in this group because of the uneven method of reporting by screening teams and the general confusion that still exists on the lower military echelons about the classification of Ukrainians by citizenship and nationality. However, I can make a report of the general situation with regard to Ukrainians.

3. Several camps have been screened that contain large Ukrainian groups and a few all-Ukrainian camps have been screened. For example, Cornberg, Team 518, an all-Ukrainian camp with a population of about 2,500, was screened a few weeks ago with no special events. There were evictions but the number was small. The Ukrainians were about evenly classified as Polish and Russian although certainly this figure cannot be judged as particularly accurate. Hindenburg Kaserne, Team 114, had about 700 Ukrainians screened; Kapellenschule, Team 114, had about 160 Ukrainians screened; Muhldorf, Team 154, had about 230 persons classified as Russians, mostly all of whom are Ukrainians; Dillingen, Team 308, had 200 Polish Ukrainians screened; and

smaller groups of Ukrainians have been screened in many other camps. Other large Ukrainian camps, like Team 612 in Aschaffenburg, with a population of over 2,000, and Team 517 in Kastel, with over 2,000 Ukrainians, have not yet been screened. In all of these camps reported as being screened there has been only one incident of irregularity reported.

4. This incident occurred in Hindenburg Kaserne where about 230 persons were evicted because they were "Soviet citizens." These persons were in actuality Russian Ukrainians. This eviction was carried out by the Army screening team under the 9th Division's interpretation of directives to the effect that any person who is a Soviet citizen is not eligible for DP care. This seems to be an interpretation that has long been used in the Bavarian district by both the Military Government and Tactical Troops. I immediately challenged this interpretation of 9th Division's and caused to have USFET bulletin of 4 January on the subject "Repatriation of Soviet Citizens Under The Yalta Agreement" re-interpreted to the 9th Division by 3rd Army Headquarters. The interpretation was to the effect that Soviet citizens are eligible for DP care excepting those three categories in Para. 2a, b, and c which call for involuntary repatriation by Soviet authorities. This interpretation is now in effect with screening teams and there have been no other incidences of eviction of Soviet citizens. The UNRRA team was instructed to assist those persons unjustly evicted at Hindenburg Kaserne to make appeals to the 9th Division Review Board. This is being carried out insofar as possible, although it is quite difficult, because within two or three days' time many of the evictees were scattered in refugee centers throughout a wide area of the American Zone.

5. In general, the screening of Ukrainians is without event. There is no special consideration being given to them or demanded by them, and there have been no incidences revealing that they are especially guilty of collaboration with the enemy or in other ways are particularly different from any other nationality of DPs as to eligibility for UNRRA care. It still may be seriously questioned whether or not even screening teams are able to make proper classification of Ukrainians as to citizenship although screening teams and UNRRA personnel assigned to the teams are certainly aware of this difficulty.

J.H. WHITING
Zone Director

Source: United Nations (UNRRA) Archives, New York. PAG – 4/3.0.11.0, 1.4:2, "Eligibility (Screening), Liaison Officers."

17. The Condition of Displaced Persons

SEPTEMBER 1946

REPORT OF THE EXECUTIVE STAFF
OF THE UNITED NATIONS RELIEF AND REHABILITATION
ADMINISTRATION (UNRRA), U.S. ZONE HEADQUARTERS,
TO THE DIRECTOR GENERAL OF UNRRA

The purpose of this report and of this action is to bring to the personal attention of the Director General of UNRRA a realistic view of the deplorable and rapidly deteriorating position of the Displaced Persons in the U.S. Zone of Occupation in Germany. For the reasons which are explained further herein, it is the conclusion of the Executive Staff of UNRRA U.S. Zone Headquarters that immediate action is required by the highest level of authority to initiate steps for the earliest possible *removal of non-repatriable Displaced Persons and Refugees from Germany*.

It is the conclusion of UNRRA U.S. Zone personnel that the ideology which ineradicably permeates the minds of the German people is successfully exerted with such consistent pressure upon the Military Government and the Army of Occupation as to render them incapable of securing for the DP a safe haven in Germany; that to retain them in Germany for any protracted length of time, under any conditions, would be to perpetuate the crimes of Nazism and the injustices of other circumstances which have caused them to be uprooted from their normal lives, with the loss of relatives, friends and possessions; that to oblige them to continue their present form of existence would be to contribute to the creation of a "barrack race," a demoralized, hopeless mass of stranded humanity.[1]

The agencies upon whom it had been expected that the responsibility for resettlement would fall, have proven inadequate to meet the situation. It is known that the Economic and Social Council of UNO [United Nations Organization] have recognized the seriousness and urgency of the problem, but unfortunately the plans of this body do not call for any form of initial action before September 1946.

It therefore remains for UNRRA, who has lived in close human touch with these unfortunate people for many months, to take the initiatives in their behalf. While it may be argued that such action does not come within the scope of UNRRA responsibility as governed by its charter and resolutions, it is the consensus of the UNRRA personnel in the field that, because of the effort which has been put forth, and in order not to shatter the last remaining hope and faith which the DPs are placing in it, there *has* developed the inescapable moral obligation and responsibility upon UNRRA to see the problem through, either directly or indirectly.

It has therefore been resolved to place before the Director General of UNRRA the urgent request that he take the lead in developing a solution for the Displaced Persons in Germany. Known as a man of direct, forceful action, unfettered by political or diplomatic considerations, but bound rather by strong human instincts to the sufferings of oppressed and downtrodden people, it is hoped that he will use his strength and prestige to awaken world consciousness to the urgency of this need; that he will take direct and energetic action with the Governments of Canada, Australia, New Zealand, Brazil, and any other interested nations to hasten the opening of their gates to these people; that he will take steps to spur the Economic and Social Council of UNO into more rapid action on their behalf; and that he will take necessary action with the Government of the United States in order that, pending their final resettlement, the genuine DP and refugees in Germany will be given asylum, hospitality and protection in the true spirit of American tradition.

I. GENERAL SITUATION OF DP, U.S. MILITARY AND GERMAN AUTHORITIES

. . . In countries other than Germany and not under military occupation, the lot of the DP is not critical. He lives among former Allies with fairly equal economic, educational and general living opportunities. His ultimate settlement can be a plan of the future, without causing him undue suffering and hardships in the meanwhile.

The DP and refugees remaining in Germany, whether in camps or in the community, do not have such an equal chance. They are living in a country hostile to them, which is itself being subjected to a punitive economy under military control with lowered standards of living and restricted occupational and educational opportunities. They are held in the greatest contempt by the Germans, who lose no opportunity to discredit them in the eyes of the American Military Authorities. The effect of this derogatory influence has been strong and widespread to the point where it has seeped up from the operating levels to even the highest military echelons. The DP problem has always been a nuisance to the Army. With redeployment and the introduction of new, untrained and unoriented military personnel, there is now an almost complete lack of knowledge and understanding of the factors which created the DP situation in the first place; and the subjection of the Americans [sic] mind to German influence has been such that there is even less human sympathy and consideration than there is understanding. The DP are generally considered by military personnel as "lousy Poles" and "Goddam DP" who should be sent back where they came from whether they like it or not.

The combat troops who originally liberated the DP, who saw the conditions to which they had been subjected, were human and considerate in their treatment of them. The directives of General Eisenhower, reflecting the policies of the U.S. Government and people, recognized the DP on the level of Allied citizens and decreed that, pending final repatriation or resettlement, they would be cared for on a high standard at the expense of the German community, and that *priority* was to be given to their requirements over those of the Germans.

Insofar as it has affected and continues to affect the DP situation, we can state authoritatively that the U.S. military establishment has broken down completely. The directives of General Eisenhower have not been and are not being properly implemented in the field. The majority of officials are woefully ignorant of the problem and the few officers remaining who have knowledge of, and sympathy for it are unable to make their influence felt at the troop level. Occasional instances of sympathetic and cooperative treatment by military authorities at the field level are usually the product of the individual intelligence and humanity of a particular officer and of his resistance to German influence.

That the contempt for the DP and forgetfulness of his proper status has also permeated the higher military echelons, is evidenced by recent policies. Most revealing of the loss of regard toward the DP, and of the absence of elemental psychological understanding, is the granting of authority for the use of German police in carrying out raids and searches in DP installations. That the average DP has long been subjected to German brutal force is established fact. That he will resent and resist the intrusion of this, to him, same brutal force into his so-called "liberated" situation, is a foregone conclusion.

This policy has provoked several serious situations, and has culminated in the incident at Stuttgart, where over 200 armed German police, under the supervision of a few MP [military police] troops with *no* commissioned officer, using a number of dogs on leashes, surrounded and attempted to search a camp of approximately 1,500 Polish-Jewish Displaced Persons. This resulted in the shooting to death by the German police of one Polish-Jew (survivor of a concentration camp and only recently reunited with his wife and two children) and the wounding by gunshot of three other DPs.

Another activity carried out on the basis of military necessity has been the wholesale transferring of DP populations from one camp to another. That this is a policy of subtle coercion toward repatriation has been confirmed by the statements of high officers who did not want the DP to become too "settled" in their living conditions.

Further to this attitude is the evident and proclaimed desire of the military to "liquidate" the DP problem by integrating DPs into the German community. This has taken the form of more or less official announcements in the press relative to the imminent closing of DP camps and various instructions given by U.S. officers at field level that UNRRA DP camps were to be closed as of certain dates, without any indication as to the future fate of the DP.

Another indication is the great emphasis which is being placed on the criminality of DPs. Continuous allegations by German civil authorities of black market activities of DPs, and the general conclusion that DP camps are largely populated by collaborators, by SS, etc., have created the tendency to class all remaining DPs as criminals and collaborators. These allegations and conclusions are founded more on assumptions than on facts. On the allegations of black market activities, and sometimes possession of arms, shake-down raids have been carried out at some time or other in almost every DP camp in the U.S. Zone. These have often been carried out by U.S. troops, untrained, unoriented, and undisciplined, without adequate officer supervision, in the crudest and roughest manner, with deliberate destruction and theft by the troops of DPs' personal possessions. These raids have in general failed to produce the evidence of large-scale black market activities by DPs as would justify such violent action. Likewise, what screening has been accomplished thus far has failed to reveal any large percentage of collaborators or otherwise undeserving persons in DP camps which would factually sustain the general assumption which is being taken.

The deterioration of the Military attitude toward the DPs, and the arbitrary, provoking and often violent actions which are being taken against them, have served to place them again in the position of inferiority and baseness, in the eyes of the Germans, that they occupied under the Nazi regime; this time, however, with the apparent concurrence of the Americans. More and more authority is being delegated to the German Civil Government and the DPs are receiving proportionately less and less protection from the U.S. Military.

Living in an uncertain status, lacking any clearly defined juridical rights and representation, the DP in his contacts with German authorities is again the victim of discriminations and ruthless treatment.

II. PRESENT LIVING CONDITIONS AND MORALE OF DPS IN THE U.S. ZONE

The living conditions of DPs and their material and spiritual lot can be generally estimated as being about ten per cent of the requirements necessary to achieve a minimum acceptable standard.

Most of the DPs live in former troops barracks, often partially destroyed, in primitive conditions of housing and feeding. The directives of General Eisenhower calling for the provision of normal living accommodations, even at the expense of German housing, were intended to restore to the DPs some opportunity for the home life which had been denied them for many years. These directives always met with resistance by Military Government and have been implemented only to an insignificant degree. This fact is self-evident since the DPs have continued to live in the most demoralizing conditions of overcrowding, with large numbers of people in single rooms, often with mixed sexes, mixed families and with children of all ages observers of adult intimacies. Within the compass of one room, without separation or privacy of any kind, are affected by groups of people the daily activities of dressing and undressing, of eating and sleeping, and of conjugal relations. These barracks constructed only for the use of regimented men are totally inadequate in the basic requirements of sanitation. The waste disposal, washing facilities and toilets were intended for a population of men, not women and children. The difficulties in obtaining materials and tools for alterations have prevented any substantial degree of correction of these conditions. Only by virtue of the initiative and persistence of UNRRA team personnel were some of the badly damaged barracks repaired sufficiently to enable the DPs to withstand the past winter. The facilities for food preparation and messing are equally dismal. While sufficient food is provided to retain average health (not, however, for workers) the lack of balance, the monotony of diet, and the method of preparation, dispensation, contribute to the general despondency. The DP diet contains very little, if any, fresh foods of any kind. Military Government regulations forbid the procurement of fresh foods, other than potatoes from indigenous sources for DPs. Any efforts by the DPs to secure such foods independently are immediately attacked by M.G. [Military Government] and German authorities as black marketing activities.

There are few facilities which can be adapted to use as central messes and this idea is generally resisted by the DP; for, although his main meal usually consists of the eternal soup or stew, in which most of the available ingredients are combined, he prefers to carry it in a container of any description to the room where, supplemented by some dry rations, on a box or other flat surface, he goes through the parody of setting the family table.

The DP's clothing is not calculated to restore or sustain this self respect. He has been provided with a covering for his body, generally a second hand, ill fitting garment. The legal issue has been limited to a single item, i.e., one trouser, one jacket, one dress, one pair of shoes, without due allowance for cleaning, mending or replacement, resulting in considerable difficulty in making ends meet. This condition has been particularly demoralizing for the women. Independent efforts by the DP to obtain supplementary clothing are again attacked as black market activities; in fact, items of clothing legitimately possessed by the DP are often confiscated by U.S. troops or German police during shakedown raids. The German civilian is still unusually well dressed and presents a neat respectable appearance. In contrast the DP looks like a bum, and this difference does not fail to make its impression on the U.S. troop. The German looks like a gentleman (or a lady) and the U.S. soldier accepts him as such; the DP man or woman looks like a bum or a tramp and that is the way they are regarded. The medical aspect of the care for DP has been far in advance of any other. Fortunately, UNRRA was able to discharge directly this professional service by having doctors on its teams; but even here, the difficulties of securing medical supplies and instruments for DP use have been a great obstacle to an adequate program. Until recently, UNRRA's medical services were limited to camp infirmaries, to deliveries, inoculations and minor injuries. Patients suffering from major illnesses or requiring surgical treatment were generally placed in German hospitals, with varying degrees of acceptance by the Germans. At present, however, UNRRA has direct administrative control of hospitals for DP to the extent of nine thousand beds, which is resulting in a great improvement for hospitalized cases.

It is a tribute to the zeal of UNRRA medical personnel that no serious outbreak of disease has occurred among DP. It is also significant that the program has been successful, in the one field of professional work where UNRRA services could be directly applied in the field, without great dependency on the military organization.

The foregoing paragraphs have dealt with the basic physical requirements to sustain life and health among the DP and the shabby manner in which they are met.

Even more serious are the tremendous deficiencies in those aspects of a normal life which develop character and spiritual values, i.e., employment opportunities, work incentives, education, vocational training, religion and recreation; and as long as the DP remain in Germany their possibilities for realizing these activities are non-existent.

Understandably enough the DP refuse to work for Germans or under German supervision, the latter being generally a condition of working for the Army. They have no desire to assist in the reconstruction of Germany, nor to be again subjected to German regimentation and discrimination against foreigners. There is plenty of hard labor to be done in Germany, but the DP who are highly trained professional and technical people (especially the Balts), such as engineers, scientists, architects, lawyers, doctors, teachers and scholars, administrators, etc., have no prospect whatsoever of following their individual pursuits or of establishing themselves once more with any degree of independence.

The maximum employment of DP has been between 12 and 14%. All but a very few of these work in assembly center administration, maintenance and workshops. On the principle that the Germans must bear the cost of DP maintenance, directives provide that the wages of such workers must be paid by the Bürgermeisters. This policy is meeting with growing resistance on the part of Bürgermeisters and Military Government.

Army directives have always stated that priority in employment be given to DPs, yet consistent discrimination has been practiced against this group by all Army echelons. This, the one possibility for acceptable employment outside of assembly centers, has never been realized. The UNRRA Employment Branch presented to the Displaced Persons Division at USFET a practical operating procedure for DP employment pools in October 1945. This division took no action until 13 March 1946, despite constant urging of this branch. On this date, a directive was again issued stressing the priority to be given DPs in employment by the Army. In view of the delegation of procurement responsibility to German civil authorities and of their recognized antagonistic attitude toward the DP, its effective implementation is not probable.

It is now a year since their liberation, and the majority of DPs have remained in comparative idleness. That they are idle by nature cannot be accepted, since the nationalities they represent are traditionally hard workers; but lacking adequate opportunities, motivation of private family life and responsibility, incentives of remuneration in convertable currencies, supplementary workers' rations and, most important, a future for which to strive, it is inevitable that every passing day adds to the deterioration of character, self-respect and the urge for independence.

Equally discouraging in effect are the extreme limitations in educational and training opportunities. The desire for education is unusually high and UNRRA welfare personnel have exploited existent possibilities to the fullest extent. However, it is estimated that only about five per cent of the children, youth and adults are having their educational and training needs properly fulfilled to desirable standards. The lack of space for school facilities, inability to procure adequate books and school supplies and the dearth of teachers, particularly in the Polish and Jewish groups, have all contributed to this deplorable situation.

German high schools, technical schools and universities have been ordered to make available ten per cent of their enrollment to DPs, but here again exists a language barrier, since these schools are conducted in German and [there is] the natural reluctance of the DP to accept German-style education, even under Military Government supervision. In any case, these facilities would meet only about one-tenth of the need.

Opportunities for vocational training are equally limited by lack of machinery and materials, with obvious reluctance on the part of Military Government to make such facilities available for DPs. A case in point was the action considered necessary by Military Government to forbid supplies of leather for DP centers. This leather was being used in cobbler workshops, set up in centers for two purposes: to repair shoes and for apprentice cobblers. DP shoes subsequently had to be sent to German factories for repair.

Religion and recreation have found a measure of native self-expression, despite dire limitations of facilities and materials. Because of its suppression under the Germans, religion assumed greater significance than ever for these people. Psychologically, the DP has had to cope with the effect of years aimed at the degradation of the human spirit, and with the months since liberation spent under conditions which have afforded little opportunities for private family living, little chance for constructive employment, little hope for the future. Serious handicaps have been the absence of a Greek Orthodox Church in Germany, of synagogues, and of facilities for Roman Catholics, notably the Poles, who do not choose to use churches frequented by the Germans. Spiritual leadership is also lacking as well as materials such as bibles, prayerbooks, etc. UNRRA and the voluntary agencies are doing all in their power to facilitate religious services and the observance of major religious holidays, the first such holidays to be observed since the war began.

The recreational activities of the DP instinctively take the forms best calculated to buoy their flagging spirits. National zeal is manifest through their music, dramatics, crafts, legend and lore. The exuberance of children and youth finds expression in sports and games, under any conditions.

This bright spot of cultural recovery, while serving to hide the tragedy and hopelessness which lie in their hearts, is also an indication of their ability to adjust and and of their potential contribution to any community in which they may live and work with equal freedom and opportunity.

At this stage, the morale of the Displaced Persons is at its lowest ebb. The change of attitude and treatment by the U.S. Military leaves them utterly bewildered. The incomprehensible moves of entire population from one camp to another, abruptly destroying whatever meager roots they may have established, fills them with dismay. The increase of German authority over them and the announced prospect of their being dumped into the German community and left to their own resources, is draining their very last hopes. Their faith in UNRRA is dying, for they cannot understand that the U.S. Military are the only responsible and commanding authority as far as the DPs are concerned.

The U.S. Immigration program, at first a light on the horizon, is being recognized in all its inadequacy, and the silence of other nations on the subject of refuge fills them with despair.

On every side, the future is dark and forbidding. The job that started with liberation, in all its glorious, humanitarian brightness, has been left to drift and disintegrate. The world of charity and understanding is breaking faith with a part of humanity.

But the job *must* be completed. The impoverished "little people," caught like grains of sand between the millstones of power, cannot be left to the "tender mercies" of a German populace, nor to the degrading effects of substandard institutional living. They *must* be removed from Germany and given the ordinary opportunities of human beings.

Every sincere UNRRA employee feels in his heart, "It is up to UNRRA to take the lead and point the way" – now, urgently, without delay.

Source: United Nations (UNRRA) Archives, New York. PAG-4/3.0.11. 3.0-9, "Confidential Report on the General Situation of DPs."

Notes

1 American policy in the U.S. Zone of Occupied Germany stressed the principle that administrative functions should be delegated as rapidly as feasible to politically reliable Germans. By October 1945, three state administrations had been set up in the zone – Bavaria, North Württemberg-Baden, and Greater Hesse – in addition to the separate administration for the Bremen enclave. In each *Land*, or state, appointed officials headed by a Minister-President were assigned full responsibility for internal affairs not involving security. All aspects of German administration were carefully scrutinized and supervised by U.S. military government, which, by January 1946, was separately constituted as the Office of Military Government (OMGUS). Even such important tasks as denazification were turned over to the German administration. (Ed.)

18. Report on the Screening of the First Ukrainian Division

21 FEBRUARY 1947

REFUGEE SCREENING COMMISSION REPORT
ON UKRAINIANS IN SURRENDERED ENEMY PERSONNEL
(SEP) CAMP NO. 374 ITALY

LACAB/18 RSC/RIC   21 February 1947

1. This camp consists entirely of male Ukrainians who were either captured in German uniform or were working in Germany as civilians and attached themselves to the 1st Ukrainian Division shortly before its surrender. The proportion of civilians is small, and doubt exists about exactly how many come into this category and about exactly when they joined up with the Division. I refer to this in more detail in paragraph 7 below. The number of inmates varies from time to time due to escapes, transfers to hospitals, etc., but the figure on which we have been working, and which was confirmed on 16th February by the British camp authorities as accurate, is a total of 8,272, which includes 218 permanently employed outside the camp on working parties. None had been screened previously by any British authority and no British records either on individuals or of a general nature were available to us here.

2. Individual screening by us being impossible, it was decided to question a small cross section chosen in accordance with their *Wehrmacht* formations. A full nominal roll broken up into these formations was prepared for us by the Ukrainian camp leader, Major Jaskewycz, which gave the following breakdown:

1,203 Offrs and ORs of the 1st Infantry Regt of the 1st Ukrainian Div.
1,058 Offrs and ORs of the 2nd Infantry Regt of the 1st Ukrainian Div.
1,150 Offrs and ORs of the 3rd Infantry Regt of the 1st Ukrainian Div.
  938 Offrs and ORs of the Artillery (actually with 4th Regt) of the 1st Ukrainian Div.
  320 Offrs and ORs of the Supply Section of the 1st Ukrainian Div.
  305 Offrs and ORs of the Engineer Bn. of the 1st Ukrainian Div.
  205 Offrs and ORs of the Signals Unit of the 1st Ukrainian Div.

2,230 Offrs and ORs of the Recruiting Regt of the 1st Ukrainian Div.
  76 Offrs and ORs of the Workshop Coy. of the 1st Ukrainian Div.
 281 Offrs and ORs of the Fusilier Bn. of the 1st Ukrainian Div.
 221 Offrs and ORs of the Sanitary Section of the 1st Ukrainian Div.
 156 Offrs and ORs of the Anti Tank Section of the 1st Ukrainian Div.
 125 Offrs and ORs of the Divisional Staff of the 1st Ukrainian Div.
   4 Offrs and ORs of the Army Staff of the 1st Ukrainian Div.
 _____
 8,272

3. At the same time Major Jaskewycz gave us his version of the history of the 1st Ukrainian Division and the various units that composed it. It should be emphasized that all these nominal rolls and the short history of the Division were supplied entirely by the Ukrainians themselves and that we had no information here of any kind against which they could be checked; and virtually none of the men had any identifying documents of any use, such as German Army pay books, though one or two of them had pre-war Polish civilian identity cards. I feel satisfied, however, that Major Jaskewycz has done his best to provide accurate and complete information, as far as he was able.

4. Our next step was to select a cross section of these people for questioning. We concentrated on the first three regiments and the Artillery Regiment in order to try to build up a Battle Order. Fifty officers and men were chosen at random from the nominal rolls of these four regiments, but in actual practice it proved impossible to question only 47 of the 1st Regiment, 49 of the 2nd Regiment, 46 of the 3rd Regiment and 47 of the Artillery Regiment. A few others were chosen from the Signals Unit, the Supply Section and the Engineer Battalion, and 30 from the Recruiting or Reserve Regiment. Except in the case of Mr. Brown, who was able to question the men in Russian, Ukrainian-speaking interpreters, who were actually inmates of the camp, had to be used.

5. When the questioning had been completed the individual statements of each man were checked against each other and against the information supplied by Major Jaskewycz about the Division and its various units. No serious discrepancies were discovered, nor did any particularly suspicious individual come to light, except in so far as some of them stated that they had volunteered for armed service with the Germans as early as July 1943, whereas the 1st Ukrainian Division does not appear to have been formed until the late summer of 1944. Nineteen men were therefore selected for further questioning, which disclosed that they had been enlisted in the summer of 1943 in the 1st Galician Division or the 14th Galician Grenadier Division. As it was not clear from the interrogations whether this was one and the same Division or two separate ones, I questioned the three senior officers in the Camp on this point, and established that it was called by the Germans the 14th Galician *Waffen* Grenadier Division and consisted of three Infantry and one Artillery Regiments. I do not see anything suspicious in some of the men not knowing exactly what unit they were in, and they probably referred to it as the 1st Galician Division because it was for them the first Division to be formed out of Ukrainians from Galicia. This Division suffered heavy losses at Brody in July 1944 and ceased to exist. The 1st Ukrainian Division was formed round its

remnants. One of the officers of the 14th Galician *Waffen* Grenadier Division has stated that it was originally called by the Germans a *Waffen-SS* Division but the *SS* was dropped from its title, on the Ukrainians protesting, and that it subsequently became an ordinary German Army Division. It seems, however, to have had some *SS* training, which would account for some of its officers having given their ranks as *Untersturmfuehrer*, which is a *SS* rank and not an ordinary German Army rank.

6. As far as the 1st Ukrainian Division is concerned, the short history supplied by Major Jaskewycz was borne out by the individual interrogations and we were able to draw up a nucleus of its Battle Order. The Division appears to have been formed about September 1944 and actually to have fought for only about one month in the late stages of the campaign in Austria (April 1945); the rest of its time was occupied in training and guard duties in Austria and Yugoslavia. It surrendered to us in Austria in May 1945. The men we questioned were nearly all of the simple peasant type, and made a good impression, showing no signs of either prevarication or truculence; a high proportion of them, and, from what we have seen, of the whole camp, are under 30 years of age. I myself questioned the three senior officers in the camp, Lt. Cols. Sylenko and Nikitin, and Major Jaskewycz. The other senior officers, namely two full colonels and one Lt. Col, were not available, but I feel sure that their story is similar to the history of the others. These three officers' stories were much the same. They were all born in the 1890s in Russia, became regular Tsarist army officers and fought in the 1914 war against the Germans. After the revolution of 1917 they fought for the Whites against the Bolsheviks in the Ukrainian Army; and when these hostilities came to an end all three settled in Poland as political emigrees [sic] with Nansen passports. None of them has this passport now, but Sylenko produced, as though it were a highly valuable objet d'art, a passport issued in 1918 by the Democratic Government of the Ukraine. He told me with pride that this was now very rare. They kept themselves in Poland from 1922 to 1939 by working in various civil jobs and continued in these jobs during and after the German occupation of Poland in 1939. They claimed that their status as political emigres exempted them from service in the Polish Army and all were insistent that they had never acquired Polish nationality. Some of the men, however, admit to having served in the Polish Army in 1939 and in a few cases were able to produce authentic-looking documents in support of their claim to Polish nationality. No officer or man that we saw admitted to having served in the Red Army, nor do I think it likely that any of these Ukrainians did do so. About 10% are of the Orthodox faith. On the crucial point whether any of them are Soviet citizens by our definition we have no evidence other than that supplied by the men themselves. Many of the places which they have given as their place of birth and/or habitual residence are small villages and hamlets which are not likely to be marked on any but the largest maps; but I think we can safely assume that the great majority of those born after 1919 were born in Poland, and were resident in Poland on 1st September 1939, and that the great majority of those born before Poland existed were not resident in the Soviet Union on 1st September 1939. The general impression which we have formed of all the men in the camp is favourable, as they strike us all as being decent, simple-minded sort of people. The national emblem of the Ukraine, in the form

of a trident, is freely displayed all over the camp, and the inmates clearly regard themselves as a homogeneous unit, unconnected either with Russia or Poland, and do not seem conscious of having done any wrong.

7. Our attention has been concentrated on trying to build up a Battle Order and a general picture of the Division, and we have for this reason paid no attention to any of the miscellaneous units except the Signals Unit, the Supply Section, and the Engineer Battalion. Some of the real villains of the piece, if there are any, may be sheltering behind these innocuous sounding units, but that is a risk which we have to take. We did, however, question thirty of the Recruiting or Reserve Regiment, the largest single unit in the camp. We did not expect these interrogations to throw much light on the Division as a whole, which proved to be the case; but we were anxious to question some men in this regiment, as the camp leader had told us that a fair proportion of them were really civilians such as Todt workers, who had only attached themselves to the regiment shortly before its surrender, as a means of escaping from the Germans. It so happened that of the thirty men we picked, none admitted to having been a Todt worker, although six of them said that they had not been enlisted in the regiment until the early part of 1945, and that before this date they had been working in various factories in Germany. Time prevented us from pursuing the matter further, but this omission is not important, as if any of the men were really civilians that must be considered a point in their favour rather than the reverse.

8. During the course of our enquiries we discovered that nearly all these Ukrainians had already been screened by an official Soviet Mission (they were then in a different camp at Bellaria). The first part of the Soviet Mission arrived on 13 August 1945, with the primary object of weeding out all the Ukrainians who were not Soviet citizens according to the Soviet definition, by which all people who were resident in that part of pre-war Poland bounded on the west by the Curzon line and on the east by the then Polish-Soviet frontier were considered Soviet citizens if they were still resident in that area by the time the Red Army occupied it in late September 1949(?). Three hundred and ninety-seven officers and men who had claimed not to be Soviet citizens, were screened by the Soviet Mission and 127 of them were passed as not being Soviet citizens and were forthwith removed from the Ukrainian camp (most of them are now back in it). The remainder were kept in the camp. On 17th August 1945 Col. Jakovlev arrived in order to discuss administrative matters. He maintained that all those left in the camp after the Soviet screening should be administered on lines laid down by the Soviet Union, and that they were eligible for the scale of rations, clothing and pay to which free Soviet citizens were entitled under the Yalta agreement. This contention was rejected. Colonel Jakovlev thereupon decided to begin a drive in the camp for voluntary repatriation, and to break down the general resistance to such repatriation by having what he called the "stubborn Fascist minority" removed from the camp. A supplementary Soviet Mission under General Vasilov arrived on the 20th August for this purpose, but only succeeded in securing 50 volunteers for repatriation, who were forthwith removed from the camp and reclassified as Free Soviet citizens. They are presumably back in the Soviet Union. The General and his personal staff left the camp on the 25th August, having met with a hostile reception and

having apparently abandoned any further attempt to secure more volunteers. The task which General Vasilov had begun of identifying the stubborn Fascist minority was continued by the original members of the mission who had arrived on the 13th August and was not completed until the end of September. Some attempt was made at thoroughness in dealing with the officers, but most of the men appear to have been treated in a remarkably high-handed and abrupt manner. When the mission had finished they stated to the British authorities that a minority in the camp was definitely responsible for terrorising the great majority from volunteering for repatriation, and that once this minority had been removed from the camp most of the remainder would eventually come forward as volunteers. Eleven men were in fact removed at the request of the Soviet Mission, but were subsequently allowed by the British authorities to return. I am satisfied that there are no grounds for the Soviet Mission's complaint of terrorisation. No official report of their activities was supplied by the Soviet Mission to the local British authorities, and the information given in this paragraph was supplied by Major Hills, GSI(b) of this Sub-Area, who was present when the visits took place.

9. The only effect, which the Soviet Mission's visit appears to have had on the Ukrainians, was to convince any waverers there might have been never to return to the Soviet Union, and to cause a great deal of probably justified anxiety to those who still had relatives there. We must, I think, accept as a definite fact, that all those Ukrainians now in Camp 374 who were screened by the Soviet Mission – that is to say the great majority – are now regarded by the Soviet Government as Soviet citizens, and that having failed to secure their voluntary repatriation the Soviet Government will demand their forcible repatriation as War Criminals when the Italian Treaty comes into force.

10. Attached you will find the following results of our activities:

*i) Nominal rolls of all the inmates of the camp broken up into their various Wehrmacht Units.

ii) Information about each unit supplied by Major Jaskewycz.

iii) Names of those chosen for questioning.

iv) Case sheets of the results of this questioning (enclosed in a separate folder).

v) Summary of information taken from cases.

vi) Battle Order for the first three Regiments, the Artillery Regiment and the Recruiting Regiment compiled from the individual questionnaires and from Major Jaskewycz's histories.

*Note: These are not forwarded with this report.

11. We have thus obtained a reasonably consistent picture as far as it goes, and as far as it can go within the limits of our time and resources. The men may be all or in part lying, and even their names may be false. No attempt at cross examination was made except where some obscurity or glaring discrepancy was revealed during the course of the interrogation; the work in fact which the screeners have done has largely consisted of taking down through an interpreter the men's answers to a limited number of set questions. If, however, we are to get anywhere we must, and in my opinion, can safely, assume that by

and large the men are what they say they are and did what they say they did. It would seem therefore that the only further screening processes that can usefully be applied:

i) To see if any of the men listed in the nominal rolls figure in UNWCC or CROWCASS lists or have been specifically accused by the Russian or other government of War Crimes.

ii) To see if any of the units to which the men belong have particularly bad war records.

iii) To see if the short history of the various units and of the Division as a whole, as ascertained by interrogation, corresponds to the known facts about them. It might be possible to locate some of the German officers of the Division and have them questioned. None are known to be in this area.

If this further screening confirms the history of the units and produces no bad units and no wanted men, then the solution of the problem resolves itself into taking a decision on the following general considerations:

A. It seems likely that the great majority, at least of the men, are not Soviet citizens by our definition. It must, however, be borne in mind that an official Soviet Mission has questioned nearly all of them, and that the Soviet Government merely regards nearly all of them as Soviet citizens; and that there *may* be among them a number who are Soviet citizens by our definition. We may, therefore, if we get them all accepted as DPs render ourselves liable to a valid charge of sheltering Russian traitors. (It might be worthwhile noting in this connection that on the nationality issue these men are really having the best of both worlds. They do not qualify as Soviet citizens because their place of birth and/or habitual domicile on 1.9.39 were in Poland, and they therefore by our definition escape all punishment by the Russians for their having assisted the enemy; and they are not presumably eligible now for punishment by the Polish authorities because that part of the country from which they came is no longer part of Poland.)

B. The great majority of them voluntarily enlisted in the German Armed Forces and fought against our Allies, Soviet Russia and Jugoslavia. There are some grounds for believing that some of those whom we have questioned have stated that they were volunteers, because if they said that they had been conscripted they would then be told that they would have nothing to fear if they returned to the Ukraine. The number of volunteers may thus be smaller than would at first appear. Nonetheless, also allowing for intimidation, and dislike of forced labour, the majority for our purpose must be regarded as volunteers. There are, therefore, prima facie grounds for classifying them as traitors, i.e., as ineligible for IRO status according to the 1st section of paragraph two of the definition sheet. The term "traitor" is vague and has been defined for our guidance by Professor Royse as embodying, among other things, "civilians who voluntarily offer their services to the enemy and, in general sense, people who gave aid and comfort to the enemy." This definition undoubtedly applies to most, if not all, of these Ukrainians.

C. We must, however, I think take into account their motives for having voluntarily offered their services to the enemy, even though by so doing one might be able, as a reductio absurdum [sic], to prove Quisling himself as eligible for IRO assistance. There seem to be four main reasons for their having taken this step:

a) The hope of securing a genuinely independent Ukraine.
b) Without knowing exactly what they were doing, e.g., because other Ukrainians whom they knew had already volunteered.
c) As a preferable alternative to forced labour, etc., or to living in Soviet-controlled territory.
d) To have a smack at the Russians, whom they always refer to as "Bolsheviks".

They probably were not, and certainly do not now seem to be at heart pro-German, and the fact that they did give aid and comfort to the Germans can fairly be considered to have been incidental and not fundamental.

D. The desire among their leaders for an independent Ukraine, naive and unreal as it is, is nonetheless genuine.

E. They are obsessed by a terror and hatred, bordering in some cases almost on hysteria, of Soviet Russia. It seems clear that when the Russians occupied Eastern Poland in 1939–40 many of these people's wives and families were ruthlessly taken away from their homes to Siberia and other remote parts of the Soviet Union and have not been seen or heard of since. They also seem to have suffered a good deal at the hands of the Red Army during the Russo-German campaign, and also on occasion at the hands of the Germans.

F. None of them wish to return to the Ukraine, with the exception of one man, who, after securing an interview with one of the Commissioners and stating to him that he did wish to return to the Ukraine, was subsequently found to be suffering from the last stages of consumption and was not expected to live very much longer. He is now in the hospital.

G. No one in the camp has been sentenced by any British military authority to one year's imprisonment or over. Their behaviour indeed since their surrender to us has been exemplary. They have not indulged in any subversive activities, nor do I think they will do so in the future. They seem resigned to the fact that there is now no place in Europe for them and that those of them who have wives and families in the Soviet Union will never see them again. We must not, however, expect most of them ever to become well disposed toward the Soviet Union.

12. I am not competent from here to judge the issue as far as our relations with the Soviet Union (or with Poland) are concerned; nor do I know whether our policy is to interpret strictly or liberally the instructions as to who is eligible for DP status and who not. I can only speak from the experience gained from our actually having seen the men and from humanitarian instincts common to us all; and on this basis and taking into account the long time that has elapsed from the end of the war, I recommend most strongly that all these Ukrainians should be classified as DPs; and I would add, with all the emphasis I can command, that, if this is accepted, immediate action, not high-sounding resolutions, is necessary either to ensure that the IRO or the IGCR can give them effective protection as DPs from being handed over to the Soviet Government by the

Italian Government under the Treaty, or to have them removed lock, stock and barrel from Italy before the Treaty comes into force.[1]

(signed) D. Haldane Porter
Refugee Screening Commission
In charge S.E.P. Camp 374

Source: Public Archives of Canada, Ottawa, Citizenship and Immigration Branch, RG 26 vol. 147, file 3-43-1 (copy).

Note

1 The British feared that Italy, after the withdrawal of British troops, would not be able to resist Soviet pressure to forcibly repatriate division members. It was therefore decided that most of the division members would be removed from Italy and brought to work camps in England, in place of the repatriated German prisoners of war. In May 1947 the men were moved to Britain, where they retained their prisoner of war status until the end of 1948. About 500, however, were allowed to join their families in West Germany and did not go to Britain. For a history of the division during the war, see the article by Myroslav Yurkevich in this volume. (Ed.)

19. British Foreign Office Assessment of the First Ukrainian Division

5 SEPTEMBER 1950

Imm. B53802   Ottawa File
Our File 232-L-40   No. 232-L-40
Despatch No. 2087
Date 5th September 1950   Security Classification
CONFIDENTIAL

FROM: The High Commissioner for Canada in the United Kingdom

TO: The Secretary of State for External Affairs, Canada

REFERENCE: Your despatch No. C229 dated 14th August 1950

SUBJECT: Admission into Canada of Ukrainian Surrendered Enemy
Personnel

The information which you requested on behalf of the Minister of Citizenship and Immigration, in your above-referenced despatch, regarding the past record of Ukrainian refugees now in the United Kingdom and who served in the German armed forces, has to-day been received from the United Kingdom authorities in response to our enquiry on the subject, and I quote below from the Foreign Office letter dated the 4th September:

While in Italy these men were screened by Soviet and British missions and neither then nor subsequently has any evidence been brought to light which would suggest that any of them fought against the Western Allies or engaged in crimes against humanity. The behaviour since they came to this country has been good and they have never indicated in any way that they are infected with any trace of Nazi ideology.

When they surrendered to the Allied forces at the end of the war, they were members of the 1st Ukrainian Division of the Wehrmacht which was formed about September 1944 and which was only in action once (against the Red Army in Austria during April 1945), being employed in training and guard duties in Austria and Yugoslavia during the rest of its existence. Some of its members, however, appear to be survivors of an earlier formation known as the 14th Galician Grenadier Division. This was also a Wehrmacht unit, an attempt made by the Germans to make it into an SS Division having apparently been resisted by the Ukrainians themselves. This unit seems to have been formed about July 1943 and to have been destroyed at the Battle of Brody in June 1944.

From the reports of the special mission set up by the War Office to screen these men, it seems clear that they volunteered to fight against the Red Army from nationalistic motives which were given greater impetus by the behaviour of the Soviet authorities during their earlier occupation of the Western Ukraine after the Nazi-Soviet Pact. Although Communist propaganda has constantly attempted to depict these, like so many other refugees, as "quislings" and "war criminals" it is interesting to note that no specific charges of war crimes have been made by the Soviet or any other Government against any member of this group.

No. of Enclosures

Post File   Signed: L.D. WILGRESS
AR. 408/7   High Commissioner

Source: Public Archives of Canada, Ottawa, Immigration Branch, RG 76, vol. 656, file 1353802 1-2.

20. Address by Ivan Dziuba at Babyn Iar

29 SEPTEMBER 1966

There are events, tragedies, the enormity of which make all words futile and of which silence tells incomparably more – the awesome silence of thousands of people. Perhaps we, too, should keep silent and only meditate. But silence says a lot only when everything that could have been said has already been said. If there is still much to say, or if nothing has yet been said, then silence becomes a partner to falsehood and enslavement. We must, therefore, speak and continue to speak whenever we can, taking advantage of all opportunities, for they come so infrequently.

I want to say a few words – one-thousandth of what I am now thinking and what I would like to say here. I want to address you as men – as my brothers in humanity. I want to address you Jews as a Ukrainian – as a member of the Ukrainian nation to which I proudly belong.

Babyn Iar is a tragedy of all mankind, but it happened on Ukrainian soil. And, therefore, a Ukrainian has no more right to forget it than a Jew has. Babyn Iar is our common tragedy, a tragedy for both the Jewish and the Ukrainian nations.

This tragedy was brought on our nations by fascism.

Yet one must not forget that fascism neither begins nor ends in Babyn Iar. Fascism begins in disrespect to man and ends in the destruction of man, in the destruction of nations – though not necessarily in the manner of Babyn Iar.

Let us imagine for a moment that Hitler had won, that German fascism had been victorious. One can be sure that the victors would have created a brilliant and "flourishing" society that would have attained a high level of economic and technical development and made the same scientific and other discoveries that we have made. Probably the mute slaves of fascism would eventually have "tamed" the cosmos and flown to other planets to represent humanity and earthly civilization. Moreover, this regime would have done everything in order to consolidate its own "truth" so that men would forget the price they paid for such "progress," so that history would excuse or forget their enormous crimes, so that their inhuman society would seem normal to people and even the best in the world. And then, not on the ruins of the Bastille but on the desecrated, forgotten sites of national tragedy, thickly choked with sand, there would have been an official sign: "Dancing Here Tonight."

We should therefore judge each society not by its external technical achievements but by the position and meaning it gives to man, by the value it puts on human dignity and human conscience.

Today, in Babyn Iar, we commemorate not only those who died here. We commemorate millions of Soviet warriors – our fathers – who gave their lives in the struggle against fascism. We commemorate the sacrifices and efforts of millions of Soviet citizens of all nationalities who unselfishly contributed to the victory over fascism. We should remember this so that we may be worthy of their memory and of the duty that has been imposed upon us by the countless sacrifices of human lives, hopes, and aspirations that were made.

Are we worthy of this memory? Apparently not, since even now various forms of human hatred are found among us – including one we call by the worn-out, banal, and yet terrible [name], anti-Semitism. Anti-Semitism is an "international" phenomenon. It has existed and still exists in all societies. Sadly enough, even our own society is not free of it. Perhaps there is nothing strange about this – after all, anti-Semitism is the fruit and companion of age-old barbarism and slavery, the foremost and inevitable result of political despotism. To conquer it – in entire societies – is not an easy task, nor can it be done quickly. But what is strange is the fact that no struggle has been waged here against it during the postwar decades; what is more, it has often been artificially nourished. It seems that Lenin's instructions concerning the struggle against anti-Semitism are forgotten in the same way as his precepts regarding the national development of Ukraine.

In Stalin's day, there were open and flagrant attempts to use prejudices as a means of playing off Ukrainians and Jews against each other – to limit the Jewish national culture on the pretext of Jewish bourgeois nationalism, Zionism, and so on, and to suppress the Ukrainian national culture on the pretext of Ukrainian bourgeois nationalism. These cunningly prepared campaigns wrought damage on both nationalities and did nothing to further friendship between them. They only added one more sad memory to the harsh history of both nations and to the complex history of their relationship.

We must return to these memories not in order to open old wounds but in order to heal them once and for all.

As a Ukrainian, I am ashamed that there is anti-Semitism here, as in other nations; that those shameful phenomena we call anti-Semitism – and which are unworthy of mankind – exist here.

We Ukrainians must fight against all manifestations in our midst of anti-Semitism or disrespect toward the Jews. . . .

You Jews must fight against those in your midst who do not respect Ukrainian people, Ukrainian culture, and the Ukrainian language – against those who unjustly see a potential anti-Semite in every Ukrainian.

We must outgrow all forms of human hatred, overcome all misunderstandings, and by our own efforts win true brotherhood.

It would seem that we ought to be the two nations most likely to understand each other, most likely to give mankind an example of brotherly cooperation. The history of our nations is so similar in its tragedies that, in the Biblical motifs of his "Moses," Ivan Franko recreated the story of the Ukrainian nation in terms of the Jewish legend. Lesia Ukrainka began one of her best poems about Ukraine's tragedy with the line: "And you fought once, like Israel. . . ."

Great sons of both our nations bequeathed to us mutual understanding and friendship. The lives of the three greatest Jewish writers – Sholom Aleichem, Itskhok Peretz, and Mendele Moykher-Sforim – are bound up with Ukraine. . . . The brilliant Jewish publicist Vladimir Zhabotinsky fought on the Ukrainian side in Ukraine's struggle against Russian Tsarism and called upon the Jewish intelligentsia to support the Ukrainian national liberation movement and Ukrainian culture.

One of Taras Shevchenko's last civic acts was his well-known protest against the anti-Semitic policies of the tsarist government. Lesia Ukrainka, Ivan Franko, Borys Hrinchenko, Stepan Vasylchenko, and other leading Ukrainian writers well knew and highly valued the greatness of Jewish history and of the Jewish spirit, and they wrote of the suffering of the Jewish poor with sincere sympathy.

Our common past consists not only of blind enmity and bitter misunderstanding – although there was much of this, too. Our past also shows examples of courageous solidarity and co-operation in the fight for our common ideals of freedom and justice, for the well-being of our nations.

We, the present generation, should continue this tradition and not the tradition of distrust and reserve.

But, sadly enough, there are a number of factors which are not conducive to letting this noble tradition of solidarity take firm root.

One of these factors is the lack of openness and publicity given to the nationalities question. As a result, a kind of "conspiracy of silence" surrounds the problem. The attitude in socialist Poland could serve as a good example for us. We know how complicated the relations between Jews and Poles were in the past. Now there are no traces of past ill-feeling. What is the "secret" of this success? In the first place, the Poles and the Jews were brought closer together by the common evil of the Second World War. But we, too, had this evil in common.

Second – and this we do not have – in socialist Poland, relations between nationalities are the subject of scientific sociological study, public discussion, inquiries in the press and literature, and so on. All this creates a proper atmosphere for successful national and international enlightenment.

We, too, should care about and exert ourselves – in deed rather than just in word – on behalf of this kind of enlightenment. We must not ignore anti-Semitism, chauvinism, disrespect toward any nationality, a boorish attitude toward any national culture or national language. There is plenty of boorishness in our midst, and, in many of us, it begins with the rejection of ourselves – of our nationality, culture, history, and language – even though such a rejection is not always voluntary nor is the person involved always to be blamed.

The road to true and honest brotherhood lies not in self-oblivion but in self-awareness, not in rejection of ourselves and adaptation to others but in being ourselves and respecting others. Jews have a right to be Jews and Ukrainians have a right to be Ukrainians in the full and profound, not merely the formal, sense of the word. Let Jews know Jewish history, Jewish culture, and the Yiddish language and be proud of them. Let Ukrainians know Ukrainian history, Ukrainian culture and language and be proud of them. Let them also know each other's history and culture and the history and culture of other nations, and let them know how to value themselves and others –as brothers.

It is difficult to achieve this – but better to strive for it than to shrug one's shoulders and swim with the current of assimilation and adaptation, which will bring about nothing except boorishness, blasphemy, and veiled human hatred.

With our very lives, we should oppose civilized forms of hatred for mankind and social boorishness. There is nothing more important for us at the present time, because, without such opposition, all our social ideals will lose their meaning.

This is our duty to millions of victims of despotism; this is our duty to the better men and women of the Ukrainian and Jewish nations who have urged us to mutual understanding and friendship; this is our duty to our Ukrainian land in which we live together; this is our duty to humanity.

Source: Viacheslav Chornovil, ed., *Lykho z rozumu: portrety dvadtsiaty "zlochyntsiv"* (The Misfortune of Intellect: Portraits of Twenty "Criminals") (Paris, 1967), 303–8. Translation from Abraham Brumberg, ed., *In Quest of Justice: Protest and Dissent in the Soviet Union Today* (New York: Praeger, 1970).

Note

Ivan Dziuba, literary critic and publicist, lives in Kiev. In the 1960s he was active in the Ukrainian dissident movement and was the author of *Internationalism or Russification?*, a *samizdat* (*samvydav*) work that demonstrated how the Soviet government had departed from Leninist nationality policy. Dziuba was arrested in 1972 and expelled from the Writers' Union of Ukraine. A year later he signed a public recantation and was released from prison. (Ed.)

APPENDIXES

Chronology of Major Events 1914–45

1914

| 28 | July | Austria-Hungary declares war on Serbia |
| 6 | August | *Ukrainski sichovi striltsi* (Ukrainian *Sich* Riflemen) formed as a national legion within the Austrian Army |

1917

| 17 | March | Ukrainian Central *Rada* (Council) formed in Kiev in the wake of the Russian Revolution |
| 20 | November | Central *Rada* proclaims formation of the Ukrainian People's Republic (UNR) as part of a future Russian federation |

1918

22	January	Central *Rada* proclaims Ukrainian independence
9	February	UNR signs a peace treaty with Germany and the other Central Powers
1	November	Western Ukrainian People's Republic (ZUNR), encompassing the Ukrainian lands formerly belonging to Austria-Hungary, is proclaimed in Lviv. The Polish-Ukrainian war begins

1919

| 22 | January | The UNR and ZUNR unite |
| 16 | July | Polish forces push the Ukrainian Galician Army out of Galicia, after unsuccessful mediation attempts by the Allied Powers |

	Summer– Autumn	Period of intense civil war and chaos in Eastern Ukraine. UNR forces led by Symon Petliura battle with the Bolsheviks, Russian White Guards, and Nestor Makhno's anarchists; peasant bands nominally allied with the combatants, including Petliura, stage pogroms

1923

15	March	Council of Ambassadors recognizes Poland's claim to Galicia

1926

25	May	Symon Petliura assassinated in Paris by Samuel Schwartzbard, ostensibly to avenge pogroms against Jews

1929

28 2	January– February	First Congress of the Organization of Ukrainian Nationalists (OUN) held in Vienna

1930

9	March	Show trial of forty-five Ukrainian intellectuals begins in Kharkiv; they are charged with forming the Union for the Liberation of Ukraine and plotting to overthrow the government. All of them "confess" and are deported to concentration camps in Siberia
16	September	Polish government initiates a pacification campaign against the Galician Ukrainian population in retaliation for OUN activities

1932

25	January	USSR-Poland non-aggression pact concluded

1933

30	January	Adolf Hitler appointed Chancellor of Germany
23	March	Hitler granted dictatorial powers
1	April	Persecution of Jews in Germany begins with national boycott of all Jewish businesses and professions
17	November	United States recognizes the Soviet Union. Famine caused by Soviet government actions sweeps Soviet Ukraine, claiming millions of victims

1934

26	January	Germany and Poland sign a non-aggression pact
14	June	OUN assassinates Bronisław Pieracki, Poland's Minister of the Interior, in Warsaw. In the wake of this attack, a concentration camp is established near Bereza Kartuzka for Ukrainian nationalists and other anti-government activists
14	September	USSR admitted to the League of Nations

1935

15	January	Stalin's Great Purge begins in the USSR with the trial of Zinoviev and other prominent Bolsheviks
16	March	Germany repudiates disarmament clauses of the Versailles Treaty
15	September	Nuremberg laws outlaw Jews and make the swastika the official symbol of Nazi Germany

1936

7	March	In violation of the Treaty of Versailles, German forces occupy the demilitarized zone of the Rhineland
18	July	Spanish Civil War begins with the army revolt led by General Francisco Franco
24	November	Anti-Comintern Pact between Japan and Germany signed

1937

12	June	Stalin purges Soviet generals and much of the Red Army officer corps

1938

11	March	German troops enter Austria, declared part of the Third Reich on 13 March
23	May	Assassination of OUN leader Ievhen Konovalets in Rotterdam
1–14	October	German troops occupy the Sudetenland
8–14	November	Anti-Jewish pogroms break out in Germany; anti-Semitic legislation introduced in Italy on 10 November

1939

15	March	German troops occupy Bohemia and Moravia; Carpatho-Ukraine is proclaimed an independent state
16		Carpatho-Ukraine occupied by Hungary with the tacit approval of Germany and Italy
28		Hitler denounces Germany's 1934 non-aggression pact with Poland
22	May	Hitler and Mussolini sign the Pact of Steel, a ten-year political and military alliance
18	August	Soviet-German commercial agreement concluded
23		USSR and Germany sign the Molotov-Ribbentrop Pact, a non-aggression agreement. The Anti-Comintern Pact collapses
27		Second OUN congress in Rome confirms Andrii Melnyk as leader
1	September	Germany invades Poland and annexes Danzig
3		Britain and France declare war on Germany
7		Germany overruns Pomerania and Silesia; by 10 September all of western Poland is under German control
17		USSR breaks its non-aggression treaty with Poland, invades it from the east, and annexes lands inhabited by Ukrainians and Belorussians to the Ukrainian SSR and the Belorussian SSR
20–22		Legal Western Ukrainian parties are dissolved under the Soviet occupation. Sovietization begins with the prohibition of Ukrainian political and cultural organizations; arrests and deportations to Siberia follow
28		German armies reach Warsaw
30		German-Soviet treaty of amity settles the partition of Poland
8	October	Germany incorporates western Poland into the Third Reich
10		Deportation of Polish Jews to Lublin begins
12		German-occupied Polish territory reconstituted as the *Generalgouvernement* within the Third Reich
26–28		*Narodni Zbory Zakhidnoi Ukrainy* (People's Assembly of Western Ukraine), elected from a single slate of candidates on 22 October, meets to endorse a request for annexation

1	November	USSR Supreme Soviet approves the annexation of Western Ukraine
29		USSR attacks Finland
14	December	USSR is expelled from the League of Nations

1940

10	February	The Revolutionary Leadership of the OUN, headed by Stepan Bandera, is formed in Cracow. The OUN splits into the Bandera and Melnyk factions, the OUN-B and OUN-M
10–11		Mass deportation of pre-war Polish colonists in Western Ukraine to Kazakhstan and Siberia
12	March	Finland signs peace treaty with USSR, ceding the Karelian Isthmus and shores of Lake Ladoga
9	April	Germany invades Norway and Denmark
15		Ukrainian Central Committee, headed by Volodymyr Kubiiovych, is formed in Cracow to act as the representative of the Ukrainian population of the *Generalgouvernement*
2	May	Germany invades Holland, Luxemburg, and Belgium
21		Massacre of an estimated ten thousand Polish army officers in the Katyn forest, probably by the Soviets
17	June	USSR occupies Lithuania, Latvia, and Estonia
22		France concludes an armistice with Germany
27		USSR invades Romania after the refusal of King Carol to cede Bessarabia and Bukovyna. Romania appeals in vain for German aid
9	July	Romania places itself under German protection

1941

5	April	Soviet-Yugoslav friendship treaty
6		German ultimatum to Greece and Yugoslavia
13		USSR signs neutrality pact with Japan
	May	Germans begin training *Nachtigall* and *Roland* military units composed of OUN-B volunteers
9		USSR withdraws recognition of Yugoslavia

3	June	USSR withdraws recognition of Greece
22		Germany invades the USSR. *Reichssicherheitshauptamt* (RSHA) forms the *Einsatzgruppen SS* (mobile killing units). Their main targets are Jews, Communists, and later Ukrainian nationalists
23–26		Before retreating from Ukraine, the NKVD (Soviet security police) massacres approximately 19,000 prisoners in Lviv and other cities. Outbreaks of violence against Jews and suspected Communists follow discovery of the bodies
28		German troops capture Minsk
30		OUN-B proclaims Ukrainian statehood in Lviv. Iaroslav Stetsko forms a provisional government
1–6	July	*Einsatzgruppen* units C and D commence operations on Ukrainian territory; on 7 July, 7,000 Jews are shot in Lviv. By the end of the year, these and other German units are responsible for more than 850,000 executions; most victims are Jews
6		Soviet troops abandon occupied Poland and the Baltic states, retiring to the Stalin Line on the former frontier with Poland
12		OUN-B leaders Stetsko and Roman Ilnytzkyj are detained and deported to Germany to join Bandera, who is under German house arrest. British-Soviet agreement of mutual assistance signed in Moscow
16		German troops pierce the Stalin Line and take Smolensk
		Romania occupies northern Bukovyna and Bessarabia. Ukrainian territory between the Boh and Dniester rivers is annexed to Romania and renamed Transnistria
29		Soviet Army invading Romania withdraws to the Dniester
30		*Ukrainska natsionalna rada* (Ukrainian National Council) formed in Lviv to represent Ukrainian political interests before the German authorities
1	August	Galicia is annexed to the former Polish lands as the fifth district of the *Generalgouvernement*
20		Erich Koch appointed *Reichskommissar* of Ukraine
	September	Members of OUN-B task forces in Eastern Ukraine are systematically eliminated by the *Einsatzgruppen*
3		Germans advance to the outskirts of Leningrad and on 8

		September take Schlüsselburg, completing the land blockade of Leningrad
19		German troops take Kiev
11		First issue of the nationalist newspaper *Ukrainske slovo*, edited by OUN-M member Ivan Rohach, is published in Kiev
15		Bandera, Stetsko, and Ilnytzkyj are sent to a concentration camp
29–30		Three thousand Jews are murdered in Babyn Iar (Babi Yar) near Kiev; they are the first of 150,000 Jews, Ukrainians, and others to die there
1	October	German forces advance from Smolensk toward Moscow
2		German forces take Orel
5		*Ukrainska natsionalna rada*, with Mykola Velychkivsky as president, is formed in Kiev but suppressed after eight weeks
16		Germans advance to within sixty miles of Moscow. The Soviet government is transferred to Kuibyshev, but Stalin stays in Moscow
16		Odessa falls
24		Germans take Kharkiv
25		First German offensive against Moscow fails
3	November	German troops take Kursk
16		Second German offensive against Moscow begins
27		Red Army General Semen Tymoshenko launches a counter-offensive, forcing the Germans to evacuate Rostov, taken on 23 November
29		Soviet counter-offensive in the Moscow sector begins
12	December	*Ukrainske slovo*, a Kiev newspaper, is suppressed by the Germans. Hitler decides on his "final solution" (*Endlösung*) to the "Jewish question" in Europe. This plan was agreed upon at the Wannsee Conference on 20 January 1942

1942

9	February	Ivan Rohach, the poetess Olena Teliha, and other OUN-M activists are shot by the Nazis in Babyn Iar near Kiev

	Spring	*Polissian Sich* partisan group, commanded by Taras Bulba-Borovets, turns against Germans after initially fighting Soviet partisans
8	May	German troops attack Kerch Peninsula in the Crimea
13		Soviet forces make gains in the Kharkiv region
20		German troops take Kerch Peninsula
26		British-Soviet twenty-year alliance signed in London
28	June	German counter-attack launched in the Kharkiv region
	Summer	Large-scale manhunts net the first of 2.3 million Ukrainian forced labourers (*Ostarbeiter*) who are sent to Germany
3	July	German forces take Sevastopol
28		German forces take Rostov and overrun the northern Caucasus
26	August	German forces reach Stalingrad
13	September	German all-out attack on Stalingrad begins
19	November	Soviet counter-offensive from Stalingrad surrounds the besieging German Army
1	December	*Nachtigall* dissolved after its members refuse to re-enlist; its officers are arrested by the Germans

1943

26	January	Soviets are victorious at Voronezh
30		Soviet forces destroy the German Army southwest of Stalingrad
31		General Paulus surrenders at Stalingrad
8	February	Soviet troops take Kursk
14–16		Soviet troops recapture Rostov and Kharkiv
15	March	Soviet troops forced to evacuate Kharkiv
26		USSR breaks off diplomatic relations with the Polish government-in-exile in London
28	April	Proclamation of the formation of the Galician Division
30	June	The District of Galicia's *SS* Commander, Katzmann, declares the district "free of Jews" (*Judenfrei*). Up to 27 June, 434,329 Jews were "evacuated" from Galicia

5	July	German offensive on Soviet front opens with Battle of Kursk
12–15		Soviet counter-offensive against Orel
13–17		An international medical commission with representation from neutral powers examines the graves of 9,439 victims of NKVD shootings (1937–8) in Vinnytsia
12	August	Soviet troops recapture Kharkiv
21–25		Third OUN-B Congress modifies the organization's platform, condemns National Socialism, and calls for democratic rights
24	September	Soviet forces cross the Dnieper River north of Kiev
25		Soviet forces take Smolensk
	October 1943–June 1944	Nazis publicly execute 1,541 OUN and UPA members in Galicia
6		Kuban Peninsula is in Soviet hands
6	November	Soviet forces take Kiev
26		Soviet forces take Homel
26	December	Soviet forces succeed in recapturing two-thirds of Soviet territory captured by the Germans

1944

26	January	Andrii Melnyk, under house arrest since 1941, is detained and sent to Sachsenhausen concentration camp
22	February	Soviet troops take Kryvyi Rih
2	April	Soviet forces enter Romania
11		Soviet forces re-enter the Crimea
	May	Germany attempts to co-operate with the UPA against Soviet forces
21		Allies break through the Hitler Line in Italy
10	June	Murder of OUN-M deputy leader Oleh Olzhych-Kandyba in Sachsenhausen concentration camp
3	July	Soviet troops take Minsk, capturing 100,000 Germans
11–15		Ukrainian Supreme Liberation Council formed as the political co-ordinating body of the Ukrainian underground

17–22		Galician Division routed at the Battle of Brody; 3,000 retreat, and 7,000 are killed, taken prisoner by the Soviets, or join local UPA units
23	July	Soviet troops cross the Curzon Line in Poland
26		USSR recognizes the pro-Soviet Lublin Committee of Polish Liberation as the authority for liberated Poland
28		Soviet troops take Brest-Litovsk
20	August	Soviet offensive in Bessarabia and Romania
30		Soviet troops enter Bucharest
5	September	USSR declares war on Bulgaria
29		Soviet forces invade Yugoslavia
	September–October	Release of Stepan Bandera, Andrii Melnyk, and other Ukrainian political leaders; Germans attempt to win them back as allies
27	December	Soviet troops surround Budapest

1945

17–23	January	Soviet forces take Warsaw, Cracow, and Tilsit
17	March	Creation of the Ukrainian National Committee and Army Command, headed by General Pavlo Shandruk
29	March	Soviet forces cross the Austrian frontier
30		Soviet troops take Danzig
1	April	30th (2d Ukr.) Regiment of the Galician Division temporarily disarmed by the Germans in Maribor, Slovenia
20		Soviet offensive on Berlin begins
26		U.S. and Soviet forces take Torgau
27		Galician Division transferred to the Ukrainian National Army commanded by General Shandruk and renamed the 1st Ukrainian Division of the Ukrainian National Army
30		Hitler commits suicide in Berlin
1	May	Surrender of the German Army on the Italian front
2		Berlin surrenders to Soviets
3		Allied forces enter Hamburg

6	May	British command agrees to accept the Ukrainian Division as surrendered enemy personnel
8		General Alfred Jodl oversees the capitulation of Germany to General Dwight Eisenhower
9		Soviets take Prague
29	June	Czechoslovakia cedes Subcarpathian Ruthenia (Transcarpathia) to USSR
17	July	Conference attended by Stalin, Truman, and Churchill is held at Potsdam to settle the occupation of Germany
20	November	Trial of Nazi war criminals before the Allied tribunal opens at Nuremberg

APPENDIX B

The Canadian Commission of Inquiry on War Criminals

On 7 February 1985 the Honourable John C. Crosbie, Minister of Justice and Attorney General of Canada, announced the establishment of a Commission of Inquiry on War Criminals to be conducted by the Honourable Mr. Justice Jules Deschênes of the Superior Court of Quebec.

The Commission, established under Part I of the *Inquiries Act*, is to conduct an investigation into alleged war criminals in Canada. It is also to attempt to determine whether any such persons are now resident in Canada.

The government has stipulated a reporting date of 31 December 1985 for the Commission's findings and recommendations.

TERMS OF REFERENCE

WHEREAS concern has been expressed about the possibility that Joseph Mengele, an alleged Nazi war criminal, may have entered or attempted to enter Canada;

WHEREAS there is also concern that other persons responsible for war crimes related to the activities of Nazi Germany during World War II (hereinafter referred to as war criminals) are currently resident in Canada;

AND WHEREAS the Government of Canada wishes to adopt all appropriate measures necessary to ensure that any such war criminals currently resident in Canada or hereafter found in Canada, are brought to justice;

THEREFORE, the Committee of the Privy Council, on the recommendation of the Prime Minister, advise that, pursuant to the *Inquiries Act*, a Commission do issue under the Great Seal of Canada, appointing the Honourable Mr. Justice Jules Deschênes, of the Superior Court of Quebec, to be Commissioner under Part I of the *Inquiries Act* "to conduct such investigations regarding alleged war criminals in Canada, including whether any such persons are now resident in Canada and when and how they obtained entry to Canada, as in the opinion of the Commissioner are necessary in order to enable him to report to the Governor in Council his recommendations and advice relating to what further action might be taken in Canada to bring to justice such alleged war criminals who might be residing within Canada, including recommendations as to what

legal means are now available to bring to justice any such persons in Canada or
whether and what legislation might be adopted by the Parliament of Canada to
ensure that war criminals are brought to justice and made to answer for their
crimes."

The Committee of the Privy Council further advise that:

a) the Commissioner be authorized to adopt such procedures and methods as
he may from time to time deem expedient for the proper conduct of the
Inquiry and to sit at such times and at such places within or outside of
Canada as he may decide from time to time;

b) the Commissioner be authorized to have complete access to personnel and
all relevant papers, documents, vouchers, records and books of any kind in
the possession of departments and agencies of the Government of Canada
and be provided with adequate working accommodation and clerical
assistance;

c) the Commissioner be authorized to engage the services of such staff and
counsel as he deems necessary or advisable at such rates of remuneration
and reimbursement as may be approved by the Treasury Board;

d) the Commissioner be authorized to rent office space and facilities for the
Commission's purposes in accordance with Treasury Board policy;

e) the Commissioner be required to submit a report to the Governor in Council
embodying his findings and recommendations and advice on or prior to
December 31, 1985 and file with the Clerk of the Privy Council his papers and
records as soon as reasonably may be after the conclusion of the inquiry;

f) the Commissioner be directed that the proceedings of the inquiry be held in
camera in all matters where the Commissioner deems it desirable in the
public interest or in the interest of the privacy of individuals involved in
specific cases which may be examined;

g) the Commissioner be directed to follow established security procedures
with regard to his staff and technical advisers and the handling of classified
information at all stages of the inquiry;

h) the Commissioner be directed, in making his report, to consider and take all
steps necessary to preserve:
  a) the secrecy of sources of security information within Canada; and
  b) the security of information provided to Canada in confidence by other
  nations;

i) the inquiry be known as the Commission of Inquiry on War Criminals;

j) the Commissioner be authorized to engage the services of such experts and
other persons as are referred to in section 11 of the *Inquiries Act* who shall
receive such remuneration and reimbursement as may be approved by the
Treasury Board; and

k) pursuant to section 37 of the *Judges Act*, the Honourable Mr. Justice Jules
Deschênes be authorized to act as Commissioner in the said inquiry.

ABBREVIATIONS AND GLOSSARY

ABWEHR (*Amt Auslandsnachrichten und Abwehr*). Intelligence and counterespionage service of the German armed forces high command.

ALLGEMEINE SS. General *SS*; main body of the prewar *SS*, composed of volunteers.

BAHNSCHUTZ. Armed, uniformed security police who defended railway lines.

BAUDIENST. Compulsory labour service.

BEKANNTMACHUNG. Official proclamation.

BUND DER DEUTSCHEN OFFIZIEREN. Union of German Officers.

CHEKA (*Vserossiiskaia Chrezvychainaia komissiia po borbe s kontrrevoliutsiei, spekuliatsiei i sabotazhem*). All-Russian Extraordinary Commission for Struggle against Counter-Revolution, Speculation, and Sabotage. Soviet security police established in 1917; renamed GPU in 1922.

CJC. Canadian Jewish Congress.

CROWCASS. Central Registry of War Criminals and Security Suspects.

DUN (*Druzhyny ukrainskykh natsionalistiv*). Brotherhoods (Legions) of Ukrainian Nationalists.

DPs. Displaced Persons.

DYVIZIIA "HALYCHYNA" (GALICIA, GALIZIEN). See GALICIAN DIVISION.

EINSATZGRUPPE, EINSATZGRUPPEN (EG) DER SICHERHEITSPOLIZEI UND DES SD. Special Operations Group(s) of the Security Police and the Security Service of the *SS*: *SS/SD* Special Task Force ("action team") for the liquidation of "undesirable" elements.

EINSATZKOMMANDO (EK) DER SICHERHEITSPOLIZEI UND DES SD. Special Operations Detachment of the Security Police; sub-unit of an EINSATZGRUPPE.

FORCES FRANÇAISES DE L'INTÉRIEUR (French Interior Forces). Group of Resistance units in France during World War II.

GALICIAN (GALIZIEN) DIVISION. Ukrainian volunteer military formation recruited by the Germans largely in the district of Galicia (Halychyna). It was one of many non-German units in the WAFFEN-SS.

GAULEITER. Nazi Party leader responsible for party administration in a province or federal state.

GENERALGOUVERNEMENT (General Government for Occupied Poland). Polish territory conquered by Germany and placed by Hitler under a civilian administration on 25 October 1939. The portions of western Poland incorporated into the Reich were Danzig, East Prussia, the Wartaland, and the administrative district of Zeichenau and Upper Silesia; Galicia was added on 1 August 1941.

GESTAPO (*Geheime Staatspolizei*). State Secret Police.

GULAG (*Glavnoe upravlenie lagerei NKVD*). The central administration of prison camps. The term has come to refer to the network of Soviet prison camps and prisons.

HILFSWILLIGE (HIWIS). Volunteer auxiliaries used by German armed forces, chiefly to handle supplies.

HROMADSKI HOSPODARSTVA. Community farms; term applied to collective farms retained under German rule.

IADC. Information and Anti-Defamation Commission of the Ukrainian Canadian Committee (Montreal Chapter).

IGCR. Intergovernmental Committee on Refugees.

INS. Immigration and Naturalization Service; the U.S. government agency in charge of prosecuting alleged Nazi war criminals until 1979.

INTEGRAL NATIONALISM. A political doctrine based on the idea of the nation as the supreme value, on mystically conceived ideas of the solidarity of all the individuals making up the nation, and on the subordination of rational and analytical thought to "intuitively correct" emotions. Expression of the "national will" is carried out through a charismatic leader and an elite of nationalists organized in a single party.

IRO. International Refugee Organization.

JUDENRÄTE. Jewish Elected Councils. Established by decree of the *Generalgouvernement*, 28 November 1939; responsible for helping enforce Nazi orders affecting Jews, and for administration of all Jewish ghettos.

KGB (*Komitet gosudarstvennoi bezopasnosti*). Committee for State Security; the official name of the Soviet security police since 1954.

KHLIBOROBSKA SPILKA. Agricultural association; the second stage of decollectivization under German rule.

KOLKHOZ (*Kollektivnoe khoziaistvo*). Soviet collective farm.

KOMSOMOL (*Kommunisticheskii soiuz molodezhi*). The Young Communist League.

LANDWIRTSCHAFTSFÜHRER or LA-FÜHRER. Local German agricultural supervisor in the *Reichskommissariat*.

LUBIANKA. KGB headquarters, investigation, and isolation prison in Dzerzhinsky Square in Moscow.

MP. Member of Parliament.

MVD (*Ministerstvo vnutrennikh del*). Ministry of Internal Affairs; the name of the Soviet security organs, 1946–53.

NASA. National Aeronautics and Space Agency of the United States.

NATO. North Atlantic Treaty Organization.

NKVD (*Narodnyi komissariat vnutrennikh del*). The People's Commissariat for Internal Affairs; an arm of the Soviet security organization, 1934–46.

OBLAST. Province.

ODVU (*Orhanizatsiia derzhavnoho vidrodzhennia Ukrainy*). Organization for the Rebirth of Ukraine; an affiliate of the OUN-M in the United States.

OSI. Office of Special Investigations, U.S. Justice Department.

OSS. Office of Strategic Services of the U.S. government; predecessor of the Central Intelligence Agency.

OSTARBEITER. Eastern European (forced) labourer during Nazi rule.

OSTMINISTERIUM. Short form of *Reichsministerium für die besetzten Ostgebiete*. Reich Ministry for the Occupied Eastern Territories; headed by Alfred Rosenberg.

OSTTRUPPEN. Low-level German military units comprised of Eastern Europeans.

OUN (*Orhanizatsiia ukrainskykh natsionalistiv*). Organization of Ukrainian Nationalists. It split into two factions: the OUN-B, headed by Stepan Bandera, and the OUN-M, headed by Andrii Melnyk.

POKHIDNI HRUPY. OUN expeditionary groups organized by both factions.

POW. Prisoner of war.

PROSVITA. Ukrainian adult-education (enlightenment) society.

RCMP. Royal Canadian Mounted Police.

REICHSKOMMISSAR. Reich Commissioner; title of a Nazi chief of civilian administration in the occupied areas of Europe.

REICHSKOMMISSARIAT UKRAINE. Major territorial unit of German civil administration, in this case, of Ukraine; it included six sub-regions (*Generalbezirke*): Volhynia-Podillia, Zhytomyr, Kiev, Dnipropetrovske, Mykolaiv, and Crimea.

REICHSSICHERHEITSHAUPTAMT (RSHA). Reich Central Security Office: SS department that controlled administration of the *SD*, the *Gestapo*, and *Kripo* (Criminal Police).

ROA (*Russkaia osvoboditelnaia armiia*). Russian Liberation Army under General Andrei Vlasov.

SAMIZDAT. "Self-published" illegal underground dissident works in the Soviet Union.

SCHUTZMANNSCHAFTEN. Local militia and auxiliary police under German supervision in occupied areas.

SD (*Sicherheitsdienst*). Security and intelligence service of the *SS*.

SEP CAMPS. Surrendered Enemy Personnel Camps (British).

SHTETL. Jewish settlements in Eastern Europe.

SICHERHEITSPOLIZEI. Security Police (*Sipo*); component of the *SS*.

SONDERKOMMANDO. Special assignment detachment; sub-unit of EINSATZGRUPPE(N).

SS. Abbreviation for *Schutzstaffel* (Protection Squad). Originally an elite Nazi para-military organization. Under the leadership of Heinrich Himmler it came to control the police and security service and created its own military force, the WAFFEN-SS.

SS DIVISION HALYCHYNA. See GALICIAN DIVISION.

TODT. A German military organization responsible for capital construction projects, named after its founder, a Nazi engineer.

UCC. Ukrainian Canadian Committee.

UHA (*Ukrainska halytska armiia*). Ukrainian Galician Army.

UHVR (*Ukrainska holovna vyzvolna rada*). Ukrainian Supreme Liberation Council.

UNA (*Ukrainska natsionalna armiia*). Ukrainian National Army.

UNC (*Ukrainskyi natsionalnyi komitet*). Ukrainian National Committee.

UNDO (*Ukrainske natsionalno-demokratychne obiednannia*). Ukrainian National Democratic Union.

UNO (*Ukrainske natsionalne obiednannia*). Ukrainian National Union.

UNR (*Ukrainska narodnia respublika*). Ukrainian People's Republic.

UNRA (*Ukrainska narodnia revoliutsiina armiia*). Ukrainian National Revolutionary Army.

UNRRA. United Nations Relief and Rehabilitation Administration.

UNTERMENSCHEN. Sub-humans; Nazi term for Slavs, Jews, and other "non-Aryans".

UNWCC. United Nations War Crimes Commission.

UPA (*Ukrainska povstanska armiia*). Ukrainian Insurgent Army.

USFET. United States Forces, European Theatre.

USS (*Ukrainski sichovi striltsi*). Ukrainian *Sich* Riflemen.

UVV (*Ukrainske vyzvolne viisko*). Ukrainian Liberation Army.

VOLKSDEUTSCHE. Ethnic Germans residing outside German territories.

VVN (*Viiskovi viddily natsionalistiv*). Armed nationalist detachments of the OUN.

WAFFEN-SS. Military branch of the *SS*, which fought alongside the Wehrmacht.

WAFFEN-SS DIVISION GALICIA. See GALICIAN DIVISION.

WEHRMACHT. German Armed Forces.

WERKSCHUTZ. Factory police, factory guards.

YAD VASHEM. Israeli Martyrs' and Heroes' Remembrance Authority, Jerusalem; research and documentation centre on the Holocaust.

ZAKORDONNE PREDSTAVNYTSTVO UHVR. The Foreign Representation of the Ukrainian Supreme Liberation Council.

ZÖGLINGE. *SS* auxiliary anti-aircraft brigades composed of fourteen-to-seventeen-year-olds. In 1944 "non-Aryan" boys and girls were forcibly recruited.

SOURCES AND BIBLIOGRAPHY

This selected bibliography is divided into four parts:
I.   a brief listing of archival and manuscript materials in the Public Archives of Canada;
II. selected published sources that include:
    1. bibliographies, guides, and aids to research;
    2. documents, memoirs, and other primary sources by language (English, French, German, Polish, and Ukrainian); for Russian-language sources see the Parrish bibliography on p. 270;
    3. secondary sources by language;
III. a subject bibliography on Ukrainians in Nazi concentration camps;
IV. a subject bibliography on U.S. cases and materials on denaturalization, deportation, and suspected Nazi war criminals, prepared by David Springer, an attorney with a Chicago law firm.

I. ARCHIVAL AND MANUSCRIPT MATERIALS

Note: Several authors in this volume cited sources in archival and manuscript repositories. Among these are the records of Holocaust survivors in Yad Vashem, Jerusalem, Israel; German government and military records in both the National Archives in Washington, D.C., and in Koblenz, West Germany; and the United Nations (UNRRA) records in New York. For more precise details, see the chapter endnotes and the source locations in the documents section. The following archival materials on the 1st Ukrainian Division's immigration to Canada and other related issues are housed in the Public Archives of Canada (Ottawa).

1. *Immigration Branch Records*

RG 76 vol. 656, file B53802 (1–2) Ukrainian Refugees, Surrendered Enemy Personnel (SEP) 1946–52.
RG 76 vol. 800, file 547-1 Security examinations – regulations and procedures 1946–53.
RG 76 vol. 854, file 554-12 Cossack refugees – general file 1947–53.

RG 76 vol. 855, file 554-20 Kalmyk refugees – general file 1946–53.

RG 76 vol. 856, file 554-33 Ukrainian refugees – general file 1947–62.

RG 76 vol. 866, file 555-55 Resettlement in Canada of political refugees in co-operation with the United States 1952–53.

RG 76 vol. 866, file 555-57 Admission of 5,000 Displaced Persons (DPs) from Europe 1947–50 (P.C. 2180).

RG 76 vol. 866, file 556-61 Return to Canada of Canadian citizens who served in enemy forces – general file 1946–54.

RG 76 vol. 870, file 556-19-637 Admission and resettlement of Displaced Persons (DPs) in the United States 1946–65.

2. *External Affairs – Canada House*

RG 25 External Affairs, Special Research Bureau, 1936–1945. Information on war crime matters (restricted).

RG 25 A12 vol. 2087, file AR 22/13 Enemy Nationals – Enforced Repatriation to respective countries from United Nations Territories 1946–48.

RG 25 A12 vol. 2109, file AR 405/4/12 United Nations War Crimes Commission (UNWCC) – Canadian War Crimes Investigations Unit 1945–51.

RG 25 F3d vols. 2607-09, War Crimes Documents, 1945–46. List of names and documents (6,000 pages) relating to the Central Registry of War Criminals, distributed by Allied governments. A list of files is available.

RG 28 F2c vols. 952–954, United Nations War Crimes Commission, 1944–1947. A list of files is available.

3. *Citizenship and Immigration*

RG 26 vol. 122, file 3–32–13 *Volksdeutsch* Refugees 1947–50.

RG 26 vol. 130, file 3–33–34 Admission to Canada of Ukrainians 1947–57.

RG 26 vol. 147, file 3–43–1 Includes Report on Ukrainians in Surrendered Enemy Personnel (SEP) Camp No. 374 Italy by Refugee Screening Commission, 21 February 1947.

RG 26 vol. 166, file 3–25–11 (parts 1–3) Overseas Security Screening (with much policy material on admissibility of Nazi Party and *Waffen-SS* members, Nazi collaborators), 1947–58.

MG 28, V120 Canadian Lutheran World Relief, vol. 24, file 17, *Waffen-SS*, including reports 1949–55.

MG 28, V9 Ukrainian Canadian Committee, vol. 5, file "Galician" Division 1946–51.

Notice to Researchers: Researchers interested in obtaining information about individual applications for immigration to Canada from Europe during the period 1946–56 should write to Employment and Immigration Canada, Place du Portage, Phase IV, 140 Promenade du Portage, Ottawa, Ontario K1A 0J9. The Public Archives of Canada in the Immigration Branch Record Collection (RG 76) has policy and general administrative and procedural files. There are some files dealing with individual cases that were perceived to be irregular or exceptional cases in the collection. In some cases these files are restricted.

The Public Archives of Canada does not have files on individual immigrants or applicants who wished to immigrate to Canada from Europe.

II. SELECTED PUBLISHED SOURCES

1. Bibliographies, Guides, and Aids to Research

Baudot, Marcel et al., eds. *The Historical Encyclopedia of World War II*. New York: Facts on File, 1980.

Bayliss, Gwyn M. *Bibliographic Guide to the Two World Wars: An Annotated Survey of English-Language Reference Materials*. New York-London: Bowker, 1977.

Bieńkowski, Wiesław, ed. *Bibliografia Historii Polski*. Vol. 3, pt. 1, *1918–1945*. Warsaw: Państwowe Wydawnictwo Naukowe, 1974.

Bloomberg, Marty, and Hans H. Weber. *World War II and Its Origins: A Select Bibliography of Books in English*. Littleton, Colo.: Libraries Unlimited, 1975.

Boshyk, Yury, and Boris Balan. *Political Refugees and "Displaced Persons," 1945–1954: A Select Bibliography and Guide to Research, with Special Reference to the Ukrainians*. Research Report No. 2. Edmonton: Canadian Institute of Ukrainian Studies, 1982.

Boshyk, Yury, and Włodzimierz Kiebalo, comps. *Publications by Ukrainian "Displaced Persons" and Political Refugees: The John Luczkiw Collection, Thomas Fisher Rare Book Library, University of Toronto*. Edmonton: Canadian Institute of Ukrainian Studies. Forthcoming.

Dallin, Alexander. "The German Occupation of the U.S.S.R. in World War II: A Bibliography." External Research Paper. Washington, D.C.: Office of Intelligence Research, Department of State, 1955.

Davies, Norman. *Poland, Past and Present: A Select Bibliography of Works in English*. Newtonville, Mass.: Oriental Research Partners, 1977.

Dekhtiarova, N.A. et al., comps. "Ukrainska RSR u Velykii Vitchyznianii viini: pokazhchyk literatury za 1975–1985 rr." *Ukrainskyi istorychnyi zhurnal* (Kiev), no. 3 (288) (March 1985): 145–58; no. 5 (290) (May 1985): 153–8.

Enser, A.G.S., ed. *A Subject Bibliography of the Second World War: Books in English*. Lexington, Mass.: Lexington Books, 1977.

Funk, Arthur L., comp. *The Second World War: A Select Bibliography of Books in English since 1975*. Claremont, Calif.: Regina Books, 1985.

Gilbert, Martin. *Atlas of the Holocaust*. London: Michael Joseph in association with the Board of Deputies of British Jews, 1982.

Held, Walter, ed. *Verbände und Truppen der deutschen Wehrmacht und Waffen-SS in Zweiten Weltkrieg: Eine Bibliographie der deutschsprachigen Nachkriegsliteratur*. Osnabrück: Biblio Verlag, 1978.

Hundert, Gershon David, and Gershon C. Bacon. *The Jews in Poland and Russia: Bibliographical Essays*. Bloomington, Ind.: Indiana University Press, 1984.

Kehr, Helen, and Janet Langmaid, comps. *The Nazi Era, 1919–1945: A Select Bibliography of Published Works from the Early Roots to 1980*. London: Mansell, 1982.

Magocsi, Paul Robert. *Galicia: A Historical Survey and Bibliographical Guide.* Toronto: University of Toronto Press in association with the Canadian Institute of Ukrainian Studies and the Harvard Ukrainian Research Institute, 1983.

Parrish, Michael. *The U.S.S.R. in World War II: An Annotated Bibliography of Books Published in the Soviet Union, 1945–1975, with an Addenda for the Years 1975–1980.* 2 vols. New York-London: Garland, 1981.

Petryshyn, Roman W., and Natalia Chomiak, comps. *Political Writings of Post-World War Two Ukrainian Émigrés: Annotated Bibliography and Guide to Research.* Research Report No. 4. Edmonton: Canadian Institute of Ukrainian Studies, 1984.

Phillips, Jill M. *The Second World War in History, Biography, Diary, Poetry, Literature, and Film: A Bibliography.* New York: Gordon, 1983.

Robinson, Jacob, and Henry Sachs, comps. *The Holocaust: The Nuremberg Evidence. Part 1: Documents Digest, Index and Chronological Tables.* Jerusalem: Yad Vashem and the YIVO Institute for Jewish Research, 1976.

Smith, Myron J. *The Secret Wars: A Guide to Sources in English.* Vol. 1, *Intelligence, Propaganda and Psychological Warfare, Resistance Movements, and Secret Operations, 1939–1945.* Santa Barbara: ABC-Clio, 1980.

– *World War II, The European and Mediterranean Theaters: An Annotated Bibliography.* New York: Garland, 1984.

Snyder, Louis L. *Encyclopedia of the Third Reich.* New York: McGraw-Hill, 1976.

Subject Bibliography of the Second World War: Books in English 1914–1978. London: Gower, 1977.

Tessin, Georg. *Verbände und Truppen der deutschen Wehrmacht und Waffen SS im Zweiten Weltkrieg 1939–1945.* 13 vols. Osnabrück: Biblio Verlag, 1965–.

Tuider, Othmar, Anton Legler, and Hans-Egon Wittas, eds. *Bibliographie zur Geschichte der Felddivisionen der deutschen Wehrmacht und Waffen-SS 1939–1945.* Vienna: Heeresgeschichtliches Museum (Militärwissenschaftliches Institut Militärwissenschaftl. Abteilung), 1976.

Walker, Malvin. *Chronological Encyclopedia of Adolf Hitler and The Third Reich.* New York: Carlton Press, 1978.

Wistrich, Robert. *Who's Who in Nazi Germany.* New York: Macmillan, 1982.

Ziegler, Janet. *World War Two: A Bibliography of Books in English, 1945–1965.* Stanford: Hoover Institution Press, 1971.

2. Documents, Memoirs, and Other Primary Sources

ENGLISH

Anatoli, A. (Kuznetsov, Anatoly). *Babi Yar: A Document in the Form of a Novel.* Translated by David Floyd. New York: Farrar, Straus and Giroux, 1970.

Arad, Yitzhak, Yisrael Gutman, and Abraham Margaliot, eds. *Documents on the Holocaust: Selected Sources on the Destruction of the Jews of Germany and Austria, Poland, and the Soviet Union.* Jerusalem: Yad Vashem in co-operation with the Anti-Defamation League and Ktav Publishing House, 1981.

Bialer, Seweryn, ed. *Stalin and His Generals: Soviet Military Memoirs of World War II.* New York: Pegasus, 1969.

Dawidowicz, Lucy S., ed. *A Holocaust Reader*. New York: Behram House, 1976.

Detwiler, Donald S., ed. *World War II German Military Studies*. Vol. 19, pt. 7, *The Eastern Theatre*. New York-London: Garland, 1979.

Documents on German Foreign Policy, 1918–1945, from the Archives of the German Foreign Ministry. Series C and D. 18 vols. Washington, D.C.: U.S. Government Printing Office, 1949–64. London: Her Majesty's Stationery Office, 1949–64.

Ehrenburg, Ilya, and Vasily Grossman, eds. *The Black Book: The Ruthless Murder of Jews by German-Fascist Invaders Throughout the Temporarily-Occupied Regions of the Soviet Union and in the Death Camps of Poland During the War of 1941–1945*. Translated by John Glad and James S. Levine. New York: Holocaust Library, 1980.

Grudzinska-Gross, Irena, and Jan Tomasz Gross, eds. *War Through Children's Eyes: The Soviet Occupation of Poland and the Deportations, 1939–1941*. Stanford: Hoover Institution, 1981.

Hilberg, Raul, comp. *Documents of Destruction: Germany and Jewry, 1933–1945*. Chicago: Quadrangle, 1971.

International Military Tribunal. *Trial of the Major War Criminals before the International Military Tribunal*. 42 vols. Nuremberg: Secretariat of the Tribunal, 1947–9.

Kugelmass, Jack, and Jonathan Boyarin, eds. and trans. *From a Ruined Garden: The Memorial Books of Polish Jewry*. Geographical index and bibliography by Zachary M. Baker. New York: Schocken Books, 1983.

Neumann, Peter. *The Black March: The Personal Story of an SS Man*. Translated by Constantine FitzGibbon. New York: William Sloane Associates, 1959.

Nomberg-Przytyk, Sara. *Auschwitz: True Tales from a Grotesque Land*. Edited by Eli Pfefferkorn and David H. Hirsch. Translated by Roslyn Hirsch. Chapel Hill, N.C.: University of North Carolina Press, 1985.

Panchuk, Gordon R. Bohdan. *Heroes of Their Day: The Reminiscences of Bohdan Panchuk*. Edited and with an introduction by Lubomyr Y. Luciuk. Toronto: Multicultural History Society of Ontario, 1983.

Potichnyj, Peter J., and Yevhen Shtendera, eds. *The Political Thought of the Ukrainian Underground*. Edmonton: Canadian Institute of Ukrainian Studies. Forthcoming.

Ross, Graham, ed. *The Foreign Office and the Kremlin: British Documents on Anglo-Soviet Relations 1941–45*. Cambridge: Cambridge University Press, 1984.

Shandruk, Pavlo. *Arms of Valor*. Translated by Roman Olesnicki. New York: Robert Speller and Sons, 1959.

Shumuk, Danylo. *Life Sentence: Memoirs of a Ukrainian Political Prisoner*. Foreword by Nadia Svitlychna. Edited by Ivan Jaworsky. Translated by Ivan Jaworsky and Halya Kowalska. Edmonton: Canadian Institute of Ukrainian Studies, 1984.

Strik-Strikfeldt, Wilfried. *Against Stalin and Hitler: Memoir of the Russian Liberation Movement, 1941–1945*. London: Macmillan, 1970.

Trials of War Criminals before the Nuernberg Military Tribunals under Control Council Law No. 10. 15 vols. Washington, D.C.: U.S. Government Printing Office, 1949–54.

United States, Chief of Counsel for the Prosecution of Axis Criminality. *Nazi Conspiracy and Aggression*. 8 vols. and supplements A and B. Washington, D.C.: U.S. Government Printing Office, 1946–48.
Wells, Leon W. [eliczker]. *The Death Brigade (The Janowska Road)*. 2d ed. New York: Holocaust Library, 1978.

FRENCH

Petit, Victor. "Journal de Marche 1944." [Commandant du Bataillon Ukrainien]. Lyon: Comité du Souvenir des soldats Ukrainiens morts pour la France, 1985 (mimeographed).

GERMAN

Frank, Hans. *Das Diensttagebuch des deutschen Generalgouverneurs in Polen 1939–1945*. Stuttgart: Deutsche Verlags-Anstalt, 1975.
Ilnytzkyj, Roman. *Deutschland und die Ukraine, 1934–1945: Ein Vorbericht*. 2 vols. Munich: Osteuropa-Institut, 1955.

UKRAINIAN

Bulba-Borovets, Taras. *Armiia bez derzhavy: slava i trahediia ukrainskoho povstanskoho rukhu. Spohady*. Winnipeg: Tovarystvo Volyn, 1981.
Hunchak, Taras, ed. *UPA v svitli nimetskykh dokumentiv*. Vols. 6 and 7 of *Litopys Ukrainskoi povstanskoi armii*. Edited by Ievhen Shtendera and Petro Potichny. Toronto: Litopys UPA, 1983.
– and Roman Solchanyk, eds. *Ukrainska suspilno-politychna dumka v 20 stolitti: dokumenty i materiialy*. 3 vols. New York: Suchasnist, 1983.
Kalba, Myroslav, ed. *U lavakh druzhynnykiv: spohady uchasnykiv*. Denver: Ukrapress, 1982.
Kary, Lukian. *Krakh: dokumentalnyi roman z chasiv Druhoi svitovoi viiny*. Baltimore-Toronto: Smoloskyp, 1985.
Kubiiovych, Volodymyr. *Meni 70*. Paris-Munich: Naukove tovarystvo im. Shevchenka, 1970.
– *Meni 85*. Paris-Munich: Molode Zhyttia, 1985.
OUN v svitli postanov Velykykh Zboriv, Konferentsii ta inshykh dokumentiv z borotby 1929–1955 r.: zbirka dokumentiv. n.p.: Zakordonni chastyny Orhanizatsii ukrainskykh natsionalistiv, 1955.
Pankivsky, Kost. *Vid derzhavy do komitetu: lito 1941 roku u Lvovi*. New York: Kliuchi, 1951. 2d ed. New York: Kliuchi, 1970.
– *Roky nimetskoi okupatsii*. New York: Kliuchi, 1965. 2d ed. New York: Naukove tovarystvo im. Shevchenka, 1983.
Rudnytska, Milena, ed. *Zakhidnia Ukraina pid bolshevykamy, IX. 1939 – VI. 1941*. New York: Naukove tovarystvo im. Shevchenka v Amerytsi, 1958.
Shandruk, Pavlo. "Tse bulo tak." *Visti Bratstva kolyshnikh voiakiv I-oi Ukrainskoi dyvizii UNA*, no. 3–4 (53–54) (1955): 2–6.
Shtendera, Ievhen, and Petro Potichny (Potichnyj), eds. *Litopys Ukrainskoi povstanskoi armii*. 10 vols. Toronto: Litopys UPA, 1976–.

3. *Secondary Sources*

ENGLISH

Abella, Irving, and Harold Troper. *None is Too Many: Canada and the Jews of Europe, 1933–1948*. Toronto: Lester and Orpen Dennys, 1982.

Arad, Yitzhak. "Jewish Family Camps in the Forests: An Original Means of Rescue." In *Rescue Attempts During the Holocaust: Proceedings of the Second Yad Vashem International Historical Conference*, 333–53. Edited by Yisrael Gutman and Ephraim Zuroff. Jerusalem: Yad Vashem, 1977.

Armstrong, John A. *Ukrainian Nationalism*. 2d rev. ed. New York: Columbia University Press, 1963. Reprint. Littleton, Colo.: Ukrainian Academic Press, 1980.

– ed. *Soviet Partisans in World War II*. Madison: University of Wisconsin Press, 1964.

– "Collaborationism in World War II: The Integral Nationalist Variant in Eastern Europe." *Journal of Modern History* 40, no. 3 (September 1968): 396–410.

Aster, Howard, and Peter J. Potichnyj. *Jewish-Ukrainian Relations: Two Solitudes*. Oakville, Ont.: Mosaic Press, 1983.

– eds. *Ukrainian-Jewish Relations in Historical Perspective*. Edmonton: Canadian Institute of Ukrainian Studies. Forthcoming.

Bardakjian, Kevork B. *Hitler and the Armenians*. Cambridge, Mass.: Zoryan Institute, 1985.

Bender, Roger James, and Hugh Page Taylor. *Uniforms, Organization and History of the Waffen-SS*. San Jose: R. James Bender, 1975.

Bethell, Nicholas. *The Last Secret: Forcible Repatriation to Russia, 1944–47*. London: André Deutsch, 1974.

Bilinsky, Yaroslav. *The Second Soviet Republic: The Ukraine After World War II*. New Brunswick, N.J.: Rutgers University Press, 1964.

Budurowycz, Bohdan. "Poland and the Ukrainian Problem, 1921–1939." *Canadian Slavonic Papers* 25, no. 4 (December 1983): 473–500.

Buss, Phillip H., and Andrew Mollo. *Hitler's Germanic Legions: An Illustrated History of Western European Legions with the SS* [in Russia], *1941–1943*. New York: Beekman House, 1978.

Carrell, Paul (Schmidt, Paul K.). *Scorched Earth: The Russian-German War, 1943–1944*. Translated from the German by Ewald Osers. Boston: Little, Brown, 1970.

Childs, David. *The GDR: Moscow's German Ally*. Boston: Allen and Unwin, 1983.

Ciechanowski, Jan M. *The Warsaw Rising of 1944*. New York-London: Cambridge University Press, 1974.

Clark, Alan. *Barbarossa: The Russian-German Conflict, 1941–45*. New York: William Morrow, 1965.

Cooper, Matthew. *The Phantom War: The German Struggle Against Soviet Partisans, 1941–1944*. London: Macdonald and Jane's, 1979.

Dallin, Alexander. *The Kaminsky Brigade, 1941–1944: A Case Study of German Military Exploitation of Soviet Dissatisfaction*. Cambridge, Mass.: Russian Research Center, Harvard University, 1956.

- *Odessa, 1941–1944: A Case Study of Soviet Territory Under Foreign Rule.* Santa Monica: Rand Corporation, 1957.
- *German Rule in Russia, 1941–1945: A Study of Occupation Policies.* London: Macmillan, 1957. 2d rev. ed. Boulder, Colo.: Westview Press, 1981.

Davies, Norman. *God's Playground: A History of Poland.* Vol. 2, *1795 to the Present.* New York: Columbia University Press, 1982.

Dawidowicz, Lucy. *The War Against the Jews, 1933–1945.* New York: Holt, Rinehart and Winston, 1975.

De Jong, Louis. *The German Fifth Column in the Second World War.* Chicago: University of Chicago Press, 1956.

Dinnerstein, Leonard. *America and the Survivors of the Holocaust.* New York: Columbia University Press, 1982.

Dmytryshyn, Basil. "The Nazis and the SS Volunteer Division 'Galicia'." *American Slavic and East European Review* 15, no. 1 (February 1956): 1–10.

Elliott, Mark R. *Pawns of Yalta: Soviet Refugees and America's Role in Their Repatriation.* Urbana, Ill.: University of Illinois Press, 1982.

Erickson, John. *The Road to Stalingrad: Stalin's War with Germany.* New York: Harper and Row, 1975.
- *The Road to Berlin: Continuing the History of Stalin's War with Germany.* Boulder, Colo.: Westview Press, 1983.

Ferencz, Benjamin B. *Less Than Slaves: Jewish Forced Labor and the Quest for Compensation.* Cambridge, Mass.: Harvard University Press, 1979.

Fireside, Harvey. *Icon and Swastika: The Russian Orthodox Church under Nazi and Soviet Control.* Cambridge, Mass.: Harvard University Press, 1971.

Fischer, George. *Soviet Opposition to Stalin: A Case Study in World War II.* Cambridge, Mass.: Harvard University Press, 1952.

Fleming, Gerald. *Hitler and the Final Solution.* Berkeley: University of California Press, 1984.

Friedman, Philip. *Their Brothers' Keepers.* New York: Crown, 1957. 2d ed. New York: Holocaust Library, 1978.
- "Ukrainian-Jewish Relations during the Nazi Occupation." *YIVO Annual of Jewish Social Science* 12 (1958–59): 259–96. Reprinted in his *Roads to Extinction: Essays on the Holocaust,* 176–208. New York-Philadelphia: Conference on Jewish Social Studies and The Jewish Publication Society of America, 1980.

Gelwick, Robert A. "Personnel Policies and Procedures of the Waffen SS." Ph.D. dissertation, University of Nebraska, 1971.

Gross, Jan Tomasz. *Polish Society under German Occupation: The Generalgouvernement, 1939–1944.* Princeton, N.J.: Princeton University Press, 1979.

Hamerow, Theodore S. "The Hidden Holocaust." *Commentary* 79, no. 3 (March 1985): 32–42.

Higgins, Trumbull. *Hitler and Stalin: The Third Reich in a Two-Front War, 1937–1943.* New York: Macmillan, 1966.

Hilberg, Raul. *The Destruction of the European Jews.* Chicago: Quadrangle, 1961. Rev. ed. 3 vols. New York: Holmes and Meier, 1985.

Hildebrand, Klaus. *The Third Reich.* Translated by P.S. Falla. Winchester, Mass.: Allen and Unwin, 1985.

Homze, Edward L. *Foreign Labor in Nazi Germany.* Princeton, N.J.: Princeton University Press, 1967.

Isajiw, Wsevolod, Yury Boshyk, and Roman Senkus, eds. *"Displaced Persons" and Political Refugees: The Ukrainian Experience, 1945–54*. Edmonton: Canadian Institute of Ukrainian Studies. Forthcoming.

Kamenetsky, Ihor. *Hitler's Occupation of Ukraine, 1941–1944: A Study of Totalitarian Imperialism*. Milwaukee: Marquette University Press, 1956.

– *Secret Nazi Plans for Eastern Europe: A Study of Lebensraum Policies*. New York: Bookman Associates, 1961; College and Universities Press, 1964.

– "The National Socialist Policy in Slovenia and Western Ukraine during World War II." *Annals of the Ukrainian Academy of Arts and Sciences in the United States* 14, no. 37–38 (1978–80): 39–67.

Kochan, Lionel, ed. *The Jews in Soviet Russia since 1917*. Introduction by Leonard Schapiro. London-New York: Oxford University Press, 1970.

Koehl, Robert L. *RKFDV: German Resettlement and Population Policy, 1939–1945: A History of the Reich Commission for the Strengthening of Germandom*. Cambridge, Mass.: Harvard University Press, 1957.

– *The Black Corps: The Structure and Power Struggles of the Nazi SS*. Madison: University of Wisconsin Press, 1983.

Kolasky, John. *The Shattered Illusion: The History of Ukrainian Pro-Communist Organizations in Canada*. Toronto: Peter Martin Associates, 1979.

Kosyk, Wolodymyr. "Ukraine's Losses During the Second World War." *The Ukrainian Review* 33, no. 2 (Summer 1985): 9–19.

Krawchenko, Bohdan. *Social Change and National Consciousness in Twentieth-Century Ukraine*. London: Macmillan, 1985.

Levin, Dov. "The Jews and the Inception of Soviet Rule in Bukovina." *Soviet Jewish Affairs* 6, no. 2 (1976): 52–70.

Littlejohn, David. *The Patriotic Traitors: A History of Collaboration in German Occupied Europe, 1940–1945*. London: Heinemann, 1972.

Luciuk, Lubomyr Y. "Searching For Place: Ukrainian Refugee Migration to Canada after World War II." Ph.D. dissertation, University of Alberta, 1984.

Lyons, Graham, ed. *The Russian Version of the Second World War*. New York: Facts on File, 1983.

Mace, James. "The Man-Made Famine of 1933 in the Soviet Ukraine." In *Toward the Understanding and Prevention of Genocide*, 67–83. Edited by I. Charny. Boulder, Colo.: Westview Press, 1984.

Marples, David. "The Ukraine in World War II." *Radio Liberty Research Bulletin*, RL Supplement 1/85. Munich: Radio Liberty, 6 May 1985 (mimeograph).

– "Western Ukraine and Western Belorussia Under Soviet Occupation: The Development of Socialist Farming, 1939–1941." *Canadian Slavonic Papers* 27, no. 2 (June 1985): 158–77.

Marrus, Michael R. *The Unwanted: European Refugees in the Twentieth Century*. New York: Oxford University Press, 1985.

Mastny, Vojtech. *The Czechs Under Nazi Rule: The Failure of National Resistance, 1939–1942*. New York: Columbia University Press, 1971.

– *Russia's Road to the Cold War: Diplomacy, Strategy, and the Politics of Communism, 1941–1945*. New York: Columbia University Press, 1980.

Medvedev, Roy A. *Let History Judge: The Origins and Consequences of Stalinism*. New York: Knopf, 1971.

Mendelsohn, Ezra. *The Jews of East Central Europe between the World Wars.* Bloomington, Ind.: Indiana University Press, 1983.

Motyl, Alexander J. *The Turn to the Right: The Ideological Origins and Development of Ukrainian Nationalism, 1919–1929.* Boulder, Colo.: East European Monographs, 1980.

– "Ukrainian Nationalist Political Violence in Inter-War Poland, 1921–1939." *East European Quarterly* 19, no. 1 (March 1985): 45–55.

Nekrich, Aleksandr M. *The Punished Peoples: The Deportation and Fate of Soviet Minorities at the End of the Second World War.* New York: W.W. Norton, 1978.

The Onslaught: The German Drive to Stalingrad. New York: W.W. Norton, 1985.

Orbach, Wila. "The Destruction of the Jews in the Nazi-Occupied Territories of the USSR." *Soviet Jewish Affairs* 6, no. 2 (1976): 14–51.

Palij, Michael. "The Problem of Displaced Persons in Germany, 1939–1950." In *Almanakh Ukrainskoho narodnoho soiuzu na rik 1985*, 28–37. Jersey City, N.J.: Svoboda, 1985.

Pearson, Raymond. *National Minorities in Eastern Europe, 1848–1945.* London, Macmillan, 1983.

Petryshyn, Roman. "Britain's Ukrainian Community: A Study of the Political Dimension in Ethnic Community Development." Ph.D. dissertation, University of Bristol, 1980.

Piotrowski, Stanisław. *Hans Frank's Diary.* Warsaw: Państwowe Wydawnictwo Naukowe, 1961.

Polonsky, Antony. *Politics in Independent Poland, 1921–1939: The Crisis of Constitutional Government.* Oxford: Clarendon Press, 1972.

– and Boleslaw Drukier. *The Beginnings of Communist Rule in Poland, December 1943–June 1945.* London: Routledge and Kegan, 1980.

Prociuk, Stephan G. "Human Losses in the Ukraine in World War I and II." *Annals of the Ukrainian Academy of Arts and Sciences in the United States* 13, no. 35–36 (1973–77): 23–50.

Procyk, Oksana, Leonid Heretz, and James E. Mace. *Famine in the Soviet Ukraine 1932–1933: A Memorial Exhibition.* Cambridge, Mass.: Harvard College Library, 1986.

Raschhofer, Hermann. *Political Assassination: The Legal Background of the Oberländer and Stashinsky Cases.* Tübingen: Fritz Schlichtenmayer, 1964.

Redlich, Shimon. "The Jews in the Soviet-Annexed Territories, 1933–41." *Soviet Jewish Affairs* 1, no. 1 (June 1971): 81–90.

– *Propaganda and Nationalism in Wartime Russia: The Jewish Antifascist Committee in the USSR, 1941–1948.* Boulder, Colo.: East European Monographs, 1982.

Reitlinger, Gerald. *The House Built on Sand: The Conflicts of German Policy in Russia, 1939–1945.* New York: Viking Press, 1960. Reprint. Westport, Conn.: Greenwood Press, 1975.

– *The Final Solution: The Attempt to Exterminate the Jews of Europe, 1939-1945.* 2d rev. and augm. edition. London: Valentine, Mitchell, 1968. New York: Beechurst Press, 1953. Reprint. New York: Yoseloff, 1968.

– *The SS: Alibi of a Nation, 1922–1945.* New York: Viking Press, 1968.

Rich, Norman. *Hitler's War Aims.* 2 vols. New York: W.W. Norton, 1973–4.

Ryan, Allan A., Jr. *Quiet Neighbors: Prosecuting Nazi War Criminals in America.* New York: Harcourt Brace Jovanovich, 1984.

Saidel, Rochelle G. *The Outraged Conscience: Seekers of Justice for Nazi War Criminals in America.* Albany: State University of New York Press, 1984.

Seaton, Albert. *The Russo-German War, 1941–45.* New York: Praeger, 1971.

– *The German Army, 1933–45.* New York: St. Martin's Press, 1982.

Stehle, Hansjacob. *Eastern Politics of the Vatican, 1917–1979.* Translated by Sandra Smith. Athens, Ohio: Ohio University Press, 1981.

Stein, George H. *The Waffen SS: Hitler's Elite Guard at War, 1939–1945.* Ithaca, N.Y.: Cornell University Press, 1966.

Stephan, John J. *The Russian Fascists: Tragedy and Farce in Exile, 1925–1945.* New York: Harper and Row, 1978.

Syndor, Charles W., Jr. *Soldiers of Destruction: The SS Death's Head Division, 1933–1945.* Princeton, N.J.: Princeton University Press, 1977.

Szporluk, Roman. "War By Other Means." *Slavic Review* 44, no. 1 (Spring 1985): 20–26.

Thorwald, Jürgen. *The Illusion: Soviet Soldiers in Hitler's Armies.* Translated by Richard and Clara Winston. New York-London: Harcourt Brace Jovanovich, 1975.

Tolstoy, Nikolai. *Victims of Yalta.* Toronto: Hodder and Stoughton, 1977. U.S. edition. *The Secret Betrayal: 1944–47.* New York: Scribner's, 1978.

– *Stalin's Secret War.* New York: Holt, Rinehart and Winston, 1982.

Trunk, Isaiah. *Judenrat: The Jewish Councils in Eastern Europe under Nazi Occupation.* New York: Macmillan, 1972.

Tys-Krokhmaliuk, Yuriy. *UPA Warfare in Ukraine: Strategical, Tactical and Organizational Problems of Ukrainian Resistance in World War II.* Translated by Walter Dushnyck. New York: Society of Veterans of the Ukrainian Insurgent Army, 1972.

The Ukrainian Insurgent Army in the Fight for Freedom. New York: United American Ukrainian Organization Committee of New York, 1954.

"Ukrainians in World War II: Views and Points." *Nationalities Papers* 10, no. 1 (Spring 1982): 1–39.

Ukrainian Resistance: The Story of the Ukrainian National Liberation Movement in Modern Times. New York: Ukrainian Congress Committee of America, 1949.

United States, General Accounting Office. Report by the Comptroller General of the United States. "Nazis and Axis Collaborators Were Used to Further U.S. Anti-Communist Objectives in Europe – Some Immigrated to the United States." Washington, D.C.: General Accounting Office, 28 June 1985 (GAO/GGD-85-66).

Vago, Bela, and George L. Mosse, eds. *Jews and Non-Jews in Eastern Europe, 1918–1945.* New York-Toronto: John Wiley and Sons, 1974.

Werth, Alexander. *Russia at War, 1941–1945.* New York: Carroll and Graf, 1984.

Wyman, David S. *The Abandonment of the Jews: America and the Holocaust, 1941–1945.* New York: Pantheon, 1984.

Wynot, Edward. "'A Necessary Cruelty': The Emergence of Official Antisemitism in Poland, 1936–39." *American Historical Review* 76, no. 4 (October 1971): 1035–58.

Wytwycky, Bohdan. *The Other Holocaust: Many Circles of Hell.* Washington, D.C.: The Novak Report, 1980.

Żarnowski, Janusz, ed. *Dictatorships in East Central Europe 1918–1939. Anthologies.* Translated by Janina Dorosz. Wroclaw: Wydawnictwo Polskiej Akademii Nauk, 1983.

FRENCH

De Launay, Jacques. *La Grande Débâcle, 1944–1945: Sept millions de civils fuient devant l'Armée rouge.* Paris: Albin Michel, 1985.

GERMAN

Buchsweiler, Meier. *Volksdeutsche in der Ukraine am Vorabend und Beginn des Zweiten Weltkriegs – ein Fall doppelter Loyalität?* Gerlingen: Bleicher Verlag, 1984.

Fleischhauer, Ingeborg. *Das Dritte Reich und die Deutschen in der Sowjetunion.* Stuttgart: Deutsche Verlags-Anstalt, 1983.

Heike, Wolf-Dietrich. *Sie wollten die Freiheit: Die Geschichte der Ukrainischen Division 1943–1945.* Dorheim: Podzun-Verlag, n.d. [1973].

Hoffmann, Joachim. *Die Geschichte der Wlassow-Armee.* Freiburg: Verlag Rombach, 1984.

Kosyk, Wolodymyr. "Die Opfer der Ukraine während des Zweiten Weltkriegs." *Jahrbuch der Ukrainekunde 1984,* 116–26. Munich: Ukrainische Wissenschafte e.V., 1984.

Krausnick, Helmut. *Hitlers Einsatzgruppen: Die Truppe des Weltanschauungskrieges, 1938–1942.* Frankfurt: Fischer Taschenbuch Verlag, 1985.

– and Hans-Heinrich Wilhelm. *Die Truppe des Weltanschauungskrieges: Die Einsatzgruppen der Sicherheitspolizei und des SD, 1938–1942.* Stuttgart: Deutsche Verlags-Anstalt, 1981.

Neufeldt, Hans-Joachim, Jurgen Huck, and Georg Tessin. *Zur Geschichte der Ordnungspolizei, 1936–1945.* Koblenz: [Bundesarchiv], 1957.

Thorwald, Jürgen. *Wen sie verderben wollen: Bericht des grossen Verrats.* Stuttgart: Steingrüben-Verlag, 1952.

Weber, Hermann. *Die Bukowina im Zweiten Weltkrieg: Völkerrechtliche Aspekte der Lage der Bukowina im Spannugsfeld zwischen Rumänien, der Sowjetunion und Deutschland.* Frankfurt-Main: In Kommission beim A. Metzner, 1972.

POLISH

Szczęśniak, Antoni, and Wiesław Z. Szota. *Droga do nikąd: działalność Organizacji Ukraińskich Nacjonalistów i jej likwidacja w Polsce.* Warsaw: Wojskowy Instytut Historyczny, 1973.

Torzecki, Ryszard. *Kwestia ukraińska w polityce III Rzeszy, 1933–1945.* Warsaw: Książka i Wiedza, 1972.

UKRAINIAN

Akademiia nauk Ukrainskoi RSR, Instytut istorii. *Istoriia Ukrainskoi RSR: Ukrainska RSR u Velykii Vitchyznianii viini Radianskoho Soiuzu, 1941–1945.* Vol. 7. Kiev: Naukova dumka, 1977.

Boiko, Iurii et al., eds. *Ievhen Konovalets ta ioho doba*. Munich: Fundatsiia im. Ievhena Konovaltsia, 1974.

Druzhyny ukrainskykh natsionalistiv u 1941–1942 rokakh. Munich: Nasha knyhozbirnia, 1953.

Haike, Volf-Ditrikh [Heike, Wolf-Dietrich]. *Ukrainska dyviziia "Halychyna": istoriia formuvannia i boiovykh dii u 1943–1945 rokakh*. Translated by Roman Kolisnyk. Toronto: Bratstvo kol. voiakiv I-oi Ukrainskoi dyvizii UNA, 1970.

Hirniak, Kost. *Ukrainskyi lehion samooborony: prychynky do istorii*. Toronto: Nakladom starshyn i voiakiv lehionu, 1977.

Horak, Stepan. "Ukraintsi i Druha svitova viina: dosvid u spivpratsi z Nimechchynoiu, 1941–1942." *Ukrainskyi istoryk* 16, no. 1–4 (1979): 23–40; 17, no. 1–4 (1980): 58–70.

Kalba, Myroslav. *"Nakhtigal" (Kurin DUN) u svitli faktiv i dokumentiv*. Denver: Ukrapress, 1984.

Kedryn, Ivan. "Velykyi iskhod." In *Almanakh Ukrainskoho narodnoho soiuzu na 1985 rik*, 17–27. Jersey City, N.J.: Svoboda, 1985.

Korduba, Feliks. "Der Generalplan Ost: u 40-richchia pokhodu III Raikhu proty SRSR." *Ukrainskyi istoryk* 18, no. 1–4 (1981): 153–73.

Krokhmaliuk, Roman. *Zahrava na skhodi: spohady i dokumenty z pratsi u Viiskovii upravi "Halychyna" v 1943–1945 rokakh*. Toronto-New York: Bratstvo kolyshnikh voiakiv I-oi Ukrainskoi dyvizii UNA, 1978.

Kubiiovych, Volodymyr. "Pochatky Ukrainskoi dyvizii 'Halychyna'." *Visti Bratstva kolyshnikh voiakiv I-oi Ukrainskoi dyvizii UNA*, no. 3–4 (41–42) (1954): 2–5.

– *Ukraintsi v Heneralnii hubernii, 1939–1941: istoriia Ukrainskoho tsentralnoho komitetu*. Chicago: Mykola Denysiuk, 1975.

Lebed, Mykola. *Ukrainska povstanska armiia: ii geneza, rist i dii u vyzvolnii borotbi ukrainskoho narodu*. Vol. 1, *Nimetska okupatsiia Ukrainy*. n.p.: Presove biuro UHVR, 1946.

Levytsky, Myron, ed. *Istoriia ukrainskoho viiska*. 2d rev. ed. Winnipeg: Ivan Tyktor, 1953.

Lysiak, Oleh, ed. *Bii pid Brodamy: zbirnyk stattei u trydtsiatlittia*. Munich: Bratstvo kolyshnikh voiakiv I-oi Ukrainskoi dyvizii UNA, 1951. 2d rev. and augm. ed. New York: Bratstvo kolyshnikh voiakiv I-oi Ukrainskoi dyvizii UNA, 1974.

Maruniak, Volodymyr. *Ukrainska emigratsiia v Nimechchyni i Avstrii po druhii svitovii viini*. Vol. 1, *Roky 1945–1951*. Munich: Akademichne vydavnytstvo Petra Beleia, 1985.

Matla, Zynovii. *Pivdenna pokhidna hrupa*. Munich: Nasha knyhozbirnia, 1952.

Melnyk, Kost, Oleh Lashchenko, and Wasyl Veryha, eds. *Na zov Kyieva*. Toronto: Olzhych Institute, 1985.

Nebeliuk, Myroslav. *Pid chuzhymy praporamy*. Paris-Lyon: Persha ukrainska drukarnia u Frantsii, 1951.

Orhanizatsiia ukrainskykh natsionalistiv, 1929–1954. Paris: Persha ukrainska drukarnia u Frantsii, 1955.

Ortynsky, Liubomyr. "Druzhyny ukrainskykh natsionalistiv (DUN)." *Visti Bratstva kolyshnikh voiakiv I-oi Ukrainskoi dyvizii UNA*, no. 6–7 (20–21) (1952): 4–7.

OUN u viini 1939–1945. n.p.: Informatsiinyi viddil OUN, 1946 (mimeograph).
Rebet, Lev. *Svitla i tini OUN.* Munich: Ukrainskyi samostiinyk, 1964.
Shankovsky, Lev. *Pokhidni hrupy OUN: prychynky do istorii pokhidnykh hrup OUN na tsentralnykh i skhidnikh zemliakh Ukrainy v 1941–1943 rr.* Munich: Ukrainskyi samostiinyk, 1958.
– *Ukrainska armiia v borotbi za derzhavnist.* Munich: Dniprova khvylia, 1958.
Shuliak, O. (Oleh Shtul-Zhdanovych). *V imia pravdy: do istorii povstanchoho rukhu v Ukraini.* Rotterdam: Provid ukrainskykh natsionalistiv, 1947.
Tytarenko, Petro. "Protypantsyrna bryhada Vilna Ukraina." *Visti Bratstva kolyshnikh voiakiv I-oi Ukrainskoi dyvizii UNA,* no. 6–7 (20–21) (1952): 3.
Veryha, Vasyl. *Dorohamy Druhoi svitovoi viiny: legendy pro uchast ukraintsiv u zdushuvanni Varshavskoho povstannia v 1944 r. ta pro Ukrainsku dyviziiu "Halychyna."* 2d rev. ed. Toronto: Bratstvo kolyshnikh voiakiv I-oi Ukrainskoi dyvizii UNA, 1981.
– *Pid sontsem Italii.* Toronto: Bratstvo kolyshnikh voiakiv I-oi Ukrainskoi dyvizii UNA, 1984.
Zelenko, Kostiantyn. "Shche pro dyviziiu 'Halychyna'." *Ukrainskyi samostiinyk* 23, nos. 11–12 (November–December 1972): 26–32; 24, no. 1 (January 1973): 25–32; 24, no. 2 (February 1973): 30–41.
Zeleny, Zenon. *Ukrainske iunatstvo v vyri Druhoi svitovoi viiny.* Toronto: Bratstvo kolyshnikh voiakiv I-oi Ukrainskoi dyvizii UNA, 1965.
Zlochyny komunistychnoi Moskvy v Ukraini vliti 1941 roku. New York: Prolog, 1960.

III. UKRAINIANS IN NAZI CONCENTRATION CAMPS

Note: All RB numbers refer to an accession number in the Thomas Fisher Rare Book Library catalogue, University of Toronto. These sources can be found in Yury Boshyk and Włodzimierz Kiebalo, comps., *Publications by Ukrainian "Displaced Persons" and Political Refugees: The John Luczkiw Collection, Thomas Fisher Rare Book Library, University of Toronto* (Edmonton: Canadian Institute of Ukrainian Studies; forthcoming). The archives of the *Liga Ukrainskykh Politychnykh Viazniv* (League of Ukrainian Political Prisoners) are now in the possession of Mykhailo H. Marunchak, Winnipeg, Canada.

Bazhansky, Mykhailo. *Mozaika kvadriv viaznychnykh.* Aschaffenburg: Tovarystvo ukrainskykh politychnykh viazniv, 1946. (RB 127206)
Beskyd [Tarnovych], Iuliian. *Liudy bez prizvyshch.* Regensburg: Ukrainske slovo, 1946. (RB 127683)
Dansky, O. *Khochu zhyty: obrazky z nimetskykh kontsentratsiinykh taboriv.* Munich: Ukrainska vydavnycha spilka, 1946. (RB 127187)
Ianiv, Volodymyr. *Nimetskyi kontsentratsiinyi tabir: sproba kharakterystyky. Dopovid na pershu naukovu konferentsiiu NDIUM.* Munich: Naukovo-doslidnyi instytut ukrainskoi martyrolohii, 1948. (RB 127789)
Ilkiw, Mykhailo. *German Concentration Camps: Memoirs.* New York: Former Ukrainian Political Prisoners, 1983.
Informatsii Holovnoi upravy Tovarystva ukrainskykh politychnykh viazniv (Munich), nos. 1–3 (1946). (RB 130233)

Izhyk, Semen. "Christmas in a Nazi Concentration Camp." *Ukrainian Echo* (Toronto), 16 February 1983.

K.V. and T.A. *Chomu svit movchyt? Ukraintsi v kontsentratsiinykh taborakh Nimechchyny 1940–1945 rr.* 2d ed. Paris: n.p., 1945–6. (RB 127593)

Kalendarets ukrainskoho politviaznia. Munich: Liga ukrainskykh politviazniv, 1947. (RB 130383)

Kyshenevyi kalendarets ukrainskoho politviaznia (1948). Munich: Vasyl Pasichniak, 1948. (RB 130379)

Litopys politviaznia (Munich), nos. 1–11 (1946–7). (RB 130252)

Maletych, I. *Try khresty: opovidannia z zhyttia ostarbaiteriv.* Regensburg: Promin, 1948. (RB 127860)

Malashchuk, Roman. "Return from the Dead, Easter 1945." *Ukrainian Echo,* 9 May 1979.

Martynets, Volodymyr. *Brätz – nimetskyi kontsentratsiinyi tabir: spohady viaznia.* Stuttgart: Tovarystvo ukrainskykh politviazniv, 1946. (RB 127132)

Marunchak, Mykhailo H. *Systema nimetskykh kontstaboriv i polityka vynyshchuvannia v Ukraini.* Winnipeg: Zahalna biblioteka "UKT," 1963.

– *Za gratamy drotamy natsional-sotsiialistychnoi Nimechchyny.* Winnipeg: Committee of Former Ukrainian Political Prisoners, 1985.

Mirchuk, Petro. *U nimetskykh mlynakh smerty: spomyny z pobutu v nimetskykh tiurmakh i kontslaherakh, 1941–1945.* New York-London: Ukrainskyi soiuz politychnykh viazniv, 1957.

– *In the German Mills of Death.* New York: Vantage Press, 1976.

Mostovych, Leonidas. "Recollections: Former Prisoner Recalls Life and Death in Nazi Camps." *Ukrainian Weekly* (Jersey City) 8, no. 36 (8 September 1985): 7.

Obvynuvachuvalnyi vnesok ukrainskoi hromadskosty do mizhnarodnoho sudu nad natsional-sotsiialistychnymy kerivnykamy Nimechchyny. Geneva: Orhanizovana ukrainska hromadskist, 1946. (RB 128581)

Osynka, Paladii. *Albom politviaznia.* Munich, 1946. (RB127123)

Pershyi kongres ukrainskykh politychnykh viazniv. Munich: Liga ukrainskykh politychnykh viazniv, 1946. (RB 129855)

Politviazen: biuleten Ligy ukrainskykh politychnykh viazniv (Munich) nos. 1–4 (1946). (RB 130287)

Rozdolsky, Roman. "Nevilnyky i smertnyky (Spomyn pro Osventsim i Birkenau)." *Oborona* (Newark), no. 7 (January 1956). Reprint. *Diialoh* (Toronto), no. 10 (1984): 84–8.

V pamiat poliahlykh ukrainskykh politychnykh viazniv. n.p.: Tovarystvo ukrainskykh politychnykh viazniv – Tsentralia, 1946. (RB 128414)

Zavdannia ukrainskoi martyrolohii. Munich: Liga ukrainskykh politychnykh viazniv, 1947. (RB 128457)

IV. U.S. CASES AND MATERIALS ON DENATURALIZATION, DEPORTATION, AND SUSPECTED NAZI WAR CRIMINALS

1. *Cases*

Afroyim v. *Rusk,* 387 U.S. 253 (1967)

Baumgartner v. *United States,* 322 U.S. 665 (1944)

Chaunt v. *United States*, 364 U.S. 350 (1960)

Johannessen v. *United States*, 225 U.S. 227 (1912)

Kennedy v. *Mendoza-Martinez*, 372 U.S. 144 (1963)

Klapprott v. *United States*, 335 U.S. 601 (1949)

Knauer v. *United States*, 328 U.S. 654 (1946)

Laipenieks v. *INS*, 750 F.2d 1427 (9th Cir. 1985)

Luria v. *United States*, 231 U.S. 9 (1913)

Ng Fung Ho v. *White*, 259 U.S. 276 (1922)

Nowak v. *United States*, 356 U.S. 660 (1958)

Rogers v. *Bellei*, 401 U.S. 815 (1971)

Schneider v. *Rusk*, 377 U.S. 163 (1964)

Schneiderman v. *United States*, 320 U.S. 118 (1943)

Simons v. *United States*, 333 F.Supp. 855 (S.D.N.Y.), *aff'd*, 452 F.2d 1110 (2d Cir. 1971)

Tutun v. *United States*, 270 U.S. 568 (1926)

United States v. *Demjanjuk*, 518 F.Supp. 1362 (N.D.Ohio 1981), *aff'd per curiam*, 680 F.2d 32 (6th Cir.), *cert. denied*, 459 U.S. 1036 (1982)

United States v. *Dercacz*, 530 F.Supp. 1348 (E.D.N.Y. 1982)

United States v. *Fedorenko*, 455 F.Supp. 893 (S.D. Fla. 1978), *rev'd*, 597 F.2d 946 (5th Cir. 1979), *aff'd*, 449 U.S. 490 (1981)

United States v. *Ginsberg*, 243 U.S. 472 (1917)

United States v. *Kowalchuk*, 571 F.Supp. 72 (E.D.Pa. 1983), *rev'd*, 744 F.2d 301 (3d Cir. 1984), *panel opinion vacated and rehearing en banc granted*

United States v. *Koziy*, 540 F.Supp. 25 (S.D.Fla 1982), *aff'd* 728 F.2d 1314 (11th Cir.), *cert. denied*, – U.S. – , 105 S.Ct. 130 (1984)

United States v. *Kungys*, 571 F.Supp. 1104 (D.N.J.), *appeal docketed* (3d Cir. 1983)

United States v. *Linnas*, 527 F.Supp. 426 (E.D.N.Y. 1981), *aff'd per curiam without opinion*, 685 F.2d 427 (2d Cir. 1982)

United States v. *Mansour*, 170 F. 671 (S.D.N.Y. 1908), *aff'd per curiam without opinion*, 226 U.S. 604 (1912)

United States v. *Minerich*, 250 F.2d 721 (7th Cir. 1957)

United States v. *Ness*, 245 U.S. 319 (1917)

United States v. *Oates*, 560 F.2d 45 (2d Cir. 1977)

United States v. *Oddo*, 314 F.2d 115 (2d Cir.), *cert. denied*, 375 U.S. 833 (1963)

United States v. *Osidach*, 513 F.Supp. 51 (E.D.Pa. 1981)

United States v. *Palciauskas*, 559 F.Supp. 1294 (M.D.Fla. 1983), *aff'd*, 734 F.2d 625 (11th Cir. 1984)

United States v. *Profaci*, 274 F.2d 289 (2d Cir. 1960)

United States v. *Riela*, 337 F.2d 986 (3d Cir. 1964)

United States v. *Rossi*, 299 F.2d 650 (9th Cir. 1962)

United States v. *Schellong*, 717 F.2d 329 (7th Cir. 1983), *cert. denied*, – U.S. – , 104 S.Ct. 1002 (1984)

United States ex rel. Leibowitz v. *Schlotfeldt*, 94 F.2d 263 (7th Cir. 1938)

United States v. *Stromberg*, 227 F.2d 903 (5th Cir. 1955)

United States v. *Theodorovich*, 102 F.R.D. 587 (D.D.C. 1984)

United States v. *Tooma*, 187 F.Supp. 928 (E.D.Mich. 1960)

United States v. *Trifa*, 662 F.2d 447 (6th Cir. 1981), *cert. denied*, 102 S. Ct. 2239 (1982).

United States v. *Walus*, 453 F.Supp. 699 (N.D. Ill. 1978), *rev'd*, 616 F.2d 283 (7th Cir. 1980)
United States v. *Wong Kim Ark*, 169 U.S. 649 (1898)
Vance v. *Terrazas*, 444 U.S. 252 (1980)

2. *Other Material*

Alleged Nazi War Criminals: Hearings Before the Subcommittee on Immigration, Citizenship, and International Law of the House Committee on the Judiciary. 95th Congress, 1st Session, 1977.
Alleged Nazi War Criminals: Hearings Before the Subcommittee on Immigration, Citizenship and International Law of the House Committee on the Judiciary. 95th Congress, 2d Session, 1978.
Baltic States Investigation: Hearings Before the Select Committee to Investigate the Incorporation of the Baltic States into the U.S.S.R., Part 1, House of Representatives. 83rd Congress, 1st Session, 1953.
Bittman, Ladislav. *The Deception Game: Czechoslovak Intelligence in Soviet Political Warfare.* Syracuse, N.Y. : Syracuse University Research Corporation, 1972.
Blum, M. *Wanted! The Search for Nazis in America.* New York: Quadrangle/The New York Times Book Co., 1977.
Cermack, John F., Jr. "The Effect of Government Knowledge on Denaturalization Proceedings: A Return to Illegal Procurement?" *American University Law Review* 30, no. 2 (Winter 1981): 519–76.
Cohen, Robert A. "United States Exclusion and Deportation of Nazi War Criminals: The Act of October 30, 1978." *International Law and Politics* 13 (1980): 101–33.
"Comment, Denaturalization of Nazi War Criminals: Is There Sufficient Justice for Those Who Would Not Dispense Justice?" *Maryland Law Review* 40 (1981): 39–89.
Communist Bloc Intelligence Activities in the United States: Hearings Before the Subcommittee to Investigate the Administration of the Internal Security Act and Other Internal Security Laws of the Senate Committee on the Judiciary. 94th Congress, 1st Session, 1975. Washington, D.C.: U.S. Government Printing Office, 1975.
Communist Bloc Intelligence Activities in the United States, Part 2: Hearings Before the Subcommittee to Investigate the Administration of the Internal Security Act and Other Internal Security Laws of the Senate Committee on the Judiciary. 94th Congress, 2d Session, 1976. Washington, D.C.: U.S. Government Printing Office, 1976.
Communist Forgeries: Hearings Before the Subcommittee to Investigate the Administration of the Internal Security Act and Other Internal Security Laws of the Committee on the Judiciary, United States Senate, June 2, 1961. Washington, D.C.: U.S. Government Printing Office, 1961.
Concurrent Resolution with Respect to the Baltic States and Soviet Claims of Citizenship Over Certain Citizens of the United States: Senate Report. 96th Congress, 1st Session, 1979. Washington, D.C.: U.S. Government Printing Office, 1979.

Country Reports on Human Rights Practices: Report Submitted to the Committee on International Relations, U.S. House of Representatives, and the Committee on Foreign Relations, U.S. Senate, by the Department of State, February 3, 1978. Washington, D.C.: U.S. Government Printing Office, 1978.

Country Reports on Human Rights Practices for 1979: Report Submitted to the Committee on Foreign Affairs, U.S. House of Representatives, and the Committee on Foreign Relations, U.S. Senate, by the Department of State, February 4, 1980. Washington, D.C.: U.S. Government Printing Office, 1980.

Country Reports on Human Rights Practices: Report Submitted to the Committee on Foreign Relations, U.S. Senate, and the Committee on Foreign Affairs, U.S. House of Representatives, for the Department of State, February 2, 1981. Washington, D.C.: U.S. Government Printing Office, 1981.

Country Reports on Human Rights Practices for 1981: Report Submitted to the Committee on Foreign Relations, U.S. Senate, and the Committee on Foreign Affairs, U.S. House of Representatives, by the Department of State, February 1981. Washington, D.C.: U.S. Government Printing Office, 1982.

"Denaturalization and the Right to Jury Trial." *Journal of Criminal Law and Criminology* 71, no. 1 (1980): 46–50.

Gerson, Allan. "Beyond Nuremberg." *Commentary* 72, no. 4 (October 1981): 62–6.

Helling, Lisa L. "U.S. Human Rights Policy Toward the Soviet Union and Eastern Europe During the Carter Administration." *Denver Journal of International Law and Policy* 9, no. 1 (Winter 1980): 85–118.

Human Rights and the Baltic States: Hearing Before the Subcommittee on International Organizations of the House Committee on Foreign Affairs. 96th Congress, 1st Session. Washington, D.C.: U.S. Government Printing Office, 1979.

Human Rights Practices in Countries Receiving U.S. Security Assistance: Report Submitted to the Committee on International Relations, House of Representatives, by the Department of State, April 25, 1977. Washington, D.C.: U.S. Government Printing Office, 1977.

Immigration and Naturalization Service Oversight: Hearings Before the Subcommittee on Immigration, Citizenship and International Law of the House Committee on the Judiciary. 93rd Congress, 2d Session. Washington, D.C.: U.S. Government Printing Office, 1974.

Immigration and Naturalization Service: Hearings Before the Subcommittee on Immigration, Refugees and International Law of the House Committee on the Judiciary. 96th Congress, 1st Session. Washington, D.C.: U.S. Government Printing Office, 1979.

Investigation of Communist Takeover and Occupation of Poland, Lithuania and Slovakia: Sixth Interim Report of Hearings Before the Subcommittee on Poland, Lithuania and Slovakia of the Select Committee on Communist Aggression, House of Representatives. 83rd Congress, 2d Session. Washington, D.C.: U.S. Government Printing Office, 1954.

Investigation of Communist Takeover and Occupation of the Non-Russian Nations of the U.S.S.R.: Eighth Interim Report of Hearings Before the Select Committee on Communist Aggression, House of Representatives. 83rd Congress, 2d Session. Washington, D.C.: U.S. Government Printing Office, 1954.

Lehman, William. "Nazi War Criminals Living in the United States."

Congressional Record – *Extensions of Remarks*, no. 18 (2 March 1982), E690.

The MacNeil/Lehrer Report: Human Rights. New York: MacNeil/Lehrer Report, 10 February 1981.

Maxey, David W. "Loss of Nationality: Individual Choice or Government Fiat?" *Albany Law Review* 164 (1962): 151.

Quinlan, James. "Due Process and the Deportable Alien: Limitation on State Department Participation in Withholding of Deportation Inquiry." *Catholic Lawyer* 22 (Autumn 1976): 275–86.

Remeikis, Thomas. *Opposition to Soviet Rule in Lithuania 1945–1980*. Chicago: Institute of Lithuanian Studies Press, 1980.

– ed. *The Violations of Human Rights in Soviet Occupied Lithuania: A Report for 1979–80*. Glenside, Pa.: The Lithuanian American Community, 1981.

Report of the Select Committee to Investigate Communist Aggression and Forced Incorporation of the Baltic States into the U.S.S.R. : Third Interim Report of the Select Committee on Communist Aggression, House of Representatives. 83rd Congress, 2d Session. Washington, D.C.: U.S. Government Printing Office, 1954.

Roche, John P. "Comments: Pre-Statutory Denaturalization." *Cornell Law Quarterly* 35 (1949): 120–37.

Second Interim Report of the Select Committee on Communist Aggression, House of Representatives. 83rd Congress, 2d Session. Washington, D.C., 1954.

Solovyov, Vladimir. "Knowing the KGB." *Partisan Review*, no. 2 (1982).

Soviet "Active Measures": Forgery, Disinformation, Political Operations, October 1981. U.S. Department of State, Bureau of Public Affairs, Special Report No. 88. Washington, D.C.

Soviet Covert Action (The Forgery Offensive): Hearings Before the Subcommittee on Oversight of the Permanent Select Committee on Intelligence, House of Representatives. 96th Congress, 2d Session, 6 and 19 February 1980. Washington, D.C.: U.S. Government Printing Office, 1980.

Staff of the Commission on Security and Cooperation in Europe: Reports of Helsinki Accord Monitors in the Soviet Union. 1978.

Taylor, Telford. *Courts of Terror: Soviet Criminal Justice and Jewish Immigration*. New York: Alfred A. Knopf, 1976.

INDEX

10.-